★★★★★★★★★★ HARCOURT **HORIZONS**

HARCOURT HORIZONS

The Pledge of Allegiance

I pledge allegiance to the Flag

of the United States of America,

and to the Republic

for which it stands,

one Nation under God, indivisible,

with liberty and justice for all.

HARCOURT HORIZONS

North Carolina

Harcourt

Orlando   Austin   Chicago   New York   Toronto   London   San Diego

Visit *The Learning Site!*
www.harcourtschool.com

HARCOURT HORIZONS

NORTH CAROLINA

General Editor

Dr. Michael J. Berson
Associate Professor
Social Science Education
University of South Florida
Tampa, Florida

Contributing Author

Dr. Ted S. Henson
Center Fellow
North Carolina Center for the
  Advancement of Teaching
Cullowhee, North Carolina

Series Consultants

Dr. Robert Bednarz
Professor
Department of Geography
Texas A&M University
College Station, Texas

Dr. Asa Grant Hilliard III
Fuller E. Callaway Professor
  of Urban Education
Georgia State University
Atlanta, Georgia

Dr. Thomas M. McGowan
Chairperson and Professor
Center for Curriculum and Instruction
University of Nebraska
Lincoln, Nebraska

Dr. John J. Patrick
Professor of Education
Indiana University
Bloomington, Indiana

Dr. Cinthia Salinas
Assistant Professor
Department of Curriculum and Instruction
University of Texas at Austin
Austin, Texas

Dr. Philip VanFossen
Associate Professor,
  Social Studies Education,
  and Associate Director,
  Purdue Center for Economic Education
Purdue University
West Lafayette, Indiana

Dr. Hallie Kay Yopp
Professor
Department of Elementary, Bilingual, and
  Reading Education
California State University, Fullerton
Fullerton, California

Content Reviewers

Dr. Karl E. Campbell
Assistant Professor
History Department
Appalachian State University
Boone, North Carolina

Dr. Gary Freeze
Associate Professor
History Department
Catawba College
Salisbury, North Carolina

Margaret P. Inman
Lecturer
School of Education
University of North Carolina at Pembroke
Pembroke, North Carolina

Dr. LuAnn Jones
Assistant Professor of History
Department of History
East Carolina University
Greenville, North Carolina

Maps
researched and prepared by

Readers
written and designed by

Take a Field Trip
video tour segments provided by

Copyright © 2003 by Harcourt, Inc.

All rights reserved. No part of this publication may be reproduced or transmitted in any form or by any means, electronic or mechanical, including photocopy, recording, or any information storage and retrieval system, without permission in writing from the publisher.

Requests for permission to make copies of any part of the work should be mailed to:

School Permissions and Copyrights
Harcourt, Inc.
6277 Sea Harbor Drive
Orlando, Florida 32887-6777
Fax: 407-345-2418

HARCOURT and the Harcourt Logo are trademarks of Harcourt, Inc., registered in the United States of America and/or other jurisdictions. TIME FOR KIDS and the red border are registered trademarks of Time Inc. Used under license. Copyright © by Time Inc. All rights reserved.

Acknowledgments appear in the back of this book.

Printed in the United States of America

ISBN 0-15-321347-7

2 3 4 5 6 7 8 9 10 032 10 09 08 07 06 05 04 03

Contents

· UNIT · 1

The Land and Early People

· UNIT ·
2

The Coastal Plain Region

· UNIT ·

3

The Piedmont Region

The Mountain Region

· UNIT ·

5

North Carolina in the Modern World

Reference

Features You Can Use

Maps

Time Lines

Reading Your Textbook

Getting Started

Your textbook is divided into five units.

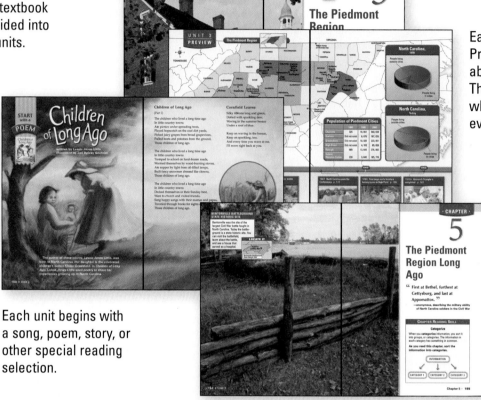

Each unit has a Unit Preview that gives facts about important events. The Preview also shows where and when those events took place.

Each unit begins with a song, poem, story, or other special reading selection.

Each unit is divided into chapters, and each chapter is divided into lessons.

The Parts of a Lesson

This statement gives you the lesson's main idea. It tells you what to look for as you read.

This statement tells you why it is important to read the lesson.

These are the new vocabulary terms you will learn in the lesson.

LESSON

1

MAIN IDEA
Read to learn about the groups of European immigrants that settled in the North Carolina backcountry.

WHY IT MATTERS
Many North Carolina ideas and traditions can be traced to groups of European settlers.

VOCABULARY
backcountry
pioneer
relocate
diversity
self-sufficent

Settling the Backcountry

1700   1800   1900
    1730–1770

In the early 1700s most North Carolina towns and cities were located on the Coastal Plain. Few settlements existed west of the Fall Line. People called this vast western region the **backcountry** because it was away from, or in back of, the Coastal Plain. Poor roads, the waterfalls, and rapids made travel to the backcountry difficult. By the 1730s, however, pioneers were streaming into the backcountry. A **pioneer** is a person who is among the first to settle in a place.

The Great Wagon Road

By the 1730s good farmland had become hard to find in Pennsylvania, Maryland, and Virginia. Colonists began going south to **relocate**, or move to a new location. In the North Carolina backcountry, land was cheap and plentiful. The newcomers traveled down the Great Wagon Road, once a pathway used by Native Americans. The Great Wagon Road

FAST FACT Travel on the Great Wagon Road was slow. People could not go any faster than their feet could carry them. In 1784 it took Ninian Riley and his family almost a month to walk from Maryland to Surry County, North Carolina. Today you can fly from Maryland to North Carolina in about an hour and a half!

156 ▪ Unit 3

Lesson title

This part of the time line shows the period when the events in the lesson took place.

Each new vocabulary term is highlighted in yellow and defined.

Each lesson is divided into several short sections.

Each lesson, like each chapter and each unit, ends with a review. There may be a Summary Time Line that shows the order of the events covered in the lesson. Questions and a performance activity help you check your understanding of the lesson.

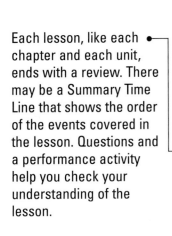

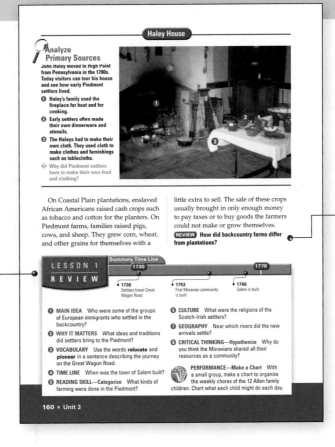

Each short section ends with a **REVIEW** question that will help you check whether you understand what you have read. Be sure to answer this question before you continue reading the lesson.

Skills

Your textbook has lessons that will help you build your reading, citizenship, chart and graph, and map and globe skills.

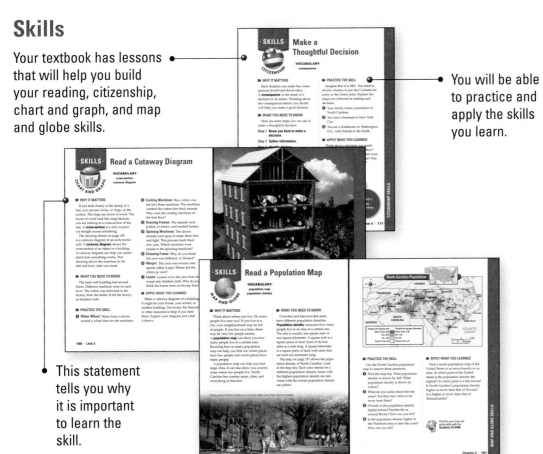

You will be able to practice and apply the skills you learn.

This statement tells you why it is important to learn the skill.

Special Features

The feature called Examine Primary Sources shows you ways to learn about different kinds of objects and documents.

The Visit feature lets you "visit" many interesting places.

Atlas

The Atlas provides maps and a list of geography terms with illustrations.

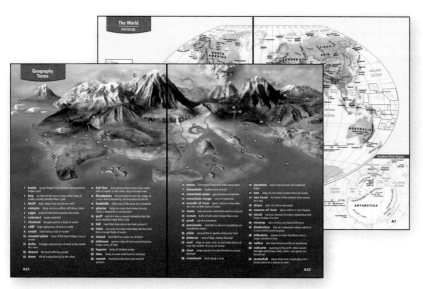

For Your Reference

At the back of your textbook, you will find the reference tools listed below.

- Almanac
- Biographical Dictionary
- Gazetteer
- Glossary
- Index

You can use these tools to look up words and to find information about people, places, and other topics.

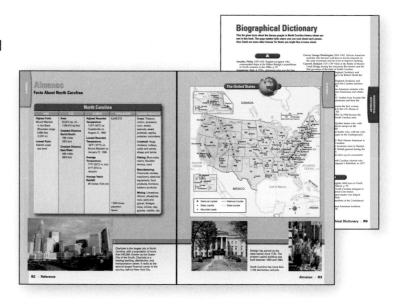

Atlas

 Map and Globe Skills

·SKILLS·
Read a Map

VOCABULARY

grid	locator	compass rose
map title	inset map	cardinal direction
map key	map scale	intermediate direction

▶ WHY IT MATTERS

Maps help you see where places are located in the world. They show the position of cities, states, and countries. They also identify where mountains, valleys, rivers, and lakes are found. Knowing how to read a map is an important skill for learning social studies.

▶ WHAT YOU NEED TO KNOW

A map is a drawing that shows some or all of Earth on a flat surface. Mapmakers often include features to help people use maps more easily.

Mapmakers sometimes draw grids on their maps. A **grid** is made up of lines that cross to form a pattern of squares. You can use a grid to locate places on a map. Look at the grid on the map of North Carolina.

North Carolina

Index to Major Cities

Asheville	C-2	Greensboro	C-3
Cary	C-4	High Point	C-3
Charlotte	C-2	Jacksonville	D-4
Durham	C-4	Raleigh	C-4
Fayetteville	D-4	Wilmington	D-4
Gastonia	C-2	Winston-Salem	C-3

★ State capital

Metropolitan area

- A **map title** tells the subject of the map. The title may also help you know what kind of map it is.
  - Political maps show cities, states, and countries.
  - Physical maps show kinds of land and bodies of water.
  - Historical maps show parts of the world as they were in the past.

- A **map key**, or legend, explains the symbols used on a map. Symbols may be colors, patterns, lines, or other special marks.

- A **locator** is a small map or picture of a globe that shows where the place shown on the main map is located.

Raleigh Area

Northside
Gorman
Youngsville
Durham
Falls Lake
Wake Forest
Rolesville
Neuse
Farrington
Morrisville
B. Everett Jordan Lake
Cary
Knightdale
Green Level
Garner
Raleigh
Apex
New Hill
Holly Springs
Clayton
McCullers
Neuse River

0   5   10 Miles
0   5   10 Kilometers

KENTUCKY

TENNESSEE

Asheville

Great Smoky Mountains National Park

GEORGIA

A2

Around the grid are letters and numbers. The letters label the rows, which run left and right. The numbers label the columns, which run up and down. Each square on the map can be identified by a letter and a number. For example, the top row of squares in the map includes squares A-1 through A-5.

Mapmakers may also include smaller maps within larger maps called **inset maps**. Inset maps show a larger view of an area on the main map. Look at the map of North Carolina below. The inset map allows you to see the Raleigh area more clearly than you can on the main map. Some inset maps may also show areas not shown on the main map.

▶ PRACTICE THE SKILL

Use the map of North Carolina to answer these questions.

1️⃣ What cities are located in square C-4?

2️⃣ In what direction would you travel to go from Charlotte to Greensboro?

3️⃣ Find the map key. What symbol is used to show the state capital?

4️⃣ How many miles is it from Durham to Fayetteville?

5️⃣ Look at the inset map of the Raleigh area. About how far is it from Wake Forest to Durham?

▶ APPLY WHAT YOU LEARNED

Write ten questions about finding places on the North Carolina map. You can ask questions about distance, direction, and location. Then exchange questions with a classmate. See if you can answer all your classmate's questions.

• A **map scale** is used to compare a distance on the map to a distance in the real world. It helps you find the real distance between places. Notice that the map scale shows both miles and kilometers.

• A **compass rose**, or direction marker, shows directions.

• The **cardinal directions**, or main directions, are north, south, east, and west.

• The **intermediate directions**, or directions between the cardinal directions, are northeast, northwest, southeast, and southwest.

The World
POLITICAL

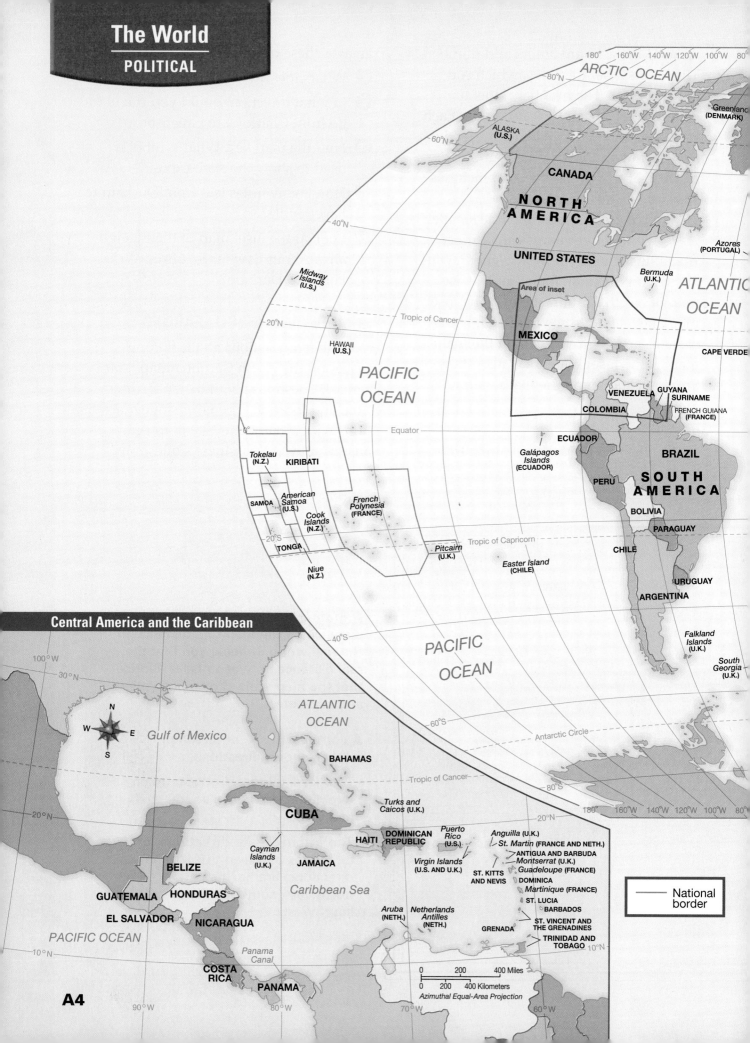

ARCTIC OCEAN

180° 160°W 140°W 120°W 100°W 80°

80°N

60°N

Greenland (DENMARK)

ALASKA (U.S.)

CANADA

40°N

NORTH AMERICA

UNITED STATES

Azores (PORTUGAL)

ATLANTIC OCEAN

Bermuda (U.K.)

20°N

Tropic of Cancer

Area of inset

MEXICO

CAPE VERDE

Midway Islands (U.S.)

HAWAII (U.S.)

PACIFIC OCEAN

VENEZUELA GUYANA SURINAME

COLOMBIA

FRENCH GUIANA (FRANCE)

0° Equator

ECUADOR

Tokelau (N.Z.)

KIRIBATI

Galápagos Islands (ECUADOR)

BRAZIL

PERU

SOUTH AMERICA

SAMOA

American Samoa (U.S.)

French Polynesia (FRANCE)

BOLIVIA

Cook Islands (N.Z.)

PARAGUAY

20°S

TONGA

Pitcairn (U.K.)

Tropic of Capricorn

CHILE

URUGUAY

Niue (N.Z.)

Easter Island (CHILE)

ARGENTINA

40°S

PACIFIC OCEAN

Falkland Islands (U.K.)

South Georgia (U.K.)

60°S

Antarctic Circle

80°S

180° 160°W 140°W 120°W 100°W 80°

Central America and the Caribbean

100°W

30°N

N
W E
S

Gulf of Mexico

ATLANTIC OCEAN

Tropic of Cancer

BAHAMAS

20°N

CUBA

Turks and Caicos (U.K.)

Cayman Islands (U.K.)

HAITI

DOMINICAN REPUBLIC

Puerto Rico (U.S.)

Anguilla (U.K.)
St. Martin (FRANCE AND NETH.)
ANTIGUA AND BARBUDA
Montserrat (U.K.)
Guadeloupe (FRANCE)

BELIZE

JAMAICA

Virgin Islands (U.S. AND U.K.)

ST. KITTS AND NEVIS

DOMINICA

Martinique (FRANCE)

GUATEMALA HONDURAS

Caribbean Sea

ST. LUCIA

BARBADOS

EL SALVADOR NICARAGUA

Aruba (NETH.)

Netherlands Antilles (NETH.)

ST. VINCENT AND THE GRENADINES

GRENADA

TRINIDAD AND TOBAGO

PACIFIC OCEAN

10°N

Panama Canal

COSTA RICA

PANAMA

90°W

80°W

70°W

60°W

10°N

20°N

─── National border

0   200   400 Miles
0   200   400 Kilometers
Azimuthal Equal-Area Projection

A4

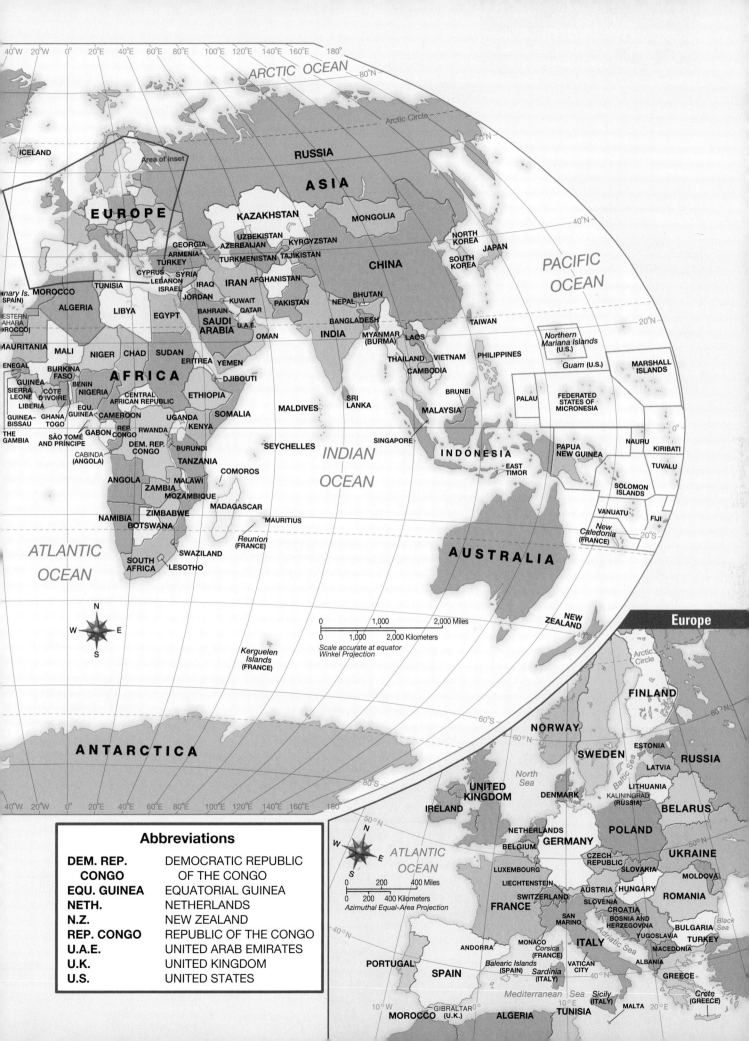

40°W 20°W 0° 20°E 40°E 60°E 80°E 100°E 120°E 140°E 160°E 180°

ARCTIC OCEAN

80°N

Arctic Circle

60°N

ICELAND

RUSSIA

EUROPE

ASIA

KAZAKHSTAN

MONGOLIA

40°N

Area of inset

GEORGIA

UZBEKISTAN KYRGYZSTAN

AZERBAIJAN

ARMENIA

NORTH
KOREA

TURKEY

TURKMENISTAN TAJIKISTAN

JAPAN

CYPRUS

SYRIA

CHINA

SOUTH
KOREA

PACIFIC
OCEAN

LEBANON

IRAQ

IRAN AFGHANISTAN

ISRAEL

JORDAN

KUWAIT

BAHRAIN

QATAR

PAKISTAN

BHUTAN

NEPAL

nary Is. MOROCCO
(SPAIN)

TUNISIA

20°N

ALGERIA

LIBYA

EGYPT

SAUDI
ARABIA

U.A.E.

BANGLADESH

TAIWAN

ESTERN
AHARA
OROCCO)

OMAN

INDIA

MYANMAR
(BURMA)

LAOS

Northern
Mariana Islands
(U.S.)

MARSHALL
ISLANDS

MAURITANIA

MALI

NIGER

CHAD

SUDAN

ERITREA

YEMEN

THAILAND

VIETNAM

PHILIPPINES

Guam (U.S.)

ENEGAL

BURKINA
FASO

AFRICA

DJIBOUTI

CAMBODIA

GUINEA

BENIN

NIGERIA

CENTRAL
AFRICAN REPUBLIC

ETHIOPIA

SRI
LANKA

BRUNEI

PALAU

FEDERATED
STATES OF
MICRONESIA

SIERRA
LEONE

CÔTE
D'IVOIRE

MALDIVES

0°

LIBERIA

GHANA

EQU.
GUINEA

CAMEROON

UGANDA

SOMALIA

MALAYSIA

GUINEA-
BISSAU

TOGO

KENYA

INDONESIA

PAPUA
NEW GUINEA

NAURU

KIRIBATI

THE
GAMBIA

GABON

REP.
CONGO

RWANDA

SINGAPORE

TUVALU

SÃO TOMÉ
AND PRÍNCIPE

DEM. REP.
CONGO

BURUNDI

SEYCHELLES

INDIAN

EAST
TIMOR

SOLOMON
ISLANDS

CABINDA
(ANGOLA)

TANZANIA

OCEAN

VANUATU

FIJI

ANGOLA

COMOROS

New
Caledonia
(FRANCE)

20°S

MALAWI

ZAMBIA

MOZAMBIQUE

MADAGASCAR

ZIMBABWE

MAURITIUS

NAMIBIA

BOTSWANA

AUSTRALIA

ATLANTIC

Reunion
(FRANCE)

SWAZILAND

OCEAN

SOUTH
AFRICA

LESOTHO

0 1,000 2,000 Miles

N

0 1,000 2,000 Kilometers

W E

Scale accurate at equator
Winkel Projection

NEW
ZEALAND

S

40°S

Kerguelen
Islands
(FRANCE)

60°S

Europe

FINLAND

ANTARCTICA

80°S

NORWAY

Arctic
Circle

ESTONIA

SWEDEN

RUSSIA

LATVIA

North
Sea

LITHUANIA

UNITED
KINGDOM

DENMARK

KALININGRAD
(RUSSIA)

BELARUS

IRELAND

50°N

NETHERLANDS

POLAND

GERMANY

UKRAINE

BELGIUM

CZECH
REPUBLIC

SLOVAKIA

Abbreviations

DEM. REP. CONGO	DEMOCRATIC REPUBLIC OF THE CONGO
EQU. GUINEA	EQUATORIAL GUINEA
NETH.	NETHERLANDS
N.Z.	NEW ZEALAND
REP. CONGO	REPUBLIC OF THE CONGO
U.A.E.	UNITED ARAB EMIRATES
U.K.	UNITED KINGDOM
U.S.	UNITED STATES

ATLANTIC

LUXEMBOURG

LIECHTENSTEIN

AUSTRIA

HUNGARY

MOLDOVA

OCEAN

ROMANIA

SWITZERLAND

SLOVENIA

N

W E

FRANCE

SAN
MARINO

CROATIA

BOSNIA AND
HERZEGOVINA

S

0 200 400 Miles

MONACO

YUGOSLAVIA

BULGARIA

Black
Sea

0 200 400 Kilometers

Corsica
(FRANCE)

ITALY

Adriatic
Sea

MACEDONIA

TURKEY

Azimuthal Equal-Area Projection

ANDORRA

VATICAN
CITY

ALBANIA

40°N

PORTUGAL

SPAIN

Balearic Islands
(SPAIN)

Sardinia
(ITALY)

GREECE

10°W

0°

Mediterranean Sea

Sicily
(ITALY)

Crete
(GREECE)

MOROCCO

GIBRALTAR
(U.K.)

10°E

ALGERIA

TUNISIA

MALTA

20°E

The World
PHYSICAL

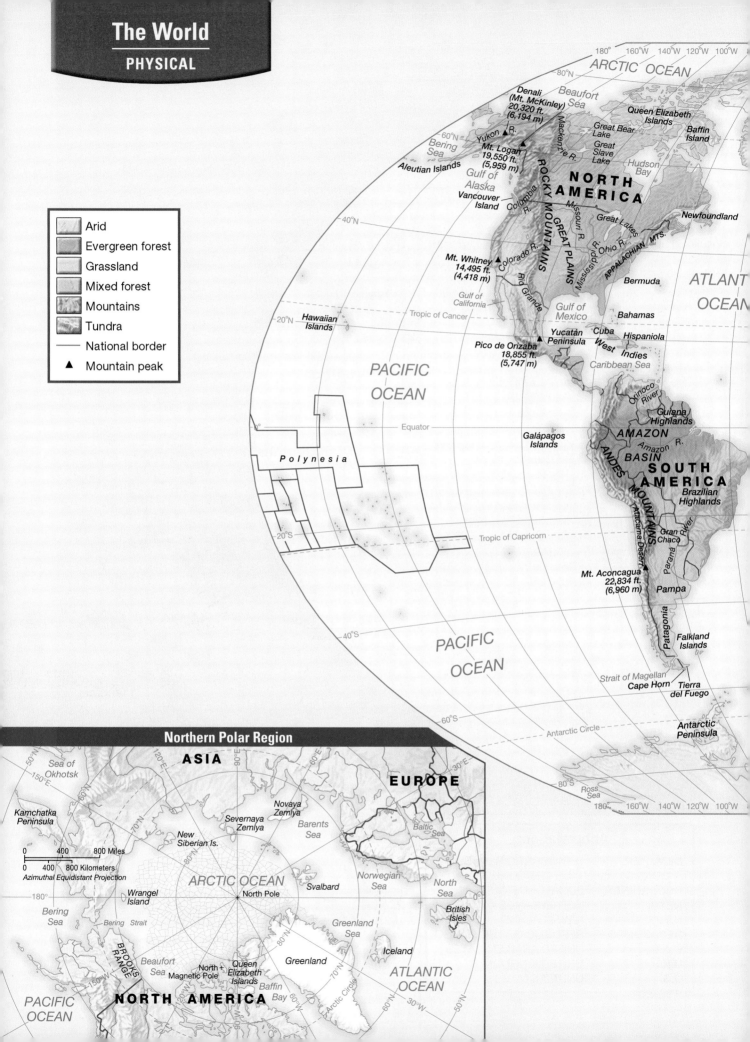

Legend

- Arid
- Evergreen forest
- Grassland
- Mixed forest
- Mountains
- Tundra
- National border
- ▲ Mountain peak

ARCTIC OCEAN

180° 160°W 140°W 120°W 100°W
80°N

Beaufort Sea

Denali (Mt. McKinley) 20,320 ft. (6,194 m) ▲

Queen Elizabeth Islands

Baffin Island

60°N

Yukon R.

Mt. Logan 19,550 ft. (5,959 m) ▲

Great Bear Lake

Great Slave Lake

Hudson Bay

Aleutian Islands

Gulf of Alaska

Mackenzie R.

NORTH AMERICA

40°N

Vancouver Island

Columbia R.

ROCKY MOUNTAINS

GREAT PLAINS

Missouri R.

Great Lakes

Newfoundland

Mt. Whitney 14,495 ft. (4,418 m) ▲

Colorado R.

Mississippi R.

Ohio R.

APPALACHIAN MTS.

Bermuda

ATLANTIC OCEAN

Rio Grande

Gulf of California

Gulf of Mexico

Bahamas

Tropic of Cancer

20°N

Hawaiian Islands

Pico de Orizaba 18,855 ft. (5,747 m) ▲

Yucatán Peninsula

Cuba

Hispaniola

West Indies

Caribbean Sea

PACIFIC OCEAN

Equator

Galápagos Islands

Orinoco River

Guiana Highlands

AMAZON BASIN

Amazon R.

SOUTH AMERICA

Polynesia

ANDES MOUNTAINS

Brazilian Highlands

20°S

Atacama Desert

Gran Chaco

Paraná River

Tropic of Capricorn

Mt. Aconcagua 22,834 ft. (6,960 m) ▲

Pampa

40°S

PACIFIC OCEAN

Patagonia

Falkland Islands

Strait of Magellan

Cape Horn

Tierra del Fuego

60°S

Antarctic Circle

Ross Sea

Antarctic Peninsula

80°S

180° 160°W 140°W 120°W 100°W

Northern Polar Region

ASIA

EUROPE

Sea of Okhotsk

150°E

120°E

90°E

60°E

30°E

Novaya Zemlya

Severnaya Zemlya

Barents Sea

Baltic Sea

Kamchatka Peninsula

New Siberian Is.

70°N

Norwegian Sea

North Sea

0   400   800 Miles
0   400   800 Kilometers
Azimuthal Equidistant Projection

ARCTIC OCEAN

Wrangel Island

North Pole

Svalbard

British Isles

180°

Bering Sea

Bering Strait

BROOKS RANGE

Beaufort Sea

North Magnetic Pole

Queen Elizabeth Islands

Greenland Sea

Greenland

Iceland

ATLANTIC OCEAN

PACIFIC OCEAN

NORTH AMERICA

Baffin Bay

Arctic Circle

30°W

50°W

60°N

70°N

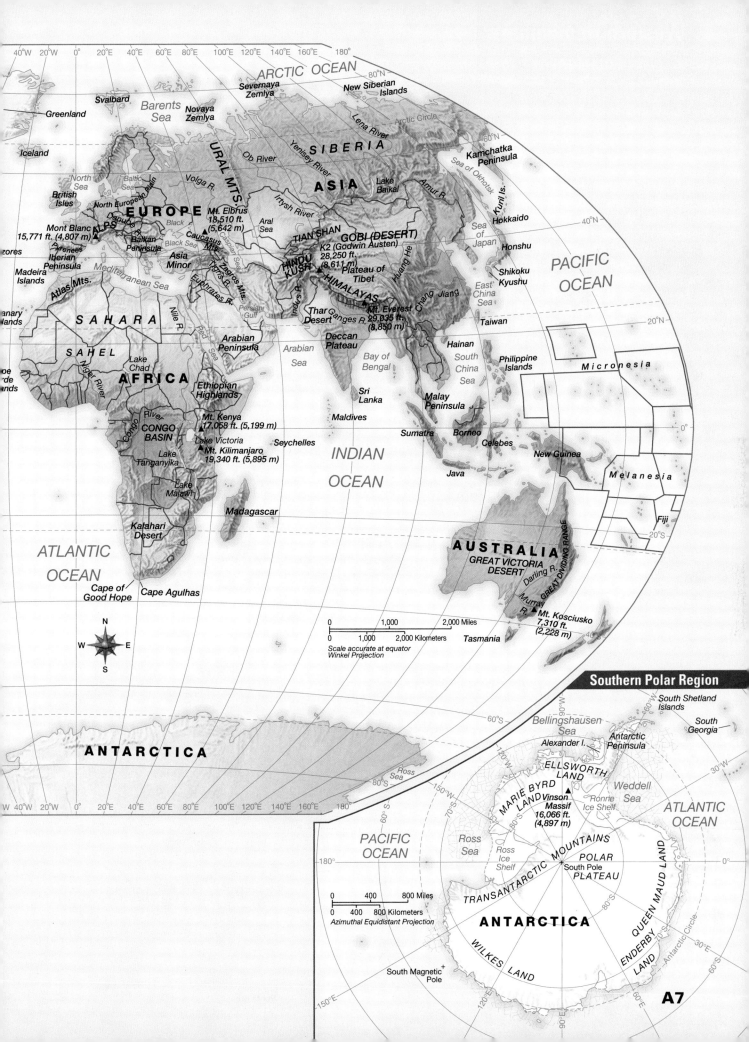

ARCTIC OCEAN

40°W 20°W 0° 20°E 40°E 60°E 80°E 100°E 120°E 140°E 160°E 180°

80°N

Greenland

Svalbard

Barents Sea

Severnaya Zemlya

Novaya Zemlya

New Siberian Islands

Arctic Circle

Iceland

North Sea

Baltic Sea

British Isles

SIBERIA

Lena River

60°N

URAL MTS.

Ob River

Yenisey River

ASIA

Kamchatka Peninsula

Sea of Okhotsk

North European Plain

EUROPE

Volga R.

Irtysh River

Lake Baikal

Amur R.

40°N

Mt. Elbrus 18,510 ft. (5,642 m)

Aral Sea

Kuril Is.

Hokkaido

Mont Blanc 15,771 ft. (4,807 m)

ALPS

Danube R.

Black Sea

Caucasus Mts.

Balkan Peninsula

Black Sea

Caspian Sea

TIAN SHAN

GOBI (DESERT)

K2 (Godwin Austen) 28,250 ft. (8,611 m)

Sea of Japan

Honshu

Shikoku

Kyushu

Pyrenees

Azores

Iberian Peninsula

Asia Minor

Zagros Mts.

HINDU KUSH

Plateau of Tibet

Huang He

East China Sea

Madeira Islands

Mediterranean Sea

Tigris R.

Euphrates R.

Indus R.

HIMALAYAS

Mt. Everest 29,035 ft. (8,850 m)

Chang Jiang

Atlas Mts.

Nile R.

Persian Gulf

Thar Desert

Ganges R.

Taiwan

20°N

Canary Islands

SAHARA

Red Sea

Arabian Peninsula

Deccan Plateau

Hainan

Cape Verde Islands

SAHEL

Lake Chad

Niger River

AFRICA

Arabian Sea

Bay of Bengal

South China Sea

Philippine Islands

Micronesia

0°

Ethiopian Highlands

Mt. Kenya 17,058 ft. (5,199 m)

Sri Lanka

Malay Peninsula

Congo River

CONGO BASIN

Lake Victoria

Mt. Kilimanjaro 19,340 ft. (5,895 m)

Seychelles

Maldives

INDIAN

Sumatra

Borneo

Celebes

New Guinea

Melanesia

Lake Tanganyika

Java

OCEAN

Lake Malawi

Madagascar

Fiji

20°S

Kalahari Desert

AUSTRALIA

GREAT VICTORIA DESERT

Darling R.

GREAT DIVIDING RANGE

ATLANTIC

OCEAN

Cape of Good Hope

Cape Agulhas

Murray R.

Mt. Kosciusko 7,310 ft. (2,228 m)

N
W   E
S

0   1,000   2,000 Miles
0   1,000   2,000 Kilometers
Scale accurate at equator
Winkel Projection

Tasmania

40°S

ANTARCTICA

W 40°W 20°W 0° 20°E 40°E 60°E 80°E 100°E 120°E 140°E 160°E 180°

Ross Sea

80°S

South Shetland Islands

South Georgia

60°S

Bellingshausen Sea

Antarctic Peninsula

Alexander I.

ELLSWORTH LAND

Weddell Sea

PACIFIC OCEAN

MARIE BYRD LAND

Vinson Massif 16,066 ft. (4,897 m)

Ronne Ice Shelf

ATLANTIC OCEAN

Ross Sea

Ross Ice Shelf

TRANSANTARCTIC MOUNTAINS

POLAR PLATEAU

South Pole

QUEEN MAUD LAND

0   400   800 Miles
0   400   800 Kilometers
Azimuthal Equidistant Projection

ANTARCTICA

ENDERBY LAND

WILKES LAND

South Magnetic Pole

Antarctic Circle

A7

Western Hemisphere
POLITICAL

ARCTIC OCEAN

Viscount Melville Sound

Beaufort Sea

Baffin Bay

Greenland (DENMARK)

Bering Strait

ALASKA (U.S.)

Yukon River

Fairbanks

Anchorage

Gulf of Alaska

Bering Sea

Whitehorse

Juneau

Mackenzie River

Great Bear Lake

Liard River

Peace River

Yellowknife

Great Slave Lake

CANADA

Lake Athabasca

Athabasca R.

Edmonton

Calgary

Saskatoon

Saskatchewan R.

Regina

Lake Winnipeg

Winnipeg

James Bay

Hudson Bay

Thunder Bay

Davis Strait

Arctic Circle

Labrador Sea

Foxe Basin

Hudson Strait

60°N

St. John's

Vancouver

Puget Sound

Seattle

Portland

Columbia R.

Boise

Snake R.

UNITED STATES

Great Salt Lake

Salt Lake City

Reno

San Francisco

Las Vegas

Los Angeles

San Diego

Tucson

Phoenix

Colorado R.

Denver

Missouri R.

St. Louis

Memphis

Mississippi R.

Chicago

Detroit

Cleveland

Indianapolis

Great Lakes

Ottawa

Quebec

Montreal

St. John

Halifax

Albany

Boston

New York City

Philadelphia

Washington, D.C.

Richmond

Norfolk

Raleigh

Atlanta

Charleston

Savannah

Jacksonville

Orlando

Tampa

Miami

Gulf of St. Lawrence

St. Lawrence River

Toronto

Dallas

New Orleans

Houston

San Antonio

El Paso

Hermosillo

Chihuahua

Rio Grande

Gulf of California

MEXICO

Durango

Monterrey

Gulf of Mexico

BAHAMAS

Nassau

Havana

CUBA

HAITI

Port-au-Prince

Santo Domingo

JAMAICA

Kingston

Puerto Rico (U.S.)

DOMINICAN REPUBLIC

León

Tampico

Guadalajara

Mexico City

Puebla

Veracruz

Acapulco

BELIZE

Belmopan

GUATEMALA

Guatemala City

San Salvador

EL SALVADOR

Tegucigalpa

HONDURAS

Managua

NICARAGUA

San José

COSTA RICA

Panama City

PANAMA

Caribbean Sea

Maracaibo

Caracas

VENEZUELA

GUYANA

Georgetown

SURINAME

Paramaribo

Cayenne

FRENCH GUIANA (FRANCE)

Medellín

Cali

Bogota

COLOMBIA

Quito

ECUADOR

Guayaquil

Iquitos

Manaus

Rio Negro

Amazon R.

Belém

Fortaleza

Recife

Trujillo

PERU

Lima

Cuzco

Lake Titicaca

La Paz

Arequipa

BOLIVIA

Sucre

Tapajós River

Xingu R.

Tocantins R.

São Francisco R.

BRAZIL

Brasília

Goiânia

Salvador

Belo Horizonte

Rio de Janeiro

Campo Grande

São Paulo

Curitiba

Antofagasta

PARAGUAY

Salta

Asunción

Paraguay R.

San Miguel de Tucumán

CHILE

Córdoba

Pôrto Alegre

URUGUAY

Valparaíso

Santiago

Rosario

Buenos Aires

La Plata

Montevideo

Rio de la Plata

Concepción

Mar del Plata

Valdivia

Bahía Blanca

ARGENTINA

Punta Arenas

Falkland Islands (U.K.)

South Georgia (U.K.)

Paraná R.

30°N

ATLANTIC OCEAN

Tropic of Cancer

Honolulu

HAWAII (U.S.)

PACIFIC OCEAN

0°

Equator

Galápagos Islands (ECUADOR)

French Polynesia (FRANCE)

Papeete

Tropic of Capricorn

30°S

0   1,000   2,000 Miles

0   1,000   2,000 Kilometers

Miller Cylindrical Projection

— National border

⊛ National capital

• City

A8

N
W   E
S

150°W   120°W   90°W   60°W

3

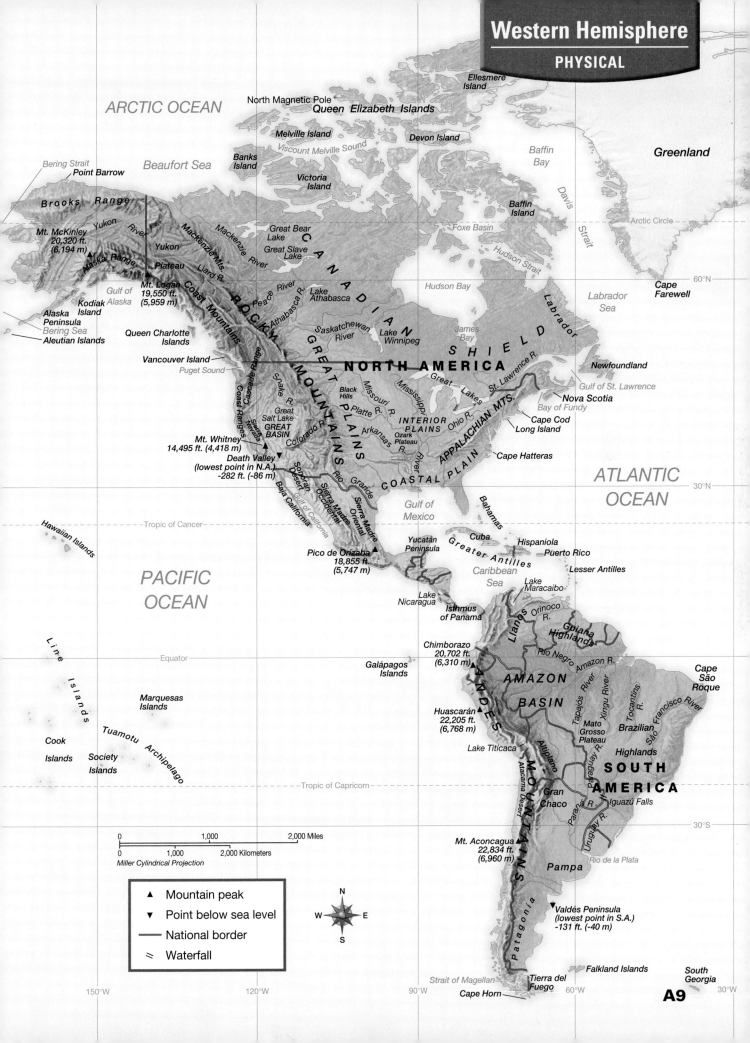

ARCTIC OCEAN

Bering Strait

Point Barrow

Beaufort Sea

Brooks Range

Mt. McKinley
20,320 ft.
(6,194 m)

Yukon River

Yukon

Alaska Range

Plateau

Mackenzie Mts.

Mackenzie River

Liard R.

Gulf of Alaska

Mt. Logan
19,550 ft.
(5,959 m)

Coast Mountains

Peace River

Athabasca R.

Banks Island

Victoria Island

Viscount Melville Sound

Melville Island

Queen Elizabeth Islands

North Magnetic Pole

Devon Island

Ellesmere Island

Baffin Bay

Greenland

Baffin Island

Davis Strait

Arctic Circle

Cape Farewell

60°N

Labrador Sea

Alaska Peninsula

Kodiak Island

Bering Sea

Aleutian Islands

Queen Charlotte Islands

Vancouver Island

Puget Sound

Cascade Range

Coast Ranges

Sierra Nevada

Snake R.

Great Salt Lake

GREAT BASIN

Colorado R.

Mt. Whitney
14,495 ft. (4,418 m)

Death Valley
(lowest point in N.A.)
-282 ft. (-86 m)

Baja California

Gulf of California

Sonoran Desert

Sierra Madre Occidental

Rio Grande

Sierra Madre Oriental

C A N A D I A N

ROCKY MOUNTAINS

GREAT PLAINS

Great Bear Lake

Great Slave Lake

Lake Athabasca

Saskatchewan River

Lake Winnipeg

S H I E L D

Hudson Bay

Foxe Basin

Hudson Strait

James Bay

Labrador

NORTH AMERICA

Black Hills

Missouri R.

Platte R.

Arkansas

Ozark Plateau

Mississippi

INTERIOR PLAINS

Ohio R.

Great Lakes

St. Lawrence R.

APPALACHIAN MTS.

COASTAL PLAIN

Newfoundland

Gulf of St. Lawrence

Nova Scotia

Bay of Fundy

Cape Cod

Long Island

Cape Hatteras

ATLANTIC OCEAN

30°N

Tropic of Cancer

Gulf of Mexico

Pico de Orizaba
18,855 ft.
(5,747 m)

Yucatán Peninsula

Bahamas

Cuba

Greater Antilles

Hispaniola

Puerto Rico

Lesser Antilles

Caribbean Sea

Lake Maracaibo

HAWAIIAN Islands

PACIFIC OCEAN

Lake Nicaragua

Isthmus of Panama

Llanos

Orinoco R.

Guiana Highlands

Rio Negro

Amazon R.

Chimborazo
20,702 ft.
(6,310 m)

Galápagos Islands

Equator

Line Islands

Marquesas Islands

Tuamotu Archipelago

Cook Islands

Society Islands

Huascarán
22,205 ft.
(6,768 m)

Lake Titicaca

A N D E S

AMAZON BASIN

Tapajós River

Xingu River

Mato Grosso Plateau

Tocantins

São Francisco River

Cape São Roque

Brazilian Highlands

SOUTH AMERICA

Altiplano

Atacama Desert

M O U N T A I N S

Gran Chaco

Paraguay R.

Paraná R.

Iguazú Falls

Uruguay R.

Tropic of Capricorn

Mt. Aconcagua
22,834 ft.
(6,960 m)

Rio de la Plata

Pampa

30°S

Valdés Peninsula
(lowest point in S.A.)
-131 ft. (-40 m)

Patagonia

Falkland Islands

South Georgia

Strait of Magellan

Tierra del Fuego

Cape Horn

0   1,000   2,000 Miles

0   1,000   2,000 Kilometers

Miller Cylindrical Projection

▲ Mountain peak

▼ Point below sea level

─ National border

≈ Waterfall

N
W — E
S

150°W   120°W   90°W   60°W   30°W

A9

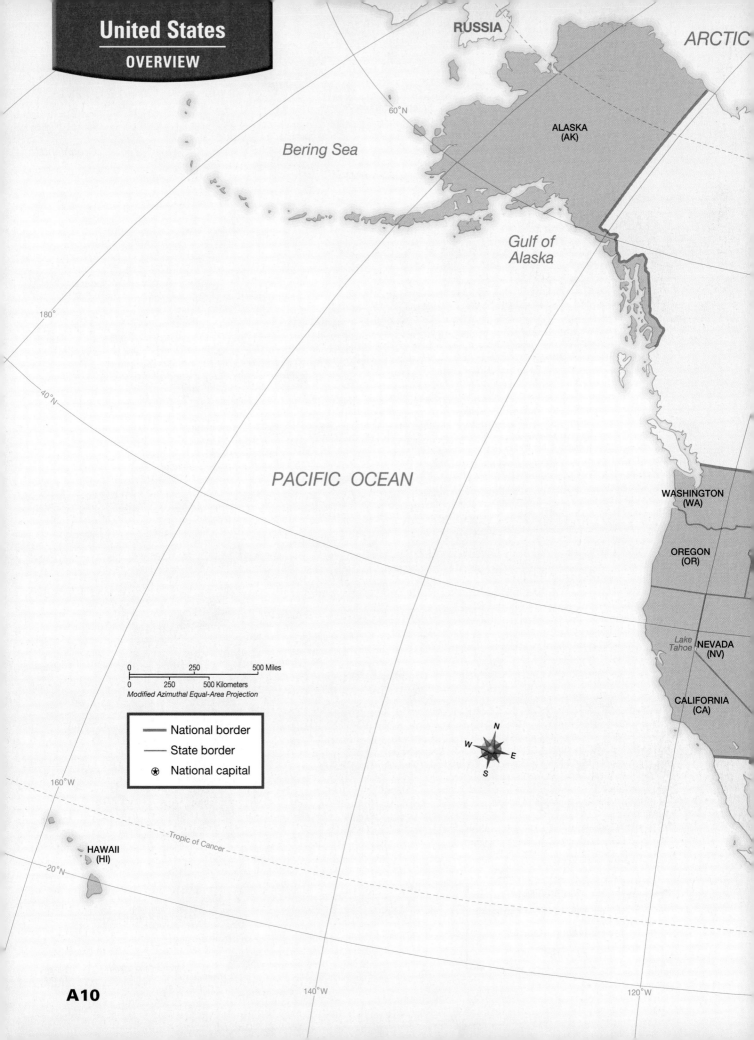

United States
OVERVIEW

RUSSIA

ARCTIC

60°N

Bering Sea

ALASKA
(AK)

Gulf of
Alaska

180°

40°N

PACIFIC OCEAN

WASHINGTON
(WA)

OREGON
(OR)

Lake
Tahoe

NEVADA
(NV)

```
0          250          500 Miles
0      250      500 Kilometers
```
Modified Azimuthal Equal-Area Projection

CALIFORNIA
(CA)

N
W   E
S

—— National border

—— State border

⊛ National capital

160°W

Tropic of Cancer

HAWAII
(HI)

20°N

140°W

120°W

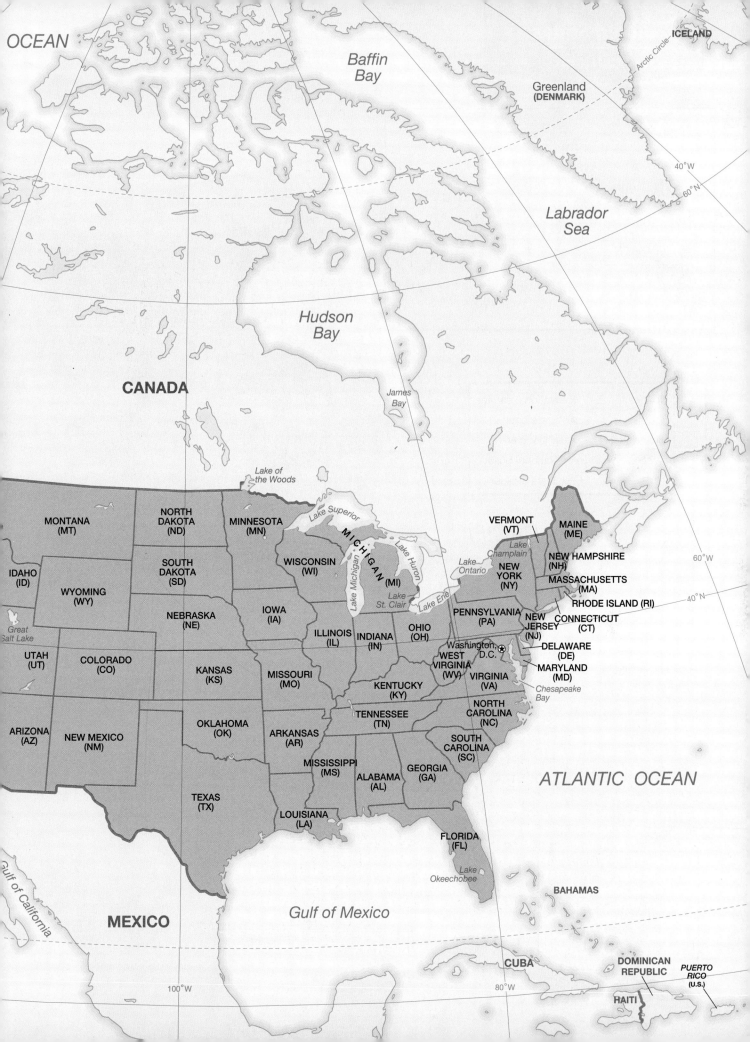

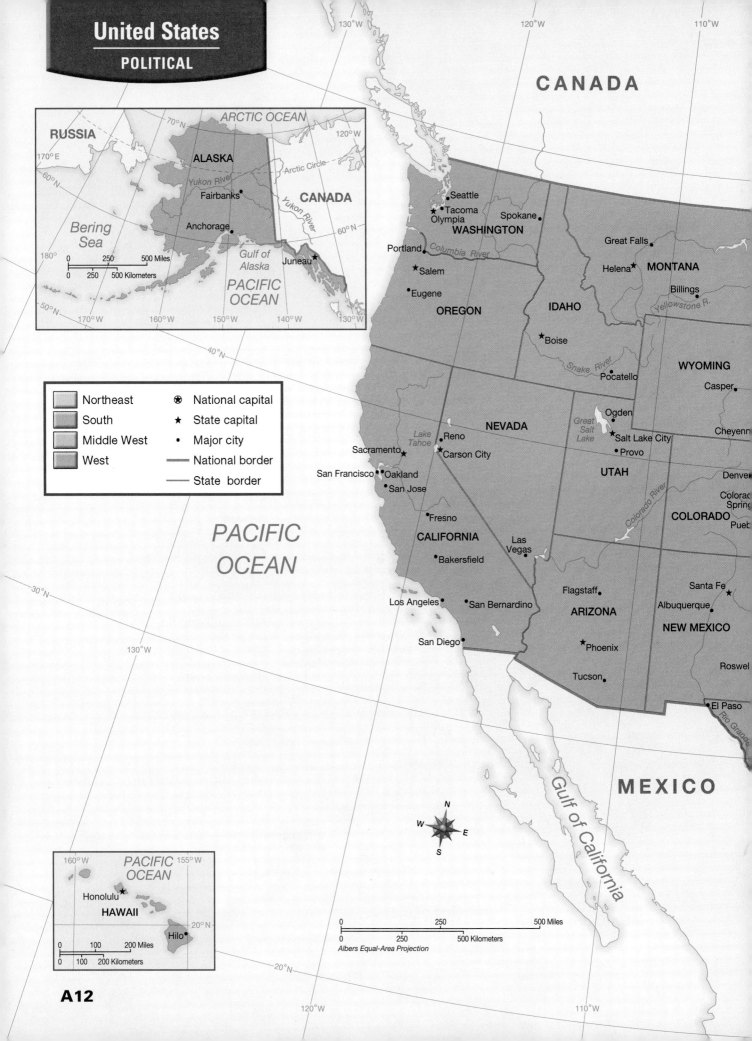

United States
POLITICAL

CANADA

Alaska Inset
RUSSIA
ARCTIC OCEAN
170° E
70° N
120° W
ALASKA
Arctic Circle
Fairbanks
CANADA
Yukon River
60° N
Bering Sea
Anchorage
60° N
180°
Gulf of Alaska
Juneau
PACIFIC OCEAN
250 500 Miles
250 500 Kilometers
170° W   160° W   150° W   140° W   130° W
50° N

40° N

PACIFIC OCEAN

Legend
Northeast
South
Middle West
West
⊛ National capital
★ State capital
• Major city
— National border
— State border

Main map
130° W   120° W   110° W

CANADA

Seattle
★ Tacoma
Olympia   Spokane
WASHINGTON
Great Falls
Portland   Columbia River
Helena ★   MONTANA
★ Salem
Billings
Eugene
Yellowstone R.
OREGON   IDAHO
★ Boise
Snake River
WYOMING
Pocatello
Casper
Great Salt Lake   Ogden
NEVADA
Cheyenne
Lake Tahoe   Reno
★ Salt Lake City
Sacramento ★   Carson City
Provo
San Francisco • Oakland
UTAH
Denver
• San Jose
Colorado River
Colorado Springs
Fresno
COLORADO
Pueb
CALIFORNIA   Las Vegas
• Bakersfield
Santa Fe
Flagstaff
★
Los Angeles   Albuquerque
30° N
• San Bernardino
ARIZONA
NEW MEXICO
San Diego   ★ Phoenix
Roswel
130° W
Tucson
El Paso
Rio Grande

PACIFIC OCEAN

N
W   E
S

MEXICO

Gulf of California

500 Miles
250
250   500 Kilometers
Albers Equal-Area Projection

Hawaii Inset
160° W   PACIFIC OCEAN   155° W
Honolulu ★
HAWAII
20° N
100 200 Miles
100 200 Kilometers
Hilo

20° N
120° W   110° W

United States
PHYSICAL

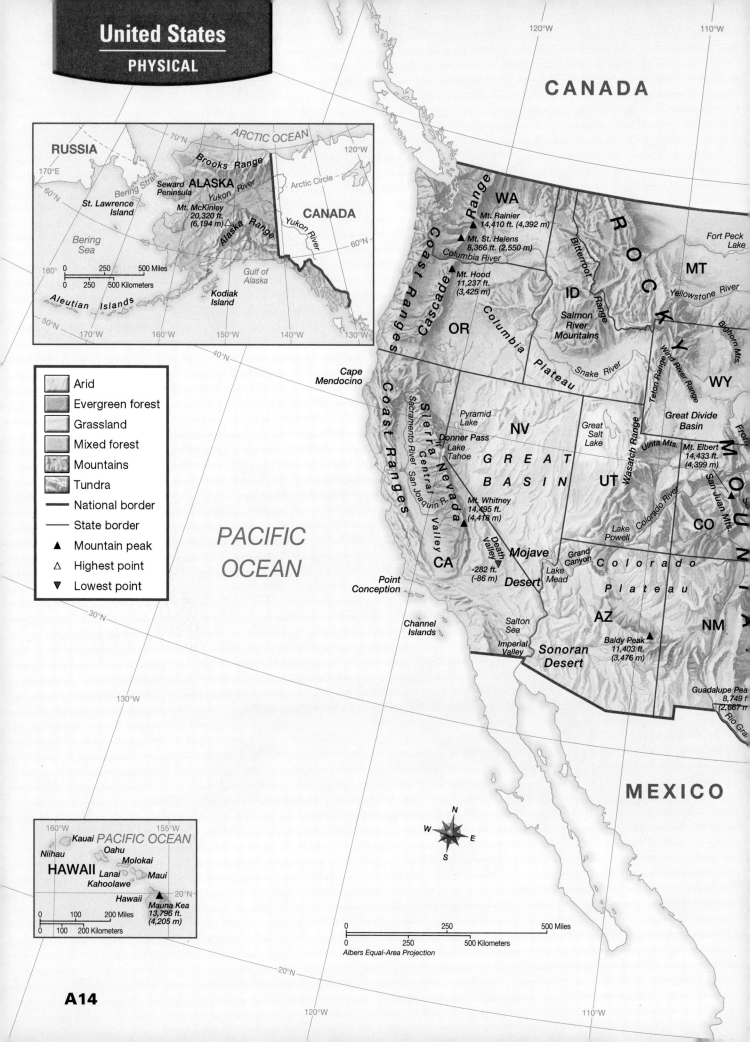

CANADA

RUSSIA

ARCTIC OCEAN

70°N

Brooks Range

170°E

Seward Peninsula

ALASKA

Yukon River

120°W

Arctic Circle

60°N

CANADA

St. Lawrence Island

Mt. McKinley 20,320 ft. (6,194 m) △

Alaska Range

Yukon River

60°N

Bering Sea

Bering Strait

Gulf of Alaska

0   250   500 Miles
0   250   500 Kilometers

Aleutian Islands

Kodiak Island

180°   50°N   170°W   160°W   150°W   140°W   130°W

40°N

120°W   110°W

WA

Coast Range

Mt. Rainier 14,410 ft. (4,392 m) ▲

Cascade

▲ Mt. St. Helens 8,366 ft. (2,550 m)

Columbia River

Bitterroot Range

ROCKY

Fort Peck Lake

MT

Yellowstone River

Mt. Hood 11,237 ft. (3,425 m) ▲

ID

Salmon River Mountains

Bighorn Mts.

OR

Columbia Plateau

Snake River

Teton Range

Wind River Range

WY

Cape Mendocino

Coast Ranges

Sacramento River

Sierra Nevada

Central Valley

San Joaquin R.

Pyramid Lake

Donner Pass

Lake Tahoe

NV

GREAT BASIN

Great Salt Lake

Wasatch Range

Uinta Mts.

Great Divide Basin

Mt. Elbert 14,433 ft. (4,399 m) ▲

UT

San Juan Mts.

CO

Legend

	Arid
	Evergreen forest
	Grassland
	Mixed forest
	Mountains
	Tundra
—	National border
—	State border
▲	Mountain peak
△	Highest point
▼	Lowest point

PACIFIC OCEAN

Mt. Whitney 14,495 ft. (4,418 m) ▲

Death Valley

Mojave

-282 ft. (-86 m) ▼

Lake Mead

Grand Canyon

Lake Powell

Colorado River

Colorado Plateau

Point Conception

CA

Desert

30°N

Channel Islands

Salton Sea

Imperial Valley

Sonoran Desert

Baldy Peak 11,403 ft. (3,476 m) ▲

AZ

NM

Guadalupe Pea 8,749 f (2,667 m)

Rio Gra

130°W

MEXICO

160°W   155°W

Kauai

PACIFIC OCEAN

Niihau

Oahu

HAWAII

Molokai

Lanai

Maui

Kahoolawe

Hawaii

Mauna Kea 13,796 ft. (4,205 m) ▲

20°N

0   100   200 Miles
0   100   200 Kilometers

N
W   E
S

0   250   500 Miles
0   250   500 Kilometers

Albers Equal-Area Projection

20°N

120°W   110°W

100°W 90°W 80°W 70°W

50°N

CANADA

ATLANTIC OCEAN

Gulf of Mexico

BAHAMAS

CUBA

40°N

70°N

30°N

ND
SD
MN
WI
MI
IA
NE
IL
IN
OH
PA
NY
VT
NH
ME
MA
CT
RI
NJ
MD
DE
WV
VA
KY
KS
MO
TN
NC
SC
OK
AR
MS
AL
GA
TX
LA
FL

G R E A T   P L A I N S

I N T E R I O R   P L A I N S

C E N T R A L   P L A I N S

C O A S T A L   P L A I N

A P P A L A C H I A N   M O U N T A I N S

P I E D M O N T

C O A S T A L   P L A I N

Ozark Plateau

Ouachita Mountains

Edwards Plateau

Llano Estacado

Black Hills

Sand Hills

Smoky Hills

Red Hills

Mesabi Range

Lake of the Woods

Upper Red Lake

Lower Red Lake

Leech Lake

Mille Lacs Lake

Lake Sakakawea

Lake Oahe

Missouri River

North Platte R.

South Platte R.

Platte River

Arkansas River

Canadian River

Red River

Pecos River

Rio Grande

Brazos River

Colorado River

Sabine River

Mississippi River

Wisconsin River

Lake Winnebago

Illinois River

Wabash River

Ohio River

Missouri River

Lake of the Ozarks

Harry S. Truman Reservoir

Lake Texoma

Toledo Bend Reservoir

Sam Rayburn Reservoir

Lake Maurepas

Lake Pontchartrain

Galveston Bay

Mississippi Delta

Mobile Bay

Tombigbee R.

Alabama R.

Chattahoochee R.

Cumberland R.

Cumberland Gap

Lake Barkley

Tennessee R.

Mt. Mitchell 6,684 ft. (2,037 m)

Stone Mountain

Clark Hill Lake

Savannah River

Oconee R.

Ocmulgee R.

Altamaha R.

Okefenokee Swamp

St. Johns River

Cape Canaveral

Lake Okeechobee

Tampa Bay

Everglades

Cape Sable

Florida Keys

Straits of Florida

Cape Fear

Cape Fear River

Roanoke R.

James R.

Cape Hatteras

Cape Charles

Chesapeake Bay

Albemarle Sound

Delaware Bay

Potomac R.

Allegheny Mts.

Hudson R.

Long Island

Finger Lakes

Adirondack Mountains

Lake Ontario

Niagara Falls

Lake Erie

Lake St. Clair

Lake Huron

Lake Michigan

Lower Peninsula

Upper Peninsula

Keweenaw Peninsula

Lake Superior

Isle Royale

St. Lawrence River

Lake Champlain

Green Mts.

White Mts.

Connecticut R.

Cape Ann

Cape Cod

Moosehead Lake

Mt. Katahdin 5,269 ft. (1,606 m)

Mt. Washington 6,288 ft. (1,917 m)

A15

KENTUCKY

WEST VIRGINIA

83°W   82°W   81°W   80

37°N

TENNESSEE

36°N

Norris Lake

Clinch

Nolichucky River

Douglas Lake

French Broad River

Watts Bar Lake

Little Tennessee River

Hiawassee River

Fontana Lake

35°N

Hiwassee Lake

Lake Jocasee

34°N

Lake Stanley Larner

Hartwell Lake

Russell Lake

GEORGIA

Chattahoochee River

Oconee River

Ocmulgee River

Jackson Lake

Lake Sinclair

33°N

New River

Sparta
Mt. Airy
Jefferson
Dobson   Danbury
Elkin   River   King
Boone   Stanleyville
N. Wilkesboro   Yadkinville   Kernersville
Newland   Wilkesboro   Lewisville   Winston-
Bakersville   Yadkin   Clemmons   Salem
                                                    High Point
Burnsville   Gamewell   Lenoir   Taylorsville   Archdal
Marshall   Lake   Hudson   Mocksville   Thomasville
                James   Granite Falls   Lexington
Woodfin   Black   Valdese Hickory   Statesville
         Mtn.   Marion Morganton Icard Conover   Salisbury Spencer
Canton Asheville   Newton   White Rock Lake
Cherokee Waynesville   Fletcher   Maiden Mooresville China Grove
Bryson   Davidson   Kannapolis
City Sylva   Lincolnton   Lake   Cornelius Concord
Robbinsville   Hendersonville Rutherfordton Cherryville Norman Huntersville Badin Lake
Cullowhee   Forest City Shelby Stanley Mt. Holly Albemarle
Andrews   Brevard E. Flat Columbus Kings Mtn. Gastonia Belmont Charlotte
Franklin   Rock   Mint Hill
Murphy   Pineville Matthews
Hayesville   Weddington
                                Monroe Wingate Wadesboro

Lake Keowee

Broad River

Catawba River

Lake Wateree

SOUTH CAROLINA

Lake Murray

Savannah River

Lake Marion

Lake Moultrie

—	State border
★	State capital
•	Other city

A16

84°W   83°W   82°W   81°W   80

VIRGINIA

Smith Mountain Lake

James River

Roanoke River

Leesville Lake

Dan River

Kerr Reservoir

Buggs Island Lake

37°N

Chesapeake Bay

Eden
Wentworth
Reidsville
Yanceyville
Roxboro
Warrenton
Roanoke Rapids
Jackson
Murfreesboro
Winton
Gatesville
Elizabeth City
Camden
Currituck
Currituck Sound

Burlington
Mebane
Hillsborough
Graham
Oxford
Henderson
Halifax
Ahoskie
Hertford
Gatesville
Greensboro
Flat River
Tar River
Louisburg
Enfield
Scotland Neck
Edenton
Albemarle Sound
Kill Devil Hills
36°N
Manteo

Haw River

Falls Lake

Durham
Wake Forest
Nashville
Rocky Mount
Tarboro
Williamston
Windsor River
Columbia
Plymouth
Phelps Lake
Lake Mattamuskeet

Chapel Hill
Randleman
Cary
Raleigh ★
Wendell
Zebulon
Wilson
Asheboro
Garner
Clayton
Farmville
Greenville
Washington
Winterville
Ayden
Snow Hill
Swan Quarter
Pamlico Sound
Cape Hatteras

Troy
Carthage
Lillington
Erwin
Benson
Dunn
Selma
Smithfield
Goldsboro
La Grange
Kinston
Neuse River
Bayboro
35°N

Pinehurst
Southern Pines
Spring Lake
Mt. Olive
Trenton
New Bern

Aberdeen
Fayetteville
Clinton
Warsaw
Havelock
Newport
Beaufort

Rockingham
Hamlet
Raeford
Hope Mills
Kenansville
New River
Piney Green
Morehead City
Lumber River

Red Springs
Wallace
Jacksonville
Cape Lookout

Laurinburg
Lumberton
Elizabethtown
Burgaw
Onslow Bay

Pee Dee River

Whiteville
Lake Waccamaw
Waccamaw River
Wilmington
Wrightsville Beach
34°N

Bolivia
Carolina Beach

Long Beach
Cape Fear

Long Bay

Santee River

ATLANTIC OCEAN

33°N

NORTH CAROLINA

N
W   E
S

0   50   100 Miles
0   50   100 Kilometers

Albers Equal-Area Projection

A17

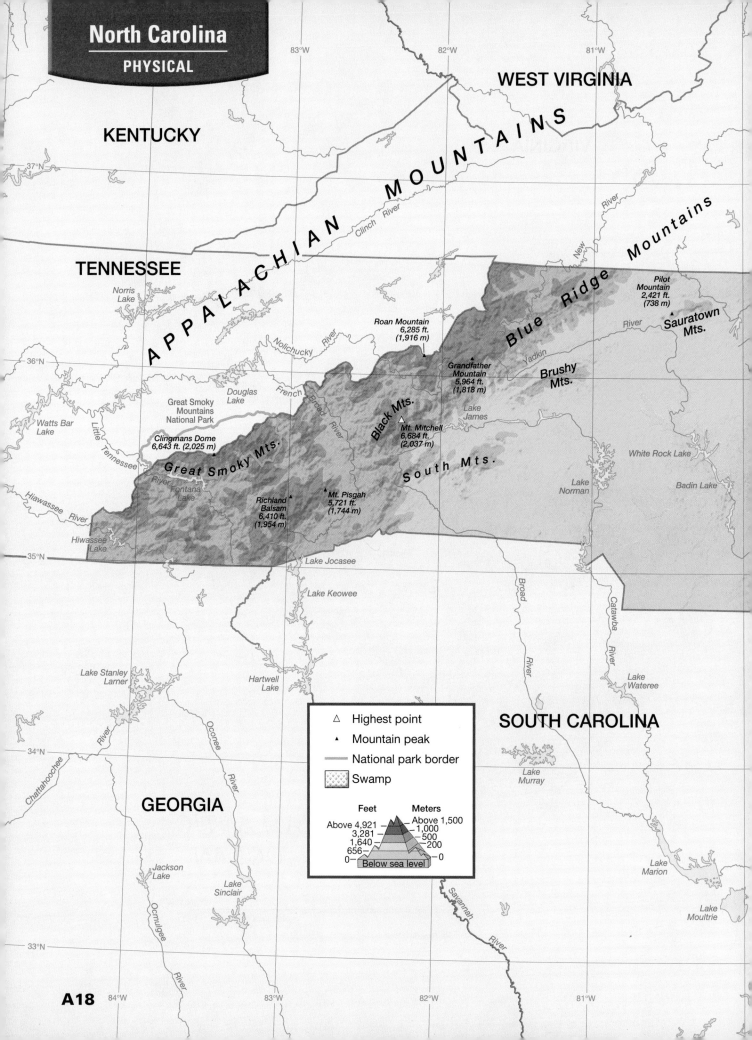

North Carolina
PHYSICAL

KENTUCKY

WEST VIRGINIA

TENNESSEE

A P P A L A C H I A N   M O U N T A I N S

Clinch River

Norris Lake

New River

Blue Ridge Mountains

Yadkin River

Pilot Mountain 2,421 ft. (738 m)

Sauratown Mts.

Roan Mountain 6,285 ft. (1,916 m)

Nolichucky River

French Broad River

Douglas Lake

Grandfather Mountain 5,964 ft. (1,818 m)

Brushy Mts.

Great Smoky Mountains National Park

Black Mts.

Lake James

Watts Bar Lake

Little Tennessee River

Clingmans Dome 6,643 ft. (2,025 m)

Great Smoky Mts.

Mt. Mitchell 6,684 ft. (2,037 m)

White Rock Lake

South Mts.

Fontana Lake

Hiawassee River

Richland Balsam 6,410 ft. (1,954 m)

Mt. Pisgah 5,721 ft. (1,744 m)

Lake Norman

Badin Lake

Hiwassee Lake

Lake Jocasee

Lake Keowee

Broad River

Catawba River

Chattahoochee River

Lake Stanley Larner

Hartwell Lake

Oconee River

SOUTH CAROLINA

Lake Wateree

GEORGIA

Lake Murray

Jackson Lake

Lake Sinclair

Ocmulgee River

Savannah River

Lake Marion

Lake Moultrie

	Highest point
△	Highest point
▲	Mountain peak
━	National park border
▨	Swamp

Feet   **Meters**

Above 4,921 — Above 1,500
3,281 — 1,000
1,640 — 500
656 — 200
0 — 0
Below sea level

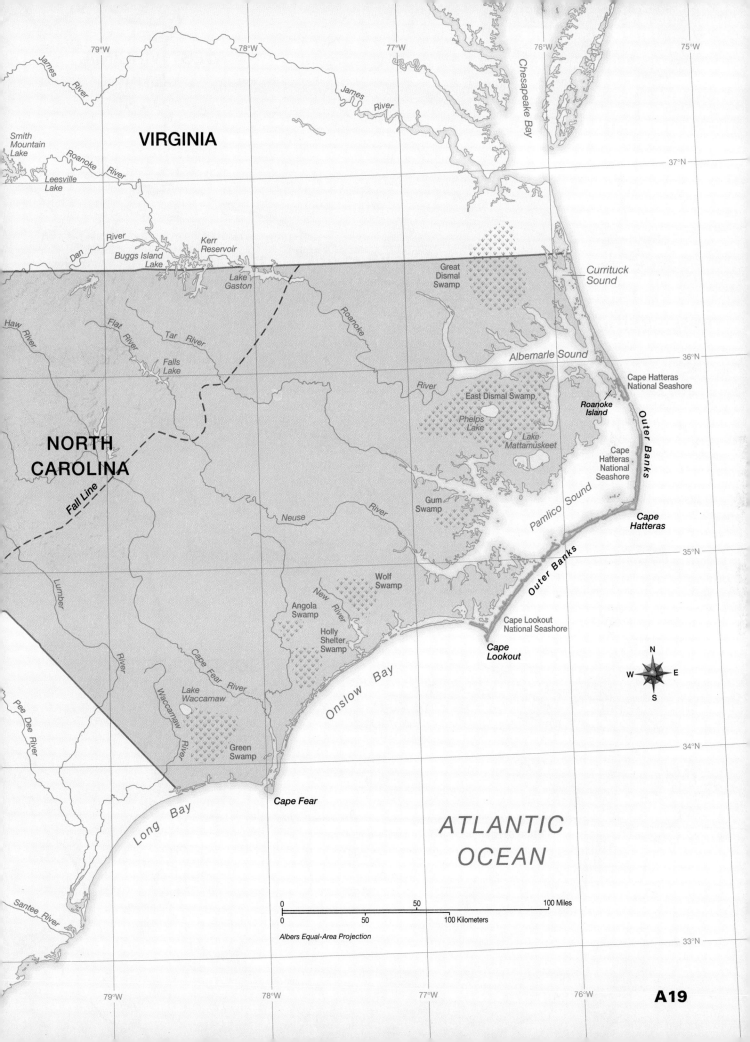

79°W · 78°W · 77°W · 76°W · 75°W

James River

VIRGINIA

Smith Mountain Lake

Roanoke River

Leesville Lake

Chesapeake Bay

37°N

Dan River

Kerr Reservoir

Buggs Island Lake

Lake Gaston

Great Dismal Swamp

Currituck Sound

Haw River

Flat River

Tar River

Falls Lake

Roanoke

Albemarle Sound

36°N

River

Cape Hatteras National Seashore

NORTH CAROLINA

East Dismal Swamp

Phelps Lake

Roanoke Island

Outer Banks

Lake Mattamuskeet

Cape Hatteras National Seashore

Fall Line

Neuse

River

Gum Swamp

Pamlico Sound

Cape Hatteras

Lumber

Wolf Swamp

Outer Banks

35°N

New River

Angola Swamp

Holly Shelter Swamp

Cape Lookout National Seashore

Cape Lookout

Cape Fear River

Waccamaw

Lake Waccamaw

Onslow Bay

N
W · E
S

Pee Dee River

River

Green Swamp

34°N

Cape Fear

Long Bay

ATLANTIC
OCEAN

Santee River

0 · 50 · 100 Miles

0 · 50 · 100 Kilometers

Albers Equal-Area Projection

33°N

79°W · 78°W · 77°W · 76°W

A19

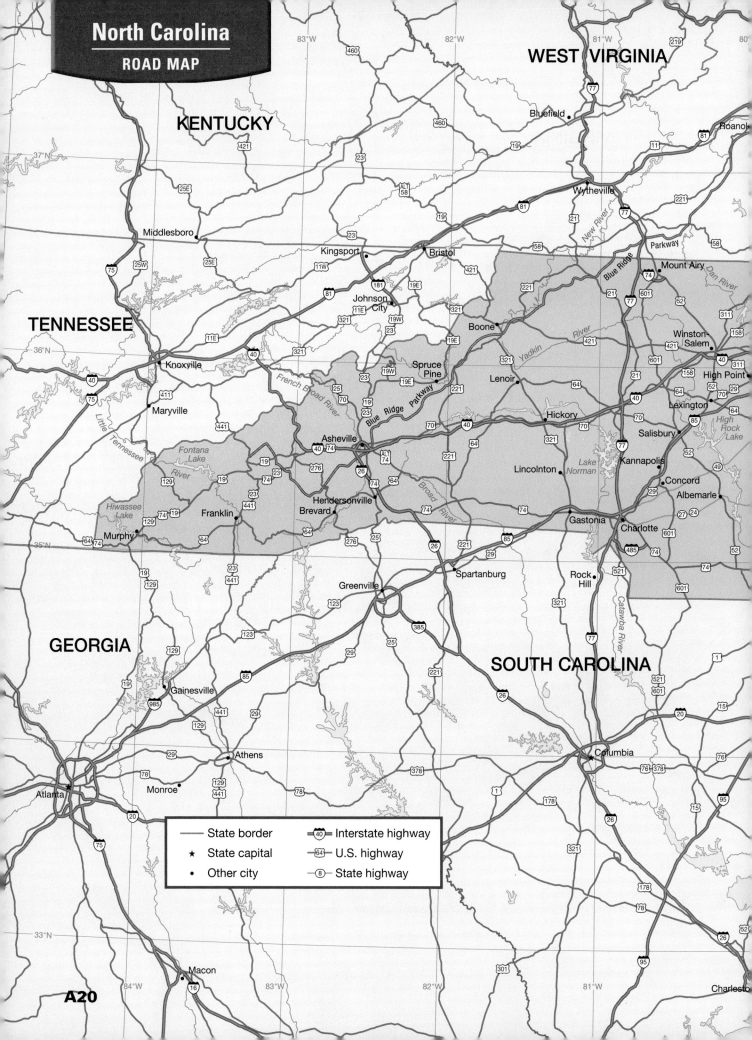

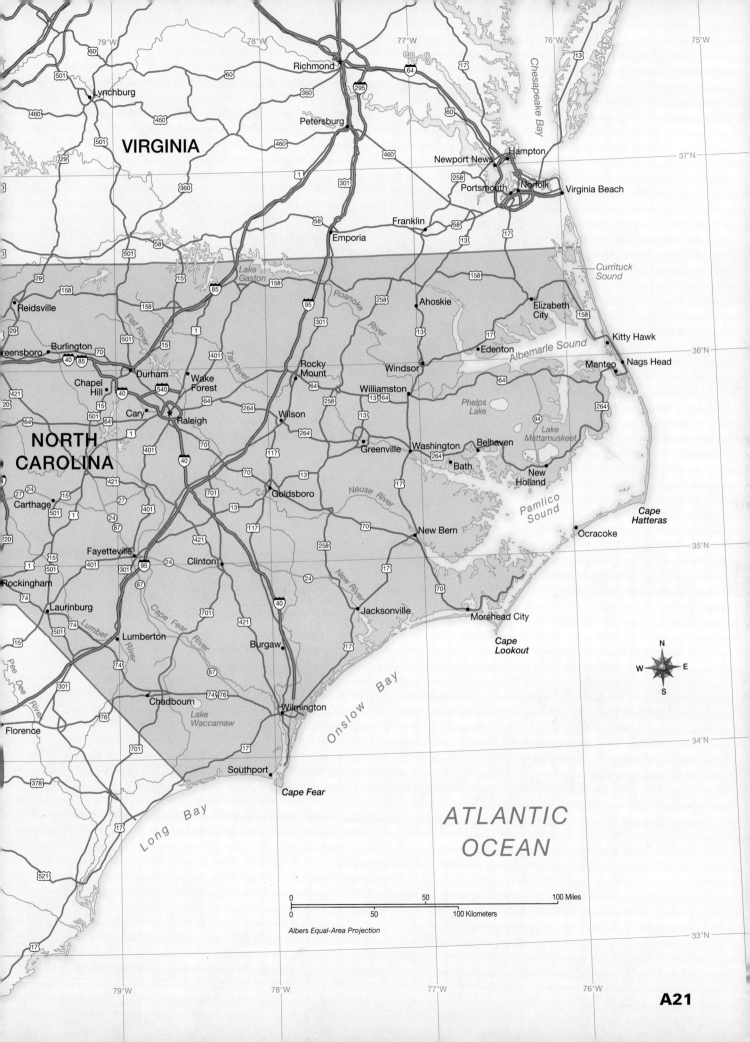

Geography Terms

1. **basin** bowl-shaped area of land surrounded by higher land
2. **bay** an inlet of the sea or some other body of water, usually smaller than a gulf
3. **bluff** high, steep face of rock or earth
4. **canyon** deep, narrow valley with steep sides
5. **cape** point of land that extends into water
6. **cataract** large waterfall
7. **channel** deepest part of a body of water
8. **cliff** high, steep face of rock or earth
9. **coast** land along a sea or ocean
10. **coastal plain** area of flat land along a sea or ocean
11. **delta** triangle-shaped area of land at the mouth of a river
12. **desert** dry land with few plants
13. **dune** hill of sand piled up by the wind

14. **fall line** area along which rivers form waterfalls or rapids as the rivers drop to lower land
15. **floodplain** flat land that is near the edges of a river and is formed by silt deposited by floods
16. **foothills** hilly area at the base of a mountain
17. **glacier** large ice mass that moves slowly down a mountain or across land
18. **gulf** part of a sea or ocean extending into the land, usually larger than a bay
19. **hill** land that rises above the land around it
20. **inlet** any area of water extending into the land from a larger body of water
21. **island** land that has water on all sides
22. **isthmus** narrow strip of land connecting two larger areas of land
23. **lagoon** body of shallow water
24. **lake** body of water with land on all sides
25. **marsh** lowland with moist soil and tall grasses

#	Term	Definition
26	**mesa**	flat-topped mountain with steep sides
27	**mountain**	highest kind of land
28	**mountain pass**	gap between mountains
29	**mountain range**	row of mountains
30	**mouth of river**	place where a river empties into another body of water
31	**oasis**	area of water and fertile land in a desert
32	**ocean**	body of salt water larger than a sea
33	**peak**	top of a mountain
34	**peninsula**	land that is almost completely surrounded by water.
35	**plain**	area of flat or gently rolling low land
36	**plateau**	area of high, mostly flat land
37	**reef**	ridge of sand, rock, or coral that lies at or near the surface of a sea or ocean
38	**river**	large stream of water that flows across the land
39	**riverbank**	land along a river
40	**savanna**	area of grassland and scattered trees
41	**sea**	body of salt water smaller than an ocean
42	**sea level**	the level of the surface of an ocean or a sea
43	**slope**	side of a hill or mountain
44	**source of river**	place where a river begins
45	**strait**	narrow channel of water connecting two larger bodies of water
46	**swamp**	area of low, wet land with trees
47	**timberline**	line on a mountain above which it is too cold for trees to grow
48	**tributary**	stream or river that flows into a larger stream or river
49	**valley**	low land between hills or mountains
50	**volcano**	opening in the earth, often raised, through which lava, rock, ashes, and gases are forced out
51	**waterfall**	steep drop from a high place to a lower place in a stream or river

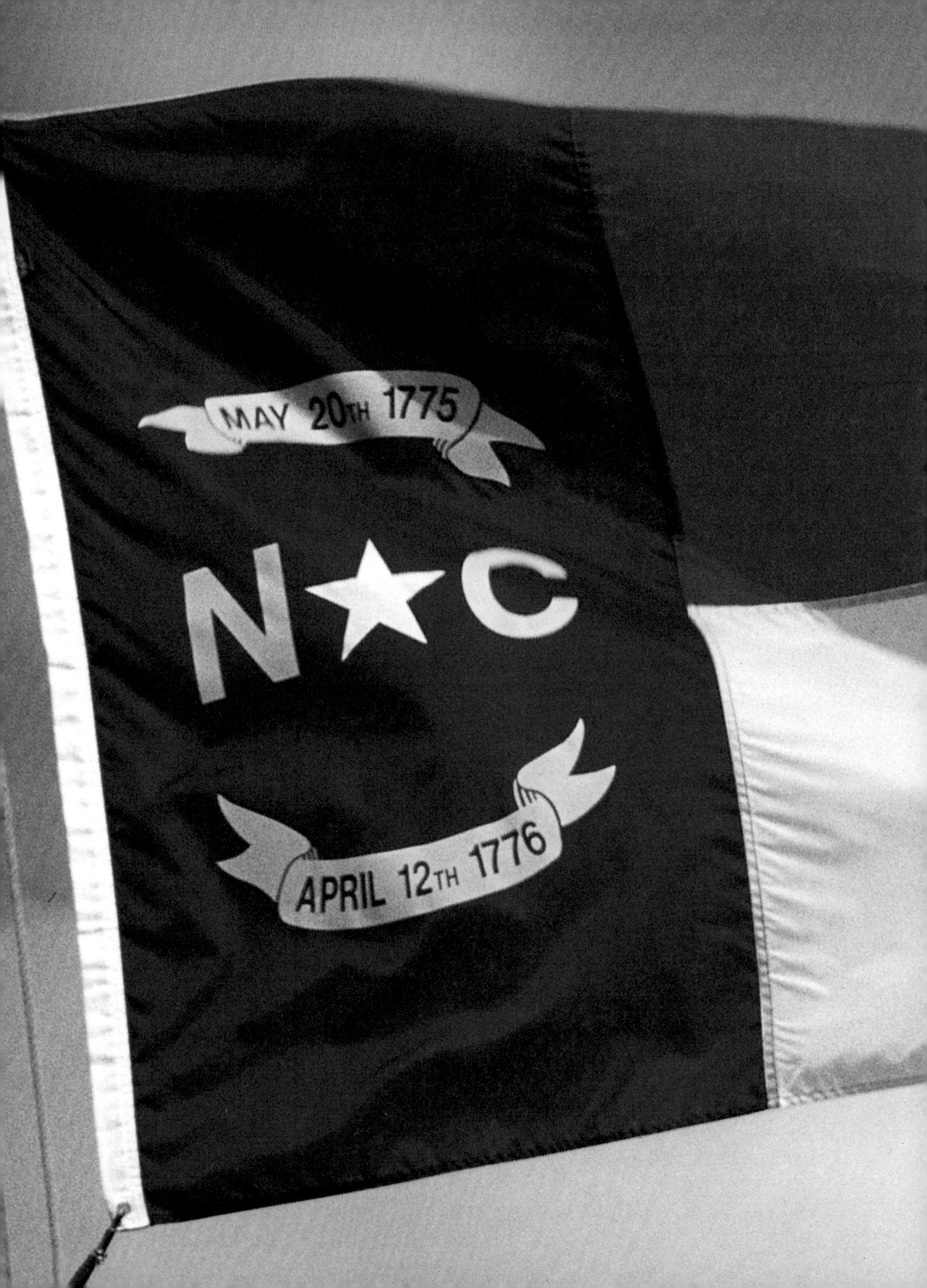
MAY 20TH 1775
N C
APRIL 12TH 1776

Introduction

66 Here's to the land of the long leaf pine,
The summer land where the sun doth shine,
Where the weak grow strong
   and the strong grow great,
Here's to 'Down Home,' the Old North State! 99

— from the poem "The State Toast" by
   Leonora Martin and Mary Burke Kerr, 1904

Learning About North Carolina

North Carolinians are proud of their state. As you read this book, you will find out why. You will learn about the state's interesting past. You will also learn about the land, water, and climate of North Carolina. In addition, you will find out about the many different people of North Carolina. All of these things will help you understand why people are proud to be citizens of North Carolina.

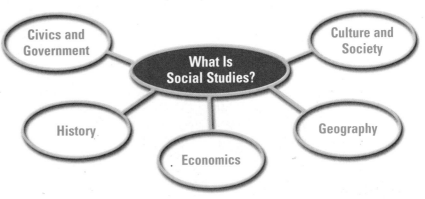

Why History Matters

VOCABULARY

history   historian   oral history   analyze
chronology   evidence   point of view

History is the study of people, places, and events in the past. History teaches us how events from the past affect the present. In addition, studying history can help us prepare for future events.

History is very important to people in North Carolina. In this book you will learn about the ways of life of North Carolinians long ago. You will also find out how North Carolina has changed over the years.

Learning About Time

Understanding history requires knowing when events took place. The order in which events take place is called **chronology** (kruh•NAH•luh•jee). **Historians**, or people who study the past, look closely at the chronology of events. This helps them better understand how one event affects another. They can also discover how the past and the present connect.

The North Carolina Museum of History in Raleigh is a good place to find out about important North Carolina events.

Finding Evidence

How do historians learn about the past? One way is to find **evidence**, or proof, of when, why, where, and how things happened. Historians read books and newspapers from long ago. They study old diaries, letters, and postcards. They look at paintings and photographs from the past. They also listen to oral histories. An **oral history** is a story of an event told aloud. Historians use these different kinds of evidence to piece together the history of a place.

Historians study artifacts, or objects made by people. The lantern (left) and wig-powder bellows (below) were used in the 1700s.

Identifying Points of View

Historians think about why different people of the past said or wrote what they did. They try to understand different people's points of view. A **point of view** is based on a person's beliefs and ideas. It can be affected by whether a person is young or old, male or female, or rich or poor. Background and experiences also affect point of view. A person's point of view is how he or she sees things. People with different points of view may have different ideas about the same event.

To understand points of view about an event, historians learn about the people who took part in the event. They find out as much as possible about how people lived long ago. This helps them get a better idea of the actions and feelings of people of the past.

Drawing Conclusions

After historians have identified the facts about a historical event, they still have work to do. They need to analyze the event. To **analyze** an event is to examine each part of it. Analyzing an event allows historians to draw conclusions about how and why it happened.

REVIEW What is history?

Background and experience help determine point of view. Above are some of the many faces of North Carolina.

·SKILLS·
READING

Compare Primary and Secondary Sources

VOCABULARY

primary source

secondary source

▶ WHY IT MATTERS

People who study the past look for evidence, or proof. They want to be sure they know what really happened. They look for evidence in two different kinds of sources—primary sources and secondary sources.

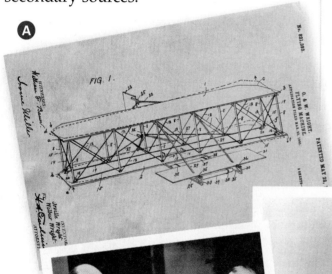

▶ WHAT YOU NEED TO KNOW

Primary sources are records made by people who saw or took part in an event. They may have written their thoughts in a journal or a diary. They may have told their story in a letter, a poem, or a song. They may have given a speech. They may have painted a picture or taken a photograph. An object made or used during an event can also be a primary source. As you can see, primary sources give the real words and pictures of people who saw what happened.

This sketch of an early airplane **Ⓐ**, this photograph of the Wright brothers **Ⓑ** , and this photograph of the Wright flyer **Ⓒ** are all primary sources.

Secondary sources are records of an event made by people who were not there. Books written by authors who only heard or read about an event are secondary sources. So too are magazine articles and newspaper stories written by people who did not take part in the event. Paintings or drawings by artists who did not see the event are also secondary sources.

➡ PRACTICE THE SKILL

On December 17, 1903, the first successful flight of a powered airplane took place at Kill Devil Hills near Kitty Hawk, North Carolina. The inventors and pilots of the airplane were brothers Orville and Wilbur Wright. Examine the artifacts, documents, and photographs about the Wright brothers' first flight. Use the sources to answer the questions.

❶ Which source was made by someone who witnessed the Wright brothers' first flight? How do you know?

❷ Which sources would help you most in writing about the first flight?

❸ Why might sources D, E, and F also be considered primary sources?

➡ APPLY WHAT YOU LEARNED

Work with a partner to find examples of primary and secondary sources in your textbook. Discuss why you think each source is either a primary source or a secondary source.

Ⓓ

Wright Brothers Memorial

Wright Brothers National Memorial and Visitors Center:

- Near Kitty Hawk and Kill Devil Hills. Containing a recently refurbished replica of the original Wright Flyer as well as other memorabilia of the First Flight, the Wright Brothers National Memorial and Visitor Center commemorates one of America's historic moments.

A nearby sand dune supports the Memorial Pylon. On the extensive grounds around the visitor center/museum there are historical markers and a reconstructed hanger and shop.

As the centennial anniversary of the famous flight made by Orville Wright on December 17, 1903 nears, the Memorial will be gearing up for the celebration. The Visitor Center is open daily from 9am-6pm. Entrance fee.

The Wright Brothers Photographs

Ⓔ

THE WRIGHT BROTHERS
How They Invented the Airplane

Russell Freedman
With Original Photographs by Wilbur and Orville Wright

Ⓕ

the Wright Brothers of Dayton

"From the time we were little children my brother Orville and myself lived together, played together, worked together and, in fact, thought together."

This Internet site **Ⓓ**, this book **Ⓔ**, and this museum display **Ⓕ** are secondary sources.

Why Geography Matters

VOCABULARY

geography   physical feature   region
geographer   human feature
location   interact

Geography is the study of Earth and the people who live on it. People who study geography are called **geographers**. Geographers do much more than find places on maps. They learn all they can about places and the people who live there.

Themes of Geography

Geographers sometimes divide geography into five themes, or key topics. Most of the maps in this book focus on one of the five themes. Keeping the themes in mind will help you think like a geographer.

Location
Everything on Earth has its own **location**— the place where it can be found.

Human-Environment Interactions
Humans and their surroundings **interact**, or affect one another. The actions of people change the environment. The environment also affects people.

Movement
People, things, and ideas move every day. Each movement affects the world in some way.

Place
Every location on Earth has features that make it different from all other locations. Features formed by nature are called **physical features**. Physical features include landforms, bodies of water, and plant life. Features created by people are **human features**. Human features include buildings, roads, and people themselves.

Regions
Areas on Earth whose features make them different from other areas can be called **regions**. A region can be described by its physical features or by its human features.

Essential Elements of Geography

Geographers use six other topics to understand Earth and its people. These topics are the six essential elements, or most important parts, of geography. Thinking about the six essential elements of geography will help you learn more about the world and your place in it.

• GEOGRAPHY •

The World in Spatial Terms

Spatial means "having to do with space." Every place on Earth has its own space, or location. Geographers want to know where places are located and why they are located where they are.

Places and Regions

Geographers often group places into regions. They do this to show that all the places in a group have a similar physical or human feature.

Physical Systems

Geographers study the physical parts of the surface of Earth. For example, they study climate, landforms, and bodies of water.

Human Systems

Geographers study where people have settled, how they earn a living, and what laws they have made.

Environment and Society

People's actions affect the environment. The environment also affects people's actions.

The Uses of Geography

Knowing how to use maps, globes, and other geographic tools helps people in their day-to-day lives.

REVIEW What is geography?

Why Economics Matters

VOCABULARY
economy   economics

Hospitals, schools, banks, and stores—these are just a few of the many places where people work. Most people work to be able to buy what they need or want and to save for the future. By working, buying, and saving, they are taking part in the economy. An **economy** is the way people use resources to meet their needs. The study of how people do this is called **economics**.

In this book you will read about how North Carolinians make, buy, sell and trade goods to meet their needs. You will also discover how North Carolina's economy has changed over time and how it came to be what it is today.

REVIEW What name is given to the study of how people meet their needs and wants?

Money plays an important role in today's economy. People earn, spend, and save money.

Why Civics and Government Matter

VOCABULARY

government   civics

To live together peacefully, people form governments. A **government** is a system of leaders and laws that helps people live safely together in a community, a state, or a country. As a North Carolinian, you follow the laws of your city or town, your state—North Carolina, and your country—the United States of America.

Harcourt Horizons: North Carolina tells about the role of North Carolinians in community, state, and national governments. It also tells how North Carolina's governments came to be and how they changed over time. As you read this book, you will learn about the leaders and laws in North Carolina history.

The study of government connects with civics. **Civics** is the study of citizenship. As you read this book, you will learn about the rights and responsibilities of citizens.

REVIEW How are government and civics different?

North Carolina state government is based in Raleigh, the state's capital city. Below is the state legislative building.

Why Culture and Society Matter

VOCABULARY

culture   heritage

       society

As you read this book, you will find out how people in the past helped make North Carolina what it is today. You will learn about where North Carolina's early settlers came from, how they dressed, and what they believed in. You will also learn about the languages they spoke and the foods they ate. All these things make up a **culture**, or way of life.

Each human group, or **society**, has a culture. Many groups of people have contributed to North Carolina's culture. This book gives information about the different cultures that have come together in North Carolina. It also describes North Carolina's **heritage**, or the ways of life that have been passed down through history.

REVIEW How are the terms *culture* and *society* related?

Scottish Americans celebrate their heritage at the Highland games at Grandfather Mountain. This Karamu celebration (left) in Greensboro honors African American contributions to American culture.

The Land and Early People

A traditional
Lumbee drum

Native American festival in Charlotte, North Carolina

The Land and Early People

" . . . I think in all the world the like abundance is not to be found. "

—Arthur Barlowe in his report to
Sir Walter Raleigh, 1584

Preview the Content

Scan the chapter and lesson titles. Use them to create an outline for the unit. Write down questions you have about the land and early people of what is now North Carolina.

Preview the Vocabulary

Multiple Meanings Words often have several meanings. Use the Glossary to find the social studies meaning of each word below. Then use each word in a sentence with its social studies meaning.

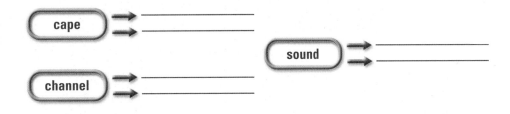

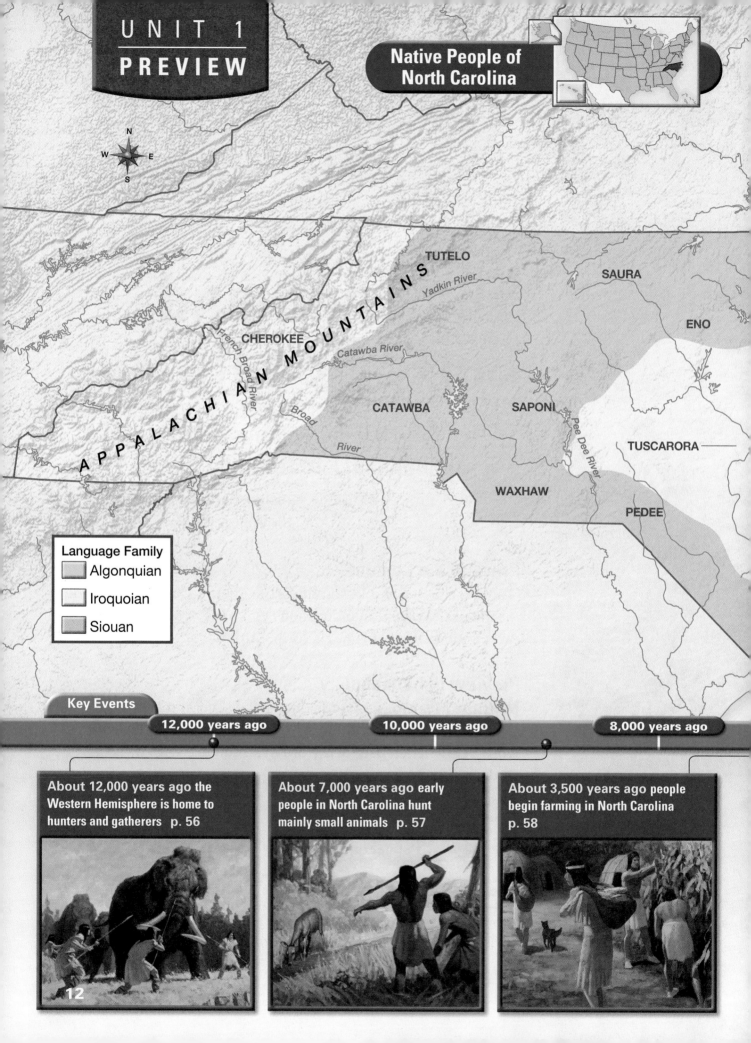

Native People of
North Carolina

N
W E
S

TUTELO

SAURA

Yadkin River

ENO

CHEROKEE

APPALACHIAN MOUNTAINS

French Broad River

Catawba River

CATAWBA

SAPONI

Pee Dee River

TUSCARORA

Broad

River

WAXHAW

PEDEE

Language Family
Algonquian
Iroquoian
Siouan

Key Events

12,000 years ago   10,000 years ago   8,000 years ago

About 12,000 years ago the
Western Hemisphere is home to
hunters and gatherers p. 56

About 7,000 years ago early
people in North Carolina hunt
mainly small animals p. 57

About 3,500 years ago people
begin farming in North Carolina
p. 58

12

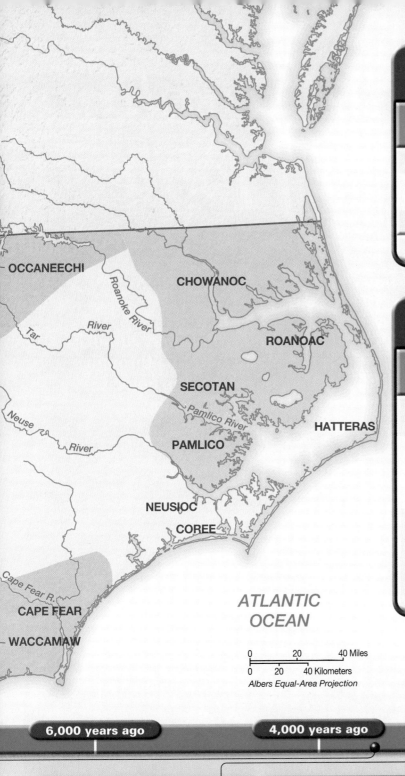

OCCANEECHI

CHOWANOC

Roanoke River

Tar River

ROANOAC

SECOTAN

Pamlico River

HATTERAS

Neuse River

PAMLICO

NEUSIOC

COREE

Cape Fear R.

CAPE FEAR

WACCAMAW

ATLANTIC
OCEAN

0   20   40 Miles
0   20   40 Kilometers
Albers Equal-Area Projection

Native American Language Families

LANGUAGE FAMILY	NUMBER
Algonquian	🏠🏠🏠🏠🏠🏠🏠🏠
Siouan	🏠🏠🏠🏠🏠🏠🏠🏠🏠🏠
Iroquoian	🏠🏠🏠🏠🏠

🏠 = 1 tribe

Natural Resources
in 1500

REGION	NATURAL RESOURCES
Coastal Plain	Longleaf pine forests Rivers and wetlands
Piedmont	Oak, hickory, and pine forests Rivers Soil
Mountains	Oak, chestnut, spruce, and fir forests Rivers Rocks, minerals, and gems Soil

6,000 years ago

4,000 years ago

2,000 years ago

About 3,000 years ago settled people in North Carolina began to specialize p. 58

About 600 years ago Mound Builders come to North Carolina p. 58

About 350 years ago more than 22,000 Cherokees live in North Carolina p. 70

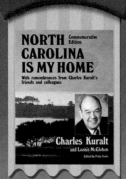

NORTH Commemorative Edition
CAROLINA
IS MY HOME
With remembrances from Charles Kuralt's
friends and colleagues

Charles Kuralt
and Loonis McGlohon
Edited by Patty Davis

North Carolina is My Home

by Charles Kuralt

In the book *North Carolina Is My Home*, author Charles Kuralt illustrates North Carolina through words and pictures. This poem from the book lists many of the names given to cities, towns, and communities throughout the state.

Yadkin. Yancey. Yorick. York.
Ripshin Ridge and Roaring Fork!
Far from home, my mind embraces
the nimble names of Tar Heel Places:
Topsail Sound and Turner's Cut
Dixon and Vixen and Devil's Gut.
Hoke, Polk, Ashe, Nash.
Calico. Calabash.
Pitt, Hyde, Clyde, Dare.
Cape Fear. Cat Square.
Take me home to Teaches Hole,
To Looking Glass Creek,
And Frying Pan Shoal,
To Bridal Veil and Blowing Rock . . .
And Currituck and Coinjock.
I'll know I'm home when I finally reach
The top of a dune at Wrightsville Beach
And stand there
with my back to the sea
Looking west toward Cherokee
And imagining the miles between . . .
From Ivanhoe to Aberdeen,
Candor and Biscoe, Uwharrie
To Gold Hill, Granite Quarry
China Grove and Cullowhee.

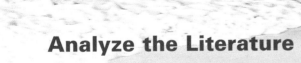

Analyze the Literature

1 What information about the places in the poem is given by their names?

2 How does the poem reflect how the author feels about North Carolina?

3 Working with a partner, choose five places in North Carolina. Research what the names of these places mean and describe how the names came to be.

READ A BOOK

START THE UNIT PROJECT

Create a Museum Display With your classmates, create a museum display to show the land and peoples of North Carolina before the Europeans arrived. As you read this unit, pay attention to key facts about the land and peoples. Note what scientists and historians have studied to learn about the past.

USE TECHNOLOGY

Visit The Learning Site at **www.harcourtschool.com/ socialstudies** for additional activities, primary sources, and other resources to use in this unit.

HANGING ROCK STATE PARK

Hanging Rock State Park is located in the northern Piedmont region of North Carolina. It is part of the Sauratown (SAWR•uh•town) Mountains. These are sometimes called the "mountains away from the mountains" because they are apart from other mountains in North Carolina. More than 300 kinds of plants grow in Hanging Rock State Park.

LOCATE IT

NORTH CAROLINA

Hanging Rock State Park

North Carolina's Geography

" From Murphy to Manteo "

—Popular North Carolina description
of the land from the mountains
to the seashore

1

Where on Earth Is North Carolina?

MAIN IDEA
Read to learn how to describe the location of North Carolina.

WHY IT MATTERS
Knowing the location of a place can help you better understand its history, geography, and economy.

VOCABULARY
region √
relative location √
continent √
hemisphere √
equator

Several years ago, the Special Olympics World Summer Games were held in Raleigh, North Carolina. More than 7,000 athletes from 150 countries came to our state.

If you were hosting visiting athletes, they might ask you, "Where on Earth do you live?" You might name your street address or your town or city. You could say that you live in North Carolina and that North Carolina is in the United States. Your street, city, state, and country are all part of your global address.

A Southern State

One way to explain North Carolina's location is to say that it is in the United States region called the South. A **region** is an area with features that make it different from other areas. Fifteen states make up the South. These states are Alabama, Arkansas, Florida, Georgia, Kentucky, Louisiana, Maryland, Mississippi, North Carolina, Oklahoma, South Carolina, Tennessee, Texas, Virginia, and West Virginia. The states in this region have similar landforms and resources. The Appalachian (a•puh•LAY•chun) Mountains run through the center of the region.

FAST FACT The highest part of the Appalachian Mountain Range is in North Carolina. The mountain range is also wider in North Carolina than anywhere else in the South.

LOCATE IT

NORTH CAROLINA

Pisgah National Forest

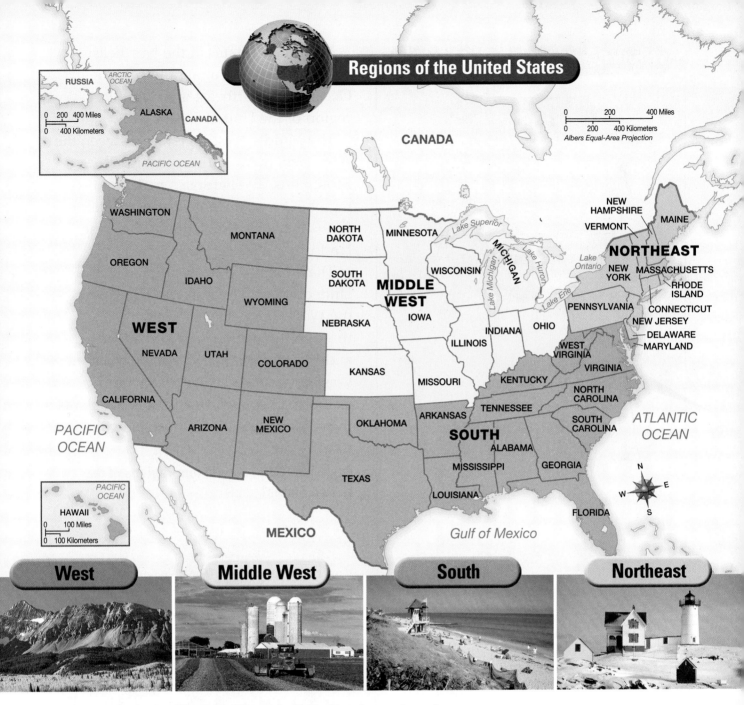

Regions of the United States

RUSSIA

ARCTIC OCEAN

ALASKA

CANADA

PACIFIC OCEAN

0 200 400 Miles

0 400 Kilometers

CANADA

0 200 400 Miles

0 200 400 Kilometers

Albers Equal-Area Projection

WASHINGTON

MONTANA

NORTH DAKOTA

MINNESOTA

Lake Superior

MICHIGAN

Lake Huron

NEW HAMPSHIRE

VERMONT

MAINE

OREGON

IDAHO

WYOMING

SOUTH DAKOTA

WISCONSIN

MIDDLE WEST

Lake Michigan

Lake Ontario

Lake Erie

NORTHEAST

NEW YORK

MASSACHUSETTS

RHODE ISLAND

PENNSYLVANIA

CONNECTICUT

WEST

NEVADA

UTAH

COLORADO

NEBRASKA

IOWA

INDIANA

OHIO

ILLINOIS

WEST VIRGINIA

NEW JERSEY

DELAWARE

MARYLAND

VIRGINIA

PACIFIC OCEAN

CALIFORNIA

ARIZONA

NEW MEXICO

KANSAS

MISSOURI

KENTUCKY

TENNESSEE

NORTH CAROLINA

SOUTH CAROLINA

ATLANTIC OCEAN

OKLAHOMA

ARKANSAS

SOUTH

ALABAMA

MISSISSIPPI

GEORGIA

PACIFIC OCEAN

HAWAII

0 100 Miles

0 100 Kilometers

TEXAS

LOUISIANA

N E W S

MEXICO

Gulf of Mexico

FLORIDA

West

Middle West

South

Northeast

GEOGRAPHY THEME

Regions The United States is divided into four main regions.

In which region is Idaho? In which region is New York?

When you describe a state's location in a region, you are describing its relative location. A state's **relative location** is its position compared to one or more other places on Earth. The location of North Carolina compared to most other states in the country is in the South.

REVIEW In what region of the United States is North Carolina located?

North Carolina's Place in the United States

North Carolina is one of the 50 states that make up the United States. Each state is in one of the country's four main regions. In addition to the South, the other regions are the Northeast, the Middle West, and the West.

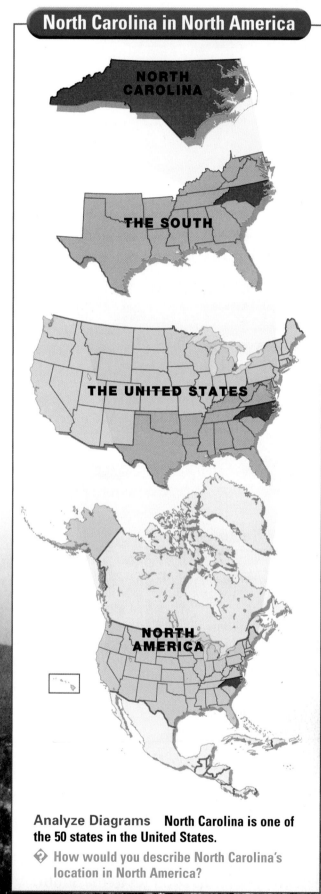

North Carolina in North America

NORTH CAROLINA

THE SOUTH

THE UNITED STATES

NORTH AMERICA

Analyze Diagrams North Carolina is one of the 50 states in the United States.

How would you describe North Carolina's location in North America?

Most of the states in the Northeast region are located along the Atlantic Ocean. The Northeast is the smallest region of the United States.

The Middle West region is between the Appalachian Mountains and the Rocky Mountains. Twelve states make up this region. One of its most distinctive land-forms is the Central Plains, where the land is good for farming.

The West is the largest region of the United States. Thirteen states make up the West. The Rocky Mountains run through this region. California, Oregon, and Washington have a Pacific coastline. Western states such as Arizona and California have warm climates. Alaska is the coldest state in the West. Hawaii is an island state.

REVIEW What are the four regions of the United States?

Most of the Appalachian Mountain Range is located in the South.

North Carolina's Place in the World

Continents are Earth's largest land areas. The United States is located on the continent of North America. North America is one of the seven continents on Earth. The other six continents are Africa, Antarctica, Asia, Australia, Europe, and South America.

On the continent of North America, Canada is our neighbor to the north. To the south, the United States shares a border with Mexico. Smaller countries, in Central America and in the Caribbean Sea, are also part of North America.

Earth is a sphere, a round object like a ball. Imagine drawing a line around the middle of this sphere, creating two halves. Each half is a **hemisphere**. *Hemi-* means "half." An imaginary line drawn north and south around Earth splits it into the Eastern Hemisphere and the Western Hemisphere. The continents of North America and South America are in the Western Hemisphere. An imaginary line drawn from east to west around the middle of Earth divides it into the Northern Hemisphere and the Southern Hemisphere. That line is called the **equator**. It lies halfway between the North Pole and the South Pole. North America, along with Europe, Asia, and parts of Africa and South America, is in the Northern Hemisphere.

REVIEW In which hemispheres is North Carolina located?

LESSON 1 REVIEW

1. **MAIN IDEA** What is North Carolina's location in the United States, in North America, and on Earth?

2. **WHY IT MATTERS** What can you learn about a place from its location?

3. **VOCABULARY** Use the words **region** and **continent** in a sentence describing North Carolina's location.

4. **READING SKILL—Main Idea and Supporting Details** What is North Carolina's relative position in the United States? Use supporting details.

5. **GEOGRAPHY** What mountain range is in the South?

6. **SCIENCE AND TECHNOLOGY** What is a hemisphere?

7. **CRITICAL THINKING—Analyze** How are the four regions of the United States similar? How are they different?

 PERFORMANCE—Make a Booklet Create an illustrated travel booklet about the South in the United States. Name the states in the region and include details about them.

Use Latitude and Longitude

VOCABULARY

absolute location	lines of longitude
lines of latitude	meridian
parallels	prime meridian

⮞ WHY IT MATTERS

One way to describe where you live is to give your **absolute location**, or exact position on Earth. You can do this by using lines of latitude and longitude.

⮞ WHAT YOU NEED TO KNOW

Lines of latitude and longitude are lines that mapmakers draw on maps and globes. One set of lines runs east and west around Earth. They are called **lines of latitude**. Lines of latitude are also called parallels. **Parallels**

(PAIR•uh•lelz) are lines that are always the same distance from each other.

Another set of lines runs from the North Pole to the South Pole. These lines are called **lines of longitude** (LAHN•juh•tood), or **meridians** (muh•RIH•dee•uhnz). Latitude and longitude are both measured in degrees (°).

The equator is the line of latitude around the middle of Earth. Other lines of latitude circle the globe between the equator and the North and South Poles. The equator is at 0°, and the North and

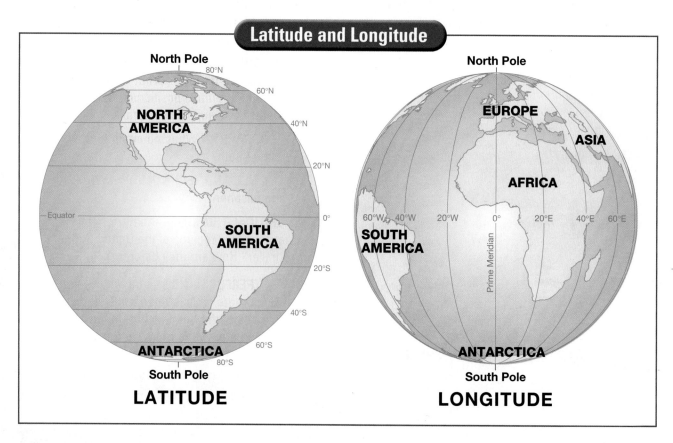

Latitude and Longitude

LATITUDE

LONGITUDE

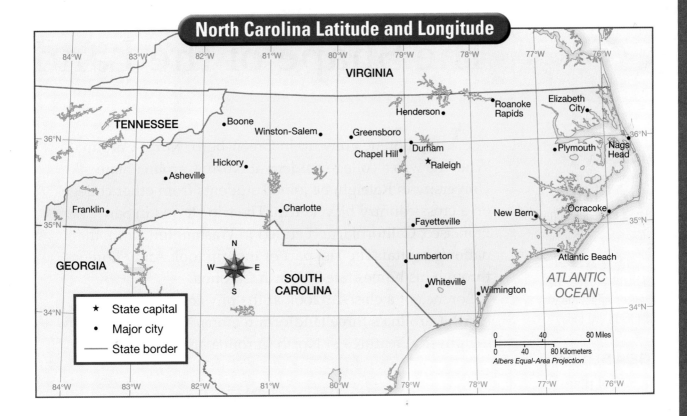

North Carolina Latitude and Longitude

South Poles are each at 90°. Lines of latitude north of the equator are labeled *N* for *North*. Lines south of the equator are labeled *S* for *South*.

The **prime meridian** is the starting place for lines of longitude. It runs through Greenwich, a town near London, England. The prime meridian is at 0°. Lines of longitude west of the prime meridian are labeled *W* for *West*. Lines east of the prime meridian are labeled *E* for *East*.

The absolute location of a place is measured by first naming the closest line of latitude and then the closest line of longitude. Find Durham on the map on this page. Durham is near 36°N latitude and 79°W longitude. Its absolute location is about 36°N, 79°W. This means that Durham is about 36 degrees north of the equator and 79 degrees west of the prime meridian.

PRACTICE THE SKILL

Now use the map to answer these questions.

1. What are the latitude and longitude of Ocracoke, Wilmington, and Charlotte?

2. What city is located near 35°N, 79°W? Which is near 36°N, 77°W?

3. Between which lines of latitude and longitude is most of North Carolina?

APPLY WHAT YOU LEARNED

Write a letter to someone in another state. Use latitude and longitude to tell where you live in North Carolina. Explain how you found your absolute location on the map.

Practice your map and globe skills with the **GeoSkills CD-ROM.**

MAIN IDEA
Read to discover the differences between North Carolina's three landform regions.

WHY IT MATTERS
North Carolina's regional differences affect the way its residents live today.

VOCABULARY

coastal plain
tide
barrier island
erosion
inlet
cape
wetland
pocosin
elevation
plateau
fall line

The Shape of the Land

Andy Lorenc grew up in Greensboro, North Carolina. When he was a college student at North Carolina State University in Raleigh, he joined students from other colleges on a cross-country bicycle trip. The trip started in San Francisco, California, and ended in Washington, D.C., the nation's capital. The last part of the trip took Andy Lorenc through his home state of North Carolina.

Lorenc got a close-up look at the physical features in North Carolina's three landform regions. You will learn how the physical features of North Carolina affected his trip.

The Coastal Plain Region

The lowest and flattest landform region in North Carolina is the Coastal Plain. A **coastal plain** is a lowland that lies along an ocean. North Carolina's Coastal Plain makes up almost half of the state's total land area. It is part of the much larger Atlantic Coastal Plain, which stretches from New Jersey to Florida, along the Atlantic Ocean.

Geographers often divide the North Carolina Coastal Plain into two parts—the Outer Coastal Plain, or Tidewater, and the Inner Coastal Plain. The Tidewater is closer to the ocean.

Its name refers to ocean tides. **Tides** are the rising and falling of the oceans and waters connected to them. The Tidewater is flat and has many swamps and salt-water marshes. Many parts of the Tidewater are at sea level or just 20 to 30 feet (6 to 9 m) above sea level.

Imagine looking at the Coastal Plain from a ship on the ocean. The first sight you might see is the Outer Banks, a 175-mile (282-km) chain of barrier islands off the mainland of North Carolina. **Barrier islands** are low, narrow islands between the ocean and the coastline of a mainland.

The barrier islands of the Outer Banks were formed over thousands of years. Over time **erosion**, or wearing away, scraped off sand, soil, and gravel from the mainland. Rivers carried the sand, soil, and gravel to the coast.

Ocean water flooded much of the low-lying land. Only the highest parts stayed dry. The remaining sand, soil, and gravel, called sand dunes, created the Outer Banks.

The openings between the islands of the Outer Banks are called **inlets**. The inlets between the islands are shallow and always changing. The shifting sands of the Outer Banks and the shallow inlets between the islands make the North Carolina coast a dangerous place for ships, especially during storms.

North Carolina's three regions have different kinds of land and water. Ocracoke Island (below) is in the Coastal Plain region. The Flat River is in the Piedmont region. Land in the Mountain region is at a high elevation.

FLAT RIVER, PIEDMONT REGION

MOUNTAIN REGION

Regions of North Carolina

VIRGINIA

TENNESSEE

GEORGIA

SOUTH CAROLINA

Great Dismal Swamp

Ahoskie

Kitty Hawk

Nags Head

Boone

Winston-Salem

Greensboro

Durham

Chapel Hill

Raleigh

MOUNTAIN

PIEDMONT

COASTAL PLAIN

Asheville

Franklin

Charlotte

Fayetteville

New Bern

Cape Hatteras

Wilmington

Cape Lookout

Cape Fear

ATLANTIC OCEAN

Yadkin River

Catawba River

French Broad R.

Little Tennessee

Pee Dee R.

Fall Line

Sandhills

Lumber

Tar River

Roanoke River

Albemarle Sound

Neuse River

Cape Fear River

Pamlico Sound

0   40   80 Miles
0   40   80 Kilometers
Albers Equal-Area Projection

N E S W

GEOGRAPHY THEME

Regions **North Carolina has three landform regions.**

In what region is Raleigh located?

The Outer Banks have many **capes**, or points of land that stick out into the ocean. Two such capes are Cape Hatteras and Cape Lookout. Cape Hatteras has earned the title Graveyard of the Atlantic because of the many shipwrecks there.

The dangers of landing on the North Carolina coast stopped many early explorers and settlers from coming ashore. They turned their ships north toward Virginia or south toward South Carolina.

The Outer Banks might have been the early sailors' worst nightmare, but Andy Lorenc thinks they are fun for riding a bike. "Most places on the Outer Banks are flat. There's a nice breeze there coming off the ocean."

Another interesting feature of the Coastal Plain is its wetlands. **Wetlands** are low-lying areas where the water level is always near or above the surface of the land. Many wetlands are salt marshes or swamps. The largest wetlands in

North Carolina are in the Tidewater area. The Great Dismal Swamp, in the northeast corner of the Tidewater, is one of the largest swamps in the United States.

Some of the Tidewater's most unusual wetland areas are called **pocosins** (puh•KOH•suhnz). These are large, swampy areas on high ground covered by bushes and shrubs. The name *pocosin* comes from an Algonquian Indian word meaning "swamp on a hill."

West of the Tidewater, the Inner Coastal Plain begins. This land is drier and higher in elevation than the Tidewater. **Elevation** is the height above sea level.

In the southwest corner of the Inner Coastal Plain are the Sandhills. The Sandhills are rolling hills of rough, sandy soil. These hills have the highest elevation on the Coastal Plain.

REVIEW What are the main differences between the Tidewater area and the Inner Coastal Plain?

The Piedmont Region

The Piedmont region, which is almost equal in size to the Coastal Plain region, is a wide, rolling plateau. A **plateau** is flat land that rises above the surrounding land. The word *piedmont* means "foot of the mountain." Unlike some plateaus, the Piedmont is not completely flat. As it stretches upward toward the mountains, it becomes hilly.

The Piedmont is at a higher elevation than the Coastal Plain. Andy Lorenc noticed a difference as he pedaled through the Piedmont. "The land was much more hilly than along the coast. There was also much more traffic. We had to watch out for cars whizzing by."

Waterfalls are created when rivers drop from higher to lower ground.

Marking the border between the Coastal Plain and the Piedmont is the Fall Line. A **fall line** is an area along which rivers drop from higher to lower ground. Along the Fall Line in North Carolina, rivers from the Piedmont form shallow pools, low waterfalls, and rapids as they drop to the Coastal Plain.

• GEOGRAPHY •

Uwharrie Mountains

Understanding Physical Systems

The oldest mountains in the United States may be in the Piedmont region of North Carolina. The Uwharrie (yoo•HAH•ree) Mountains are hundreds of millions of years old. Long ago some of the Uwharries may have been 20,000 feet (6,096 m) high. Now they are less than 1,000 feet (305 m) high. Over time, rain and wind have worn the mountains down into gently sloping ridges.

You can see the Uwharries at Morrow Mountain State Park. Uwharrie Morrow Mountain is the highest peak in the park. It is 936 feet (285 m) high.

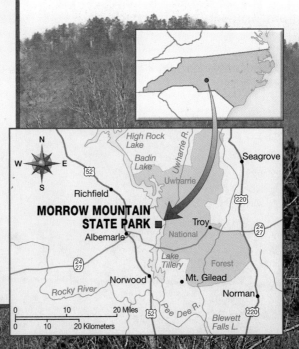

Throughout the Piedmont region, hills and low mountains add variety to the landscape. Hikers enjoy walking the trails of Morrow Mountain State Park and Uwharrie National Forest, in the Uwharrie Mountains. The Uwharries are really high hills rather than mountains. Other high areas within the Piedmont region are the Sauratown Mountains and Kings Mountain.

Andy Lorenc crossed the western edge of the Coastal Plain into the Piedmont. The land had risen from sea level to about 300 feet (91 m) and was still mostly flat. As he rode over the bigger hills, he began to huff and puff. The land at the western end of the Piedmont region rises to 1,500 feet (457 m).

Throughout North Carolina's history, the Piedmont has been easier to cross than the state's other two regions. Pioneers traveling in the Piedmont did not have to worry about dangerous waters or shifting sands. The roads and trails on which the Native Americans and settlers traveled developed into the state's first major transportation routes.

REVIEW **What are the major landforms of the Piedmont region?**

The Mountain Region

The Blue Ridge Mountains divide the Piedmont region from the Mountain region. They are part of the larger Appalachian Range. This range extends almost 2,000 miles (3,219 km) from Canada to the Great Smoky Mountains in North Carolina. The Great Smoky Mountains take their name from the bluish gray clouds that cover their peaks.

As Lorenc came to the mountains, he faced a steep upward climb. More than 40 peaks in the Appalachian Mountains are higher than 6,000 feet (1,829 m). These include Roan Mountain, Mount Pisgah, Richland Balsam Mountain, Clingmans

Great Smoky Mountains National Park is a popular place to see the Appalachian Mountains.

Satellite Images

Analyze Primary Sources

This is a satellite image, or picture, of the eastern part of North Carolina. Satellites are objects that circle Earth. Some satellites take pictures of land and water.

1 Areas that look rough are hills and mountains.

2 Different shades of green show kinds of plants.

3 The narrow line is the Outer Banks.

4 The dark blue areas are the deep water of the ocean.

◈ Can you find any rivers in the image?

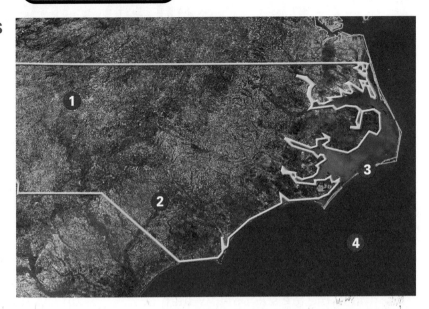

Dome, and Mount Mitchell. Mount Mitchell rises 6,684 feet (2,037 m). It is the highest peak in the eastern United States. The difficulties of crossing the mountains of North Carolina made the Mountain region the last part of the state to be settled by Europeans.

Andy Lorenc had this to say about pedaling up the steep mountain roads. "I tried to remember that every mountain road that goes up also comes down."

REVIEW What physical feature forms the border between the Piedmont region and the Mountain region?

LESSON 2
REVIEW

1 **MAIN IDEA** What are the main features of North Carolina's landform regions?

2 **WHY IT MATTERS** How do you think regional differences affect the way people in our state live today?

3 **VOCABULARY** Use **barrier island** and **cape** to describe the Coastal Plain.

4 **READING SKILL—Main Idea and Supporting Details** Why has the Piedmont been the easiest region of North Carolina to cross? Give supporting details.

5 **SCIENCE AND TECHNOLOGY** How were the Outer Banks created?

6 **GEOGRAPHY** What are pocosins?

7 **CRITICAL THINKING—Hypothesize** How might our history have been different if the mountains were easier to cross?

PERFORMANCE—Make a Classroom Map Put a large map of North Carolina on the bulletin board. With a partner, choose a landmark. Write information about the landmark on a sheet of paper and attach a picture. Mark your landmark's location on the map. Post your information sheet nearby.

·SKILLS·

MAP AND GLOBE

Read an Elevation Map

VOCABULARY

relief

➡ WHY IT MATTERS

As you travel west through North Carolina from Cape Hatteras, the elevation begins to change. There are more hills, and some are steep. How high is the land in this part of the state? How much higher is the land in the west than the land in the east? To answer these questions, you need to be able to use an elevation map.

➡ WHAT YOU NEED TO KNOW

The elevation map of North Carolina uses color to show **relief** (rih•LEEF), or differences in elevation. Shaded areas on the map help you identify hills and mountains, but they do not give you elevations. To find the elevation on the map, you must understand what each color stands for. The map key tells you that.

Notice that the map key does not give exact elevations for all places in North Carolina. Instead, each color shows a

Some parts of North Carolina, such as Mount Mitchell, have a high elevation.

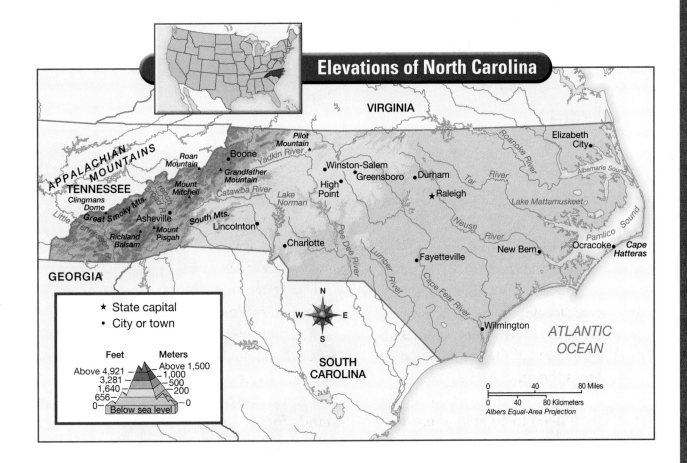

Elevations of North Carolina

range of elevations. This means the color stands for the highest and lowest elevations in an area, and all the elevations between.

All elevations are measured from sea level, usually in feet or meters. The elevation of land that is level with the sea is 0 feet (0 m). The area around Wilmington is colored green. According to the key, this means that the elevation there is between 0 and 656 feet (0 and 200 m) above sea level.

▶ PRACTICE THE SKILL

Study the map key to understand elevations in North Carolina. Then use the key to answer these questions.

1 Is the land around Raleigh higher or lower than it is around Asheville?

2 What is the elevation of the land in the Great Smoky Mountains in western North Carolina?

3 What color shows elevations of 656–1,640 feet (200–500 m)? Where in the state can these elevations be found?

▶ APPLY WHAT YOU LEARNED

Draw an elevation map of an imaginary country. Be sure to include a map key that shows which color stands for which elevations. Then trade maps with a classmate. Ask your classmate questions about your map, and see if you can answer your classmate's questions.

Practice your map and globe skills with the **GeoSkills CD-ROM**.

PRIMARY SOURCES

Tools of Geography

The tools that mapmakers use have changed greatly over time. Early maps often had mistakes. As better mapmaking tools were developed, maps improved. Today mapmakers use computers and satellites to quickly make maps that are more exact than those of the past.

FROM THE INSTITUTE AND MUSEUM OF HISTORY OF SCIENCE, FLORENCE, ITALY

This map from 1606 is one of the most detailed maps of the Southeast of its time. It shows Virginia, Florida, and the area that would become North Carolina. In the 1700s a surveying line (below left) was used to measure distances.

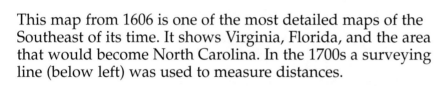

Tools such as this compass from the 1700s helped both mapmakers and explorers.

Analyze the Primary Source

❶ How do you think the surveying line worked?

❷ Why does the folding rule have a hinge? Why might mapmakers need a tool for drawing curved lines?

❸ When might someone today need to draw a map? Which of these tools would be most useful?

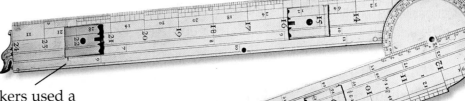

Mapmakers used a folding rule, like this one from the 1580s, to draw curved lines.

Sailors in the late 1700s used nautical protractors to find locations on maps and charts.

ACTIVITY

Draw a Map   Make an outline map of the state of North Carolina. Show major rivers in the state. Show your community and four other cities. Indicate the state capital with a star. Be sure to include a title, map key, compass rose, and scale. Then write a paragraph describing the tools that you used to make your map. Share your map with the class.

RESEARCH

Visit The Learning Site at **www.harcourtschool.com/ primarysources** to research other primary sources.

North Carolina's Rivers and Lakes

Judy Allen admits that she is crazy about rivers. She especially likes the Eno (EE•noh) River, which runs through the city of Durham, North Carolina. For six years Judy Allen has run the Festival for the Eno. She belongs to a group that is working to keep the Eno River clean and clear. The festival raises money to buy land along the banks of the river so that everyone can enjoy it.

Many people enjoy using North Carolina's rivers and lakes for fishing, boating, and other kinds of recreation. Many more people depend on the rivers to meet their daily needs. Waterways are important resources for North Carolina.

People of all ages enjoy getting wet at the Festival for the Eno. This is just one way North Carolinians use rivers and lakes.

LOCATE IT

Durham

NORTH CAROLINA

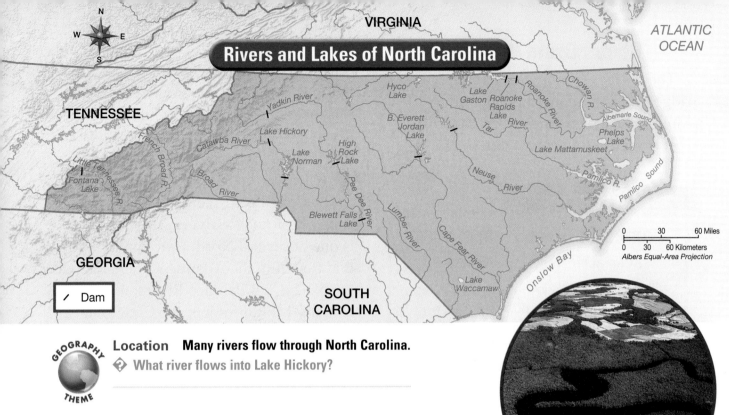

Rivers and Lakes of North Carolina

TENNESSEE

Yadkin River

Hyco Lake

Lake Gaston

Roanoke Rapids Lake

Roanoke River

Chowan R.

B. Everett Jordan Lake

Albemarle Sound

Lake Hickory

Catawba River

High Rock Lake

Tar River

Phelps Lake

Little Tennessee R.

French Broad R.

Lake Norman

Lake Mattamuskeet

Pamlico R.

Fontana Lake

Broad River

Neuse River

Pamlico Sound

Pee Dee River

GEORGIA

Blewett Falls Lake

Lumber River

Cape Fear River

Onslow Bay

SOUTH CAROLINA

Lake Waccamaw

✓ Dam

0   30   60 Miles
0   30   60 Kilometers
Albers Equal-Area Projection

Location   **Many rivers flow through North Carolina.**

❖ **What river flows into Lake Hickory?**

GEOGRAPHY THEME

Rivers Shape the Land

Sometimes rivers shape the land suddenly and swiftly. This happened in 1999, when floods covered parts of eastern North Carolina after Hurricane Floyd. More often, however, rivers shape the land at a slow and steady pace over hundreds and thousands of years.

Rivers shape land through the erosion of Earth's surface. Erosion is the wearing away of the Earth's surface. Rivers, rain, and ocean waves can wear away even the hardest rocks. The continuing movement of water slowly turns rocks into gravel, soil, and sand.

Many of North Carolina's rivers have their source, or beginning, high in the Appalachian Mountains, where the land is steep. The Roanoke River starts in the Blue Ridge Mountains of southwestern Virginia. It then flows in a southeastern direction for 380 miles (612 km). Much of its route runs through North Carolina. Above the Fall Line the Roanoke and other rivers flow swiftly in narrow

channels, or paths, toward the edge of the Piedmont. There the Roanoke River tumbles over the Fall Line in low waterfalls and rapids near the town of Roanoke Rapids.

When the Roanoke River reaches the flat land below the Fall Line, it spreads out and slows down. As rivers move more slowly over the Coastal Plain, they make changes in the land. Some sand and soil carried from the western mountains is deposited, or left, on banks and floodplains. A **floodplain** is low flat land along a river. When a river floods, water spreads out over the floodplain.

The Roanoke and many other North Carolina rivers end their journey to the sea by emptying into a sound. A **sound** is a body of water that lies between the mainland and an island. The Roanoke River flows into Albemarle Sound.

REVIEW   **How do rivers change the land?**

Rivers Drain the Land

The Eastern Continental Divide is a ridge that runs along the Blue Ridge Mountains. It separates rivers flowing east from those flowing west. In North Carolina, rivers to the east of the divide flow into the Atlantic Ocean. Those to the west eventually empty into the Mississippi River and the Gulf of Mexico. Rivers flowing west include the Hiwassee (hy•WAH•see), the French Broad, and the Watauga (wah•TAW•guh) Rivers.

The Cape Fear River is one of the state's best-known rivers. The Cape Fear is one of several North Carolina rivers that flow into the Atlantic. Others include the Neuse and Pamlico Rivers.

Many tributaries join the Cape Fear River as it flows toward the coast. A **tributary** is a river or stream that flows into a larger river. The Haw, Deep, and South Rivers are tributaries of the Cape Fear River.

• BIOGRAPHY •

James B. Duke   1856–1925
Character Trait: Inventiveness

James B. Duke's inventiveness started in his family's tobacco business. He helped develop new machines for tobacco manufacturing. His family also started a textile business in 1892. Duke decided to build dams on the Catawba River to generate electricity. Soon his company was supplying electricity to more than 300 cotton mills and other factories. In 1905 Duke's family started the Duke Power Company. Duke's inventiveness helped make his family businesses very successful. The Duke family has contributed more than a billion dollars to schools, hospitals, and other charities.

MULTIMEDIA BIOGRAPHIES
Visit The Learning Site at
www.harcourtschool.com/biographies
to learn about other famous people.

GO ONLINE

A river and its tributaries make up a river system. A **river system** drains, or carries away water, from the land around it. The Cape Fear River system drains almost one-fifth of the state's land area.

REVIEW What do river systems do?

Rivers and Lakes as Power Sources

In the 1890s James Duke and his older brother Benjamin started a textile, or cloth-making, business. Their mills needed a cheap source of power.

The Dukes turned to **hydroelectricity**, which is electricity made by using the power of rushing water. Today North Carolina's rivers and dams are an important source of hydroelectric power.

Dams are walls built to control the power of rushing water. A dam can hold back flood waters or help run generators, or machines that make electricity. Much of the electricity in North Carolina is made this way. The Catawba River leads the state in producing hydroelectricity.

REVIEW How do rivers help people meet their daily needs?

Analyze Diagrams Hydroelectric plants can generate enormous amounts of electricity.

◆ How does the water help produce electricity?

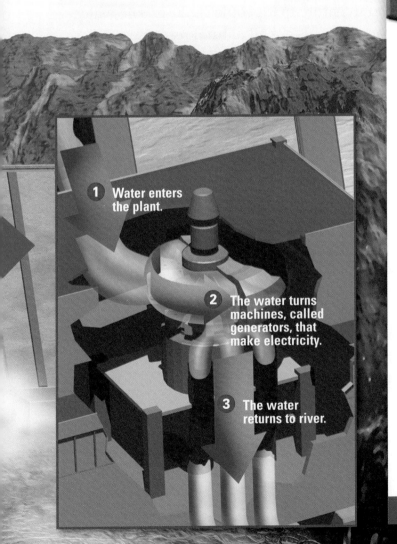

1. Water enters the plant.

2. The water turns machines, called generators, that make electricity.

3. The water returns to river.

LESSON 3 REVIEW

❶ **MAIN IDEA** How have North Carolina's rivers affected its land and people?

❷ **WHY IT MATTERS** Why are North Carolina's river systems important?

❸ **VOCABULARY** How are a **tributary** and a **river system** related?

❹ **READING SKILL—Main Idea and Supporting Details** What is the Roanoke River's path across North Carolina? Add supporting details to your answer.

❺ **ECONOMICS** Why did James and Benjamin Duke use hydroelectricity?

❻ **GEOGRAPHY** What are five major North Carolina rivers?

❼ **CRITICAL THINKING—Analyze** How has erosion helped shape the land?

 PERFORMANCE—Draw a Mural Working in a small group, create a mural showing important rivers in North Carolina and how they affect the land and people. Post your mural where other students can see it.

4

North Carolina's Resources

MAIN IDEA

Read to find out about the natural resources of North Carolina and how, they are used.

WHY IT MATTERS

People often change the environment when they use natural resources.

VOCABULARY

natural resource

product

quarry

fertilizer

broadleaf

needleleaf

habitat

pollution

extinct

One day in 1799, twelve-year-old Conrad Reed went fishing at the Little Meadow Creek on his family's farm in what is now Cabarrus (kuh•BAIR•uhs) County. He found a shiny yellow stone in the creek and gave it to his father, John. John Reed did not know what the curious stone was. For the next three years, he used it as a doorstop. Then, in 1802, he took the stone to Fayetteville and showed it to a jeweler. The jeweler knew at once that the stone was gold. Conrad Reed's find started the state's first gold rush.

Gold is one of Earth's natural resources. A **natural resource** is something found in nature that people can use. Soil, water, minerals, plants, and animals are all natural resources. Throughout North Carolina's history, these resources have helped the state succeed.

North Carolina's Soil Resources

Government leaders in North Carolina's Department of Agriculture like to use the phrase *Goodness Grows in North Carolina*. It reminds people that many of the foods they enjoy are grown right here at home. One reason for North Carolina's success in farming is its fertile soil. Good soil is one of North Carolina's most important natural resources.

At one time the state's most important crop was tobacco. Tobacco is less important today, and farmers produce many other products. A **product** is something people make or grow, usually to sell.

Gold played an important role in North Carolina's history.

North Carolina leads the nation in the production of sweet potatoes. Almost half of the sweet potatoes in the United States come from North Carolina. In 1995 state lawmakers made the sweet potato the state vegetable. The state is also one of the country's top producers of peanuts, strawberries, blueberries, apples, and cucumbers used to make pickles.

Many of the state's leading crops grow on the Inner Coastal Plain. This area has the most fertile, well-drained soil in the state. Farmers there raise most of the state's sweet potatoes, as well as cucumbers, tobacco, peanuts, corn, soybeans, cotton, and watermelons.

Red clay soil covers much of the Piedmont. Corn, grain, and hay grow well there. Farmers in the Piedmont region and in the Mountain region grow corn to feed their dairy cattle.

When someone asked a farmer about the soil in the Mountain region, he replied, "Oh, this is good, strong land. It must be, to hold up all the rocks we got around here." In the gray-brown soil of this region, farmers plant corn, hay, cabbage, and tobacco. Apple trees in the Mountain region produce all of the state's apple crop.

REVIEW **What food crops are grown in North Carolina?**

• HERITAGE •

Sweet Potatoes

For more than 500 years, sweet potatoes have been an important North Carolina crop. Sweet potatoes were an important food for Native Americans, especially in the Mountain region. Today four out of every ten sweet potatoes sold in the United States are grown in North Carolina.

North Carolina even has sweet potato festivals! One of the most popular is the North Carolina Yam Festival. Held in Tabor City at the end of October, the festival lasts for ten days. It includes events such as a sweet potato craft show, a sweet potato cook-off, and displays of award-winning sweet potatoes.

North Carolina's Mineral Resources

For many years after Conrad Reed's lucky find at Little Meadow Creek, gold was North Carolina's most important mineral. Until 1848, when gold was discovered in California, most of the nation's gold came from North Carolina.

Today, many other minerals are important to the state's economy. The state has more than 300 kinds of rocks and minerals. Most of them are found in western North Carolina. The state's most important minerals are feldspar, mica (MY•kuh), lithium (LIH•thee•uhm), and olivine (AH•luh•veen). Factories use feldspar to make glass and ceramics. Wallpaper, paint, and some fireproofing materials are made with mica. Lithium is used in batteries and as a medicine. Olivine is important in the steelmaking process.

North Carolina's most common rock resources are sand, gravel, and crushed stone. Counties in the Sandhills of the Inner Coastal Plain are the major sources of sand and gravel. These materials are used to make concrete and asphalt for road building and construction projects.

The Piedmont region is well known for its granite and clay. Mount Airy has the world's largest open-face granite quarry. A **quarry** is a place where stone is cut or blasted out of the ground. Red clay from the Piedmont is used to make bricks, sewer pipes, and roof tiles.

The emerald is the state's official gemstone. Emeralds are found near the towns of Spruce Pine in Mitchell County and Hiddenite (HIH•duhn•yt) in Alexander County. The town of Hiddenite is named for an emerald-colored gem discovered by William Hidden and found only in North Carolina.

At the Aurora phosphate mine in Beaufort County, huge cranes scoop up phosphate rock from the ground. Phosphate is used to make fertilizer. **Fertilizer** is material that is added to the soil to help plants grow.

REVIEW What are North Carolina's most important mineral resources?

This forklift moves a huge block of granite that workers have cut from the Mount Airy quarry.

Maple and oak trees are found in North Carolina's broadleaf forests (left). Pine trees are common in needleleaf forests (right).

North Carolina's Vegetation

Forests are one of the most important natural resources for North Carolina. The state is one of the most heavily forested states in the country. Many of the largest forests are found in the Mountain region. Together the Pisgah (PIZ•guh) and Nantahala Forests in western North Carolina cover more than a million acres of land.

Two kinds of trees grow in the state's forests—broadleaf and needleleaf. A **broadleaf** tree has wide, flat leaves. These leaves change color and fall off each autumn. Oaks are the state's most common broadleaf trees. In early October the oak leaves change from green to red, orange, and yellow. There are many oak, hickory, maple, and yellow poplar trees in the Mountain region.

North Carolina also has many **needleleaf** trees. These trees have thin, sharp, needlelike leaves that stay green all year. For this reason they are also known as evergreens. The pine tree is such a common sight in North Carolina that state leaders chose it as the state tree.

Today North Carolina's forests are an important economic resource. They provide timber for the furniture, paper, and lumber industries. Forest products are North Carolina's second-largest manufacturing industry.

Many people in North Carolina use the state's forests for recreation. Forests help preserve the environment by keeping air and water clean. Forests also serve as habitats for wildlife. A **habitat** is a place where animals find food and shelter.

Some of the state's valuable forests have been lost because of pollution. **Pollution** is anything that makes a natural resource dirty or unsafe to use. Trees are cut down and not replaced. The forests need to be protected so that they remain a valuable resource.

REVIEW What are some uses of North Carolina's forests?

DEMOCRATIC VALUES
Common Good

At Farmington Woods Elementary School in Cary, students work together for the common good of their school and community. They are members of the BEA (Becoming Environmentally Aware) Bunch. Students and teachers put used paper and boxes in special bins. The BEA Bunch gathers the bins so community workers can take them to recycling plants. Recycling preserves natural resources by reusing materials and also helps keep the school clean.

Analyze the Value

❶ How does the recycling project at Farmington Woods Elementary School work?

❷ How does the BEA Bunch program help Cary and the school?

❸ **Make It Relevant** Work in a group to make a list of ways you can help protect North Carolina's natural resources.

Pamlico Sound is a perfect habitat for birds such as herons and terns.

North Carolina's Animal Habitats

The forest is the natural habitat of black bears. At one time black bears lived all over North Carolina. They roamed great distances looking for grasses, leaves, nuts, berries, and fruit to eat.

As forests have disappeared, bears and other forest animals have lost their habitats. Today black bears are found only near the swamps, pocosins, and forests of the Coastal Plain and in the forests of the Appalachian Mountains. Deer, foxes, gray squirrels, opossums, rabbits, and raccoons are other forest animals. Wetlands are often nesting places for shorebirds and waterfowl. Ducks, geese, and swans make their homes in the marshes and swamps of the Tidewater. For Canadian geese, ducks, tundra swans, herons, egrets (EE•grets), and other birds, North Carolina is a stopover on their spring and fall journeys.

A great egret

A black bear

A white-tailed deer

Inland lakes and rivers are the habitats of bluegills, bass, and sunfish. Both brook trout and mountain trout are found in the lakes and rivers of the Mountain region.

Animal habitats can be easily damaged or destroyed. If their habitats are lost, animals may die out, or become **extinct**. People in North Carolina are working to protect animal habitats.

REVIEW What are two animal habitats in North Carolina today?

LESSON 4
REVIEW

1 **MAIN IDEA** What are our state's main natural resources? How are they used?

2 **WHY IT MATTERS** How can using natural resources affect the environment?

3 **VOCABULARY** What is the difference between a **natural resource** and a **product**?

4 **READING SKILL—Main Idea and Supporting Details** What are the main characteristics of North Carolina's forests? Use supporting details.

5 **ECONOMICS** What role does good soil play in the economy of North Carolina?

6 **SCIENCE AND TECHNOLOGY** Why are black bears found only in certain areas today?

7 **CRITICAL THINKING—Analyze** Why are rocks and minerals important to North Carolina's economy?

PERFORMANCE—Make a Poster Choose one natural resource in North Carolina. Learn more about the resource and its uses. Then make a poster about it for your classroom.

·SKILLS·
MAP AND GLOBE

Use a Land Use and Product Map

VOCABULARY

land use
resource

WHY IT MATTERS

The land of North Carolina is used in many ways, including farming, manufacturing, and mining. But where are there farms in North Carolina? What kinds of minerals are mined? What kinds of products are manufactured? You can find all this information on a land use and product map.

WHAT YOU NEED TO KNOW

Look at the map. It uses color to show **land use**, or how most of the land in an area is used. It also uses picture symbols to show the location of different

industries and **resources**, or products, in North Carolina. Look at the map key to see which colors and symbols are used on the map and what they stand for.

The picture symbols show the main resources for an area. The map key shows what kind of resource, or product, each picture symbol represents.

The area around Goldsboro is colored tan, which means that the land around Goldsboro is used mainly for tobacco farming. The picture symbols around Goldsboro show several animals and vegetables. According to the key, these symbols show that chickens, hogs, soybeans, sweet potatoes, and corn are found nearby.

Growing corn is one way North Carolinians use the state's land.

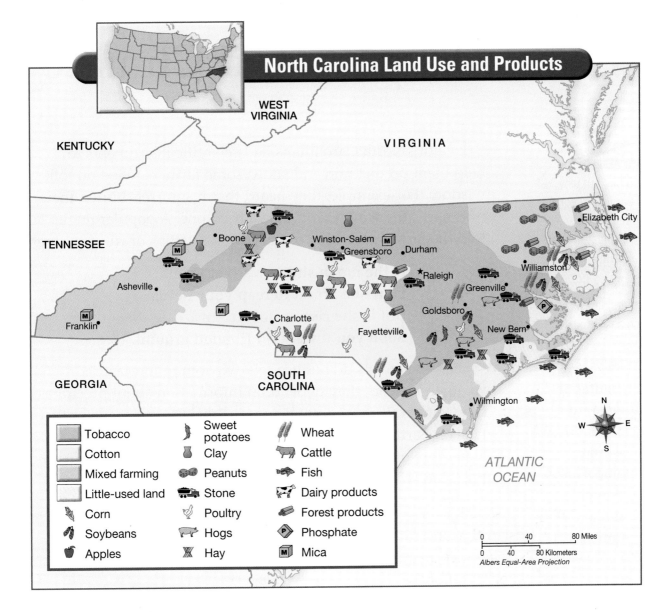

North Carolina Land Use and Products

WEST VIRGINIA

KENTUCKY

VIRGINIA

TENNESSEE

• Boone

Winston-Salem

Greensboro

• Durham

★ Raleigh

• Elizabeth City

Williamston

Greenville

Asheville •

• Charlotte

Goldsboro

Franklin•

Fayetteville•

New Bern•

GEORGIA

SOUTH CAROLINA

• Wilmington

ATLANTIC OCEAN

N
W E
S

Map Key

Tobacco	Sweet potatoes	Wheat
Cotton	Clay	Cattle
Mixed farming	Peanuts	Fish
Little-used land	Stone	Dairy products
Corn	Poultry	Forest products
Soybeans	Hogs	P Phosphate
Apples	Hay	M Mica

0   40   80 Miles
0   40   80 Kilometers
Albers Equal-Area Projection

▶ PRACTICE THE SKILL

Study the map key to understand the land use and resources of North Carolina. Then use the map and map key to answer these questions.

❶ What is the land around Fayetteville used for? What are the major products of the area?

❷ What is the land around Greenville used for? What are the major products of this area?

❸ What are the major products of the Mountain region?

▶ APPLY WHAT YOU LEARNED

Make a land use and resource map of your community. Use books, interviews, or other sources to find out what resources come from your area and how people use the land. Then draw a map of your community. Use colors to show how the land is used. Choose symbols for the resources and mark them on your map. Remember to make a map key to explain your symbols.

Practice your map and globe skills with the **GeoSkills CD-ROM**.

· LESSON ·

5

MAIN IDEA
Read to find out why North Carolina's regions have different climates and how climate affects people's lives.

WHY IT MATTERS
Climate influences our lives on a daily basis.

VOCABULARY

precipitation
temperature
weather
climate
growing season
drought
tornado
hurricane

Weather and Climate

Before North Carolinians had scientific instruments to help them predict rain and snow, some farmers relied on folk wisdom. For example, they heard that if squirrels buried their nuts early, the winter would be a hard one. A popular jingle told the farmers whether to harvest their crops or run for cover.

> **If the moon shows a silver shield,**
> **Don't be afraid to reap your field;**
> **But if she rises haloed round,**
> **Soon you'll walk on flooded ground.**

Today scientists do not use folk wisdom to forecast the weather. Instead, they depend on information about precipitation, temperature, and wind speed. **Precipitation** is water that falls on Earth's surface as rain, sleet, or snow. **Temperature** is a measure of how hot or cold the air is. Precipitation, temperature, and wind speed determine the weather.

The climate of the Mountain region makes skiing possible in western North Carolina in the winter.

LOCATE IT

NORTH CAROLINA

Appalachian Ski Mountain

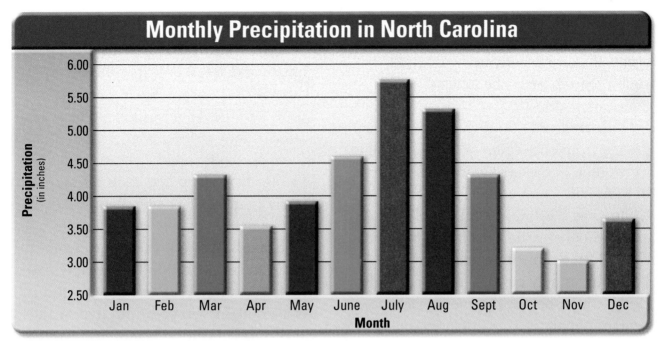

Monthly Precipitation in North Carolina

Analyze Graphs   **This graph shows the average, or usual, amount of rain and snow that North Carolina receives each month.**

◆ In which month does North Carolina usually have the most precipitation? In which month does it have the least?

The Climate of North Carolina

Weather refers to the condition of the air outside on a particular day. **Climate** is the term for the weather patterns of a place over a long time. The climate of a place depends partly on its location.

Location affects climate because some places on Earth receive more of the sun's heat than others. Places near the equator receive the most heat. They have a tropical, or very hot and wet, climate. The farther a place is from the equator, the colder it is. The coldest places on Earth are the North Pole and the South Pole.

Distance from the equator is called *latitude*. The equator is the starting point for measuring latitude. Lines of latitude are measured in degrees north (°N) and south (°S) from the equator.

They are labeled from 0° at the equator to 90° at each of the poles. Because most of North Carolina is between the latitudes of 34°N and 37°N, it is in the temperate, or moderate, climate zone.

North Carolina's climate is also influenced by elevation. Elevation is how far above or below sea level a place is. Places at higher elevations are often cooler than places at lower elevations. The higher above sea level a place is, the lower its temperature is. Geographers think that temperatures drop more than 3°F (2°C) for every 1,000 feet (305 m) of elevation.

Because of its high elevation, the Mountain region has the state's coolest temperatures. The warmest temperatures are in the Coastal Plain.

This thermometer is a tool for measuring temperature.

The Piedmont is at a higher elevation than the Coastal Plain. It also has temperatures that are usually a few degrees cooler than those of the lower Coastal Plain.

On a single day, temperatures can vary greatly from one region of North Carolina to another. In the spring and fall, families in Mountain region towns such as Cullowhee (KUHL•uh•wee), Mars Hill, and Hendersonville bundle up in warm coats. At the same time people in Wilmington may be wearing lightweight clothes. In Asheville the average temperature in January is 37°F (3°C), but in Wilmington it is 46°F (8°C).

REVIEW How does elevation affect climate in North Carolina?

A CLOSER LOOK
The Water Cycle

On Earth, water constantly moves from the oceans to the air to the ground and back to the oceans. This is called the water cycle.

❶ The heat of the sun makes water from the oceans evaporate, or turn to a gas. The gas is called water vapor.

❷ The water vapor forms into clouds.

❸ Water falls from the clouds to the ground as rain, snow, or other kinds of precipitation. Some water soaks into the ground or is absorbed by plant roots.

❹ The rest of the water flows into lakes and rivers. Rivers carry the water back to the oceans.

❖ What happens to water that falls as precipitation?

Wind, Water, and Weather

Another factor that affects the state's climate and weather is its nearness to water. As you know, North Carolina is located on the Atlantic Ocean. Places near water usually have milder weather than places far from water.

Water warms up and cools off more slowly than land. The temperature of large bodies of water, such as oceans and some lakes, does not vary much from winter to summer. Winds that blow over water take on the water's temperature. As a result, air temperatures over water do not vary as much as air temperatures over land.

In summer the ocean is cooler than the land. So winds blowing from the ocean help keep places near the coast cooler than places inland. During the coldest months of the year, the ocean water is warmer than the land. So winds blowing off the water make coastal areas warmer in winter than inland areas.

Temperatures in North Carolina change with the season, giving its residents four different seasons. Winters are cool and mild with little snow except in the Mountain region. Summers are warm to hot. Spring and fall have mild weather.

Seasonal temperature changes are caused by Earth's movement around the sun each year. This is because Earth tilts on its axis, an imaginary line through Earth from the North Pole to the South Pole. Because the axis is tilted, the Northern Hemisphere is closer to the sun for part of the year. That is when the sun's rays hit North Carolina more directly, causing summer.

Seasonal changes in temperature affect the growing season in North Carolina. The **growing season** is the time of year when the weather is warm enough for plants to grow. The growing season is measured in days. It lasts from the time of the last freeze of spring to the first freeze of fall. In North Carolina the growing season is longer in the eastern part of the state.

Climate affects which plants grow well in North Carolina.

Precipitation varies from one region of the state to another. The Mountain region averages about 60 inches (152 cm) of rain or snow a year. Snowfalls in the Piedmont are rarely more than 6 inches (15 cm) deep. The Piedmont usually gets less than 46 inches (117 cm) of rain a year. Sometimes it can have droughts. A **drought** is a time of extreme dryness that causes damage to crops.

More precipitation falls in the Coastal Plain than in the Piedmont. The Coastal Plain gets an average of more than 54 inches (137 cm) of precipitation a year.

REVIEW How does nearness to water affect the climate of the Coastal Plain?

Stormy Weather

From May through August, storm warnings often flash across the television screen. However, storms can occur at any time of year.

North Carolina has many kinds of storms. Thunderstorms often form over the state in the summer. These storms are created when cold, dry air meets warm, humid air. Along with rain, thunderstorms can bring lightning and hail, or pieces of ice that can be as large as golf balls. Sudden and strong storms can cause flooding and destroy crops.

A tornado is another kind of severe weather seen in North Carolina. A **tornado** is a funnel-shaped column of spinning air. It forms under the clouds of strong thunderstorms. The narrowest part of a tornado travels near the ground. The tornado can be spinning at more than 200 miles (321 km) an hour. Tornadoes usually affect only small areas. Dangerous tornadoes are most common in the eastern Piedmont and the Coastal Plain.

Mel Gardner, who lives in Stanly County, recalled what it was like when a tornado touched down near his church in 1999. "It sounded," he said, "like two 18-wheeler trucks coming through the church."

• SCIENCE AND TECHNOLOGY •

Doppler Radar

Radar is an electronic system used by weather forecasters. The word *radar* stands for *ra*dio *d*etection *a*nd *r*anging. Radio waves are sent out and bounce back from objects up to 250 miles (402 km) away. Signals coming back from snowflakes, hailstones, or raindrops tell how far away a storm is and its direction, speed, and strength. Doppler radar is used by the National Weather Service to measure wind speeds and wind shifts. It can even measure falling rain or snow. This information helps forecasters warn North Carolinians when a thunderstorm, tornado, hurricane, or other severe weather is coming.

Tornadoes are dangerous storms that can cause a great deal of damage.

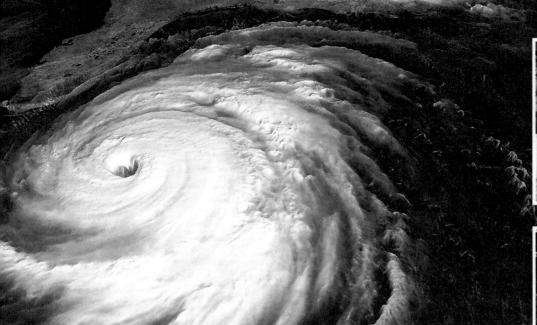

Hurricane Floyd (above) forced people to flee to shelters (top right) and flooded many places (bottom right) in North Carolina.

Hurricanes are the state's most damaging storms. A **hurricane** is a big storm with heavy rains and high winds that forms over warm ocean water. Toward the end of summer, tropical storms sometimes travel over the Caribbean Sea and southern Atlantic Ocean. When they reach wind speeds of more than 74 miles (119 km) an hour, they are called hurricanes.

Hurricane Floyd, which swept across eastern North Carolina in September 1999, caused billions of dollars in property damage. People from all over the United States gave money, food, and their time to rebuild damaged areas. Hurricane Floyd was the state's worst natural disaster.

REVIEW What kinds of storms does North Carolina get?

LESSON 5
REVIEW

1 MAIN IDEA Why are the climates of North Carolina's regions different?

2 WHY IT MATTERS How does climate affect people's lives?

3 VOCABULARY Use the words **precipitation** and **temperature** to describe the weather patterns in one of North Carolina's regions.

4 READING SKILL—Main Idea and Supporting Details Which region of North Carolina is the coldest? Why? Give supporting details.

5 GEOGRAPHY Between what latitudes does most of North Carolina lie?

6 SCIENCE AND TECHNOLOGY What is a tornado?

7 CRITICAL THINKING—Evaluate Based on climate, which region of North Carolina would you prefer to live in? Why?

PERFORMANCE—Interview Interview a weather reporter in your area by phone, by e-mail, or in person. With your class, create a list of questions before the interview.

1 Review and Test Preparation

USE YOUR READING SKILLS

Complete this graphic organizer to show that you understand the main ideas and supporting details that describe North Carolina. A copy of this graphic organizer appears on page 16 of the Activity Book.

North Carolina's Geography

MAIN IDEA → SUPPORTING DETAILS

North Carolina's Coastal Plain has several different features.

→

1. The Tidewater area is flat and has many swamps and saltwater marshes.
2. The barrier islands are low, narrow islands that stand between the ocean and the mainland.
3. _____
4. _____

_____
_____
_____
_____
_____

→

1. North Carolina has more than 300 varieties of rocks and minerals.
2. North Carolina's forests provide timber for the furniture, paper, and lumber industries.
3. _____
4. _____

THINK & WRITE

Write a Letter to the Editor Think about how North Carolina's natural resources are used. To do this, answer the following questions: Are North Carolina's natural resources being used well? How could they be used better? How do the ways people use them affect the environment? After you answer these questions, write a letter that you might send to a local newspaper.

Report on Climate Imagine that you are a weather reporter. You want to do a special report on North Carolina's climate. Conduct research to find information on the climate of one of North Carolina's regions. Write a report to describe the region's climate over the past five to ten years. Be sure to include information about any major storms or unusual weather.

USE VOCABULARY

Fill in the blank for each sentence, using the correct term from the list.

equator (p. 21)

fall line (p. 27)

sound (p. 35)

natural resource (p. 38)

growing season (p. 49)

1 Many North Carolina rivers end their journey by emptying into a ____.

2 Farmers can raise crops during the ____.

3 A ____ is the place where rivers drop from higher to lower ground.

4 The imaginary line that separates the Northern and Southern Hemispheres is called the ____.

5 Gold is one ____ found in North Carolina.

RECALL FACTS

Answer these questions.

6 What is a coastal plain?

7 What is a floodplain?

8 What are three natural resources found in North Carolina?

Write the letter of the best choice.

9 **TEST PREP** Wind speed, precipitation, and temperature are parts of the—
A elevation.
B climate zone.
C growing season.
D weather.

10 **TEST PREP** The prefix *hemi-* in the word *hemisphere* means—
F low.
G whole.
H half.
J high.

THINK CRITICALLY

11 Choose a region of North Carolina where you do not live. How would the weather and environment there change how you live?

12 Why is it important to protect animal habitats?

APPLY SKILLS

Use Latitude and Longitude
Use the map on page 23 to answer the question.

13 What line of longitude passes the closest by Wilmington?

Read an Elevation Map
Use the map on page 31 to answer the question.

14 Which is higher, Grandfather Mountain or Pilot Mountain?

Read a Land Use and Product Map
Use the map on page 45 to answer the question.

15 What is the major product of western North Carolina?

OCCANEECHI TOWN

Occaneechi Town is an important site for scientists who study the early people of North Carolina. Between 50 and 75 Native Americans lived there from 1695 to 1710. Scientists found the site in 1983. They spent three years researching the site. They found buildings and items left behind by the people who lived there.

LOCATE IT

Occaneechi Town

NORTH CAROLINA

2

The Early People of North Carolina

" They left no written records for historians. "

—Theda Perdue, historian

CHAPTER READING SKILL

Summarize

To **summarize**, restate the most important ideas, or key points, in your own words.

As you read this chapter, think about the key points of each lesson. Then write them down in your own words.

KEY POINTS SUMMARY

MAIN IDEA
Read to learn how
changes in climate and
land affected how the
earliest people lived.

WHY IT MATTERS
People's lives are still
affected by land and
climate changes.

VOCABULARY
artifact
archaeologist
migrate
nomad
scarce
atlatl
agriculture
tribe
specialize
division of labor

The Earliest People

The first people in what is now North Carolina left no written records of their lives. They lived during the time known as prehistory. Prehistory is the period of time before written records were made. Today we know about these people from the tools, weapons, and other artifacts they left behind. **Artifacts** are things people used in the past.

Early People in North Carolina

The ancestors of early people in what is now North Carolina arrived on this continent many thousands of years ago. Some archaeologists (ar•kee•AH•luh•jists) think they came on foot, from Asia, across a narrow bridge of land. An **archaeologist** is a scientist who studies artifacts to figure out what life was like long ago.

Archaeologists think these early people **migrated**, or moved, across North America and settled in what is today North Carolina. According to this theory, or idea, the first people came because they were following herds of bison and mammoths. Mammoths were huge, hairy, elephant-like animals that stood as much as 14 feet (4 m) tall.

FAST FACT When people first came to North Carolina, the coast was several miles east of where it is today. Over time, the ocean covered more of the land. Today archaeologists find Native American artifacts under water!

Prehistoric Atlatl

Early Native Americans hunted with spears. Many used a tool called an atlatl to help. An atlatl was a stick with a hook at the end to hold a spear. It acted like an extra-long arm. This meant that the hunter could throw the spear harder and farther. Often hunters tied stone weights to their atlatls. This weight helped the hunter hold the atlatl steady. Scientists think that Native Americans used atlatls in many parts of North America, including North Carolina.

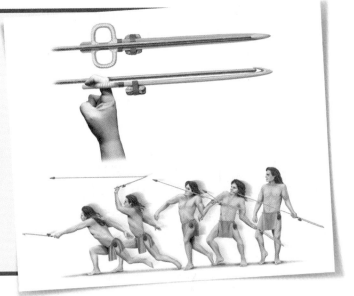

These early people were nomads. A **nomad** is a person who keeps moving from place to place. Nomads traveled in bands, or small groups of families that lived and worked together.

Their diet consisted mainly of nuts, berries, and plants they gathered in the forests. Archaeologists know that these early people also fished and hunted. They learned this from artifacts found at the Hardaway site in Stanly County.

REVIEW How did the earliest people live?

Hunters and Gatherers

By about 10,000 years ago, the climate had become warmer. Still, people traveled in search of food. They moved in a pattern based on the seasons. They traveled to where they knew they would find food at each time of the year.

In winter the people hunted rabbits and other small animals. Some larger animals became **scarce**, or hard to find. Other large animals became extinct. In spring the people fished along the coast. In summer and fall they moved inland.

The early people lived in caves or rock shelters. They built summer camps near water, where they could find fish and shellfish to eat. Their tools included scrapers, drills, and axes. They also developed the **atlatl** (AHT•lah•tuhl), a tool that hunters used for throwing spears farther.

REVIEW How did early people change their way of life when the climate changed?

Early Farmers

About 3,500 years ago people began learning how to farm. The development of **agriculture**, or farming, brought about a major change. As people discovered how to plant seeds and grow food, they no longer had to spend all their time hunting and gathering.

Early farmers settled along rivers. There they found fertile soil and plenty of water. The farmers planted beans, squash, gourds, sunflowers, and maize, which is a kind of corn.

With a steady supply of food, people lived longer, and the total number of people increased. Over time they formed tribes. A **tribe** is a group of people who share land, speak the same language, and have the same customs.

In farming groups, people began to specialize. To **specialize** is to work at just one job. There were many farming jobs to be done. These jobs were divided among different workers. This is called **division of labor**.

REVIEW How did farming change the way early people lived in the region that is now North Carolina?

The Mound Builders

In the 1450s a group related to the Creeks in what are today Alabama and Georgia migrated to the area that is now North Carolina. They built towns along the Pee Dee River. Between 1,000 and 2,000 people lived in each town. They built fences of pointed sticks to protect their settlements.

These people were farmers. Corn was their major food crop. It was also important to the religious ceremonies they held in their temples.

Today these people are known as the Mound Builders.

Early people worked together to farm. They used querns (above) to grind grain.

Town Creek Indian Mound

Understanding Human Systems

Between A.D. 1450 and 1550, Town Creek Indian Mound was the center of religion and government for the people of the Pee Dee River valley. The people held ceremonies, feasts, ball games, and burials at the mound. No one lived within the mound area except the men who were in charge of it.

The mound held a temple, houses, and burial huts. A tall fence protected the area. Today Town Creek Indian Mound is a state historic site. The mound, buildings made from clay and straw, and a palisade show what this center looked like 500 years ago.

They built flat-topped mounds, or large hills of dirt. These mounds served as temples and burial places.

The largest Mound Builder settlement in the area of what is now North Carolina was Town Creek Indian Mound. The mound served many purposes. It was a center for religious ceremonies and ball games. Today, the Town Creek Indian Mound is a state historic site.

REVIEW Why did the Mound Builders build mounds?

LESSON 1
REVIEW

❶ **MAIN IDEA** How did the first people in North Carolina adjust to changes in climate and land?

❷ **WHY IT MATTERS** How are people's lives today affected by land and climate?

❸ **VOCABULARY** How are the words **nomad** and **migrate** related?

❹ **READING SKILL—Summarize** What have you learned about how the Mound Builders lived?

❺ **SCIENCE AND TECHNOLOGY** What tools did the early people of North Carolina use?

❻ **HISTORY** What is prehistory?

❼ **CRITICAL THINKING—Synthesize** How did farming change the lives of early people?

PERFORMANCE—Make a Drawing
Create a drawing about how the early people in North Carolina lived. Choose one topic, such as hunting and gathering, farming, or mound building. Read more about your topic. Then make your drawing and present it to your class.

· SKILLS ·

CHART AND GRAPH

Read a Time Line

VOCABULARY

time line

➡ WHY IT MATTERS

To understand the early history of North Carolina, you need to know when important events happened. A **time line** is a diagram that shows the order in which events took place and the amount of time that passed between them.

➡ WHAT YOU NEED TO KNOW

You can use a time line to organize information that archaeologists have

learned about the early peoples of North Carolina. These scientists have studied many artifacts that were left behind by ancient people.

Like a map, a time line has a scale. A time line shows units of time instead of distance. On this time line, the space between each two marks stands for 2,000 years. Earlier dates are near the left end of the time line. Later dates are near the right end.

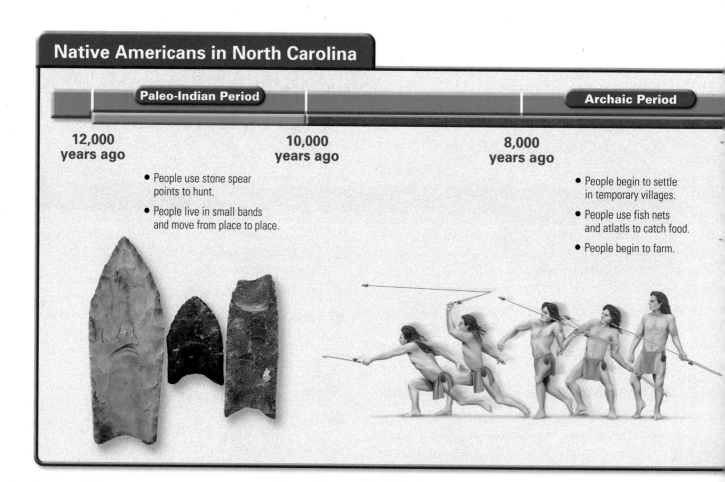

Native Americans in North Carolina

Paleo-Indian Period   **Archaic Period**

12,000 years ago   **10,000 years ago**   **8,000 years ago**

- People use stone spear points to hunt.
- People live in small bands and move from place to place.

- People begin to settle in temporary villages.
- People use fish nets and atlatls to catch food.
- People begin to farm.

Below this time line are colored bars. Each color shows when a period in history began and ended. Above the time line are labels that tell the name archaeologists use for each period shown. For example, you can see from the time line that the Paleo-Indian period began about 12,000 years ago.

There is also information below the time line. This information tells you some important facts about the ways people lived during each period.

▶ PRACTICE THE SKILL

Use the time line to answer these questions.

1 What name do archaeologists use for the period that began about 10,000 years ago and ended about 3,000 years ago? How long did this period last?

2 When was the Woodland period in North Carolina? What event marks the end of the Woodland period?

3 In which period did people first use fishnets and atlatls?

▶ APPLY WHAT YOU LEARNED

Make a time line of your life. Begin your time line with the year you were born. End it with this year. Label important periods on your time line, such as the years you have lived where you live now. You can also mark important events on your time line, such as the year you started school. Add pictures and descriptions to your time line. Display your time line in your classroom and compare it with your classmates' time lines.

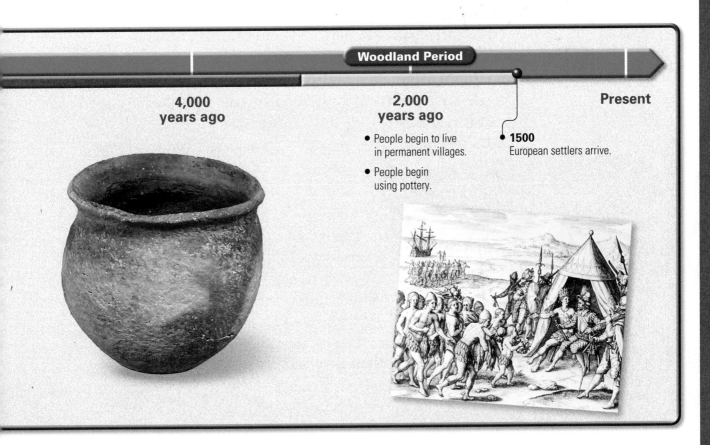

Woodland Period

4,000 years ago

2,000 years ago

Present

• People begin to live in permanent villages.
• People begin using pottery.

• **1500** European settlers arrive.

2

People of the Coastal Plain

Look at a map of North Carolina. You can see one of the ways Native Americans of long ago left their mark on our state. Throughout North Carolina, many towns, lakes, rivers, and other places have Native American names. For example, the Eno River, Perquimans (per•KWIH•muhns) County, Cape Hatteras, and the town of Waxhaw are all named for Native American peoples.

Early Native Americans in North Carolina

When Europeans first came to the area that is now North Carolina, about 30 different Native American tribes lived there. Each had its own traditions, religious beliefs, and ways of dressing, speaking, and behaving. A **tradition** is an idea or way of doing things that has been handed down. Together, beliefs, traditions, and ways of living make up a **culture**.

The early Native Americans in the North Carolina area can be divided into three major groups—Siouan (SOO•uhn), Algonquian (al•GAHN•kee•uhn), and Iroquoian (ir•uh•KWOY•uhn). These groups are based on the languages the people spoke.

This bowl and spoon were made by a Tuscarora (tuhs•kuh•ROHR•uh) carver.

Native Americans lived in heavily forested areas and relied on forest resources. That is why members of all three groups living in the region are known as Woodland people. Early Woodland people survived by hunting, by fishing, and by gathering nuts, berries, and shellfish.

REVIEW What are the three main groups of Native Americans who first lived in North Carolina?

Early Coastal Settlements

Most Native Americans who spoke Algonquian languages lived on the Coastal Plain. The Hatteras (HA•tuh•ruhs), Roanokes (ROH•uh•nohks), Croatoans (kroh•uh•TOH•unz), Secotans (SEK•uh•tanz), and Pamlicos (PAM•li•kohz) were among the Algonquian-speaking tribes on the Coastal Plain.

The Tuscaroras also lived on the Coastal Plain, in about 15 villages. Most of their villages were located between the Tar and Neuse Rivers. Although they did some hunting and gathering, agriculture was most important to their way of life. The Tuscaroras did not speak an Algonquian language. Instead they used an Iroquoian language.

REVIEW What Native American groups settled on the Coastal Plain?

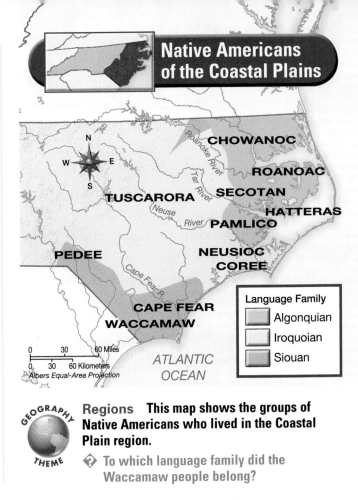

Native Americans of the Coastal Plains

Language Family
- Algonquian
- Iroquoian
- Siouan

CHOWANOC
ROANOAC
TUSCARORA
SECOTAN
HATTERAS
PAMLICO
PEDEE
NEUSIOC
COREE
CAPE FEAR
WACCAMAW
ATLANTIC OCEAN

Roanoke River
Tar River
Neuse River
Cape Fear R.

0   30   60 Miles
0   30   60 Kilometers
Albers Equal-Area Projection

GEOGRAPHY THEME

Regions This map shows the groups of Native Americans who lived in the Coastal Plain region.

To which language family did the Waccamaw people belong?

The Village of Pomeiock

Analyze Primary Sources

This is a watercolor painting by English explorer John White. It shows the Algonquian village of Pomeiock (PAH•mee•ahk) on Pamlico Sound near Lake Mattamuskeet (ma•tuh•MUHS•keet). This is one of more than 70 watercolors of Native Americans that White painted between 1577 and 1590.

❶ A palisade protected the village from enemies.

❷ Several families lived in each large house.

❸ Small buildings were probably used for storage.

❹ This fire was a place for the villagers to gather.

How many people do you think lived in this village?

The Coastal People

By the late 1500s, Native Americans in what is now North Carolina had become skilled farmers. They slowly cleared areas of forests for farming and stayed in one place for several years at a time. However, when their crops failed and firewood was scarce, they moved.

As farming skills got better, the population grew because there were more kinds of food to eat. In some areas coastal people built large villages near rivers.

• SCIENCE AND TECHNOLOGY •

Weirs

Native Americans in North Carolina's Tidewater region used weirs to catch fish. Weirs are fence-like wooden barriers placed across a sound, a river, or a stream and held in place with sticks or rocks. Once fish were trapped by the weir, people caught them with a spear or a net that hung from a long wooden pole.

Villages usually had from 10 to 30 long rectangular houses called **longhouses**. These longhouses were made of wood frames with rounded roofs covered with bark or grass.

Several related families lived together in a single longhouse. The longhouse was divided into as many as five rooms with a family in each room.

In the daily life of the coastal people, men and women worked together to farm. For Algonquian farmers, corn was the main crop, but they also planted pumpkins and beans.

The Algonquians often hunted with bows and arrows. They also captured ducks and geese at night by building a fire in a canoe. The birds, attracted by the light, came close enough to be captured. Sometimes the Algonquians also trapped fish in the same way.

Along the shore, women gathered clams and oysters. The mounds made up of oyster shells found along the coast show how important oysters were as food for coastal people. The shells were as valuable as the tiny creatures inside. Many coastal tribes made strings of beads cut from shells. They called the beads **wampum**. Both shells and wampum were important trade goods for coastal peoples. They exchanged the wampum for goods such as clay, salt, or mica from other tribes living in the Piedmont and Mountain regions.

REVIEW How did the Native Americans of the Coastal Plain use natural resources to survive?

People of the Coastal Plain region made beads from shells.

LESSON 2
REVIEW

1. **MAIN IDEA** What were some of the customs of the Coastal Plain people?

2. **WHY IT MATTERS** How have people used the Coastal Plain's resources to meet their needs?

3. **VOCABULARY** Use the words **tradition** and **culture** in a sentence.

4. **READING SKILL—Summarize** What were the main ways the Algonquian people hunted for food?

5. **HISTORY** What were some foods that Coastal Plain people ate?

6. **CULTURE** Why was wampum an important trade good?

7. **CRITICAL THINKING—Hypothesize** Why was trading important for Coastal Plain people?

 PERFORMANCE—Act Out a Scene With a small group, write a short scene about life in the Coastal Plain region long ago. Each person in your group should have a role to play. Perform your scene for the class.

MAIN IDEA
Read to learn about the customs and government of the Piedmont people.

WHY IT MATTERS
The Piedmont people had a system of government that is similar to the government of the United States.

VOCABULARY
government
council
democracy

People of the Piedmont

Vance Eller of Salisbury, North Carolina, is an amateur archaeologist. He has spent much time studying the ways of life of early Native American people in the Piedmont. He traces his interest in archaeology to an exciting discovery in his childhood. "My cousin Clarence was fishing in a little creek," he explained. "Then he came running across a field to me. He'd picked up an arrowhead, and he showed it to me. That did it." Eller has been a hunter of artifacts ever since.

In the 1940s Eller led an archaeological team to a site at High Rock Lake. The scientists discovered some of the most important artifacts ever found in Rowan County. Through work by Eller and archaeologists, we have learned a lot about the people who lived in the Piedmont.

Archaeologists have found important artifacts near High Rock Lake.

Early Piedmont Settlements

Almost all the 15 Siouan-speaking groups in what is now North Carolina lived in the Piedmont. They included the Catawbas, Enos, Keyauwees, Occaneechis, Saponis, Cheraws, Shakoris, Sissipahaws, Tutelos, and Waxhaws. Like the people of the Coastal Plain, these groups are called Woodland people by archaeologists.

The Siouan-speaking peoples lived in small villages made up of round, domed houses. The Siouan peoples hunted and gathered food, but they also farmed. They cleared fields just outside their villages, where they grew corn, beans, squash, peas, and melons. They were skilled potters who used the red clay of the Piedmont to make all kinds of pottery.

REVIEW Who were the early peoples of the Piedmont, and what was their daily life like?

The Piedmont Peoples

The peoples of the Piedmont lived in different places at different times of year. In fall and winter they camped and hunted near wooded areas in the hillier part of the Piedmont.

Hunters came up with clever ways to capture their prey. Sometimes they hunted alone, covering themselves in deerskins with the deer head still attached. With this disguise they could creep up on deer.

In spring and summer the peoples of the Piedmont moved to the land along rivers and streams. They planted beans, corn, and squash in small mounds of dirt.

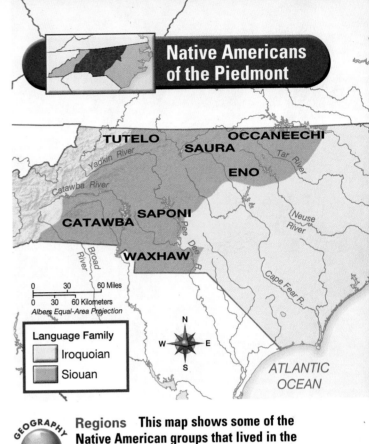

Native Americans of the Piedmont

Regions This map shows some of the Native American groups that lived in the Piedmont region.

❓ Which Piedmont group lived the farthest south?

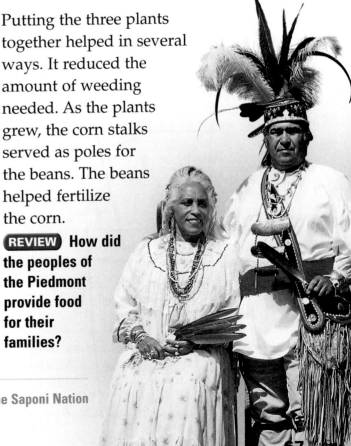

Putting the three plants together helped in several ways. It reduced the amount of weeding needed. As the plants grew, the corn stalks served as poles for the beans. The beans helped fertilize the corn.

REVIEW How did the peoples of the Piedmont provide food for their families?

Members of the Occaneechi Band of the Saponi Nation

The Catawbas had a representative government. In a representative government, each group chooses one person to be their representative. The representative listens to the people's ideas. Then he or she shares those opinions with leaders. This makes it easier for leaders to know what the people want. The Catawba representatives were part of a council that helped the leaders make decisions.

Analyze the Value

1. In a representative government, why is it important to involve as many people as possible?

2. Would it be easier to have a representative government or to let the people make their own decisions? Explain.

3. **Make It Relevant** The United States also has a representative government. Find out who represents your community in the North Carolina government and in the United States government. Write a letter or an e-mail message to one of your representatives telling your opinion about an important issue. Share your letter with your classmates before you send it.

The Catawbas

With between 5,000 and 6,000 members, the Catawbas were the largest of the Siouan groups living in the Piedmont. They wore animal skins and jewelry made of shells, animal teeth, or copper.

The Catawbas, like other Piedmont peoples, chose to live along rivers. They called themselves People of the River.

Also like other Native Americans, they built villages surrounded by palisades. Inside the palisades were from 5 to 15 round houses made of wooden frames covered with tree bark. Each house held ten or more people, usually from the same family. Children lived with their parents, grandparents, aunts, uncles, and cousins.

The meeting house was the largest building in each village. It had to be big enough to hold everyone in the village. It was long rather than round like the houses. There everyone in the community met to discuss problems and make plans. The meeting house was the center of government for each village. A **government** is a system for making decisions for a group of people. The decisions include how to protect the group from enemies or other threats, keep order, and settle conflicts. A government's leaders have the authority, or power, to make rules and see that they are followed.

Catawba villagers gathered at the meeting house to talk about matters of importance to the tribe. Although everyone attended these meetings, a **council**, or group of advisers, made the final decisions. The council consisted of older men who had earned the respect of the community. This government was somewhat like a **democracy**, a government in which the people take part. The chief was the leader, but he could not force council members to do as he wanted.

REVIEW In what ways was the government of the Catawbas like a democracy?

· **HERITAGE** ·

Native American Place Names

A map of North Carolina shows that many places have Native American names. Counties such as Cherokee, Pamlico, and Catawba get their names from Native American groups.

- The village of Saxapahaw is named after the Sissipahaw people.
- *Pasquotank*, the name of a county, means "where the current divides."
- *Cullowhee*, the name of a township, means "place of the lilies."
- *Nantahala*, the name of a river and of a national forest, comes from the Cherokee word *Nan-toh-ee-yah-heh-lih*, which means "land of the noonday sun."

Look at a map. Are there places near you that have Native American names? See if you can find out what they mean.

LESSON 3 REVIEW

❶ **MAIN IDEA** What kinds of villages, food, and government did the people of the Piedmont have?

❷ **WHY IT MATTERS** How was the Catawba system of government similar to the United States system of government?

❸ **VOCABULARY** Use the word **government** to describe a **democracy**.

❹ **READING SKILL—Summarize** How did the Piedmont people farm? Summarize the main ideas.

❺ **CIVICS/GOVERNMENT** What power did the chief of a Catawba village have?

❻ **CULTURE** How did the early Piedmont people make clothing, jewelry, and pottery?

❼ **CRITICAL THINKING—Evaluate** What job would you have liked if you were a Catawba? Why?

PERFORMANCE—Write a Diary Entry You are an archaeologist working in the Piedmont region. Write a diary entry about an important discovery. What does the discovery mean to you? What does it tell you about the Piedmont people?

4

MAIN IDEA
Read to find out about the customs and government of the Cherokees.

WHY IT MATTERS
The Mountain people believed that respect and teamwork were important to community life, just as Americans do today.

VOCABULARY
clan
confederation
Green Corn Ceremony

People of the Mountains

The Cherokees called themselves the *Ani-Yun'-wiya*, meaning "leading people" or "principal people." The name *Cherokee* comes from a Creek word, *Tisolkioe* or *Tciloki*, meaning "people of different speech." The Cherokees made their home in the Appalachian Mountains. For more than 1,000 years, they lived in the Great Smoky Mountains and throughout the Mountain region. They also settled in what are now Tennessee, South Carolina, and Georgia.

The Principal People

By 1650 more than 22,000 Cherokees were spread out over a hunting range of 40,000 square miles (103,600 sq km). They were by far the largest Native American group in the Mountain region. They spoke a language in the Iroquoian language family.

The Cherokees settled in more than 200 villages and towns. Each town had between 30 and 60 houses. Unlike many Native Americans of this time, the Cherokees remained in their towns all year. They built large, sturdy, rectangular homes. To do this, they stretched bark and woven material over a framework of poles. They covered the walls with a mixture of grass and clay and the roof with bark or thatch, which is dried grass. A hole in the roof let out smoke from the fire pit below.

In the winter months families moved to smaller, round houses with no windows. A fire burned inside day and night

This modern Cherokee woman is making pottery the same way the early Cherokee people did.

to keep the house warm. Several generations of the same family lived together in each house.

Each family had a small garden near its house, but the villagers worked together to care for large fields that belonged to the group. In their fields they planted corn, squash, pumpkins, and beans. They planted the corn and beans together in small mounds of soil. Between these mounds, they grew squash, sunflowers, and pumpkins. Men hunted for food and assisted with the harvest, and women did most of the farming.

Although the Cherokees were skilled farmers, they relied heavily on wild game, fish, and nuts and berries for their food as well. They also gathered wild plants from the forests to make medicines.

REVIEW How did the Cherokees use the resources of the Mountain region?

Cherokee Government

Every Cherokee belonged to a **clan**, a group tracing its roots from a common ancestor. There were seven clans in the Cherokee system of kinship, or family relationships. Each clan had a special name, such as *wolf*, *deer*, or *bird*.

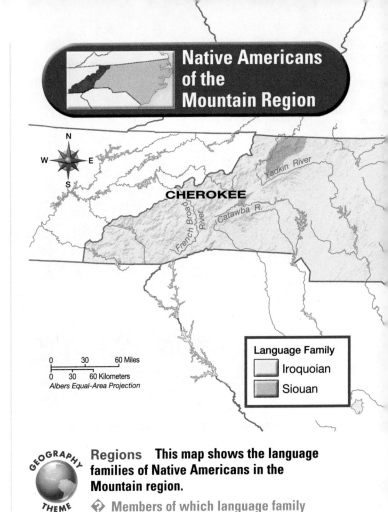

Native Americans of the Mountain Region

CHEROKEE

Yadkin River
French Broad River
Catawba R.

0   30   60 Miles
0   30   60 Kilometers
Albers Equal-Area Projection

Language Family
☐ Iroquoian
☐ Siouan

GEOGRAPHY THEME

Regions This map shows the language families of Native Americans in the Mountain region.

❖ Members of which language family lived in most of the Mountain region?

Each Cherokee town had a local government. At the center of each town was an open square with a round or seven-sided council house. The council house was divided into seven parts, one for a representative of each of the seven clans. A fire burned at all times in the central fire pit. Community leaders greeted important visitors and held religious ceremonies in the council house.

Cherokee artists made beautiful baskets.

A CLOSER LOOK
A Cherokee Village

The Cherokees lived in villages or towns. Each town was built around a central square, or open area. This drawing shows a Cherokee village during the Green Corn Ceremony.

1 The council house usually had seven sides. Sometimes it was round. The village leaders met in the council house to make decisions.

2 The Cherokee people had both summer and winter houses. In the summer they lived in open rectangular houses made of wood. In winter they lived in round houses made of earth. These houses were much warmer in the winter than the other houses were.

3 The central square was used by everyone in the village. Feasts, ball games, and ceremonies took place there.

Leaders, called chiefs, governed each village. The chiefs decided day-to-day matters. They were political and religious leaders. Women also held power in the town councils and spoke their opinions as freely as men did. The government councils were democratic. Villagers discussed each issue until they reached an agreement.

Cherokee towns and villages were part of a larger government called a confederation. A **confederation** is a large group made up of several smaller groups that work together toward the same goal. Although the Cherokee people were spread out across thousands of square miles, they had a central government that worked well. It included representatives from all the main towns.

REVIEW What form of government did the Cherokees have?

Life in a Cherokee Village

Suppose that you lived in a Cherokee village in the early 1600s. Here is what you might see on a day in late summer. All the women and the young children are in the fields, where beans and corn are growing. Nine-year-old Running Deer is helping her mother harvest the corn. Running Deer's younger sister and brother are there, too. They are supposed to be gathering twigs and branches for firewood, but Running Deer has to keep an eye on them.

Running Deer knows the younger children will be hungry in a few hours. She has brought cornbread and berries for them to eat. The Cherokees did not eat meals at set times. Instead, they ate throughout the day, whenever they were hungry.

Running Deer's mother is teaching her to cook. Yesterday Running Deer worked beside her mother, removing the kernels from the ripe corn and soaking them in water mixed with wood ashes. This removed the outer layer of the kernels. Then they pounded the corn to make flour. Running Deer will watch as her mother makes a tasty stew filled with corn over the cooking fire in their home.

Running Deer has brought food to the fields in a basket that she made herself last winter. She is very proud of this basket. She worked many days making it. She took strips of wood and bark from white oak and ash trees and wove them tightly together. Then Running Deer found orange-colored roots and maple bark to make colorful dyes to decorate the basket.

Running Deer's brother Gray Wolf is standing at the edge of the woods, practicing with his bow and arrow. This is a skill he will need when he is old enough to take part in the winter hunt.

Gray Wolf knows that he must never kill an animal for fun. The Cherokees believe that animals should be killed only for food. When a Cherokee hunter kills a deer, he must apologize to the spirit of the deer and explain that his family needs the food to survive.

In a few days everyone in Running Deer and Gray Wolf's family will go to the council house for the **Green Corn Ceremony**.

A Cherokee doll

Ball games like this one (right) were an important part of Cherokee festivals in the past. These Cherokee girls demonstrate how an early game was played, using equipment (above) like that of long ago.

The festival is a time when the entire community gives thanks. They celebrate the good harvest and the beginning of a new year. It is also a time to settle arguments. The women will present the first harvest of new green corn from the fields. It will be a symbol of the fresh start the Cherokees make each year.

Before the ceremony all the families in the village will clean their houses. Running Deer and Gray Wolf's parents will put out the fire in the fire pit of their home. Village leaders will put out the fire in the council house.

After the women present the corn, a new fire will be lit in the council house. All the villagers will use embers, or hot ashes, from this fire to relight the fires in their own houses. Then, a feast is held, followed by ball games and dances.

REVIEW What were some of the daily activties of Cherokee boys and girls?

LESSON 4
REVIEW

1 MAIN IDEA Describe the Cherokee government.

2 WHY IT MATTERS Why were teamwork and respect important to the Cherokees?

3 VOCABULARY Explain how a **clan** is related to a **confederation**.

4 READING SKILL—Summarize Write a brief summary of how the Cherokees built their homes and villages.

5 CULTURE To which language family did the Cherokee language belong?

6 GEOGRAPHY Besides North Carolina, where did the Cherokees settle?

7 CRITICAL THINKING—Apply How do you think Running Deer's life might change as she grows older?

PERFORMANCE—Build a Model Make a model of part of a Cherokee village. You might choose a house, a garden, or a council house. Do research to learn more about that part of the village. Then use cardboard, clay, or other materials to make your model.

Identify Cause and Effect

VOCABULARY

cause

effect

▶ WHY IT MATTERS

Suppose you get up late and miss your school bus. Getting up late is the cause of your missing the bus. A **cause** is something that makes something else happen. Missing your bus is the effect of your getting up late. An **effect** is what happens as a result of something else happening.

Sometimes an effect has more than one cause. Besides getting up late, you also may have watched TV before you got dressed. Understanding causes and their effects can help you make better decisions. It can also help you understand why things happen.

▶ WHAT YOU NEED TO KNOW

In Chapter 2 you read about the growth of Native American groups in North Carolina. Use the following three steps to find the causes of an event.

Step 1 **Identify the effect.**

Step 2 **Look for all the causes of that effect.**

Step 3 **Think about how the causes relate to each other and to the effect.**

▶ PRACTICE THE SKILL

Copy the chart below. Then read each of the following statements and decide if it describes a cause or an effect. Add it in the proper place on your copy.

❶ Early people learn how to farm.

❷ The population rises because people have a steady supply of food.

❸ Early people invent the atlatl.

▶ APPLY WHAT YOU LEARNED

Ask your parents about one change in their lives. What were the causes of the change? What was the effect?

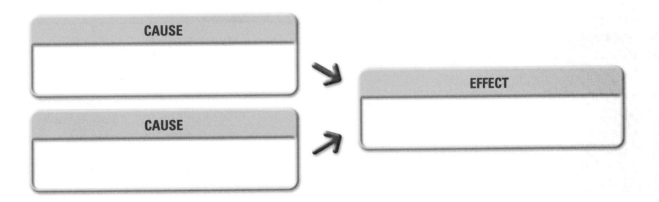

CAUSE

CAUSE

EFFECT

Review and Test Preparation

USE YOUR READING SKILLS

Complete this graphic organizer to help you summarize what you learned about the early people of North Carolina. A copy of this graphic organizer appears on page 27 of the Activity Book.

The Early People of North Carolina

GROUP → SUMMARY

The Earliest People	→	Summary: _____ _____
People of the Coastal Plain	→	Summary: _____ _____
People of the Piedmont	→	Summary: _____ _____
People of the Mountains	→	Summary: _____ _____

THINK & WRITE

Plan a Project   Plan an archaeological project. Decide what you want to know about the early peoples of North Carolina. Then think about where your project might take place. Write a plan for your project. Describe what you would need, what you would do, and what you would learn. Be sure to give a reason why your project is an important one to undertake.

Report a News Event   Imagine you are a reporter for a television news program. You are at an archaeological dig in the Mountain region. Archaeologists have dug up several pieces of Cherokee pottery and some tools. Write a short script for a television news report about the discoveries. Tell how the discoveries can help people better understand Cherokee life.

Write a sentence for each word.

1 scarce (p. 57)

2 agriculture (p. 58)

3 longhouse (p. 64)

4 council (p. 69)

5 confederation (p. 72)

RECALL FACTS

Answer these questions.

6 How did early people live before they began farming?

7 To which three language families did the early people of North Carolina belong?

8 What was the Green Corn Ceremony?

Write the letter of the best choice.

9 **TEST PREP**   Most of the Native Americans in North Carolina who spoke Algonquian languages lived—
   A on the Outer Banks.
   B in the Mountain region.
   C in the Piedmont region.
   D on the Coastal Plain.

10 **TEST PREP**   An atlatl was a—
   F tool used for planting.
   G tool used for hunting.
   H part of a council house.
   J part of the government.

THINK CRITICALLY

11 How might our knowledge of early people in North Carolina be different if no archaeological discoveries had been made?

12 How were the lives of people in the Coastal Plain, the Piedmont, and the Mountain region similar? How were they different?

APPLY SKILLS

Read a Time Line
Use the time line on pages 60–61 to answer the following questions.

13 During which time period did people begin using atlatls?

14 Between which years did people get food mainly by hunting with spears?

15 During which time period did people begin to settle in permanent villages?

Identify Cause and Effect
If the statement is a cause, write an effect of it. If the statement is an effect, write a cause for it.

16 **Cause:** Large animals became scarce.

17 **Cause:** People learned to farm.

18 **Effect:** People began to live longer.

VISIT

THE APPALACHIAN
NATIONAL SCENIC TRAIL

GET READY

The Appalachian National Scenic Trail is a 2,160-mile (3,476-km) footpath that winds its way through the Appalachian Mountains. Running from Georgia to Maine, the trail passes through 14 states, including North Carolina.

The Appalachian Trail opened in 1937. Today many people continue to enjoy hiking or back-packing along it. Some spend just an afternoon on the trail, while others hike for weeks at a time. No matter how much time you spend on the Appalachian National Scenic Trail, you will be moved by its natural beauty and enjoy its varied wildlife.

LOCATE IT

NORTH CAROLINA

Appalachian National Scenic Trail

WHAT TO SEE

Maps along the way show the path of the Appalachian National Scenic Trail.

Hikers carry backpacks containing clothing, food and water, tents, sleeping bags, and other gear they will need on the trail.

Raccoon

White-tailed deer

Black bear

Box turtle

Most of the trail is protected from development. This means that hikers can enjoy the outdoors in an area where natural, scenic, and historic resources are preserved.

TAKE A FIELD TRIP

GO ONLINE

A VIRTUAL TOUR
Visit The Learning Site at
www.harcourtschool.com/tours
to find virtual tours of other
parks and scenic areas.

CNN Turner Le@rning®

A VIDEO TOUR
Check your media
center or classroom library for a
videotape tour of the Appalachian
National Scenic Trail.

VISUAL SUMMARY

Write a Paragraph Study the pictures and captions below to help you review Unit 1. Then choose one picture. Write a paragraph that describes what the picture shows about Native American life.

USE VOCABULARY

Explain how the terms in each pair are related.

1 **hemisphere** (p. 21), **equator** (p. 21)

2 **barrier island** (p. 25), **inlet** (p. 25)

3 **specialize** (p. 58), **division of labor** (p. 58)

RECALL FACTS

Answer these questions.

4 In which region of the United States is North Carolina located?

5 Why are the early settlers of the Coastal Plain known as Woodlands people?

6 What was the Cherokee confederation?

Write the letter of the best choice.

7 **TEST PREP** Quarries are important to North Carolina because—
  A they are valuable animal habitats.
  B they are places where stone is taken from the ground.
  C they are places of rich farmland where many crops can be grown.
  D they help drain the farmland.

8 **TEST PREP** One reason the Mountain region has the coolest temperatures of North Carolina's three regions is that—
  F it is the closest to the ocean.
  G it is the farthest from the equator.
  H it has the highest elevation.
  J it has the lowest elevation.

9 **TEST PREP** Coastal Plain villages were made up of buildings called—
  A weirs.
  B wampums.
  C longhouses.
  D palisades.

Visual Summary

| 12,000 years ago | 10,000 years ago | 8,000 years ago |

About 12,000 years ago the Western Hemisphere is home to hunters and gatherers p. 56

About 7,000 years ago early people in North Carolina hunt mainly small animals p. 57

About 3,500 years ago people begin farming in North Carolina p. 58

10 TEST PREP The government of the Catawbas was like a democracy because—

F the chief decided everything alone.

G it allowed the people to take part in making decisions for the group.

H people made their own decisions.

J only the best farmers made decisions.

11 TEST PREP A confederation is a—

A group tracing its roots to a common ancestor.

B ceremony at which the entire community gives thanks.

C large group made up of several smaller groups that work together.

D representative of each of the seven clans.

THINK CRITICALLY

12 Imagine that you are going on a trip with your family to a city outside your state. As you begin to plan your trip, why would it be useful to learn about that city's relative location?

13 If you could be a farmer in any region of North Carolina, which region would you choose and why?

14 What are some difficulties the early nomadic peoples of North Carolina might have faced?

15 Why do you think some early governments allowed people to participate in council meetings?

APPLY SKILLS

Use a Land Use and Products Map

Use the land use and products map on this page to answer the following questions.

MAP AND GLOBE SKILLS

16 Which industries are located near both Charlotte and Raleigh?

17 What is the major product of North Carolina's coastal areas?

North Carolina Land Use and Products

VIRGINIA

TENNESSEE

Greensboro
Durham
Winston-Salem
Asheville ★Raleigh
Goldsboro
Charlotte
Gastonia Fayetteville New Bern
SOUTH CAROLINA
GEORGIA
0   40   80 Miles
0   40   80 Kilometers   Albers Equal-Area Projection
Wilmington
ATLANTIC OCEAN

- Electronics
- Fish
- Forest products
- Publishing
- Rocks and minerals
- Textiles

N
W   E
S

About 3,000 years ago settled people in North Carolina began to specialize p. 57

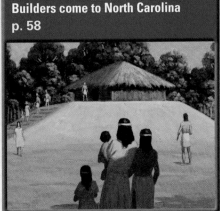

About 600 years ago Mound Builders come to North Carolina p. 58

About 350 years ago more than 22,000 Cherokees live in North Carolina p. 70

6,000 years ago   4,000 years ago   2,000 years ago

Unit Activities

 Visit The Learning Site at www.harcourtschool.com/socialstudies/activities for additional activities.

Write a Letter

Choose one of the three regions of North Carolina. Write a letter to someone who has never been to North Carolina. Tell your friend about the land, weather, industries, and early history of that region. Write about places to visit and fun things to do in the region. Read your letter to the class.

Make a Speech

Many early peoples of North Carolina had meetings to discuss issues in their communities. Choose a Native American group and imagine that you are going to speak at a community meeting. Think about important issues, people, and events. Give your speech to the class.

VISIT YOUR LIBRARY

■ *The Big North Carolina Reproducible Activity Book* by Carole Marsh. Gallopade International.

■ *North Carolina* by Kathleen Thompson. Steck-Vaughn.

■ *Living Stories of the Cherokee* by Barbara R. Duncan. University of North Carolina Press.

COMPLETE THE UNIT PROJECT

The North Carolina Museum Create pictures and models to show what you have learned about North Carolina. Be sure to show different landforms and resources. Also show how early Native Americans lived. Invite other students to visit your museum.

The Coastal Plain Region

A ship's wheel

Ocracoke lighthouse, Cape Hatteras National Seashore, North Carolina

2

The Coastal Plain Region

“ **It is the goodliest [best] and most pleasing territory of the world.** ”

—from a letter from Ralph Lane to a friend in England, 1585

Preview the Content

Scan the chapter and lesson titles. Use them to make a main idea web for each chapter.

Preview the Vocabulary

Antonyms An antonym is a word that means the opposite of another word. Match each word with its antonym.

WORD	ANTONYM
export	Loyalist
renewable resource	import
Patriot	nonrenewable resource

Meherrin River

Roanoke Rapids

Roanoke Rapids Lake

Historic Halifax ▣

Roanoke

Scotland Neck •

Tar River

Rocky Mount •

Wilson •

Greenville •

Legend:
- • City or town
- ▣ Historic site
- ■ Military base
- ⚲ Lighthouse
- ＼ Dam
- --- Fall Line
- ☐ National forest
- ☐ National seashore
- ☒ Swamp

• Smithfield

Goldsboro •

Seymour Johnson A.F.B. ■

▣ Bentonville Battlefield State Historic Site

Kinston •

Neuse River

Pinehurst •
Southern Pines •

S a n d h i l l s

Pope A.F.B. ■
• Dunn

Clinton •

Fort Bragg Military Reservation ■
Fayetteville •

Drowning Creek

Northeast Cape Fear R.

New River

Wo Swam

Laurinburg •

Jacksonville •
New River Marine Corps Air Station ■

Angola Swamp

• Lumberton

Cape Fear River

Little Pee Dee River

Lumber River

Holly Shelter Swamp

Moores Creek National Battlefield ▣

Del Mar Beach •

SOUTH CAROLINA

Lake Waccamaw

Wilmington •

Wrightsville Beach •

Green Swamp

Carolina Beach •

Onslo

Waccamaw

River

Oak Island Lighthouse ⚲

Corncake Inlet

Long Bay

Cape Fear Lighthouse ⚲

Cape Fear

Key Events

1550   1600   1650

1585 First Roanoke Island Colony is started p. 94

1663 King Charles II of England signs charter for Carolina Colony p. 99

1706 Carolina Colony establishes first town, Bath p. 102

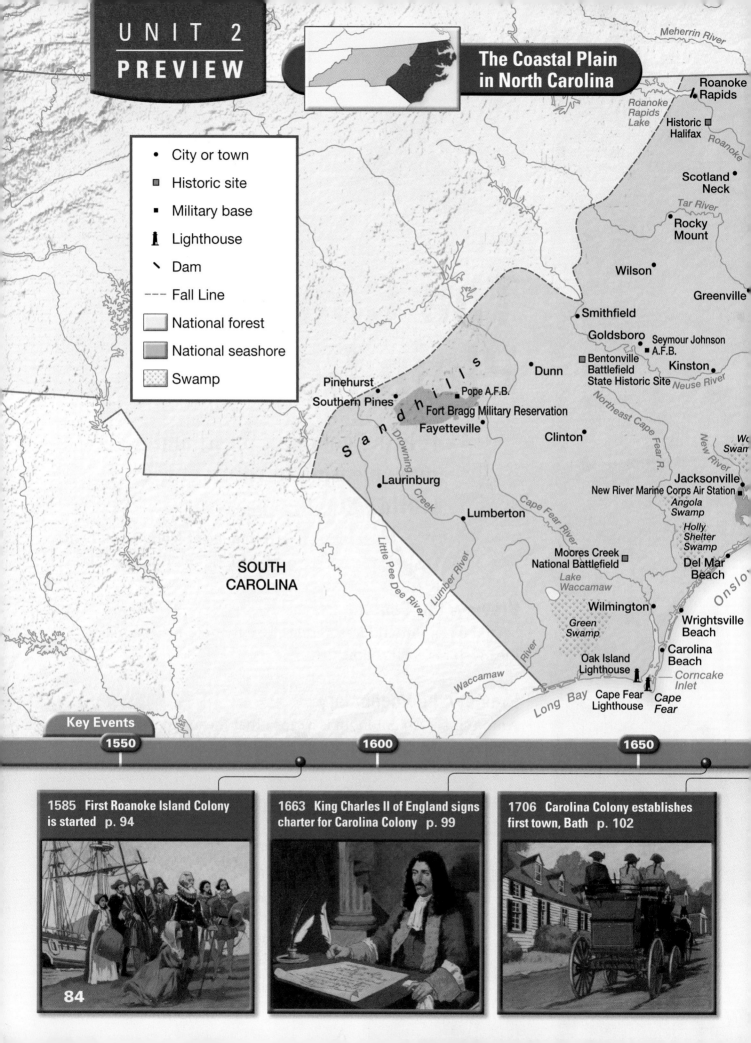

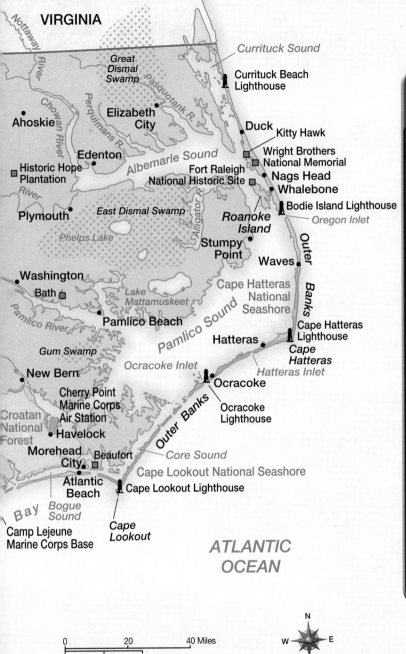

VIRGINIA

Nottaway River

Great Dismal Swamp

Currituck Sound

Currituck Beach Lighthouse

Chowan River

Perquimans R.

Pasquotank R.

Elizabeth City

Ahoskie

Duck

Kitty Hawk

Edenton

Albemarle Sound

Wright Brothers National Memorial

Fort Raleigh National Historic Site

Nags Head

Whalebone

Historic Hope Plantation

River

East Dismal Swamp

Alligator R.

Bodie Island Lighthouse

Oregon Inlet

Plymouth

Roanoke Island

Phelps Lake

Stumpy Point

Outer Banks

Washington

Lake Mattamuskeet

Waves

Bath

Cape Hatteras National Seashore

Pamlico River

Pamlico Beach

Pamlico Sound

Cape Hatteras Lighthouse

Gum Swamp

Hatteras

Cape Hatteras

New Bern

Ocracoke Inlet

Hatteras Inlet

Cherry Point Marine Corps Air Station

Ocracoke

Ocracoke Lighthouse

Croatan National Forest

Havelock

Outer Banks

Morehead City

Beaufort

Core Sound

Cape Lookout National Seashore

Atlantic Beach

Cape Lookout Lighthouse

Bay

Bogue Sound

Cape Lookout

Camp Lejeune Marine Corps Base

ATLANTIC OCEAN

0   20   40 Miles
0   20   40 Kilometers
Albers Equal-Area Projection

N W E S

The 15 Largest Towns in the Coastal Plain

TOWN	POPULATION
Laurinburg	
Roanoke Rapids	
Elizabeth City	
Lumberton	
Havelock	
New Bern	
Kinston	
Fort Bragg	
Goldsboro	
Wilson	
Rocky Mount	
Greenville	
Jacksonville	
Wilmington	
Fayetteville	

👤 = 5,000 persons

1700

1750

1800

1711 War with Tuscaroras begins
p. 103

1774 The Edenton Tea Party is held
p. 112

1776 Declaration of Independence is signed p. 115

START with a STORY

AN ISLAND SCRAPBOOK

written and illustrated by Virginia Wright-Frierson

The barrier islands in the Coastal Plain region of North Carolina are home to an amazing number of plants and animals. In *An Island Scrapbook*, author and illustrator Virginia Wright-Frierson and her daughter, Amy, explore a North Carolina barrier island together.

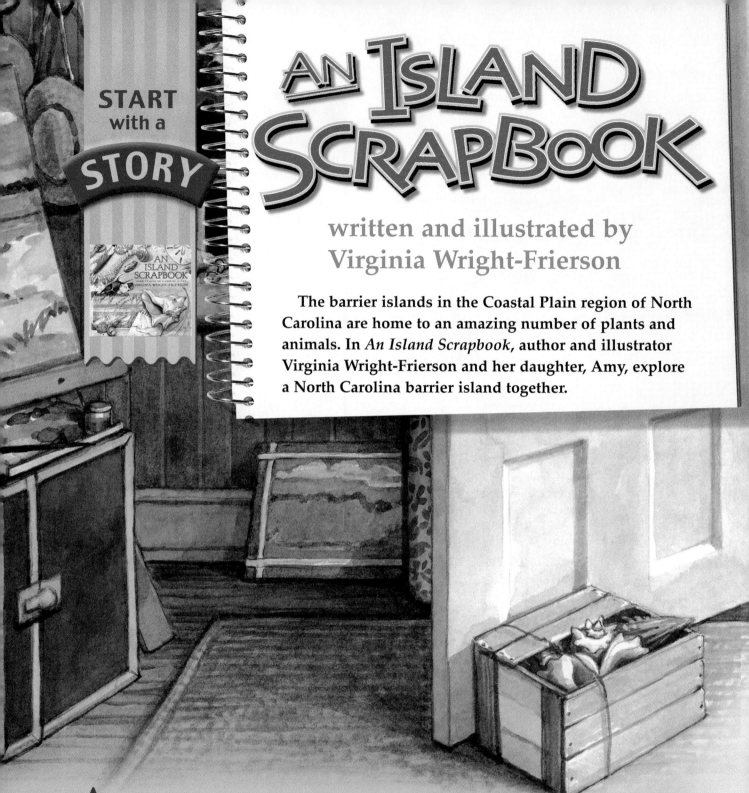

Amy and I are awake before dawn on this September morning. It is the last week at our island house until next summer, and we don't want to waste a minute of it. We dress quietly, grab our packs, and slip outside into the cool darkness of the salt marsh.

"The sun!" calls Amy. It is a fingernail sliver, glowing above the distant trees. We unpack our watercolors, brushes, and sketch pads as fast as we can. I paint a tiny study of the sunrise every few minutes until the soft orange light becomes a fireball.

Amy paints one sunrise study
with more detail of the fiery sky and
choppy water. As we work, we listen to
the whisper of the rustling cordgrass,
the lapping of the tide, the call of a clapper
rail, and the skittering and claw-clicking of
fiddler crabs. The warming breezes bring
us the rich muddy smell of the salt marsh.

One fiddler threatens us with his huge violin-shaped claw while the others vanish into their burrows. In a few hours, the water will reach the high tide mark on the dock piling. The fiddlers will plug up their tunnels with a mudball and wait for low tide to return.

We decide to walk through the maritime forest to the ocean. The springy, sandy floor is covered with acorns, palm fronds, pine cones and needles, grasses,

When our paintings are finished, we walk under the old dock to look at the mudflats teeming with fiddler crabs and patterned with the tracks of night-prowling raccoons.

and poison ivy. This ground cover provides food and shelter for deer, birds, and other forest animals.

Amy climbs up into her lookout tree for a bird's-eye view of the rainwater pond where the egrets roost at night.

She counts eight yellow-bellied turtles before they slip underwater. There are deer tracks and more raccoon prints (they look like tiny human handprints). Amy spots a great blue heron, almost as tall as she is, standing as still as a tree on the far bank, waiting to dart after a fish or frog.

We emerge from the forest shade to a beautiful view of the windswept grasses on the dunes, and the sparkling ocean stretching on forever. Pelicans fly low over the waves in a dotted line. We make our way carefully around the patches of sandspurs and prickly pear cactus to the clean, hard-packed sand of the ocean beach. Only shrimpers, fishermen, and shorebirds are out this early.

Analyze the Literature

1 How did the author and her daughter record their exploration of the barrier island?

2 What senses does the author use to describe the environment of the barrier islands?

3 Design your own scrapbook of a place you enjoy. Sketch items and write a description describing the place to others.

READ A BOOK

TIME FOR KIDS READERS
Pirates ON THE PROWL
Harcourt
by Patrick Garner

TIME FOR KIDS READERS
THE MYSTERY OF ROANOKE
Harcourt
by Leslie Goldman

TIME FOR KIDS READERS
Moving THE LIGHTHOUSE
Harcourt
by Betsy Ochester

START THE UNIT PROJECT

Stage a Play With your classmates, write and stage a play about an important event in the Coastal Plain region. As you read this unit, think about an event to show. Pay attention to how the event affected the Coastal Plain.

USE TECHNOLOGY

GO ONLINE

Visit The Learning Site at **www.harcourtschool.com/ socialstudies** for additional activities, primary sources, and other resources to use in this unit.

MANTEO

Manteo is a town on Roanoke Island. Every year in June, July, and August, actors there perform a play called *Lost Colony*. The play tells the story of the first English settlement in North Carolina. The characters include settlers, Native Americans, and English leaders.

LOCATE IT

Manteo

NORTH CAROLINA

3

The Coastal Plain Region Long Ago

❝ We let fall our Grapnel [anchor] neare the shore, & sounded with a trumpet a Call & afterward many familiar English tunes of Songs, and called to them friendly; but we had no answer. ❞

—from Governor John White's journal describing his return to Roanoke, 1590

CHAPTER READING SKILL

Sequence

Sequence is the order in which events happen. Words such as *first*, *next*, and *last* can help you put events in the correct order.

As you read this chapter, keep track of the sequence of important changes.

FIRST → NEXT → LAST

MAIN IDEA
Read to learn how people from several European nations explored and tried to settle in the Coastal Plain region in the early 1500s.

WHY IT MATTERS
The efforts of early explorers and settlers resulted in Europeans settling in what is today North Carolina.

VOCABULARY
expedition
Northwest Passage
colony
raw material
governor

Explorers and Settlers of the Coastal Plain

| 1500 | 1600 | 1700 | 1800 |

1524–1590

In the late 1500s, England and Spain each wanted to be Europe's most powerful nation. Competition led Spain and England as well as France to send sailors on expeditions to North America. An **expedition** is a journey to learn more about a land.

In 1584 Captain Philip Amadas and Captain Arthur Barlowe told England's Queen Elizabeth I about the voyage to what is now North Carolina. They said this about Roanoke Island:

> **66**a most pleasant and fertile ground, [filled] with goodly cedars and other sweet woods full of currants, of flax and many other notable commodities. Besides this island, there are many [other islands] . . . most beautiful and pleasant.**99**

The First Explorers

The first European to visit what is now North Carolina was the explorer Giovanni da Verrazano (joh•VAH•nee dah vair•uh•ZAH•noh), who sailed for the French. He stopped briefly on the Outer Banks in his search for a water route through the Americas to Asia. At that time, many people believed that there was a water route, called the **Northwest Passage**,

Giovanni da Verrazano (far left) sailed his ship *Dauphine* (near left) in his search for the Northwest Passage.

through the mainland of North America to the Pacific Ocean. In the winter of 1524, Verrazano sailed north along the east coast of North America, searching for this route. In March 1524 Verrazano and his crew landed near the mouth of the Cape Fear River and then sailed north farther along the coast.

Two years later, Spanish explorer Lucas Vásquez de Ayllón (LOO•kahs VAHS•kays day eye•YOHN) led a fleet of six ships carrying about 500 men, women, and children, including enslaved Africans. He hoped to start a Spanish colony along the Cape Fear River. A **colony** is a settlement separated from, but under the control of, a home country. Ayllón's colony lasted only a few months. Illness and the loss of supplies in a shipwreck led to the death of more than 300 settlers, including Ayllón. The discouraged survivors boarded the remaining ships and left.

In 1540 Hernando de Soto (er•NAHN• doh day SOH•toh) led a large group through what is now the southeastern

Early Explorers in North Carolina

Verrazano (France), 1524
Ayllón (Spain), 1526
De Soto (Spain), 1539–1542
Amadas and Barlowe (England), 1584

0 200 400 Miles
0 200 400 Kilometers
Azimuthal Equal-Area Projection

Movement Early explorers came to North Carolina by different routes.

From where did de Soto travel to North Carolina?

FAST FACT De Soto and his men met many Native Americans in the mountains of North Carolina. One Native American leader gave de Soto a string of pearls 12 feet long!

United States from Florida to southwestern North Carolina. De Soto and his men hoped to find gold in the mountains. When they did not, they moved on.

REVIEW What brought the first European explorers to what is today North Carolina?

Other Efforts to Start a Colony

Spanish ships from South America returned to Spain with treasure chests of gold and silver. When England captured some of these ships, Queen Elizabeth I decided that she wanted such riches for her country.

Soon adventurers were talking with the queen about plans to create an English colony in North America. One of these people was Sir Walter Raleigh (RAH•lee). In 1584 Queen Elizabeth gave Raleigh permission to set up England's first colony in North America. Raleigh sent Captain Amadas and Captain Barlowe to North America to find a good location for his colony.

Raleigh read the glowing report the captains sent back. He believed they had found a place that would provide lumber and other raw materials for England. A **raw material** is a natural resource that is later changed to make a product.

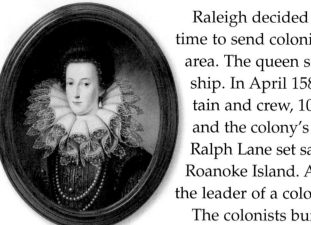

Queen Elizabeth I

Raleigh decided that it was time to send colonists to the area. The queen supplied a ship. In April 1585 the captain and crew, 108 colonists, and the colony's governor Ralph Lane set sail for Roanoke Island. A **governor** is the leader of a colony or a state.

The colonists built a fort, which they named Fort Raleigh, and several houses. By the summer of 1586, food was becoming scarce. The colonists feared that they would starve. They returned to England with Sir Francis Drake, who was visiting the colony.

REVIEW Why did Sir Walter Raleigh choose Roanoke Island for England's first colony in North America?

The Mystery of the Lost Colony

In 1587 Sir Walter Raleigh sent a second group of settlers to Roanoke Island. Raleigh chose John White as governor. White was a gifted artist who had been

Sir Walter Raleigh (below); a clue to the lost colony (right)

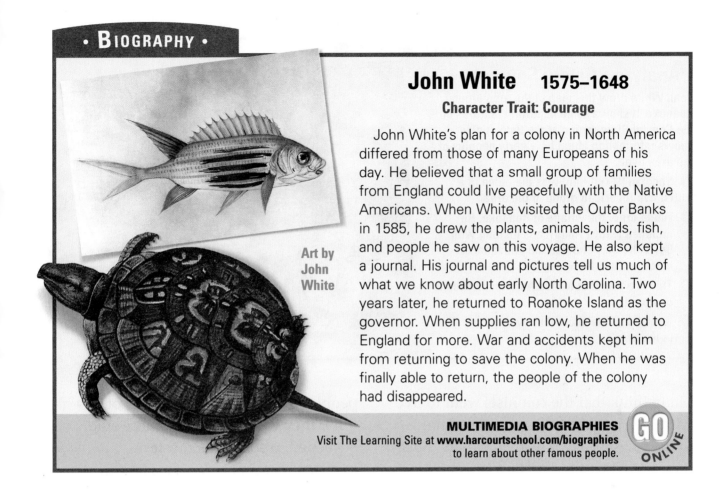

Art by John White

John White   1575–1648
Character Trait: Courage

John White's plan for a colony in North America differed from those of many Europeans of his day. He believed that a small group of families from England could live peacefully with the Native Americans. When White visited the Outer Banks in 1585, he drew the plants, animals, birds, fish, and people he saw on this voyage. He also kept a journal. His journal and pictures tell us much of what we know about early North Carolina. Two years later, he returned to Roanoke Island as the governor. When supplies ran low, he returned to England for more. War and accidents kept him from returning to save the colony. When he was finally able to return, the people of the colony had disappeared.

MULTIMEDIA BIOGRAPHIES
Visit The Learning Site at www.harcourtschool.com/biographies
to learn about other famous people.

GO ONLINE

a member of the first Roanoke Colony. When the colonists reached Roanoke Island, they rebuilt the fort, constructed new houses, and repaired the old ones. On August 18, 1587, Governor White's daughter, Eleanor White Dare, gave birth to a daughter, Virginia Dare, the first English child born in the Americas.

The colonists had arrived too late to plant crops. The colony did not have enough supplies to last until crops could be planted and harvested. In 1587 Governor White returned to England for food and other supplies. As he arrived in England, the powerful Spanish Armada, or fleet of ships, was getting ready to attack England. Queen Elizabeth declared that all English ships must remain at home to protect the country. So Governor White was unable to leave the country.

Three years passed before White was able to return to Roanoke Island. He was shocked and saddened by what he saw there. The land was overgrown with weeds, and the colonists were gone. Some of the books White had written were spread around. Their corners were torn off, and their maps had been ruined by the rain.

The only traces of the colony were the letters *CRO* carved on a tree and the word *CROATOAN* carved on a wooden post. White believed that the settlers had gone to live among friendly Native Americans elsewhere on the Outer Banks. A storm came up, and White was not able to search further for the colonists. He never saw his family again.

People began to refer to the second Roanoke settlement as the Lost Colony.

John White Map

Analyze Primary Sources

John White drew this map of the area around Roanoke. It shows some important features of the Coastal Plain region at the time. It also shows information about how early peoples of the area lived.

1. Secotan (SEK•uh•tan) was the name of a Native American group in the area.

2. White drew the village of Roanoke. He included Native Americans hunting with bows. He also showed the palisade, or fence, around the village.

3. This is a trap that Native Americans used to capture fish.

❖ How did White show that many plants grew in the area?

Many think that the colonists went to live with the Hatteras tribe or traveled north to the Chesapeake Bay area. Others think they settled on the Coastal Plain and are the ancestors of the Lumbee Indians. Many Lumbees have the last names of people from the lost colony. Still others think they were murdered. More evidence is needed to solve this mystery.

REVIEW Why is the second colony that settled on Roanoke Island now known as the Lost Colony?

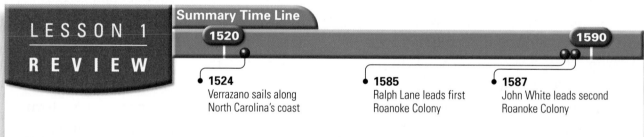

LESSON 1
REVIEW

Summary Time Line

1520 — 1590

1524
Verrazano sails along North Carolina's coast

1585
Ralph Lane leads first Roanoke Colony

1587
John White leads second Roanoke Colony

1. **MAIN IDEA** Why did European explorers first come to the Coastal Plain region?

2. **WHY IT MATTERS** What happened as a result of Amadas and Barlowe's trip to Roanoke Island?

3. **VOCABULARY** Use **governor** and **colony** in a sentence about Roanoke Island.

4. **TIME LINE** When did Ralph Lane lead the first Roanoke Island Colony?

5. **READING SKILL—Sequence** Which happened first, de Soto's expedition or Sir Francis Drake's visit?

6. **GEOGRAPHY** Why did explorers look for the Northwest Passage?

7. **HISTORY** What kept John White from returning to Roanoke Island as he had planned?

8. **CRITICAL THINKING—Hypothesize** Do you think the second Roanoke Island colony might have survived if the colonists had arrived during planting season? Why or why not?

PERFORMANCE—Make an Advertisement Make an advertisement for the Roanoke Colony. Include information about the land, water, and raw materials.

·SKILLS· READING

Predict a Likely Outcome

VOCABULARY

prediction

outcome

▶ WHY IT MATTERS

People make predictions every day. A **prediction** is a reasonable guess about what will happen next. When people make predictions, they use information they know to predict a likely **outcome**, or result. Suppose you know you need to write a report. You might predict that you will go to the library tomorrow.

▶ WHAT YOU NEED TO KNOW

You can use these steps to predict a likely outcome.

Step 1 **Think about what you know.**

Step 2 **Read or gather more information.**

Step 3 **Make a prediction.**

Step 4 **Think about whether new information that you gather supports your prediction.**

▶ PRACTICE THE SKILL

1 Think about what you know about the early colonies. For example, you learned that the land was "a most pleasant and fertile ground . . ." You also learned that colonists arrived on Roanoke Island too late in the year to plant crops.

2 Using this information and other information from the lesson, make predictions about later settlements in the Coastal Plain region.

3 Read the rest of the chapter.

4 Check to see if your predictions are accurate.

▶ APPLY WHAT YOU LEARNED

Read the weather report in last week's newspaper. Then predict this week's weather. What other information could you use to make your prediction? Check your prediction at the end of the week.

The Outer Banks was home to the early settlers.

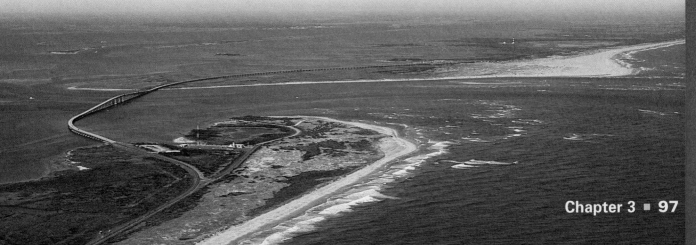

MAIN IDEA
Read to discover why settlers moved to the Albemarle Sound area and what their lives were like there.

WHY IT MATTERS
The many settlers of Virginia helped the Carolina Colony grow.

VOCABULARY
charter
cash crop
export
proprietor
assembly
tax
rebel

Settling near Albemarle Sound

1606–1677

After the disappearance of the Lost Colony, more than 70 years passed before colonists settled permanently in North Carolina. Of the 13 original English colonies, North Carolina was one of the last to be permanently settled.

There is no record of the exact date on which the first English colonists came to what is now North Carolina. By the 1660s families and small groups were arriving from the Virginia Colony at a steady pace.

Settlers from Virginia

In 1606 King James of England gave a charter to the Virginia Company to start a colony. A **charter** is a written document that gives certain rights from a government or state to a person or group of people. One year later, three ships carrying about 100 colonists reached Chesapeake Bay. There they founded

King James gave the Virginia Company a charter (left) to settle in Virginia. Later, some settlers moved south to Albermarle Sound (below).

• GEOGRAPHY •

The Great Dismal Swamp

Understanding Physical Systems

The Great Dismal Swamp is a great place to call home. At least it is for many animals, such as birds and frogs. Moss and clay keep water in the swamp from draining out of the soil. This makes the ground wet and soft. Sometimes the swamp plants are so thick that you cannot walk through them. Millions of insects come to eat these plants and to lay eggs in the swamp. More than 200 kinds of birds and more than 12 kinds of frogs feed on these insects. The swamp is home to other animals including raccoons, deer, squirrels, black bears, turtles, lizards, salamanders, and snakes. Most early settlers avoided this area. Later colonists, including George Washington, sought to harvest the trees in the swamp for lumber.

Jamestown, the first permanent English settlement in North America.

The Virginia Colony grew quickly. Its prosperity was based in part on the colonists' decision to grow tobacco as a **cash crop**, a crop that people raise to sell rather than to use themselves. Tobacco became an important export. An **export** is a product sent from one country to another to be sold.

In 1629 Sir Robert Heath received a grant of land covering the entire area from what is now the North Carolina–Virginia border to Florida. King Charles of England named this area Carolana, or Carolina, which means "land of Charles."

As the Virginia Colony grew, some Virginia colonists settled near the shores of Albemarle Sound. About 1655 fur trader Nathaniel Batts became the first permanent English settler in North Carolina.

REVIEW Where did the first English settlers in Carolina come from?

The Lords Proprietors

In 1663 Charles II named eight of his supporters Lords Proprietors of Carolina. A **proprietor** is an owner of land or of a business. The proprietors' land grant stretched from Albemarle Sound in the north to present-day Florida.

The land grant gave the proprietors the authority to set up towns and counties, build forts, and collect money. The charter also gave colonists the same rights that citizens in England had.

Chapter 3 ▪ **99**

The proprietors appointed a governor for the Carolina Colony. A council of advisers appointed by the king assisted the governor. The Carolina Colony also had an **assembly**, or group of people elected to make laws and to decide how the colony's money would be spent.

REVIEW How did the Lords Proprietors become the owners of the Carolina Colony?

The Colony's Slow Growth

Throughout the 1660s more settlers moved to the Albemarle Sound area. Most were farmers. By 1663 tobacco had become a major export crop.

The colony grew slowly for a number of reasons. Farmers had to send their tobacco overland to Virginia for shipment to England because the Carolina Colony had no deepwater port. Also, colonists received only small grants of land, and their taxes were higher than those in Virginia. A **tax** is money that a government collects from its citizens and is most often used to pay for services. A third reason for slow growth was that many of the governors made bad decisions or were dishonest.

Although the colony grew slowly, it did grow. Settlers came from the Virginia Colony, from New England, and from England. Among the new settlers were followers of the Quaker religion. The Quakers became the first organized religious group in what is now North Carolina.

REVIEW Why did the colony grow slowly?

CITIZENSHIP

DEMOCRATIC VALUES
Individual Rights

In 1678 the Carolina colonists presented the Lords Proprietors with a list of changes they wanted made to their government. Formally asking a government for a change is called petitioning. Many colonists were upset because they felt their land could be taken away at any time. One person who petitioned the Lords Proprietors was Timothy Biggs. He wrote, "... people having no assurance of [certainty about] their lands ... is a matter of great discouragement." The right to petition the government was later included in the state's Bill of Rights.

Analyze the Value

❶ Why is petitioning an important right?

❷ **Make It Relevant** Write a letter to the state government identifying a problem you would like changed.

Settlers worked together to plant and harvest tobacco and other crops.

Culpeper's Rebellion

Beginning in 1651 England passed a series of laws called the Navigation Acts. These laws required the colonists to ship their goods to England on English ships. If the colonists wanted to ship goods to other colonies, they had to pay a tax. The laws also stated that some products, such as tobacco and cotton, could be sold to England only. This meant that the colonists could no longer sell these products to other countries.

The Albemarle colonists were unhappy with these laws. In December 1677 they met to protest the tobacco tax. George Durant and John Culpeper led the protest.

When the governor's supporters tried to arrest Durant, the colonists put the governor in prison. Then protestors elected an assembly and chose John Culpeper as governor. When Culpeper went to England to make peace with the proprietors, he was arrested for treason, or

Government agents try to arrest George Durant

trying to overthrow the government. However, he was not punished.

This incident became known as Culpeper's Rebellion. It was one of the first times English colonists in North America **rebelled**, or turned against, an unfair government. It would not be the last time.

REVIEW **Why did the Albemarle colonists take part in Culpeper's Rebellion?**

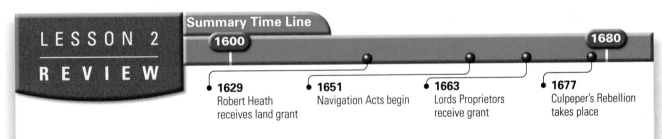

LESSON 2
REVIEW

Summary Time Line

1600 — 1680

1629
Robert Heath receives land grant

1651
Navigation Acts begin

1663
Lords Proprietors receive grant

1677
Culpeper's Rebellion takes place

1 **MAIN IDEA** Why did farmers settle in the Albemarle Sound area?

2 **WHY IT MATTERS** How did the growth of the Virginia Colony change the population near Albemarle Sound?

3 **VOCABULARY** Give the meanings of **cash crop** and **export**.

4 **TIME LINE** When did England begin passing the Navigation Acts?

5 **READING SKILL—Sequence** Put in order: Culpeper's Rebellion, the founding of Jamestown, and Heath's land grant.

6 **GEOGRAPHY** Why did Albemarle farmers take their crops to Virginia?

7 **CIVICS/GOVERNMENT** What were the responsibilities of Carolina's assembly?

8 **CRITICAL THINKING—Hypothesize** What might have helped the colony of Carolina grow more quickly?

 PERFORMANCE—Write a Letter Imagine that you are a Carolina colonist. Write a letter to the British government. Explain your opinion about the Navigation Acts. Use facts to support your opinion.

MAIN IDEA
Read to learn about the conflicts in the Carolina Colony and how they were resolved.

WHY IT MATTERS
After the conflicts were resolved, the colony grew at a faster pace.

VOCABULARY
pirate
cargo

Colonists Face Challenges

1700–1718

In 1700 English surveyor John Lawson wrote of the Native Americans on the Coastal Plain, "They are really better to us than we are to them; they always give us [food and drink] and take care we are arm'd against hunger and thirst."

As the Carolina Colony grew, so did tensions between the new settlers and Native Americans. Conflict with Native Americans was just one of the challenges the colonists faced.

Carolina Colony's First Towns

As Virginians streamed south into the Albemarle Sound area, other colonists moved away from this area and settled farther south along the Carolina coast. They settled along Pamlico Sound and on the banks of the Neuse River. In 1706 Bath on the

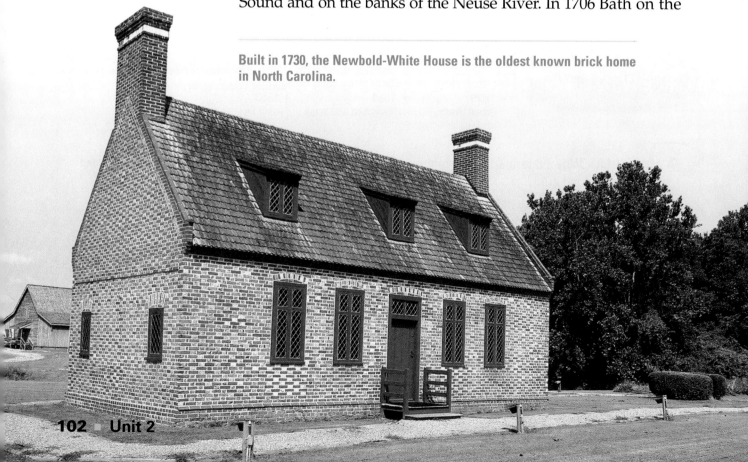

Built in 1730, the Newbold-White House is the oldest known brick home in North Carolina.

For many years before European settlers arrived, the Tuscarora people made arrowheads (top) and fished (left) on the Coastal Plain.

banks of the Pamlico River, became the colony's first town. It was built on land taken from the Pamlico Indians.

Edenton, near the mouth of the Chowan River on Albemarle Sound, was another of the colony's early towns. Named for the royal governor Charles Eden, Edenton became the Carolina Colony's capital in 1710.

Over the next few years, other settlements began springing up. In 1713 colonists drew up a plan for Beaufort Town, named after the Duke of Beaufort, one of the proprietors. In 1765 a French visitor remembered Beaufort as "a small village with fewer than 12 houses."

The town of New Bern was different. Its first residents consisted mainly of families from Switzerland and Germany. They laid out their town at the place where the Neuse and Trent Rivers meet and named it after the city of Bern in Switzerland. New Bern grew quickly. In 1770 it became the permanent center of government for the Carolina Colony.

REVIEW What were the first towns settled in the Carolina Colony?

The Tuscarora War

As more and more settlers arrived, their houses and fields began to spill over onto Native American hunting grounds. Anger and resentment grew as the settlers built their villages on Native American sites. German and Swiss settlers built New Bern by leveling the site of the Tuscarora village of Chattawka (chah•TAH•kah).

In 1711 these and other land losses pushed the Tuscaroras into war against the colonists. Early in September 1711 Tuscarora Indians captured surveyor John Lawson. They also captured Baron von Graffenried, founder of the New Bern colony, and two enslaved Africans. The Tuscaroras let the baron and the Africans go, but they killed Lawson.

A few weeks later, the Tuscaroras attacked settlements near New Bern and Bath. They hoped to frighten away the colonists. Instead, their attack began the Tuscarora War.

Tuscarora hunter, drawn by a colonist

Chapter 3 ■ **103**

Finding the *Queen Anne's Revenge*

A team of archaeologists found Blackbeard's ship at the bottom of the sea in 1996. They had been looking for almost ten years. The ship was about two miles off the North Carolina coast in shallow water. To find the ship, the scientists used a new, high-tech machine. It picked up magnetic signals from old cannons lying on the ocean bottom. Then scuba divers went down to check the ocean bottom. The divers found plates, cannons, and a bell made in 1709.

Scientists locate an anchor (above) and a cannon (right) used by Blackbeard.

Many Native Americans and European settlers lost their lives during the conflict.

In March 1713 the colonists defeated the Tuscarora people at Fort Neoheroka (noh•huh•ROH•kah), near what is now Snow Hill. During the fighting 950 Tuscaroras were killed or were captured and sold into slavery. Most of the survivors moved north to join the Iroquois. The Tuscaroras' departure opened the way for the settlers to move inland.

REVIEW **What were the causes and the outcome of the Tuscarora War?**

Danger from Pirates

While Native Americans and settlers battled on land, other troubles were brewing at sea. In 1717 British officials forced pirates to leave the Caribbean Islands. A **pirate** is someone who robs ships at sea. Many of these pirates who fled the Caribbean moved to the Carolina coast to continue their criminal activities. No ship on the Atlantic Coast was safe when pirates left their island hideaways to steal valuable **cargo**, or goods carried from one place to another.

One of North Carolina's best-known pirates was the Englishman Edward Teach, better known as Blackbeard. He was a large man with a long, bushy, black beard and wild strands of hair, making him look terrifying to his victims.

Blackbeard made his home in Bath. One of his favorite hideaways was Ocracoke Inlet. There he hid his pirate ship, the *Queen Anne's Revenge*, behind sandbars and waited to attack and seize British and colonial ships passing by. In 1718 British sailors attacked Blackbeard's hideout, and Blackbeard was killed. In 1996 divers located the wreckage of Blackbeard's ship.

Some women were pirates too. Anne Bonny was one of the most famous. She was captured and jailed. After that, the colony entered more peaceful times. With fewer threats to safety, the colony began to grow more rapidly.

REVIEW How did pirates cause problems for the colonists?

Sometimes Blackbeard put burning pieces of cloth in his beard to appear even more terrifying.

Anne Bonny was one of the few women to live the life of a pirate.

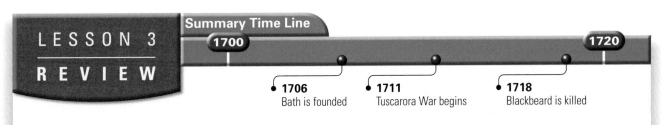

LESSON 3
R E V I E W

Summary Time Line

1700 — 1720

• 1706
Bath is founded

• 1711
Tuscarora War begins

• 1718
Blackbeard is killed

1 **MAIN IDEA** What challenges did North Carolina colonists face?

2 **WHY IT MATTERS** How did people in Carolina resolve their conflicts?

3 **VOCABULARY** Use the word **cargo** in a sentence about an eighteenth-century **pirate**.

4 **TIME LINE** Which happened first, the Tuscarora War or Blackbeard's death?

5 **READING SKILL—Sequence** Which was built later, New Bern or Bath?

6 **GEOGRAPHY** Where was Edenton built?

7 **CIVICS/GOVERNMENT** Which town became the capital of the Carolina Colony in 1710?

8 **CRITICAL THINKING—Synthesize** Why did capturing pirates help the colony grow?

PERFORMANCE—Make a Map Draw a map of the Coastal Plain region in 1715. Label important rivers, sounds, swamps, and other geographical features. Include towns and forts.

MAIN IDEA
Read to find out why different groups of people moved to the Cape Fear River area and what their lives were like.

WHY IT MATTERS
The colony grew and prospered largely due to the forced labor of enslaved African Americans.

VOCABULARY
royal colony
immigrant
indentured servant
naval stores
plantation
planter
slave

Settling near the Cape Fear River

1687–1790

During the early 1700s British colonists from South Carolina began moving north to lands along the lower Cape Fear River. They were looking for rich soil where rice, cotton, or tobacco would grow. What they found seemed far less promising. The soil was sandy, and pine trees grew every-where. However, the settlers soon found a product in the forests that helped the Cape Fear area prosper.

North Carolina Becomes a Colony

In 1689 the proprietors divided the Carolina Colony into North Carolina and South Carolina. North Carolina remained in the hands of the proprietors until 1729, when it became a

Once North Carolina became a royal colony, its population began to grow. Many settlers built homes along the Cape Fear River.

LOCATE IT

NORTH CAROLINA

Cape Fear River

North Carolina Population in the Eighteenth Century	
YEAR	NUMBER OF PEOPLE
1700	
1720	
1740	
1750	

= 10,000 persons

Analyze Graphs North Carolina's population grew quickly in the 1700s. Ads encouraged people to settle in the colonies. They brought valuables such as this tea caddy and chest.

❓ About how many more people lived in North Carolina in 1750 than in 1720?

royal colony, a colony ruled by the king. The colony grew, and settlers spread into the lower Cape Fear area.

In 1725 colonists settled Brunswick on the lower Cape Fear River. Then residents of Brunswick founded Wilmington, 15 miles (24 km) upstream. Wilmington soon became the area's leading town due in part to its major deepwater port. At last the North Carolina Colony could ship its exports directly to Europe.

By 1732 many of the new settlers were immigrants from the highlands of Scotland. An **immigrant** is a person who moves to one country from another. Some Highland Scots came as indentured servants. An **indentured servant** agreed to work for a colonist without pay for a number of years in exchange for travel to America. Once his or her years of service ended, the indentured servant was free.

The ships that brought the settlers across the Atlantic landed at either Brunswick or Wilmington. Many Highland Scots settled in what is today Fayetteville on the Cape Fear River.

REVIEW How did Wilmington's location help it grow?

New Ways of Making a Living

The Highland Scots raised corn, wheat, flax, potatoes, and tobacco on small farms. Large forests of longleaf pines covered the land along the lower Cape Fear River. The pine tree produces a sticky liquid called resin, from which tar, turpentine, and other products are made. These products are called **naval stores**. Shipbuilders used naval stores to waterproof ships' wooden hulls and to protect ropes and ladders.

Wood products were also important in the lower Cape Fear region. Lumber mills turned out boards and shingles. Colonists built ships, houses, and public buildings of wood.

REVIEW How did the Highland Scots make a living in the Cape Fear area?

Plantations in North Carolina

Some wealthy colonists from South Carolina built plantations in the lower Cape Fear area. A **plantation** is a large farm that specializes in growing a single cash crop. In the Albemarle Sound area, **planters**, the people who owned plantations, grew tobacco. Along the Cape Fear River, rice was the leading cash crop.

Both rice and tobacco plantations depended on the labor of enslaved Africans. Unlike other settlers, these people were forced to come to the colonies as slaves. A **slave** is a person who is treated as property of another person and made to work without pay.

By the mid-1700s the lower Cape Fear area had more slaves than any other part of North Carolina. Both agriculture and naval stores depended on slave labor.

Only planters who owned many slaves could grow rice for export. One of the best-known rice planters was Roger

Moore, who built Orton Plantation near Wilmington in the 1730s. The 250 enslaved Africans on the Orton Plantation helped make the plantation the source of the finest rice in the colonies.

Enslaved Africans also served as cooks, carpenters, shoemakers, tanners, tailors, and blacksmiths. They cared for the planter's home and children as well.

Throughout the 1700s free African Americans made up a very small part of the total African American population in North Carolina. In the mid-1700s only 5 to 10 of every 100 African Americans were free. Of the 105,000 living in North Carolina in 1790, about 5,000 were free.

From the American Revolution until 1835, free African American men had the right to vote. Although they had some other rights, they also faced a great deal of prejudice, or unfair treatment. Beginning in 1720, free African American families had to pay taxes that no other groups

Somerset Place was once one of the South's largest and busiest plantations. The Collins family built the plantation. It was a working plantation from 1785 to 1865. Corn, rice, and other grains were grown there, and trees were harvested for lumber. Today it is a state historic site.

❶ The owners lived in the big house. Their food came from the nearby gardens, orchards, kitchen, smokehouse, and salting house.

❷ Through the years, more than 850 enslaved people lived and worked at Somerset Place. They worked in the fields, in the big house, and in the gardens and orchards. Some worked as skilled craftspeople. They lived in cabins and got their food from a separate kitchen.

❸ The overseer lived in this house. He supervised the enslaved workers.

❹ The Lake Hospital was used by both the owners and the enslaved workers.

◈ Why was it important for the plantation to be near water?

paid. These families were not always sure of their freedom. They lived with the constant threat of being kidnapped and sold into slavery.

REVIEW Why did a successful plantation need a large workforce?

LESSON 4 REVIEW

Summary Time Line

1680 — 1730

1689
Proprietors divide the Carolina Colony

1725
Brunswick is settled

1729
North Carolina becomes a royal colony

❶ **MAIN IDEA** Describe the life of early settlers in the Cape Fear area.

❷ **WHY IT MATTERS** How did enslaved African Americans help the colony grow?

❸ **VOCABULARY** What is the difference between an **indentured servant** and a **slave**?

❹ **TIME LINE** In what year did colonists first settle in Brunswick?

❺ **READING SKILL—Sequence** Which was settled first, Brunswick or Wilmington?

❻ **ECONOMICS** How did settlers use pine trees in the Cape Fear area?

❼ **CULTURE** What group settled in Fayetteville?

❽ **CRITICAL THINKING—Analyze** Why did plantations need so many enslaved workers?

PERFORMANCE—Draw a Diagram Read more about North Carolina plantations. Draw a diagram of a plantation. Label fields and buildings, including places where enslaved Africans lived and worked.

PRIMARY SOURCES

Blackbeard's Ship

Edward Teach, also known as Blackbeard, can be called North Carolina's own pirate. Although he was not a native of the colony, he died in North Carolina in 1718. That was the same year that his most important ship, *Queen Anne's Revenge*, sank in Beaufort Inlet. *Queen Anne's Revenge* remained buried in sand for 278 years. In 1996 the Underwater Archaeology Unit (UAU) of the North Carolina Department of Cultural Resources, along with a private research company, found the wreck and began recovering artifacts. Their goal was to use the artifacts to prove that the wreck was, in fact, Blackbeard's ship.

 FROM THE NORTH CAROLINA MARITIME MUSEUM, BEAUFORT, NORTH CAROLINA

This 21-pound (10-kg) sounding weight (marked XXI) was used to check the depth of water.

This 24-pound (11-kg) cannonball recovered from the wreck supported archaeologists' beliefs that the wreck they found was the *Queen Anne's Revenge*. Smaller ships could not have carried a cannon large enough to fire it.

This bell is believed to be too small to be the ship's bell of the *Queen Anne's Revenge*. It is more likely to be a Spanish or Portuguese church bell taken from another ship by Blackbeard's pirates. The bell's surface reads "IHS [*Iesu Hominorum Salvator*] Maria."

This cutaway model shows what the *Queen Anne's Revenge* may have looked like.

ACTIVITY

Write a Story Imagine that you were one of the archaeologists recovering these artifacts. Tell how you found them. Describe each artifact in detail, and explain what information each reveals in determining whether the wreck is that of Blackbeard's ship. Share your story with a classmate.

RESEARCH

Visit The Learning Site at **www.harcourtschool.com/ primarysources** to research other primary sources.

The American Revolution

1754–1791

In January 1775 a letter from a group of women in Edenton, North Carolina, appeared in a London newspaper. The signers of this letter planned to follow the example of North Carolina's leaders "not to drink any more tea, nor wear any more British cloth."

Many colonists in North Carolina had close ties with Britain. What had made the women of Edenton angry enough to send their letter? In this lesson you will learn how the conflict started and why it grew.

The Edenton Tea Party

From 1754 until 1763, British and French forces fought for control of North America. The war was called the French and Indian War. The war was a costly one for the British. After the war, they passed laws to raise money by taxing goods going in and out of the colonies.

The colonists thought this was unfair because they did not have anyone to represent them in Britain. Colonists called this tax on them "taxation without representation."

Monument honoring the Edenton Tea Party (left); tax stamps (right)

Penelope Barker   1728–1796

Character Trait: Civic Virtue

During most of the American Revolution, Penelope Barker lived independently. She took care of her household and lands while her husband was in London on business related to the North Carolina Colony.

Penelope Barker wanted to speak out against "acts that will enslave our Native Country." On October 25, 1774, she brought 50 women of Edenton together to sign a pledge stating they would not drink British tea or wear British clothes. Under Penelope Barker's leadership, the women of Edenton showed that they supported the rebellion against England.

MULTIMEDIA BIOGRAPHIES
Visit The Learning Site at www.harcourtschool.com/
biographies to learn about other famous people.

The next tax, the Stamp Act, was passed in 1765. It made the colonists even angrier. The Stamp Act required them to pay for special stamps to use on most printed items. Throughout the 13 colonies, people protested these taxes.

In December 1773 the British put a tax on tea, which was a favorite drink in the colonies. Angry colonists boarded two ships in Boston Harbor to protest the tax. They dumped chests of tea into the water. This protest became known as the Boston Tea Party.

News of the Boston Tea Party spread throughout the colonies. On October 25, 1774, Penelope Barker called a meeting of 50 women in Edenton, North Carolina. The women decided not to drink tea or wear British cloth until the tea tax was canceled. This meeting, the Edenton Tea Party, was one of the first times colonial women united in a political activity.

REVIEW What was the purpose of the Edenton Tea Party?

The Fight for Freedom

The first conflicts of the American Revolution took place on April 19, 1775, at the towns of Lexington and Concord, in Massachusetts. A **revolution** is the sudden change or overthrow of a government. It results in a new or different government.

Tradition says that in May 1775, Scotch-Irish **Patriots**, people favoring independence, signed the Mecklenburg Resolves. According to tradition the Mecklenburg Resolves, or Declaration, stated that Americans were free and independent people.

The American Revolution was a war between Patriots and the British and **Loyalists**, those loyal to Britain. In North Carolina, one of the most famous battles was at Moores Creek Bridge.

On February 18, 1776, almost 1,600 Highland Scots Loyalists marched to meet the Patriots at Moores Creek.

The Battles of the American Revolution in North Carolina

KENTUCKY

VIRGINIA

TENNESSEE

Roanoke Rapids
Halifax
Guilford Courthouse
Greensboro
Hillsborough
Pyle's Massacre
Greenville
Ramsour's Mill
Cowan's Ford
Charlotte
NORTH CAROLINA
Fayetteville
Kinston
New Bern
Kings Mountain
Rockfish
Moores Creek Bridge
GEORGIA
Elizabethtown
Wilmington
ATLANTIC OCEAN
Brunswick
Cape Fear

Yadkin River
New River
Deep River
Tar River
Roanoke River
Chowan R.
Albemarle Sound
Neuse River
Pamlico Sound
French Broad River
Little Tennessee R.
Broad River
Pee Dee River
Lumber R.
Cape Fear R.
New R.
Onslow Bay

Battle
→ **Cornwallis' route**
— **Present-day border**

SOUTH CAROLINA

N
W E
S

0   40   80 Miles
0   40   80 Kilometers
Albers Equal-Area Projection

GEOGRAPHY THEME

Human-Environment Interactions Revolutionary battles were fought throughout the Piedmont and Coastal Plain regions of North Carolina.

❓ **Which battles were fought along Cornwallis's route?**

At Moores Creek Bridge the fight began as Loyalists and Patriots clashed. The Patriots won the battle and delayed the British plan to capture the southern colonies. The victory showed that the Patriots could challenge the British even in the countryside areas of the colonies.

On April 12, 1776, more than 80 delegates from North Carolina met in a congress in Halifax. A **congress** is a meeting where laws and decisions are made. The delegates wrote the Halifax Resolves, a paper recommending independence from Britain for the colonies.

Moores Creek Bridge (below) and a gunpowder horn used during the American Revolution (right)

The North Carolina signers of the Declaration of Independence: Joseph Hewes (left), John Penn (middle), and William Hooper (right).

North Carolina was the first colony to call officially for independence.

Delegates from all the colonies read the Halifax Resolves. The delegates met in Philadelphia to write the Declaration of Independence. The **Declaration of Independence** is a statement telling why the colonies wanted to be free from Britain.

The Declaration was signed on July 4, 1776. The North Carolina signers were Joseph Hewes, John Penn, and William Hooper.

REVIEW Why were the Halifax Resolves an important step in becoming independent from Britain?

Victory at Yorktown

The war for independence soon took North Carolinian soldiers north to fight in the American army led by General George Washington. Then, late in 1778, British General Charles Cornwallis moved his army south. By 1780 the British controlled Georgia and South Carolina. Cornwallis thought he would soon conquer the entire South.

In September 1780 a British attack on Charlotte showed Cornwallis he was wrong. The Patriots resisted so strongly that Cornwallis called the area a "hornet's nest." A month later the Patriots defeated the British army and its Loyalist supporters at the Battle of Kings Mountain.

In January 1781 Cornwallis returned to the South with a much bigger army. He chased General Nathanael Greene's troops through the Piedmont.

The two armies clashed in March 1781 at Guilford Courthouse. The British won the battle, but they lost many of their soldiers.

At Yorktown in Virginia, Cornwallis and his army were finally trapped. They faced the American army on one side and the French navy on the other.

On October 19, 1781, British General Cornwallis surrendered to General Washington. The American Revolution ended British rule in the colonies. The Patriots had won independence after a long fight.

REVIEW How did the Battle of Guilford Courthouse affect the British army?

A National Government

In 1787 delegates from the 13 independent states met in Philadelphia to write a constitution for the new country of the United States of America. A **constitution** is a plan of government.

When the delegates sent the finished Constitution to North Carolina for approval, its leaders held back. North Carolina's leaders wanted to add a Bill of Rights to the Constitution. A **Bill of Rights** is a list of rights all citizens should have, such as freedom of speech and freedom of religion.

After Congress agreed to add a Bill of Rights, North Carolina became the twelfth state to ratify, or approve, the Constitution. The Bill of Rights was finally added to the Constitution in 1791.

REVIEW Why was North Carolina one of the last states to approve the Constitution?

The Constitution of the United States

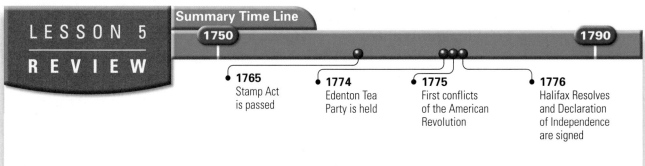

LESSON 5 REVIEW

Summary Time Line

1750 — 1790

1765 Stamp Act is passed

1774 Edenton Tea Party is held

1775 First conflicts of the American Revolution

1776 Halifax Resolves and Declaration of Independence are signed

❶ **MAIN IDEA** Why were colonists unhappy with the British government?

❷ **WHY IT MATTERS** How did the colonists work for independence?

❸ **VOCABULARY** Describe the difference between **Patriots** and **Loyalists**.

❹ **TIME LINE** When did the Edenton Tea Party take place?

❺ **READING SKILL—Sequence** Which happened first, the Battle of Moores Creek Bridge or the writing of the Halifax Resolves?

❻ **CIVICS/GOVERNMENT** What is the Bill of Rights?

❼ **CRITICAL THINKING—Evaluate** Do you think the Edenton Tea Party was successful? Why or why not?

PERFORMANCE—Perform a Skit In a small group, create a short skit about the writing of the Halifax Resolves. Brainstorm what the leaders might have talked about. Make sure each person in your group has a part in the skit. Perform your skit for the class.

·SKILLS· Resolve Conflicts

VOCABULARY
compromise
ratify

▶ WHY IT MATTERS

When individuals or groups of people disagree, it can cause great conflict. People must find peaceful ways to resolve conflicts and reach a compromise. A **compromise** happens when each side gives up some things it wants so both sides can agree.

Steps for Resolving Conflict

> Identify what is causing the conflict.

⬇

> Tell the people on the other side what you want. Listen to what they want.

⬇

> Decide which things are most important to you.

⬇

> Present a plan for compromise. Let the people on the other side present their plan. Talk about the differences in the two plans.

⬇

> Present a second plan for a compromise, giving up one of the things that is important to you. Ask the other side to do the same thing. Look for a way to let each side have most of what it wants.

⬇

> Keep talking until you agree.

⬇

> Plan your compromise so that it will work for a long time.

▶ WHAT YOU NEED TO KNOW

To resolve a conflict, you can follow the steps shown at left.

▶ PRACTICE THE SKILL

Being able to compromise and resolve conflicts is important for citizens and government leaders. In 1787, delegates from the 13 American states met to write a constitution. Think again about what happend when it came time for delegates to **ratify**, or accept, the Constitution.

① Did delegates from all the states ratify the Constitution right away?

② What did the North Carolina delegates want to add to the Constitution?

③ Did the North Carolina delegates finally ratify the Constitution? Why or why not?

▶ APPLY WHAT YOU LEARNED

Think about a time when you had a conflict with a friend. How did you and your friend resolve the conflict? How might you have resolved it differently? Make a list of three possible compromises you could have made.

· CHAPTER ·

3 Review and Test Preparation

USE YOUR READING SKILLS

Use this graphic organizer to help you put the events of Chapter 3 in order. A copy of this graphic organizer appears on page 39 of the Activity Book.

Coastal Plain Region Long Ago

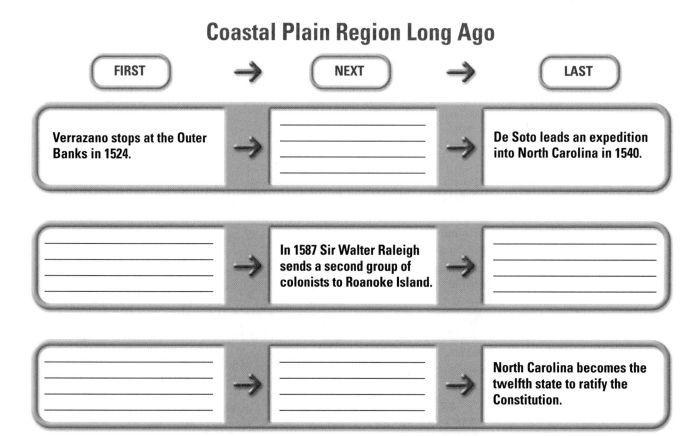

FIRST → NEXT → LAST

Verrazano stops at the Outer Banks in 1524. → → De Soto leads an expedition into North Carolina in 1540.

 → In 1587 Sir Walter Raleigh sends a second group of colonists to Roanoke Island. →

 → → North Carolina becomes the twelfth state to ratify the Constitution.

THINK & WRITE

Write a Diary Entry Think about what life was like for the early settlers of towns such as Edenton, Beaufort, and New Bern. Think about why settlers moved into these towns, how they lived, and the challenges they faced. Write a diary entry from the point of view of an early settler. Compare your entry with your classmates' entries.

Write a Speech Imagine that you live in a North Carolina town at the time of the Revolution. First, decide whether to support the Patriots or the Loyalists. Then write a speech for a town meeting giving your opinions about the British government and taxes. Give your speech to your classmates. Try to persuade your classmates to agree with you.

1587
John White leads the second Roanoke Colony

1663
Lords Proprietors receive land grant

1677
Culpeper's Rebellion takes place

1711
The Tuscarora War begins

1729
North Carolina becomes a royal colony

1774
Edenton Tea Party is held

USE THE TIME LINE

Use the chapter summary time line to answer these questions.

1 When did the Tuscarora War begin?

2 How many years after Culpeper's Rebellion was the Edenton Tea Party?

USE VOCABULARY

Fill in the blank for each sentence using the correct term from the list.

colony (p. 93)

charter (p. 98)

tax (p. 100)

pirate (p. 104)

constitution (p. 116)

3 King James gave a _____ to the Virginia Company.

4 John Culpeper protested the _____ on tobacco.

5 Leaders met in Philadelphia to write a _____ for the nation.

6 Blackbeard was a _____ who hid at Ocracoke Inlet.

7 A _____ is a settlement in one place ruled by people of another place.

RECALL FACTS

Answer these questions.

8 Whom did Sir Walter Raleigh choose as governor of the second colony on Roanoke Island?

9 What were the Navigation Acts?

10 What was the first town in the Carolina Colony?

Write the letter of the best choice.

11 **TEST PREP** The Tuscarora War ended when—

  A settlers moved into Native American lands.

  B the colonists defeated the Tuscaroras at Fort Neoheroka.

  C Tuscaroras freed Baron von Graffenried.

  D Swiss settlers destroyed the Tuscarora village of Chattawka.

12 **TEST PREP** The Halifax Resolves recommended—

  F overthrowing the British government.

  G staying a part of Britain.

  H independence from Britain.

  J support of British tax laws.

THINK CRITICALLY

13 Were the Tuscaroras right to fight the colonists? Why or why not?

14 Was refusing to buy British products a good way for colonists to protest the tax laws? Why or why not?

APPLY SKILLS

Resolve Conflict

15 Suppose you are a Patriot. Explain your views on taxes. Then explain the British government's reason for the taxes. Try to find a compromise.

Predict a Likely Outcome

16 With a partner, look through a newspaper to find an article about a conflict between two countries. Together, try to predict how this conflict might end.

THE OUTER BANKS

People come from around the world to visit the Outer Banks and enjoy its beaches and ocean waves. Many people live and work on the Outer Banks year-round as well.

LOCATE IT

NORTH CAROLINA

Outer Banks

The Coastal Plain Region Today

" Every morning, as the sun comes up on the barrier islands of the outer banks, the gulls still swoop and call above the ocean breakers . . . "

—Charles Kuralt, *North Carolina: An Intimate View*, 1986

CHAPTER READING SKILL

Compare and Contrast

When you **compare** two things, you look at how they are alike. When you **contrast** them, you look at how they are different.

As you read this chapter, pay attention to the similarities and differences between places, industries, and ways of life.

COMPARE ⟷ CONTRAST

1

Living on the Coastal Plain

When the American Revolution ended, Wilmington was a small port surrounded by rural countryside. Today it is one of North Carolina's largest cities. Fayetteville and Jacksonville are other large Coastal Plain cities. In this lesson you will learn how location affects the growth of cities and towns.

Communities near Water

North Carolina's first towns, Bath and New Bern, grew because they were near water. Bath grew on the Pamlico River, only 50 miles (80 km) from the Atlantic Ocean. It could be reached easily by boat.

This made Bath a natural trade center. A **trade center** is a community in which buying and selling goods are the main business activities. Farmers exchanged crops for goods, and merchants did a brisk trade.

FAST FACT
The USS *North Carolina*, now docked in Wilmington, was the most honored battleship of World War II. The ship earned 15 battle stars and took part in every major sea battle in the Pacific.

New Bern was settled where the Neuse and Trent Rivers meet, about 35 miles (56 km) from the Atlantic Ocean. New Bern also became a trade center.

Wilmington grew faster than Bath or New Bern. It rose up on the Cape Fear River, which flows directly into the Atlantic Ocean. Large oceangoing ships could dock there.

Today Wilmington is the state's busiest deepwater port. Cranes the size of sky-scrapers lift cargo in large containers onto ships. The port's major imports are chemicals, forest products, and metal products. An **import** is a good brought in from another country to be used or sold.

Morehead City, founded in 1853, is another deepwater port. North Carolina cargoes leaving Morehead City are unloaded in many world ports.

REVIEW Why did Wilmington grow faster than either Bath or New Bern?

Communities Along Roads and Railroads

Until the early 1800s the lack of roads slowed the growth of towns and cities in the state. As more roads were built, new towns sprang up where main roads crossed.

In the mid-1800s North Carolinians found an even faster way to get around. In 1840 the state got its first major railroad. At one time the 161-mile (259-km) Wilmington-to-Weldon Railroad was the longest in the world.

In the 1900s the Atlantic Coastline Railroad laid tracks through both Rocky Mount and Wilmington. The railroad boosted the growth of both towns. Both suffered when the railroad shut down. Wilmington later recovered when the state extended Interstate 40 to it.

REVIEW How did railroads affect the growth of towns?

Wilmington is a busy port city. Ships from around the world dock at the port every year.

Military Bases in North Carolina

Understanding Human Systems

North Carolina is home to three of the most important military bases in the United States: Fort Bragg, Camp Lejeune, and Johnson Air Force Base. Put together, these three bases make up the largest military center in the world. Some people call these three bases the "military triangle." More than 90,000 members of the United States Army, Air Force, and Marines serve on these bases. There are more servicemen and servicewomen at these three bases than in the entire army of some countries!

Communities near Military Bases

Several communities in the Coastal Plain region grew because of their location near military bases. A **military base** is a place where people train or work for the armed services, such as the army, navy, air force, or marines.

In 1918 the United States government built Fort Bragg, an army base, near Fayetteville. A year later, officials added Pope Air Force Base. The base created many new jobs in Fayetteville. The city soon needed more schools, stores, houses, and services for the soldiers and their families. Today Fayetteville is the largest city in the Coastal Plain region.

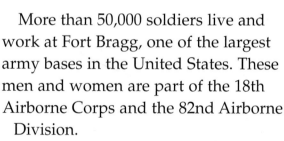

More than 50,000 soldiers live and work at Fort Bragg, one of the largest army bases in the United States. These men and women are part of the 18th Airborne Corps and the 82nd Airborne Division.

Camp Lejeune (luh•JOON), a Marine Corps training camp near Jacksonville, sparked that city's growth in the 1940s. Seymour Johnson Air Force Base near Goldsboro had a similar effect on that city. Like Fayetteville, Jacksonville and Goldsboro grew as more soldiers, families, and businesses moved to the area.

REVIEW What changes did nearby military bases bring to Fayetteville and Jacksonville?

Statue at Fort Bragg

IRON MIKE
IN HONOR OF
AIRBORNE TROOPERS
WHOSE COURAGE,
DEDICATION, AND
TRADITIONS MAKE THEM
THE WORLD'S FINEST
FIGHTING SOLDIERS

Population Growth and Decline

The census of the population in 2000 showed uneven growth in the Coastal Plain region. Some counties had lost population, while others had gained new residents. Many areas of the region, especially the Tidewater, experienced strong growth. Vacationers, as well as older people, have moved there permanently to enjoy the beaches and the golf courses that are open year-round.

At the same time, Edgecombe, Bertie, and Washington Counties lost population. The damage caused by Hurricane Floyd in 1999 led some people to move. Some left permanently, but some left just temporarily until they were able to rebuild their homes. The rebuilding of homes because of damage continues into the twenty-first century. Others left because the number of farming jobs decreased, and many textile mills in the area closed or moved overseas.

REVIEW How has location affected growth in the Coastal Plain region?

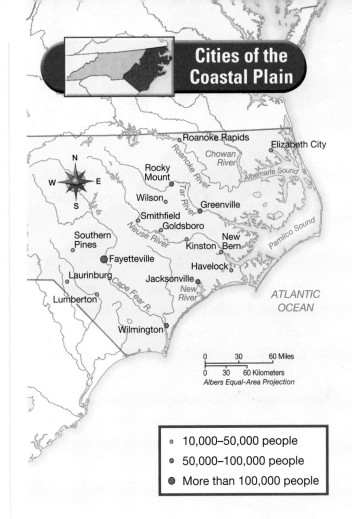

Cities of the Coastal Plain

- ○ 10,000–50,000 people
- ○ 50,000–100,000 people
- ● More than 100,000 people

GEOGRAPHY THEME

Human Environment Interactions
In the Coastal Plain, 16 cities have more than 10,000 people.

❖ Which 5 cities have the largest populations?

LESSON 1 REVIEW

1 MAIN IDEA How did the locations of Bath, New Bern, and Wilmington help the cities become trade centers?

2 WHY IT MATTERS Why have some cities in the Coastal Plain region grown while others declined?

3 VOCABULARY Use the terms **trade center** and **import** in a sentence.

4 READING SKILL—Compare and Contrast Compare and contrast the histories of Wilmington and Fayetteville.

5 GEOGRAPHY On which river was Wilmington built?

6 ECONOMICS How did the closing of the railroad affect Rocky Mount?

7 CRITICAL THINKING—Hypothesize How might Jacksonville be different if Camp Lejeune had not been built nearby?

PERFORMANCE—Make a Brochure Choose a city from this lesson, and read more about it. Then create a travel brochure for the city. Include illustrations and important travel information.

SKILLS
MAP AND GLOBE

Compare Maps with Different Scales

▶ **WHY IT MATTERS**

On these pages, you can see two maps that show North Carolina. On Map A, North Carolina looks smaller than it does on Map B. Map A shows less information about North Carolina but more information about the surrounding states. Map B has been drawn larger so that it can show more details. A **map scale** is the part of a map that compares a distance on a map to a distance in the real world.

Every inch on the map stands for a certain number of miles or kilometers.

▶ **WHAT YOU NEED TO KNOW**

Maps A and B show different amounts of land and have different scales. You might use Map A if you wanted to plan a trip in the southeastern part of the United States. You might look at Map B to write a report about the geography of North Carolina.

Map A: The Southeastern United States

- ★ State capital
- • Major city
- — State border

Albers Equal-Area Projection

Map B: North Carolina Close-up

★ State capital
• Major city
— State border

ATLANTIC OCEAN

NORTH CAROLINA

Great Smoky Mountains National Park

Murphy • Gastonia • Charlotte • Fayetteville • Wilmington • Boone Winston-Salem • Greensboro • Chapel Hill • Asheboro • Durham ★ Raleigh • Rocky Mount • Greenville • Elizabeth City

0   50   100 Miles
0   50   100 Kilometers
Albers Equal-Area Projection

▶ PRACTICE THE SKILL

Although Maps A and B have been drawn to different scales, they show the same distances between places. This is because distances on Earth do not change. You can show this for yourself by finding the distance between two cities on each map.

1 Find the numbered line, or scale, on Map A. The scale tells you the distance on Earth that one inch stands for on this map.

2 Now use your ruler to measure the distance between Charlotte and Fayetteville.

3 Use the scale to figure out the real distance between the cities. How far apart are they?

4 Do the same for Map B. Compare your answers. You can use either map to find the distance. The answer will be the same.

▶ APPLY WHAT YOU LEARNED

Find two different maps that show the same region. Use the maps' scales to find out the distance between any two places shown on both maps. Are the answers the same? What kinds of things are shown on one map but not on the other? How might you use each map?

Practice your map and globe skills with the **GeoSkills CD-ROM**.

Working on the Coastal Plain

MAIN IDEA
Read to find out about the Coastal Plain's various economic activities.

WHY IT MATTERS
The success of the Coastal Plain's industries greatly influences how people earn a living in the region.

VOCABULARY
mixed farming
livestock
food processing
renewable resource
nonrenewable resource
tourism
economy
service job

Workers on the Coastal Plain earn a living in many different ways. They are farmers, factory workers, filmmakers, and fishers. Author William Least Heat-Moon got an inside look at the seafood industry. He found work helping two Outer Banks packers in the town of Wanchese (WAHN•cheez) on Roanoke Island. They were packing crabs into crates for a trip to a factory in Bellhaven. Here is how he described his experience.

"There were more crabs than crates, and the critters kept hopping out of the overfilled boxes like popcorn in a hot skillet. I started shuffling to avoid stepping on them. A [crab] reached up and clamped onto my pant leg and slid back and forth across the floor with me until we finished."

Although very few workers on the Coastal Plain ever spend time with a crab attached to their clothing, they do work hard. They make goods or offer services that are important to people in North Carolina and throughout the country.

Fishing

The 320-mile-long (514-km) coastline of the Tidewater area, with its many sounds, bays, and marshlands, is ideal for fishing. Commercial fishing is one of the state's oldest business activities. For centuries people have made their living catching and preparing fish and shellfish.

Fishing boats called trawlers drag nets through the water to catch blue crabs, shrimp, and flounder.

Blue crabs are an important part of North Carolina's fishing industry.

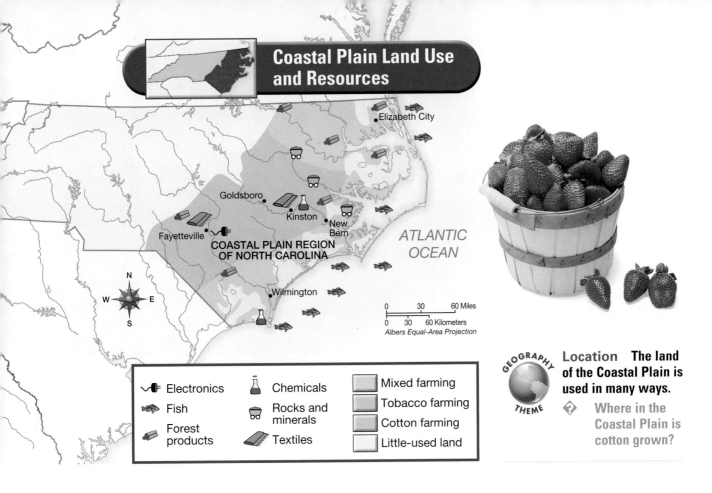

Coastal Plain Land Use and Resources

COASTAL PLAIN REGION OF NORTH CAROLINA

Elizabeth City

Goldsboro
Kinston
Fayetteville
New Bern

Wilmington

ATLANTIC OCEAN

N
W E
S

0   30   60 Miles
0   30   60 Kilometers
Albers Equal-Area Projection

Electronics   **Chemicals**   Mixed farming
Fish   **Rocks and minerals**   Tobacco farming
Forest products   **Textiles**   Cotton farming
Little-used land

GEOGRAPHY THEME

Location The land of the Coastal Plain is used in many ways.

? **Where in the Coastal Plain is cotton grown?**

The largest blue crab populations live in Albemarle and Pamlico Sounds. Shrimp are second only to blue crabs in importance. Fishing boats use nets to catch shrimp in sounds and rivers. Onshore, some of the fish and shellfish are packed in ice and taken directly to market. Other fish are taken to plants to be packaged as frozen or canned fish. Fishing is important to the Coastal Plain economy. However, poor water quality, diseases, and the loss of wetlands have greatly reduced the numbers of some shellfish in the waters of North Carolina.

In North Carolina people enjoy eating fried or broiled fish served with hush puppies and sweet tea. One kind of fish, called menhaden (men•HAY•duhn), is not used for food but mainly for animal feed, oil, fish meal, and fertilizer. Fish oil is used in paint and soap, and fish meal is fed to livestock.

Not all North Carolina's fish and shellfish are caught in oceans, lakes, rivers, or sounds. To meet today's increased demand, some people raise fish and shellfish in fish farms, ponds, or human-made oyster or clam beds in coastal waters. Catfish and crawfish are the main pond-raised species.

REVIEW **Why does North Carolina have many fish farms?**

Farming

Farming is one of the region's most important business activities. Some farmers grow basic crops such as corn, squash, soybeans, and cotton. Many Coastal Plain farmers practice mixed farming. In **mixed farming** farmers grow more than one kind of crop. They may grow corn, soybeans, and peanuts on the same farm.

Farmers in North Carolina raise cows and other kinds of livestock.

Much of the corn grown by Coastal Plain farmers is used as animal feed. Soybeans are grown throughout the region and are used both for food and for making a variety of nonfood products.

Some farmers grow specialty crops, including many vegetables and most fruits, such as blueberries. These crops are hard to grow but get high prices. Farms in Elizabethtown in Bladen (BLAY•den) County are the state's largest blueberry producers. Many farms near Chadbourn and Wallace grow straw-berries. Farms in the Sandhills area grow peaches.

North Carolina's cash crops are tobacco, sweet potatoes, corn, cotton, and wheat. The most important cash crop is tobacco. At one time, tobacco was the state's top income producer. North Carolina still produces more tobacco than any other state. In recent years, how-ever, many tobacco farmers have reduced production. Fewer people are using tobacco because of the health problems it causes.

North Carolina is the country's top producer of sweet potatoes. This cash crop comes from Harnett, Nash, Johnston, and Wilson Counties. Other important cash crops of the Coastal Plain include corn, cotton, and wheat.

The sale of **livestock**, or farm animals that are raised to be sold, brings billions of dollars into the state. North Carolina is a major producer of chickens, turkeys, and hogs. Chicken and turkey farms account for $2 billion in income in North Carolina.

Many hog farms are quite large. One farm might have more than 1,000 hogs. As hog production has increased, so have concerns about the hog wastes that pollute streams and rivers.

Corn is an important cash crop for North Carolina.

Many people in the Coastal Plain region make products from the region's crops. Companies in Mount Olive and Faison buy cucumbers grown in this area to make pickles. Before pickles and many other foods appear on grocery store shelves, they must be processed. **Food processing** is the act of turning raw foods into food products. Workers in food-processing plants clean, cook, and package foods for market.

REVIEW **What kinds of crops and livestock are important in the Coastal Plain region?**

Forestry and Paper

In earlier years people in the Coastal Plain produced lumber for ships' masts and for building, as well as naval stores. Today some people in this region still earn their living producing lumber and other wood products.

The Coastal Plain's most important forest products are wood chips and wood pulp. These products are used to make paper. North Carolina has 20 or more chipping mills where high-powered saws cut wood into chips.

To make wood pulp, workers mix wood chips with chemicals and cook the mixture to soften it. The pulp is then used to make paper.

Some paper companies have their own tree farms. Trees are renewable resources. A **renewable resource** is one that can be used and replaced. Tree farming is a way to renew the supply of trees. In contrast, oil and natural gas are nonrenewable resources. A **nonrenewable resource** is a resource that cannot be easily replaced once it is used up.

REVIEW **Why are trees a renewable resource?**

Analyze Diagrams   Paper is just one of the many uses for the trees of North Carolina.

◆ In what other ways are the trees of North Carolina used?

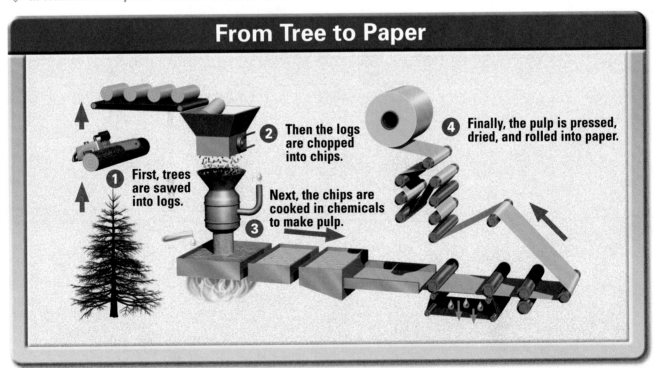

From Tree to Paper

1. First, trees are sawed into logs.
2. Then the logs are chopped into chips.
3. Next, the chips are cooked in chemicals to make pulp.
4. Finally, the pulp is pressed, dried, and rolled into paper.

Tourism and Filmmaking

North Carolina has been called the Variety Vacationland. Tourism has become a major industry for North Carolina because the state has a mild climate and both mountains and seashores to visit. **Tourism** is the selling of goods and services to travelers. Today tourism contributes to the economy of the state. The **economy** is the way people use resources to meet their needs. In the Coastal Plain, people work in many service jobs connected with tourism. A **service job** is an activity that people do for others for pay. In tourism, service workers hold jobs in restaurants, motels, water parks, and miniature golf courses.

They are tour guides, bus drivers, and lifeguards. They also rent cars and boats to tourists or work in parks.

During the summer, towns such as Kitty Hawk in Dare County and Beaufort in Carteret County depend on tourism to keep their economies going. On the Inner Coastal Plain, golf courses draw many people to Pinehurst and Southern Pines.

In the late 1990s filmmakers at Jim Henson Pictures began shooting *Muppets from Space* at Screen Gems Studios in Wilmington. Set decorators shopped at nearby antique shops and even at the military base in Jacksonville to find the furniture for the Muppets' house in the movie.

Filmmakers are able to find a variety of locations in North Carolina. Tourists also enjoy a wide range of activities.

Wilmington's mild climate and variety of riverfront, oceanfront, and rural locations have attracted many filmmakers. The city now has six studios where film crews make both movies and television shows.

Filmmaking requires materials, transportation, housing arrangements, and food for the crews. Many residents have found jobs as camera operators, sound engineers, actors, musicians, and artists. Filmmaking has boosted the region's economy. Wilmington has helped make North Carolina the third-busiest filmmaking state in the country. Only California and New York produce more movies.

REVIEW How has the film industry helped Wilmington's economy?

LESSON 2 REVIEW

❶ **MAIN IDEA** What are three important industries of the Coastal Plain?

❷ **WHY IT MATTERS** Explain how the industries of the Coastal Plain are important to the region.

❸ **VOCABULARY** Contrast the term **renewable resource** with the term **nonrenewable resource**.

❹ **READING SKILL—Compare and Contrast** How are the farming and fishing industries alike? How are they different?

❺ **SCIENCE AND TECHNOLOGY** How is wood pulp made?

❻ **ECONOMICS** What are some service jobs in the tourism industry?

❼ **CRITICAL THINKING—Evaluate** Of the industries in this lesson, which would you most want to work in and why?

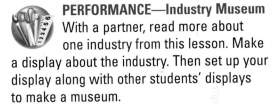

PERFORMANCE—Industry Museum With a partner, read more about one industry from this lesson. Make a display about the industry. Then set up your display along with other students' displays to make a museum.

Using Tables to Group Information

VOCABULARY

classify   compare   contrast

▶ WHY IT MATTERS

You can use tables to show many kinds of information. Tables are especially useful when you have information to **classify**, or sort into categories. You can use tables to organize your ideas and to display information clearly. You can also use tables to compare and contrast information. When you **compare** two things, you show how they are alike. When you **contrast** two things, you show how they are different.

▶ WHAT YOU NEED TO KNOW

Tables are made up of columns and rows. Columns are read from the top of the table to the bottom. Each column has a different heading. This heading tells you what kind of information is featured in the column. Look at Table A on the next page. The column on the left lists the different resources found in the Coastal Plain region. The column on the right lists the different industries that produce or use these resources.

North Carolina's rivers and forests are important natural resources that are found throughout much of the state.

Table A classifies the industries of the Coastal Plain by the resource that they use. Table B classifies the products that come from the Coastal Plain by the industry that creates them.

Rows are read across, from left to right. Look again at Table A below. The first column of the first row shows *Soil* as a resource of the Coastal Plain. In the second column, this row shows *Farming* as the industry related to this resource.

PRACTICE THE SKILL

Use the tables to answer these questions.

1. Which table would you look at to find industries that use soil? Why?

2. What industry uses fish as a resource?

3. What industry produces limestone?

4. What does farming produce?

APPLY WHAT YOU LEARNED

Make a table to compare and contrast ideas for raising money for a class trip. First, draw a three-column table. In the first column, list possible fundraising events. Think of a heading for this column. In the second column, list the benefits of each fundraising event. Think of a heading for this column. In the third column, list the problems with each fundraising event. Think of a heading for this column. Then compare the benefits and problems of each. Decide which fundraising event you think would work best.

Table A: Resources and Industries

RESOURCES OF THE COASTAL PLAIN	INDUSTRIES OF THE COASTAL PLAIN
Soil	Farming
Stone	Rock quarrying
Fish	Fishing
Trees	Lumber

Table B: Industries and Products

INDUSTRIES OF THE COASTAL PLAIN	PRODUCTS OF THE COASTAL PLAIN
Farming	Soybeans Tobacco Pork Poultry
Rock quarrying	Limestone Cement Crushed rock
Fishing	Trout Catfish
Lumber	Pulpwood Lumber

MAIN IDEA
Read to learn about the life and activities of Coastal Plain people.

WHY IT MATTERS
The people and activities of the Coastal Plain region make it an attractive place to live and to visit.

VOCABULARY
national seashore
wildlife refuge
festival

Coastal Life

When it comes to taking a vacation in North Carolina, some say that there are two kinds of people—beach people and mountain people. In her book *Show and Tell*, Tar Heel writer Suzanne Britt tells which one she is:

"On the first hot day, as I walked across the huge black parking lot . . . the smell of honeysuckle smacked me in the face, and I was transported to the beach. . . . There I was, deep in sand; my hand sifting through cool, clean mud; feeling for periwinkles. . . . I am a beach person."

Many people around the state share Britt's love of coastal North Carolina. There are many ways to enjoy the area.

By the Sea, on the Water

When people think about visiting coastal North Carolina, they imagine fishing from a pier, building sand castles, jumping ocean waves, or taking long walks on sandy beaches. All that and more is possible on the North Carolina coast. The Outer Banks has more than 100 miles (161 km) of sandy beaches. Many are in **national seashore** parks—land and water areas protected by the United States government. Cape Hatteras National Seashore, set up in 1953, was the first national seashore park in the United States.

LOCATE IT
NORTH CAROLINA
Wrightsville Beach

Wrightsville Beach, on the North Carolina coast, is a popular location for swimmers.

Analyze Diagrams Hurricanes form off the coast of Africa and gain strength as they cross the Atlantic Ocean.

◈ What do you think happens when a hurricane hits land?

The Outer Banks has the highest sand dune on the Atlantic Coast. About 140 feet (43 m) high, Jockey's Ridge near Kitty Hawk attracts visitors who enjoy flying kites or hang gliding.

A walk on the trails of a wildlife refuge is another way to enjoy the North Carolina coast. A **wildlife refuge** is a place where birds and animals are protected, usually by the government. The region has several refuges, including the Pea Island Wildlife Refuge. That refuge is a feeding and resting area for more than 260 kinds of migratory birds. At the Nags Head Woods Preserve, visitors may see an alligator nearby.

Coastal North Carolina also offers boating and fishing. Morehead City is well known for its deep-sea fishing. Sailboats, yachts, and motorboats travel the Intracoastal Waterway. The Intracoastal Waterway is an inland waterway that stretches from Massachusetts to Florida and cuts through the Tidewater.

REVIEW What are some ways visitors enjoy North Carolina's coastal areas?

Living with Hurricanes

Hurricanes are huge rotating storms. Hurricane season in North Carolina begins in June and lasts until the end of November. With wind speeds reaching from 74 to 150 miles (119 to 241 km) an hour or more, hurricanes can cause major property damage and loss of life.

Weather stations now have warning systems that give coastal residents advance notice of approaching storms. When a storm approaches, residents stay close to their radios and televisions, listening for news about the storm's path. News stations provide storm warnings and notices to evacuate, or leave, the area.

Moving Cape Hatteras Lighthouse

The Cape Hatteras Lighthouse is one of North Carolina's most famous landmarks. Wind and waves had worn away the seashore near it until the lighthouse was right on the edge of the water. To save it, engineers had to figure out how to move it half a mile uphill without destroying it. The lighthouse is 208 feet (63 m) tall. It weighs more than 2,800 tons. The engineers built tracks and a roadway of steel mats. They used special jacks to lift and push the building onto rollers. Workers moved the lighthouse about 100 feet (30 m) a day. It took 23 days to move it to safety.

People who live where there are hurricanes usually have an evacuation route they can follow. This is the route families will take to get away from the coast if it is not safe for them to stay.

As a storm nears, people board up their houses. Owners securely tie up their boats or move them inland. When hurricanes strike, emergency management officials open shelters in schools and churches where people can stay until the storm is over.

REVIEW How do people prepare for a hurricane?

Coastal Plain Celebrations and Traditions

The people of the Coastal Plain celebrate their heritage in many ways. Every spring thousands of people visit the Azalea Festival in Wilmington. A **festival** is a celebration that takes place every year at about the same time.

Many Coastal Plain festivals display the region's farm products. Edenton's Peanut Festival celebrates peanut farming with music, dancing, and a sailboat race. If you like strawberry shortcake, visit Chadbourn, where people have enjoyed parades, dancing, and strawberry-cooking contests for 60 years during the Strawberry Festival.

Many towns, including Morehead City and Shallotte (shul•LOHT), have seafood festivals. At the festivals people line up to sample tasty seafood or enjoy a fish fry.

Some festivals celebrate the cultures of the peoples who settled the region. The Lumbee, Coharie (koh•HAR•ree), and Waccamaw-Siouan peoples hold powwows. A powwow is a celebration

Native American dancers at powwows dance to drum rhythms and songs.

held by one tribe to welcome and honor others. At a powwow, Native Americans celebrate their heritage with traditional songs, dances, and games. A powwow can last several days.

REVIEW What are some ways people on the Coastal Plain celebrate their traditions and way of life?

LESSON 3 REVIEW

1 MAIN IDEA What are some activities people enjoy along the North Carolina coast?

2 WHY IT MATTERS What activities along the coast are important to tourism?

3 VOCABULARY Use the following terms **national seashore** and **wildlife refuge** in a sentence about visitors to the coast.

4 READING SKILL—Compare and Contrast How are the Cape Hatteras National Seashore and the Intracoastal Waterway similar and different?

5 CULTURE What is a powwow?

6 GEOGRAPHY What is the highest sand dune on the Atlantic Coast?

7 CRITICAL THINKING—Synthesize Why do you think people choose to live along the North Carolina coast despite the threat of hurricanes?

PERFORMANCE—Make a Poster Read more about a popular attraction located in coastal North Carolina. Then make a poster about this attraction. Include illustrations and important facts. Share your poster with your classmates.

4 Review and Test Preparation

Complete this graphic organizer to compare and contrast the major industries of the Coastal Plain. A copy of this graphic organizer is on page 46 of the Activity Book.

Industries of the Coastal Plain

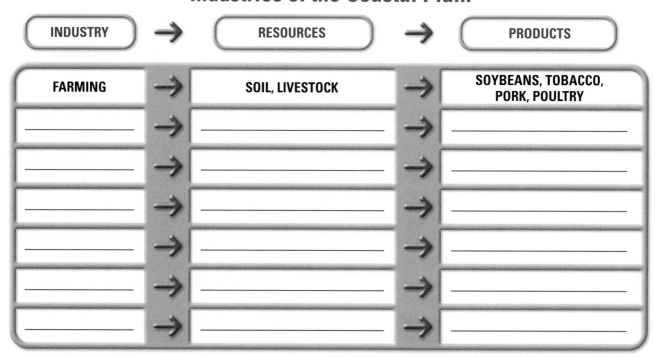

INDUSTRY	→	RESOURCES	→	PRODUCTS
FARMING	→	SOIL, LIVESTOCK	→	SOYBEANS, TOBACCO, PORK, POULTRY
_____	→	_____	→	_____
_____	→	_____	→	_____
_____	→	_____	→	_____
_____	→	_____	→	_____
_____	→	_____	→	_____
_____	→	_____	→	_____

THINK & WRITE

Make a Festival Flyer   Work with a group to begin to plan a festival on the Coastal Plain. Select a possible site. Do some research to pick a theme for the festival. Work with your group to create a flyer to advertise the festival. Post your festival flyer in your classroom alongside the flyers prepared by other groups.

Write a Job Advertisement   Suppose you are starting a new company in the Coastal Plain region. Decide what kind of company it is and what industry it is in. Write an advertisement for a newspaper telling people about jobs at your company. Explain what the company does and why people should work for it.

Use Vocabulary

For each term below, write a sentence that uses that term.

1. **trade center** (p. 122)
2. **military base** (p. 124)
3. **food processing** (p. 131)
4. **tourism** (p. 132)
5. **festival** (p. 139)

Recall Facts

Answer these questions.

6. What is the busiest port in North Carolina?

7. What are reasons that the population declined in Edgecombe, Bertie, and Washington Counties?

8. What are North Carolina's cash crops?

9. Which city is the center of North Carolina's film industry?

10. What are some festivals that take place in the Coastal Plain region?

Write the letter of the best choice.

11. **TEST PREP** How did the building of Camp Lejeune affect the city of Jacksonville?
    A It helped the city grow.
    B It hurt the city's economy.
    C It caused many people to move out of the city.
    D It harmed the industries in Jacksonville.

12. **TEST PREP** Morehead City is well known for its—
    F sweet-potato farming.
    G deep-sea fishing.
    H wildlife refuges.
    J peanut festivals.

13. **TEST PREP** Where is Fort Bragg?
    A near Jacksonville
    B near Goldsboro
    C near Wilmington
    D near Fayetteville

14. **TEST PREP** Which of the following is not a way that people in North Carolina prepare for hurricanes?
    F evacuate the area
    G board up their houses
    H move boats inland
    J add sand to beaches

Think Critically

15. Why do you think many Coastal Plain farmers practice mixed farming?

16. How did the Atlantic Coastline Railroad help the economies of Rocky Mount and Wilmington?

Apply Skills

Compare Maps with Different Scales

17. Look at the maps on pages 126 and 127. Which would you use to plan a trip from Wilmington to Great Smoky Mountains National Park?

Use Tables to Group Information

18. Use the tables on page 135. What are the products of the rock quarrying industry?

VISIT

Orton Plantation

GET READY

Orton Plantation was one of many plantations established along the Cape Fear River in the 1720s. It is located in Winnabow, near Wilmington. Once a huge rice farm, it also served as a military hospital for Union forces during the Civil War. This meant that, unlike many Southern mansions, it survived the war.

In 1910 the plantation's owners began to grow flowers instead of rice. Today Orton Plantation's beautiful gardens cover 20 acres. Visitors to Orton Plantation are impressed by the enormous live oak trees, the stately mansion, and the grand view overlooking the old rice fields and the Cape Fear River.

LOCATE IT

NORTH CAROLINA

Winnabow

WHAT TO SEE

The original house, built in 1725, was much smaller than the mansion is today. The second story and large columns were added years later.

A camellia flower

A yellow pansy

A luna moth rests on a flowerbed.

The flowerbeds in the formal gardens are laid out in unique designs.

TAKE A FIELD TRIP

GO ONLINE

A VIRTUAL TOUR
Visit The Learning Site at www.harcourtschool.com/tours to find virtual tours of other historic sites in the United States.

CNN Turner Le@rning.

A VIDEO TOUR
Check your media center or classroom library for a videotape tour of Orton Plantation.

2 Review and Test Preparation

Write a Journal Study the pictures and captions below to help you review Unit 2. Choose three events. For each event, write a journal entry from the point of view of someone who was there.

USE VOCABULARY

Define the words below.

1 **expedition** (p. 92)

2 **immigrant** (p. 107)

3 **import** (p. 123)

RECALL FACTS

Answer these questions.

4 Who sailed along the coast of North America in 1524?

5 What did John White find when he returned to the colony on Roanoke Island?

6 What was the name of the meeting that Penelope Barker led in 1774?

Write the letter of the best choice.

7 **TEST PREP** Which town became the seat of government for North Carolina in 1770?
A Bath
B New Bern
C Edenton
D Beaufort

8 **TEST PREP** The Halifax Resolves—
F showed that many colonists supported the British government.
G led many colonists to leave North Carolina.
H made North Carolina the first colony to call for independence.
J showed that many colonists opposed the Edenton Tea Party.

9 **TEST PREP** Bath grew quickly because—
A settlers could reach it easily by boat.
B it had rich mineral resources.
C it had the best farmland in the Carolina colony.
D it had the strongest leaders.

Visual Summary

1550　　　1600　　　1650

1585 First Roanoke Island Colony is started p. 94

1663 King Charles II of England signs charter for Carolina Colony p. 99

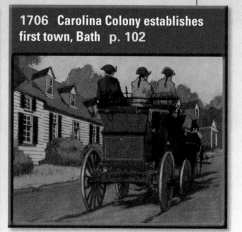

1706 Carolina Colony establishes first town, Bath p. 102

10 TEST PREP Which industry is most important to Kitty Hawk during the summer?
F forestry and paper
G mixed farming
H commercial fishing
J tourism

THINK CRITICALLY

11 How might history have been different if the colonists had been represented in the British government?

12 Why do you think some colonists chose to be Loyalists?

13 Why do some farmers grow basic crops instead of specialty crops?

14 What might be some challenges in filming a movie in North Carolina?

APPLY SKILLS

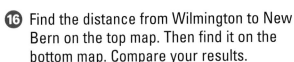

Use the maps on this page to answer the questions.

15 Which map would be easier to use to plan a trip along the Outer Banks?

16 Find the distance from Wilmington to New Bern on the top map. Then find it on the bottom map. Compare your results.

17 Which map shows more detail?

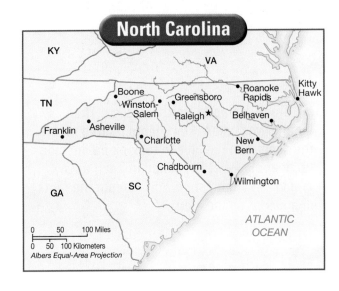

North Carolina

The Coastal Plain

1700

1750

1800

1711 Three-year war with Tuscaroras begins p. 103

1774 The Edenton Tea Party is held p. 112

1776 Declaration of Independence is signed p. 115

145

Unit Activities

Visit The Learning Site at
www.harcourtschool.com/
socialstudies/activities
for additional activities.

Make a Map

Trace a map of North Carolina. Then label towns where key events related to the American Revolution took place. Include facts about what happened in each town and when it happened. You can put the facts in a key or on the map.

Create a Mural

Choose important industries in the Coastal Plain region. As a class, create a mural showing the major industries of the region and their products. Include information about the history of particular industries and show the importance of the industry to the Coastal Plain region.

VISIT YOUR LIBRARY

■ *Storm Warriors* by Elisa Carbone. Random House.

■ *Back Home* by Gloria Jean Pinkney. Dial Books.

■ *Pale as the Moon* by Donna Campbell. Coastal Carolina Press.

COMPLETE THE UNIT PROJECT

Put on a Play   After you have finished writing your class play, assign roles to members in your group. Be sure to practice the play. Group members should also make any necessary props or costumes for the play. When you have everything together, practice the play one last time with everyone in costume. Then present the play to your classmates.

The Piedmont Region

Carved wooden
colonial figurine

Old Salem Home Moravian Church, Winston-Salem, North Carolina

The Piedmont Region

66 The Piedmont is another land. It has always been a more serious-minded land. 99

—Jonathan Daniels, *North Carolina: A Guide to the Old North State*, 1939

Preview the Content

Read the Main Idea for each lesson in this unit. Then predict what the lesson will be about. Write down any questions you may have about life in the Piedmont region.

Preview the Vocabulary

Related Words Knowing how words are related can help you understand them. Look up each pair of words below in a dictionary. Explain how each pair is related.

RELATED WORDS	
capital	capitol
capital resources	human resources
urban	suburb

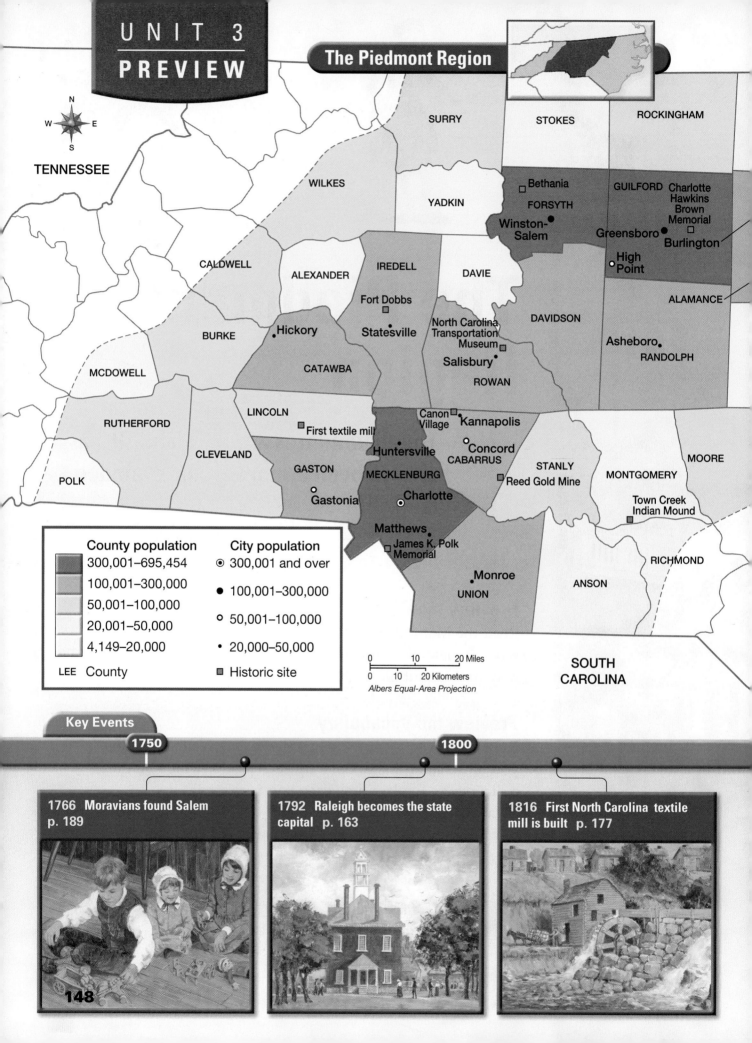

The Piedmont Region

TENNESSEE

SURRY

STOKES

ROCKINGHAM

WILKES

YADKIN

Bethania

GUILFORD   Charlotte
FORSYTH   Hawkins
                          Brown
Winston-   Memorial
Salem   Greensboro

                          Burlington

CALDWELL

ALEXANDER

IREDELL

DAVIE

High
Point

ALAMANCE

BURKE

Hickory

Fort Dobbs

Statesville

North Carolina
Transportation
Museum

DAVIDSON

Asheboro

RANDOLPH

MCDOWELL

CATAWBA

Salisbury

ROWAN

LINCOLN

First textile mill

Canon
Village

Kannapolis

RUTHERFORD

Huntersville

Concord
CABARRUS

STANLY

MOORE

MONTGOMERY

CLEVELAND

GASTON

MECKLENBURG

Reed Gold Mine

Town Creek
Indian Mound

POLK

Gastonia

Charlotte

Matthews
James K. Polk
Memorial

RICHMOND

Monroe

UNION

ANSON

County population

▨	300,001–695,454
▨	100,001–300,000
▨	50,001–100,000
▨	20,001–50,000
▢	4,149–20,000

LEE   County

City population

⊙ 300,001 and over

● 100,001–300,000

○ 50,001–100,000

• 20,000–50,000

■ Historic site

0   10   20 Miles
0   10   20 Kilometers
Albers Equal-Area Projection

SOUTH
CAROLINA

Key Events

1750   1800

1766 Moravians found Salem
p. 189

1792 Raleigh becomes the state
capital p. 163

1816 First North Carolina textile
mill is built p. 177

148

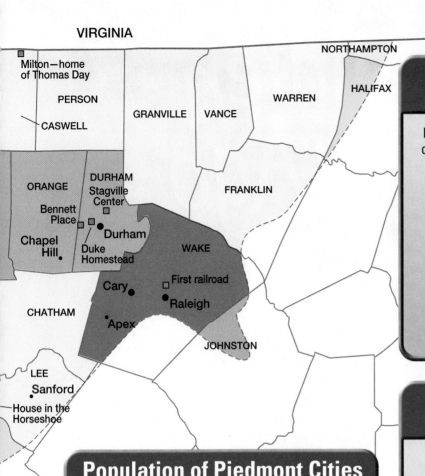

VIRGINIA

Milton—home of Thomas Day

PERSON

CASWELL

GRANVILLE

VANCE

WARREN

NORTHAMPTON

HALIFAX

ORANGE

DURHAM
Stagville Center

FRANKLIN

Bennett Place

Durham

Duke Homestead

Chapel Hill

WAKE

Cary

First railroad

Raleigh

CHATHAM

Apex

JOHNSTON

LEE
Sanford
House in the Horseshoe

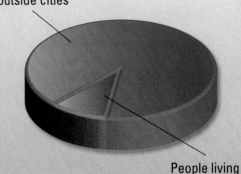

North Carolina, 1900

People living outside cities

People living in cities

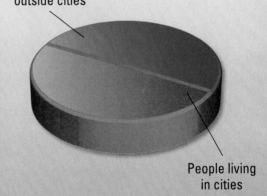

North Carolina, Today

People living outside cities

People living in cities

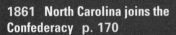

Population of Piedmont Cities

	1800	1900	2000
Charlotte	325	18, 091	540, 828
Durham	Did not exist	6, 679	187, 035
Greensboro	Did not exist	10, 035	223, 891
High Point	Did not exist	4, 163	85, 839
Raleigh	669	13, 643	276, 093
Salem/ Winston-Salem	233	3, 642	185, 776

1900

1950

1861 North Carolina joins the Confederacy p. 170

1888 First large-scale furniture factory opens in High Point p. 178

1950s Research Triangle is begun p. 187

Children of Long Ago

written by Lessie Jones Little
illustrated by Jan Spivey Gilchrist

The author of these poems, Lessie Jones Little, was born in North Carolina. Her daughter is the celebrated children's author Eloise Greenfield. In *Children of Long Ago*, Lessie Jones Little used poetry to share her experiences growing up in North Carolina.

Children of Long Ago

(Part I)

The children who lived a long time ago
In little country towns
Ate picnics under spreading trees,
Played hopscotch on the cool dirt yards,
Picked juicy grapes from broad grapevines,
Pulled beets and potatoes from the ground,
Those children of long ago.

The children who lived a long time ago
In little country towns
Tromped to school on hard-frozen roads,
Warmed themselves by wood-burning stoves,
Ate supper by light from oil-filled lamps,
Built fancy snowmen dressed like clowns,
Those children of long ago.

The children who lived a long time ago
In little country towns
Decked themselves in their Sunday best,
Went to church and visited friends,
Sang happy songs with their mamas and papas,
Traveled through books for sights and sounds,
Those children of long ago.

Cornfield Leaves

Silky ribbons long and green,
Dotted with sparkling dew,
Waving in the summer breeze
Under a roof of blue.

Keep on waving in the breeze,
Keep on sparkling, too,
And every time you wave at me,
I'll wave right back at you.

All Dressed Up

The church bell is ringing bong-bong, bong-bong.
It sounds like it's saying, "Come along, come along."

The folks are wearing their best Sunday clothes,
Miss Lossie in her seamed-back hose,
Mr. George in a straw hat with a black band,
Miss Lou carrying a big fancy fan,

Emmett in knee-pants and long black stockings,
Rubber-soled shoes for easy walking,
Little Lucy in a long-waisted, pleated dress,
With rickrack braid across the chest.

The townsfolk dress up in their nicest things
And strut to church when the church bell rings.

Children of Long Ago

(Part II)

Sometimes sad and sorry,
Sometimes jolly and glad,
    They cried,
    They laughed,
    They worked,
    They played,
    They learned,
    They loved,
Those children of long ago.

Analyze the Literature

1 When do you think these poems took place?

2 What things are important to the people in the poems?

3 Think of something that happened to you in the past. Write a poem describing the event.

READ A BOOK

START THE UNIT PROJECT

Create a Newcomers' Guide
With your classmates, create a book or a Web site guide for people moving to the Piedmont. In a small group, choose an industry or some other aspect of life in the Piedmont. As you read the unit, take notes about the history of your topic. Also think about how it affects the Piedmont today.

USE TECHNOLOGY

Visit The Learning Site at **www.harcourtschool.com/ socialstudies** for additional activities, primary sources, and other resources to use in this unit.

BENTONVILLE BATTLEGROUND STATE HISTORIC SITE

Bentonville was the site of the largest Civil War battle fought in North Carolina. Today the battleground is a state historic site. You can visit the battlefield, learn about the battle, and see a house that served as a hospital.

LOCATE IT

NORTH CAROLINA

Bentonville Battleground State Historic Site

5

The Piedmont Region Long Ago

" First at Bethel, furthest at
Gettysburg, and last at
Appomattox. "

—anonymous, describing the military ability
of North Carolina soldiers in the Civil War

CHAPTER READING SKILL

Categorize

When you **categorize** information, you sort it
into groups, or categories. The information in
each category has something in common.

**As you read this chapter, sort the
information into categories.**

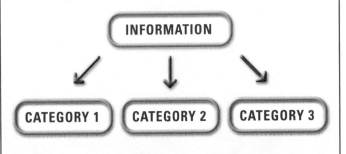

Settling the Backcountry

1730–1770

MAIN IDEA

Read to learn about the groups of European immigrants that settled in the North Carolina backcountry.

WHY IT MATTERS

Many North Carolina ideas and traditions can be traced to groups of European settlers.

VOCABULARY

backcountry
pioneer
relocate
diversity
self-sufficient

In the early 1700s most North Carolina towns and cities were located on the Coastal Plain. Few settlements existed west of the Fall Line. People called this vast western region the **backcountry** because it was away from, or in back of, the Coastal Plain. Poor roads, the waterfalls, and rapids made travel to the backcountry difficult. By the 1730s, however, pioneers were streaming into the backcountry. A **pioneer** is a person who is among the first to settle in a place.

The Great Wagon Road

By the 1730s good farmland had become hard to find in Pennsylvania, Maryland, and Virginia. Colonists began going south to **relocate**, or move to a new location. In the North Carolina backcountry, land was cheap and plentiful. The newcomers traveled down the Great Wagon Road, once a pathway used by Native Americans. The Great Wagon Road

FAST FACT Travel on the Great Wagon Road was slow. People could not go any faster than their feet could carry them. In 1784 it took Ninian Riley and his family almost a month to walk from Maryland to Surry County, North Carolina. Today you can fly from Maryland to North Carolina in about an hour and a half!

stretched from near Philadelphia, south through the Shenandoah Valley in Virginia, and into North Carolina.

The new settlers brought **diversity**, or differences, to the Piedmont. Some spoke different languages and had different religious beliefs and customs. Many of the settlers were German or Scotch-Irish immigrants. The Scotch-Irish were people whose ancestors had migrated from Scotland to Ireland. Still other new settlers were Welsh or Irish.

Most settlers belonged to Christian churches. Many of the Scotch-Irish were Baptists or Presbyterians. The Germans were often Lutherans or Moravians. Others were Quakers.

Many of the Piedmont settlers were the children or the grandchildren of European immigrants to Pennsylvania. These people settled in the valleys of the Yadkin and Catawba Rivers. They bought land in what are today Anson, Granville, Mecklenburg, Orange, and Rowan counties.

John and Rachel Allen were among these settlers. John Allen was 13 years old when he traveled with his family from Pennsylvania to Cane Creek in Orange County. As an adult, John Allen returned to Pennsylvania. He married Rachel Stout in 1779. The couple returned to Cane Creek, where they built a log cabin for their new home.

John Allen was a farmer, a merchant, and a teacher. The Allen family grew to include 12 children. The family did almost all the work on the farm.

REVIEW Who were the European immigrants who settled in the North Carolina backcountry?

· GEOGRAPHY ·

GEOGRAPHY ESSENTIAL ELEMENTS

The Great Wagon Road

Understanding the World in Spatial Terms

The Great Wagon Road did not start as a road. First it was a path that Native Americans followed when they hunted buffalo. Later, immigrants from northern colonies followed the path to Virginia and North Carolina.

The path was hard to locate and follow, though, so the immigrants made maps of it. This map from the 1750s shows where travelers could safely cross the Blue Ridge Mountains. It also shows the many rivers in this part of North Carolina.

Today actors portray the Moravians' way of life at Old Salem.

The Moravian Settlements

In 1753 a group of German-speaking immigrants called Moravians made a long and difficult journey to the Piedmont from Bethlehem, Pennsylvania. The Moravians moved to the backcountry to start a religious community. The group bought almost 100,000 acres of land in what is today Forsyth County. The people named their land Wachovia (wa•CHO•vee•uh).

In Moravian communities in North Carolina, the church owned all property. Every member of the religious group worked for the good of the whole community. They shared their resources and the money they earned. The Moravians became known for their hard work, neatness, and skill at crafts.

The Moravians first built two small farming communities called Bethabara (bee•THAH•buh•ruh) and Bethania. In 1766 they started work on their largest settlement. Their new town was called Salem, after the Hebrew word *shalom*, meaning "peace." Today's city of Winston-Salem grew out of this town.

Salem was a planned community. Workers built homes and churches, a tavern, a pottery, and other shops. Skilled craftspeople, merchants, doctors, and teachers offered their services to backcountry farmers.

For many years Salem was the leading trade center of the Piedmont. The Moravians became known throughout

The craftspeople of the community made the tools and pots settlers needed.

the region for their high-quality goods. When boys and girls were 14 years old, they left their parents' homes. The girls lived in the Single Sisters' House. There they learned to knit, weave, and sew. They also made candles, soap, gloves, straw hats, and other goods.

The boys lived in the Single Brothers' House. There they learned various trades. Some prepared to be shoemakers, carpenters, or blacksmiths. Others learned baking, brickmaking, or tailoring. At school they studied reading, writing, history, geography, geometry, and Latin. For both boys and girls, music was also important. In each house the group worked, studied, and worshiped together.

Until the late 1700s, German Moravians and African Americans who had joined their church went to the same services. In the early 1800s the Moravian church became divided. As a result, the African Americans began holding their own services in several places around the area.

Finally, in 1823 the African American Moravian group built a new church, St. Philip's Moravian Church. It is the oldest African American church in North Carolina and has been restored to the original log church.

REVIEW How did Moravian communities differ from other backcountry settlements?

Farming in the Backcountry

The farms of the backcountry were smaller than the plantations of the Coastal Plain. Few farm families had slaves. The eight boys in the Allen family helped their father with plowing and planting the crops. The girls helped their mother with cooking, sewing, spinning thread, weaving, and other household chores. Everyone helped with the harvest.

In the backcountry, families were **self-sufficient**, or able to produce almost everything they needed. They grew their food and made their clothes.

Backcountry farmers worked hard to raise crops and build homes for their families.

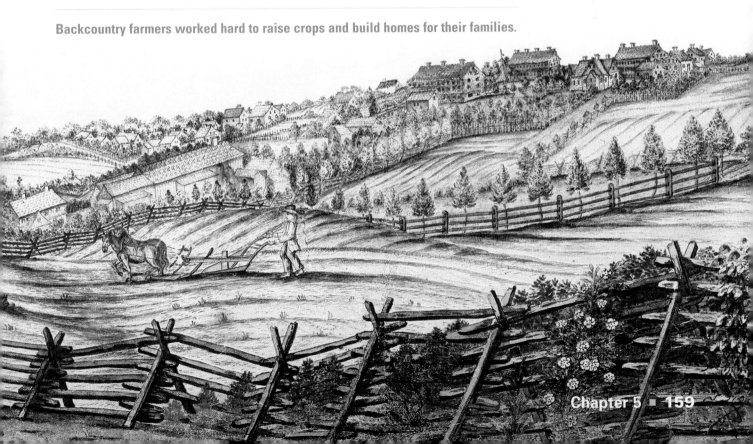

Haley House

Analyze Primary Sources

John Haley moved to High Point from Pennsylvania in the 1780s. Today visitors can tour his house and see how early Piedmont settlers lived.

1 Haley's family used the fireplace for heat and for cooking.

2 Early settlers often made their own dinnerware and utensils.

3 The Haleys had to make their own cloth. They used cloth to make clothes and furnishings such as tablecloths.

❖ Why did Piedmont settlers have to make their own food and clothing?

On Coastal Plain plantations, enslaved African Americans raised cash crops such as tobacco and cotton for the planters. On Piedmont farms, families raised pigs, cows, and sheep. They grew corn, wheat, and other grains for themselves with a little extra to sell. The sale of these crops usually brought in only enough money to pay taxes or to buy goods the farmers could not make or grow themselves.

REVIEW How did backcountry farms differ from plantations?

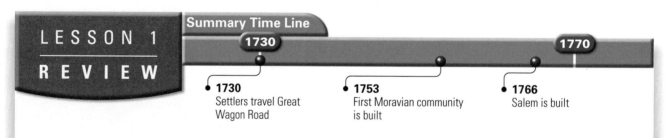

LESSON 1 REVIEW

Summary Time Line

1730 — 1770

1730 Settlers travel Great Wagon Road

1753 First Moravian community is built

1766 Salem is built

1 MAIN IDEA Who were some of the groups of European immigrants who settled in the backcountry?

2 WHY IT MATTERS What ideas and traditions did settlers bring to the Piedmont?

3 VOCABULARY Use the words **relocate** and **pioneer** in a sentence describing the journey on the Great Wagon Road.

4 TIME LINE When was the town of Salem built?

5 READING SKILL—Categorize What kinds of farming were done in the Piedmont?

6 CULTURE What were the religions of the Scotch-Irish settlers?

7 GEOGRAPHY Near which rivers did the new arrivals settle?

8 CRITICAL THINKING—Hypothesize Why do you think the Moravians shared all their resources as a community?

PERFORMANCE—Make a Chart With a small group, make a chart to organize the weekly chores of the 12 Allen family children. Chart what each child might do each day.

From a Colony to a State

1700   1800   1900

1775–1850

Several battles of the American Revolution took place in North Carolina. After the American Revolution, the state of North Carolina faced more challenges. Its growth was slow, and many North Carolinians left the state. Archibald Murphey, a lawyer and planter from the Piedmont, warned state leaders in North Carolina. He said, "Thousands of our wealthy and respectable citizens are annually moving to the west . . . and thousands of our poorer citizens follow them, being driven away by the prospect of poverty."

The Revolution Battles in the Piedmont

One of the first important battles of the American Revolution in the South took place in February 1776 at Moores Creek Bridge near Wilmington. The battle resulted in a Patriot victory. This victory kept the British from capturing the southern colonies early in the war.

MAIN IDEA
Read to find out how North Carolina changed as a result of becoming a state.

WHY IT MATTERS
Changes in government and transportation helped North Carolina grow.

VOCABULARY
capital
manufacturing
plank road
toll road

This is a diorama, or model, of the Battle of Moores Creek Bridge.

FAST FACT
The night before the battle of Moores Creek Bridge, Patriots took some of the wooden boards out of the bridge. Then they greased the rest with soap and animal fat. When the Loyalists tried to cross the bridge the next morning, it was so slippery that many of them fell into the water.

Analyze Primary Sources

This flag was made in North Carolina in the 1700s. It may have been used by Patriots at the Battle of Guilford Courthouse. Even then, red, white, and blue were the colors of the United States.

1. The flag has 6 red and 6 blue stripes now. It may have had 14 stripes when it was new.
2. The flag has 13 blue stars on a white background. One star stands for each of the original 13 colonies.
3. The flag is made of wool and cotton. It was sewn by hand.

How is the Guilford flag similar to the United States flag today? How is it different?

By 1780 the British were again fighting in the South. They controlled Georgia and South Carolina. At Ramsour's Mill, near what is today Lincolnton (LIN•kuhn•tuhn), Scotch-Irish Patriots broke up a gathering of Loyalists planning to join the British.

More British soldiers were sent to protect the main British army. They were met by a group of Patriots from the Piedmont and Mountain regions. This group was called the Overmountain Men because they came from a region west of the mountains. On October 7, 1780, they drove British troops to the top of Kings Mountain, and overcame the entire British force.

In March 1781 British and American forces met at Guilford (GIL•ferd) Courthouse in what is now Greensboro. British general Cornwallis won the battle. Still, the fighting at the Battle of Guilford Courthouse weakened

the British greatly. The final British defeat occurred at Yorktown, Virginia, less than eight months later. Cornwallis surrendered to General George Washington on October 19, 1781.

REVIEW What battles of the American Revolution took place in the Piedmont?

Choosing a State Capital

After the American Revolution, North Carolina lawmakers began thinking about moving their **capital**, or place of government. New Bern seemed too far east for many of the people who traveled to the capital for government business. Many people wanted a location closer to the center of the state. State lawmakers could not agree on a site. They turned the problem over to state leaders who were meeting in Hillsborough.

This drum was used at the Battle of Guilford Courthouse.

Delegates to the meeting recommended moving the capital to Wake County. One committee chose the exact location for the new capital. Another committee made plans to build the statehouse.

In 1792 the state bought 1,000 acres of land and laid out a street plan for the new capital city. State lawmakers named the new city Raleigh in honor of Sir Walter Raleigh, the founder of the first colony on Roanoke Island.

REVIEW Why did lawmakers decide to move their capital to Raleigh?

A Sleeping State Awakes

In the early 1800s North Carolina grew more slowly than many other states. Many farmers raised little more than they needed for their families. Few people raised cash crops. Transportation to markets where they could sell their crops was risky and costly because the roads were so poor.

North Carolina also had other economic troubles. People were leaving the state in large numbers. Between 1815 and 1850 the state lost about one-third of its population. Tar Heels moved west to such states as Tennessee, Alabama, and Ohio. In 1820 only seven towns in North Carolina had more than 1,000 people living in them. The lack of cities to serve as trade centers hurt the state's economy.

Manufacturing also developed slowly in North Carolina. **Manufacturing** is the making of goods. Most manufactured goods bought by North Carolina families came from outside the state.

This drawing shows the first statehouse, or state capitol, built in Raleigh.

Growth also slowed because the state did little to educate its citizens. In 1830 North Carolina had only a few schools. None were public schools, which are schools run by the government and paid for by taxes. The only college was the University of North Carolina at Chapel Hill, which opened in 1795.

North Carolina needed a wake-up call. Archibald Murphey, a state lawmaker between 1812 and 1818, called on the state government to build roads and canals. He wanted to improve transportation to the western part of the state.

By the late 1830s North Carolina began to make changes. In 1835 the state constitution gave people in the mountains more representation in government. The governor was elected by the people rather than by state lawmakers. The state also made plans to use tax money to put a public school in each county.

Major changes also began to take place in transportation. The state built plank roads, which could be used in all kinds of weather. **Plank roads** are made by laying heavy logs side by side across a trail.

Then planks, or thick and heavy boards, are put across the logs. To pay for the building and repair of these roads, the state made them toll roads. A **toll road** is a road that people must pay a toll, or fee, to use. Users paid their toll at toll gates.

• GEOGRAPHY •

GEOGRAPHY ESSENTIAL ELEMENTS

Raleigh
Understanding Human Systems

The railroad helped the city of Raleigh grow. In fact, the first railroad in the state was built to carry the rock used to build the state capitol. This railroad was the first of many to run through Raleigh. By 1840 trains were running between Gastonia and Raleigh. In 1849 the North Carolina Railroad Company started a railroad from Goldsboro to Charlotte. This railroad ran through Raleigh and Greensboro. Because of the railroads, Raleigh soon became one of the busiest cities in the state.

Archibald Murphey wanted North Carolinians to build better roads. Plank roads like this one made it easier for farmers to take their crops to cities where they could sell them.

By the late 1840s railroads connected cities in eastern North Carolina with the Piedmont. In 1849 the state government built the North Carolina Railroad, which connected Charlotte, Salisbury, and Greensboro with Raleigh and Goldsboro. Over time, many of these towns grew into some of the state's largest cities. By the 1850s North Carolina's decision to improve transportation and education started to pay off. North Carolina's population began to grow.

REVIEW **How did North Carolina wake up from its years of slow growth?**

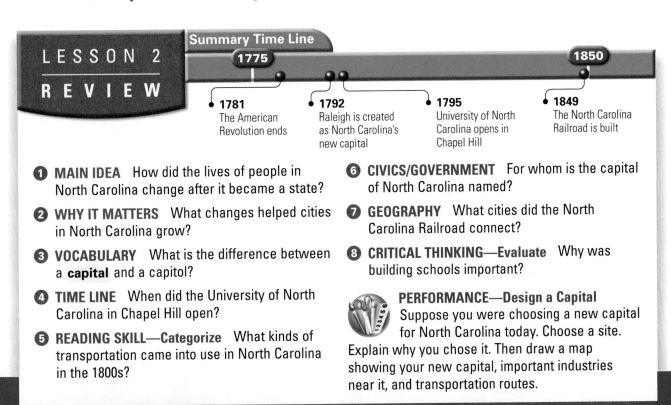

LESSON 2 REVIEW

Summary Time Line

1775 — 1850

1781 The American Revolution ends

1792 Raleigh is created as North Carolina's new capital

1795 University of North Carolina opens in Chapel Hill

1849 The North Carolina Railroad is built

1. **MAIN IDEA** How did the lives of people in North Carolina change after it became a state?

2. **WHY IT MATTERS** What changes helped cities in North Carolina grow?

3. **VOCABULARY** What is the difference between a **capital** and a capitol?

4. **TIME LINE** When did the University of North Carolina in Chapel Hill open?

5. **READING SKILL—Categorize** What kinds of transportation came into use in North Carolina in the 1800s?

6. **CIVICS/GOVERNMENT** For whom is the capital of North Carolina named?

7. **GEOGRAPHY** What cities did the North Carolina Railroad connect?

8. **CRITICAL THINKING—Evaluate** Why was building schools important?

PERFORMANCE—Design a Capital Suppose you were choosing a new capital for North Carolina today. Choose a site. Explain why you chose it. Then draw a map showing your new capital, important industries near it, and transportation routes.

MAIN IDEA
Read to find out why the Northern and Southern states disagreed over slavery, taxes, and other issues by the mid-1800s.

WHY IT MATTERS
Differences between the North and the South led to war.

VOCABULARY
slave state
free state
abolitionist
Underground Railroad
states' rights
secede
Union
Confederacy

Conflicting Views

1700	1800	1900

1850–1865

In 1861 the people of North Carolina had to take sides in a war between the Northern and Southern states. This war divided the country and sometimes even families. North Carolinians were descendants of people who had fought in the American Revolution, and they loved their country. However, they also loved their way of life in the South and felt ties to neighboring states.

Work in the South and in the North

Throughout the Piedmont the average farmer had fewer than 100 acres of land. Most farm families lived in log cabins and grew corn as their main crop. Few of these farms were worked by enslaved African Americans.

This engraving from 1863 shows African Americans leaving North Carolina near New Bern.

166

On the Coastal Plain large plantations covered hundreds of acres. Huge amounts of tobacco, cotton, and naval stores were produced by enslaved African Americans. These and other cash crops were important to the economies of Southern states.

Overall, the South had fewer people and far fewer factories than the North. Only a few people in North Carolina lived in towns. Manufactured goods came from the Northern states or from Europe. Transportation systems were not as developed as in the North.

The South relied on farming as the main part of its economy. The North, however, had more people, cities, and railroads and a stronger manufacturing base than the South.

REVIEW How were Northern states and Southern states different?

Slave States and Free States

In the 1860 census about 4 million people were counted as slaves. Most of them lived in the Southern states. These states came to be called slave states. A **slave state** was a state in which slavery was allowed by law.

Often the treatment of enslaved African Americans was very harsh. Many enslaved African Americans worked in the fields from dawn to sunset, seven days a week. Some slaves tried to escape. The risks of trying to escape were great. When caught, runaways were beaten. Some slaves did escape, however. Most headed north to reach a **free state**. In a free state slavery was not allowed.

In North Carolina and other Southern states, some people helped enslaved

African Americans escape. These people were **abolitionists**. They wanted to abolish, or end, slavery. They wanted all people to be free.

Levi Coffin, a Quaker from Guilford County in the Piedmont, helped set up escape routes known as the Underground Railroad. The **Underground Railroad** was not a railroad. It was a series of routes and safe houses where runaways could find clothing, food, and rest on their journey north to freedom. Greensboro, Jamestown, and Goldsboro were towns that had stations, or hiding places, on the Underground Railroad.

Harriet Jacobs was born into slavery. She escaped when she was 21. She wrote a book about her life as an enslaved person.

Many runaways received help from religious groups, such as the Quakers. As early as 1776, North Carolina Quakers had declared, "Keeping our fellow men in bondage is [not in keeping with] the law of righteousness."

REVIEW How did abolitionists in North Carolina show their opposition to slavery?

A Divided Nation

In the 1850s the North and the South disagreed about many issues. In the Northern states new industries were developing. The North wanted to keep taxes high on goods imported from other countries. In that way, Americans would buy goods made at home, not goods from overseas. Southern states opposed higher taxes. They wanted to sell their cotton to British cotton mills and to import goods from Britain.

The nation was also divided over whether slavery should continue and be allowed to spread to lands in the West. Many Northerners believed that slavery was wrong and should be ended. In the South, slave owners depended on slave labor for their living.

Many Southerners sided with the slave owners. They believed that the question of slavery should be decided by each state. Most of these Southerners supported **states' rights**. They felt that each state should have the right to decide for itself about slavery, taxes, and other issues.

When Abraham Lincoln won election as President in 1860, the debate over slavery ended for many Southerners. They believed that the new President would outlaw slavery. They feared the effects such an action would have on their way of life.

Abraham Lincoln was elected United States President in 1860.

Jefferson Davis was the president of the Confederacy.

Seven Southern states decided to **secede** (sih•SEED), or withdraw, from the Union. The **Union** is another name for the United States. In December 1860 South Carolina became the first state to secede. The states of Mississippi, Florida, Alabama, Georgia, Louisiana, and Texas soon followed. These states formed a new country called the Confederate States of America, or the **Confederacy**. They elected Jefferson Davis, a former senator from Mississippi, as their president.

GEOGRAPHY THEME

Regions Eleven states in all joined the Confederacy. Border states were states near the Confederacy that chose not to secede.

❖ Which states joined the Confederacy?

The Union and the Confederacy

Union state
Border state
Confederate state
Territory
(1863) Date of statehood

The attack on Fort Sumter started the Civil War. Many people in North Carolina thought the United States was wrong to fight the Confederacy.

In North Carolina, Lincoln's election alone did not provide a reason for leaving the Union. Confederate soldiers attacked Fort Sumter in South Carolina in April 1861. Then President Lincoln asked North Carolina to send troops to fight Confederates. North Carolina had not strongly favored seceding. However, being asked to send troops to South Carolina was too much for many Southerners. One month later, North Carolina, Virginia, Arkansas, and Tennessee joined the Confederacy. North Carolina was the last Southern state to secede from the United States.

REVIEW Why did the Southern states secede?

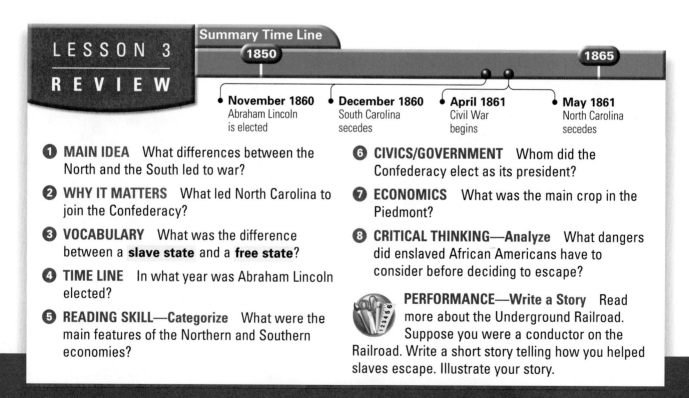

LESSON 3 REVIEW

Summary Time Line

1850 — 1865

- **November 1860** Abraham Lincoln is elected
- **December 1860** South Carolina secedes
- **April 1861** Civil War begins
- **May 1861** North Carolina secedes

❶ **MAIN IDEA** What differences between the North and the South led to war?

❷ **WHY IT MATTERS** What led North Carolina to join the Confederacy?

❸ **VOCABULARY** What was the difference between a **slave state** and a **free state**?

❹ **TIME LINE** In what year was Abraham Lincoln elected?

❺ **READING SKILL—Categorize** What were the main features of the Northern and Southern economies?

❻ **CIVICS/GOVERNMENT** Whom did the Confederacy elect as its president?

❼ **ECONOMICS** What was the main crop in the Piedmont?

❽ **CRITICAL THINKING—Analyze** What dangers did enslaved African Americans have to consider before deciding to escape?

PERFORMANCE—Write a Story Read more about the Underground Railroad. Suppose you were a conductor on the Railroad. Write a short story telling how you helped slaves escape. Illustrate your story.

·SKILLS·
CITIZENSHIP

Make a Thoughtful Decision

VOCABULARY

consequence

▶ WHY IT MATTERS

Each decision you make has consequences (KAHN•suh•kwen•sihz). A **consequence** is the result of a decision or an action. Thinking about the consequences before you decide will help you make a good decision.

▶ WHAT YOU NEED TO KNOW

Here are some steps you can use to make a thoughtful decision.

Step 1 **Know you have to make a decision.**

Step 2 **Gather information.**

Step 3 **Identify choices.**

Step 4 **Predict consequences and evaluate them.**

Step 5 **Make a choice and take action.**

▶ PRACTICE THE SKILL

Imagine that it is 1861. In each situation below, you need to decide whether to join the Confederate army or the Union army. Explain the steps you followed in making each decision.

❶ Your family owns a plantation in North Carolina.

❷ You own a business in New York City.

❸ You are a Southerner in Washington, D.C., with friends in the South.

▶ APPLY WHAT YOU LEARNED

Think about a decision you made recently. What steps did you follow? What choices did you have? What were the consequences of your choices? Was your decision a thoughtful one?

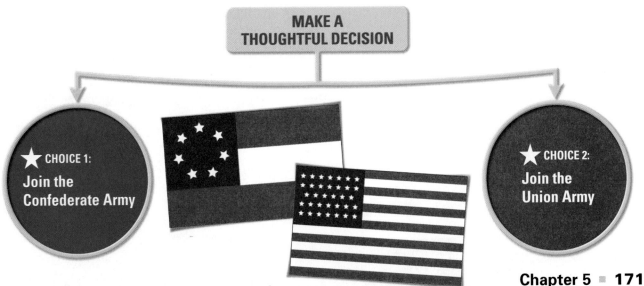

MAKE A THOUGHTFUL DECISION

★ CHOICE 1:
Join the
Confederate Army

★ CHOICE 2:
Join the
Union Army

CITIZENSHIP SKILLS

4

North Carolina in the Civil War

MAIN IDEA

Read to learn how the Civil War and the events that followed affected life in North Carolina.

WHY IT MATTERS

After the Civil War North Carolina faced many new challenges.

VOCABULARY

blockade
Emancipation Proclamation
reconstruct
amendment
sharecropper
Freedmen's Bureau
segregation

1700   1800   1900

1860–1900

The Civil War lasted from 1861 to 1865. More than 120,000 North Carolinians fought for the Confederate Army. Another 15,000 North Carolinians, including more than 5,000 enslaved African Americans, fought for the Union. Mary Anderson was an enslaved African American living in Wake County during the war years. She recalled, "There were stories of fights and freedom." Freedom did come, but it came with disappointments as well as better times.

The War in North Carolina

Early in the Civil War, Union military leaders set up a blockade along the Atlantic coast. During a **blockade** an area is blocked, or cut off, to keep people and supplies from going in or out. Union warships kept Confederate ships from

bringing in supplies or shipping goods out. The blockade hurt the Confederacy by making weapons, goods, and food scarce.

The Confederate navy attached sheets of iron to a wooden ship, the *Merrimack*, making it a new kind of ship called an ironclad. On March 8, 1862, the *Merrimack* sank several Union ships near Newport News, Virginia. The next day a Union ironclad, the *Monitor*, challenged the *Merrimack*, but neither ship won. In North Carolina the Confederate navy built an ironclad, the CSS *Neuse*. That ship is now part of a historical site in Kinston.

A CLOSER LOOK
The Ironclad *Neuse*

During the Civil War, both the Union and the Confederacy built ironclads—wooden ships covered with metal plates. The Confederacy built 22 ironclads during the war. One of them was the CSS *Neuse*.

1 The frame of the *Neuse* was made of yellow pine and covered with iron plates 4 inches (10 cm) thick. The ship was 152 feet (46 m) long and 34 feet (10 m) wide.

2 The ship's guns could be fired through gun ports. The gun ports were high to allow the people firing the guns a clearer view.

3 The engine ran on steam that was produced by burning coal to heat water in a boiler.

❓ Why do you think the builders covered the ship with iron?

Remains of CSS *Neuse*

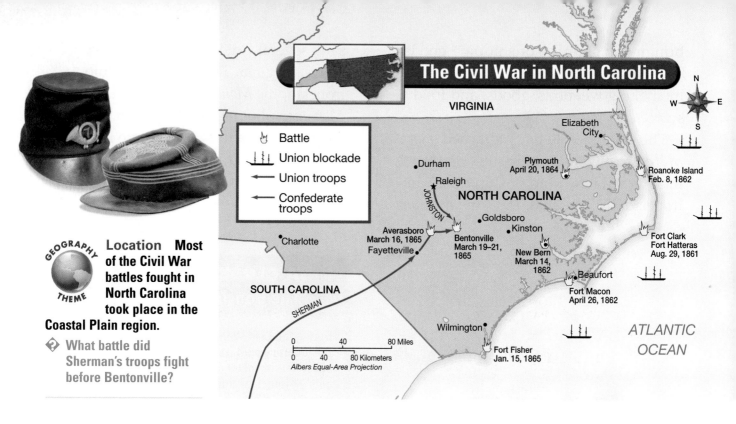

The Civil War in North Carolina

VIRGINIA

NORTH CAROLINA

SOUTH CAROLINA

ATLANTIC OCEAN

Battle
Union blockade
Union troops
Confederate troops

- Durham
- Raleigh
- Plymouth April 20, 1864
- Roanoke Island Feb. 8, 1862
- Charlotte
- Averasboro March 16, 1865
- Fayetteville
- Goldsboro
- Kinston
- Bentonville March 19–21, 1865
- New Bern March 14, 1862
- Fort Clark Fort Hatteras Aug. 29, 1861
- Beaufort
- Fort Macon April 26, 1862
- JOHNSTON
- SHERMAN
- Wilmington
- Fort Fisher Jan. 15, 1865
- Elizabeth City

0 40 80 Miles
0 40 80 Kilometers
Albers Equal-Area Projection

GEOGRAPHY THEME

Location Most of the Civil War battles fought in North Carolina took place in the Coastal Plain region.

◆ What battle did Sherman's troops fight before Bentonville?

Union forces soon gained control of most of eastern North Carolina. By 1865 the Confederacy was losing the war. Union general William T. Sherman and his troops had marched through the Confederacy, destroying houses and crops. In March 1865 Sherman's troops headed for Goldsboro, North Carolina.

At Bentonville in Johnston County, General Sherman's soldiers faced a surprise attack from Confederate troops led by General Joseph Johnston. It was the largest Civil War battle fought in North Carolina.

By April 1865 Confederate general Robert E. Lee's army was weak and exhausted. He surrendered to Union general Ulysses S. Grant on April 9, 1865. On April 26, 1865, General Johnston surrendered to General Sherman at James Bennett's farmhouse near Durham. Johnston's surrender at Bennett Place was the largest of the war.

REVIEW What was the largest battle of the Civil War fought in North Carolina?

Reconstruction

In January 1863 President Lincoln signed the **Emancipation Proclamation**, a document that freed the enslaved people in the Southern states. When the Civil War ended, the period known as Reconstruction began. The United States government directed the Southern states to **reconstruct**, or rebuild, their governments.

The years after the Civil War were hard for everyone in the South, especially for freed African Americans. When the war ended, the Thirteenth Amendment outlawed slavery. An **amendment** is a change to the Constitution. Most former slaves owned no land, and had no education. Many former slaves returned to farming and worked as sharecroppers. A **sharecropper** is a person who rents land, farms it, and pays the landowner a share, or part, of the crops.

The federal government created the **Freedmen's Bureau**, a group that helped freed African Americans by providing food, clothing, and education. Many religious groups from the North also opened schools in North Carolina. One successful school was the Palmer Institute in Sedalia, started by Charlotte Hawkins Brown in 1902.

After the war Southern states passed Black Codes. These laws took away African Americans' rights. In response, the United States Congress passed the Fourteenth Amendment in 1868 which made African Americans citizens of the United States. Every citizen was to be treated equally. In 1870 the Fifteenth Amendment gave the right to vote to African American male citizens throughout the United States.

Some white Southerners were angry at the changes Reconstruction brought. They did not like the changes to their governments. Throughout the South, new state legislatures looked for ways to take away the rights and freedoms of African Americans. One way they did this was by

After the Civil War, many African Americans voted for the first time.

passing segregation laws. **Segregation** is the practice of keeping people apart based on their race or culture.

Segregation took place in most public places, including schools. Some people challenged segregation laws in the courts. At that time, however, judges ruled segregation was legal as long as groups were treated equally.

REVIEW What challenges did African Americans face after the Civil War?

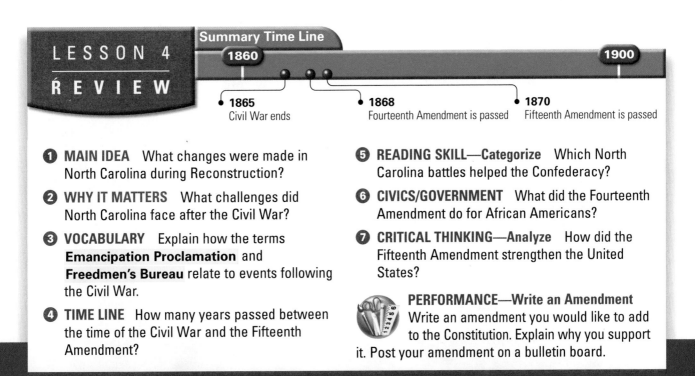

LESSON 4

REVIEW

Summary Time Line

1860 — 1900

1865
Civil War ends

1868
Fourteenth Amendment is passed

1870
Fifteenth Amendment is passed

1. **MAIN IDEA** What changes were made in North Carolina during Reconstruction?

2. **WHY IT MATTERS** What challenges did North Carolina face after the Civil War?

3. **VOCABULARY** Explain how the terms **Emancipation Proclamation** and **Freedmen's Bureau** relate to events following the Civil War.

4. **TIME LINE** How many years passed between the time of the Civil War and the Fifteenth Amendment?

5. **READING SKILL—Categorize** Which North Carolina battles helped the Confederacy?

6. **CIVICS/GOVERNMENT** What did the Fourteenth Amendment do for African Americans?

7. **CRITICAL THINKING—Analyze** How did the Fifteenth Amendment strengthen the United States?

PERFORMANCE—Write an Amendment Write an amendment you would like to add to the Constitution. Explain why you support it. Post your amendment on a bulletin board.

MAIN IDEA
Read to discover how the growth of industries changed North Carolina.

WHY IT MATTERS
The textile, tobacco, and furniture industries changed the economy of North Carolina.

VOCABULARY
free enterprise
entrepreneur
profit
human resources
capital resources

Growth and Industry

1700	1800	1900

1815–1900

Free enterprise was changing the Piedmont. **Free enterprise** is the economic system in which people are free to start and run their own businesses. For example, in 1871 William Henry Snow moved from Vermont to High Point, North Carolina. There he helped build the state's furniture industry. By the early 1900s more than 200,000 North Carolinians had left farms to find new ways to earn a living. Many of these people found jobs in the textile, tobacco, and furniture industries.

The late 1800s and early 1900s were a time of growth and change in North Carolina. North Carolina entrepreneurs (AHN•truh•pruh•NERZ) saw ways to earn more money. An **entrepreneur** is a person who starts and runs a new business or finds better ways of doing things.

THE FIRST COTTON MILL IN NORTH CAROLINA.

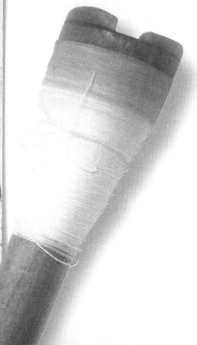

This drawing shows Michael Schenck's first cotton mill. Water from the river turned the wheel, which powered the mill's machines. Below is a bobbin used to wind yarn or thread.

Tobacco farming and processing have been important industries in North Carolina for hundreds of years.

The Textile Industry

More than 40 years before the Civil War, the textile industry began in the Piedmont. Textiles are cloth. In 1816 Michael Schenck arrived from Pennsylvania. That year Schenck built North Carolina's first waterpowered textile mill beside a fast-moving stream near Lincolnton.

Waterpower was needed to drive the machinery of the textile mills. The textile industry grew slowly because mills had to be built near rivers and streams. By the time of the Civil War, Gastonia, on the Catawba River, had become a textile center.

In 1898 James W. Cannon developed a way to make cloth for towels. Over time, Cannon Mills in Kannapolis became one of the largest makers of towels in the world.

In 1891 the Cone brothers established Cone Mills in Greensboro. It became especially well known for denim, a sturdy blue cloth used to make overalls and jeans.

Factory workers in cities no longer had time to make their own cloth or clothing. They eagerly bought the cloth produced in the mills of the South.

Early in the 1900s mills began to use electricity, and the textile industry grew rapidly. New railway lines made it easier and cheaper to ship cloth goods to the North and to the South. These changes helped North Carolina's businesses make a profit. A **profit** is the money left over after all costs have been paid. By the early 1900s textile production had become one of the state's top industries.

REVIEW What helped the textile industry develop in the Piedmont?

The Tobacco Industry

Before the Civil War many small factories in North Carolina produced chewing and smoking tobacco. Union troops liked the taste. They created a demand for this kind of tobacco outside North Carolina.

Early tobacco advertisement

Chapter 5 ▪ 177

Thomas Day   1801–1861

Character Trait: Inventiveness

Even as a young child, Thomas Day had a knack for making furniture. According to one story, he saw a piece of furniture in the house of some family friends—and then made an exact copy of it. When Day was 22 years old, he moved to Milton in Caswell County. Within four years he had saved enough money to open his own shop.

Thomas Day was a free African American, but people who worked for him came from many backgrounds. For almost 40 years Day ran a very successful business. He made furniture for government officials and wealthy citizens. People still admire Thomas Day's fine furniture. Some of the furniture is still used. Other pieces are in museums.

MULTIMEDIA BIOGRAPHIES
Visit The Learning Site at www.harcourtschool.com/ **biographies** to learn about other famous people.

THOMAS DAY, CABINET MAKER

When the Civil War ended, Washington Duke began selling the tobacco grown on his farm throughout eastern North Carolina.

A kind of tobacco known as bright leaf sold so well that in 1870 the Duke family built a tobacco factory in Durham. In the 1880s one of Washington Duke's sons, James Buchanan Duke, bought a machine that cut in half the cost of making his product. His company became very successful. Duke used much of his money to support schools, hospitals, and churches in North Carolina.

REVIEW How did James Buchanan Duke improve his family business?

The Furniture Industry

Before the Civil War one of the best-known furniture makers in North Carolina was Thomas Day. He was a free African American who lived in Milton.

Day's cabinets and other fine creations were beautiful. However, they were costly because they were made by hand. Furniture making was not a major industry in North Carolina until workers began using machines. In 1881 two brothers, David and William White, opened a factory in Mebane.

Seven years later, the first large furniture factory in North Carolina was built in High Point. It was a good place for making furniture because forests and sawmills were nearby. Also, the state's first east-west railroad passed through High Point.

A group of entrepreneurs that included William Henry Snow understood that costs could be kept low by using nearby lumber to make furniture. Before this time, wood had been used mostly for building and heating. To succeed in High Point, the furniture business needed **human resources**, or workers, to make

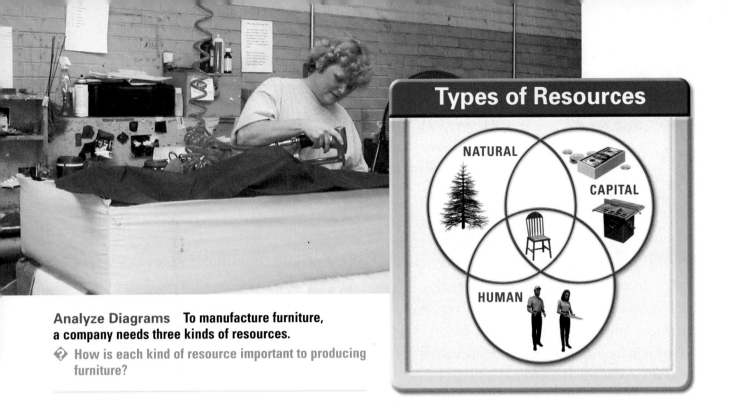

Analyze Diagrams To manufacture furniture, a company needs three kinds of resources.

◈ How is each kind of resource important to producing furniture?

Types of Resources

NATURAL

CAPITAL

HUMAN

the products. Many former tobacco farmers were hired to make the furniture. Business leaders used their own money to make the business grow. They provided the capital resources for the furniture factories. **Capital resources** are the money, buildings, machines, and tools needed to run a business. By 1910 other towns in the northern Piedmont were also building furniture factories.

REVIEW What helped make High Point the furniture industry center of North Carolina?

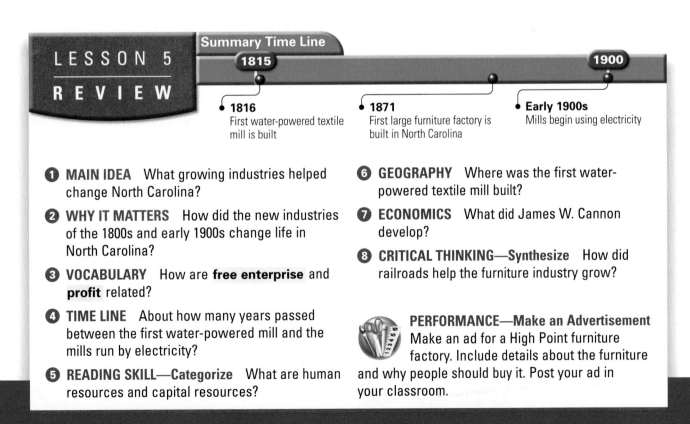

LESSON 5 REVIEW

Summary Time Line

1815 — 1900

• **1816** First water-powered textile mill is built

• **1871** First large furniture factory is built in North Carolina

• **Early 1900s** Mills begin using electricity

❶ **MAIN IDEA** What growing industries helped change North Carolina?

❷ **WHY IT MATTERS** How did the new industries of the 1800s and early 1900s change life in North Carolina?

❸ **VOCABULARY** How are **free enterprise** and **profit** related?

❹ **TIME LINE** About how many years passed between the first water-powered mill and the mills run by electricity?

❺ **READING SKILL—Categorize** What are human resources and capital resources?

❻ **GEOGRAPHY** Where was the first water-powered textile mill built?

❼ **ECONOMICS** What did James W. Cannon develop?

❽ **CRITICAL THINKING—Synthesize** How did railroads help the furniture industry grow?

PERFORMANCE—Make an Advertisement Make an ad for a High Point furniture factory. Include details about the furniture and why people should buy it. Post your ad in your classroom.

CHART AND GRAPH

Read a Cutaway Diagram

VOCABULARY

cross-section
cutaway diagram

▶ WHY IT MATTERS

If you look closely at the stump of a tree, you can see circles, or rings, on the surface. The rings are layers of wood. The layers of wood look like rings because you are looking at a cross-section of the tree. A **cross-section** is a slice or piece cut straight across something.

The drawing shown on page 185 is a cutaway diagram of an early textile mill. A **cutaway diagram** shows the cross-section of an object or a building. A cutaway diagram can help you understand how something works. This drawing shows the machines in the mill and how cloth was made.

▶ WHAT YOU NEED TO KNOW

The main mill building had several floors. Different machines were on each level. The cotton was delivered to the factory from the fields. It left the factory as finished cloth.

▶ PRACTICE THE SKILL

1 Water Wheel: Water from a stream turned a wheel that ran the machines.

2 Carding Machines: Raw cotton was fed into these machines. The machines combed the cotton into thick strands. Why were the carding machines on the first floor?

3 Drawing Frames: The strands were pulled, or drawn, and twisted loosely.

4 Spinning Machines: The drawn strands were spun to make them thin and tight. This process made them into yarn. Which machines were closest to the spinning machines?

5 Dressing Frame: Why do you think the yarn was stiffened, or dressed?

6 Warper: The yarn was wound onto spools called warps. Where did the cotton go next?

7 Looms: Looms wove the yarn from the warps into finished cloth. Why do you think the looms were on the top floor?

▶ APPLY WHAT YOU LEARNED

Make a cutaway diagram of a building. It might be your house, your school, or another building. Use books, the Internet, or other resources to help if you need them. Explain your diagram and what it shows.

A Textile Mill

CHART AND GRAPH SKILLS

· CHAPTER ·

5 Review and Test Preparation

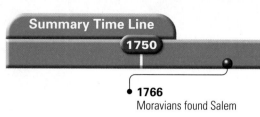
USE YOUR READING SKILLS

Complete this graphic organizer to show how the Piedmont region changed before, during, and after the Civil War. A copy of this graphic organizer appears on page 56 of the Activity Book.

PEOPLE

GOVERNMENT

THE PIEDMONT REGION LONG AGO

TRANSPORTATION

INDUSTRIES

THINK & WRITE

Write a Brochure Suppose that you are starting a school in the Piedmont in the 1840s. Write a pamphlet about your school. Describe what it will teach. Explain why it is important for children to go to school. Try to convince other citizens that the government should pay for the school.

Write an Editorial Imagine that you are living in North Carolina just before the Civil War. Write an editorial for a local newspaper about seceding from the United States. Give your opinions on the issues. Use facts to justify your opinions. Try to get other people to agree with your views.

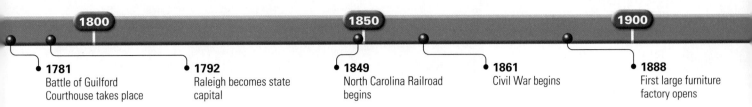

1781
Battle of Guilford
Courthouse takes place

1792
Raleigh becomes state
capital

1849
North Carolina Railroad
begins

1861
Civil War begins

1888
First large furniture
factory opens

USE THE TIME LINE

Use the chapter summary time line to answer these questions.

1 When did the Civil War begin?

2 Which happened first, the founding of Salem or the Battle of Guilford Courthouse?

USE VOCABULARY

3 Use these words to write a paragraph about changes in North Carolina's economy during the 1800s.

manufacturing (p. 163)

sharecropper (p. 174)

entrepreneur (p. 176)

profit (p. 177)

4 Use these words to write a paragraph about the Piedmont's history.

backcountry (p. 156)

capital (p. 162)

toll road (p. 164)

slave state (p. 167)

reconstruct (p. 174)

RECALL FACTS

Answer these questions.

5 Who first suggested that North Carolina should improve its roads?

6 Where did the largest Civil War battle in North Carolina take place?

7 What did Michael Schenck build in 1816?

Write the letter of the best choice.

8 **TEST PREP** The Moravians came to North Carolina to—

A find political freedom.

B start a religious community.

C escape from war.

D start new factories.

9 **TEST PREP** Furniture making became a major industry when—

F the Revolutionary War ended.

G Thomas Day began selling cabinets.

H workers began using machines to make furniture.

J the city of Raleigh was built.

THINK CRITICALLY

10 Why did backcountry settlers have to be self-sufficient?

11 Why was it important to develop new kinds of transportation?

APPLY SKILLS

Make a Thoughtful Decision

12 Suppose that you lived in the Coastal Plain region in the 1760s. Decide whether to stay there or move to the Piedmont. List the consequences of each choice before you decide.

Read a Cutaway Diagram
Use the diagram on page 181 to answer the questions.

13 How were the machines connected to the water wheel?

14 Which machines were on the top floor?

Chapter 5 ■ **183**

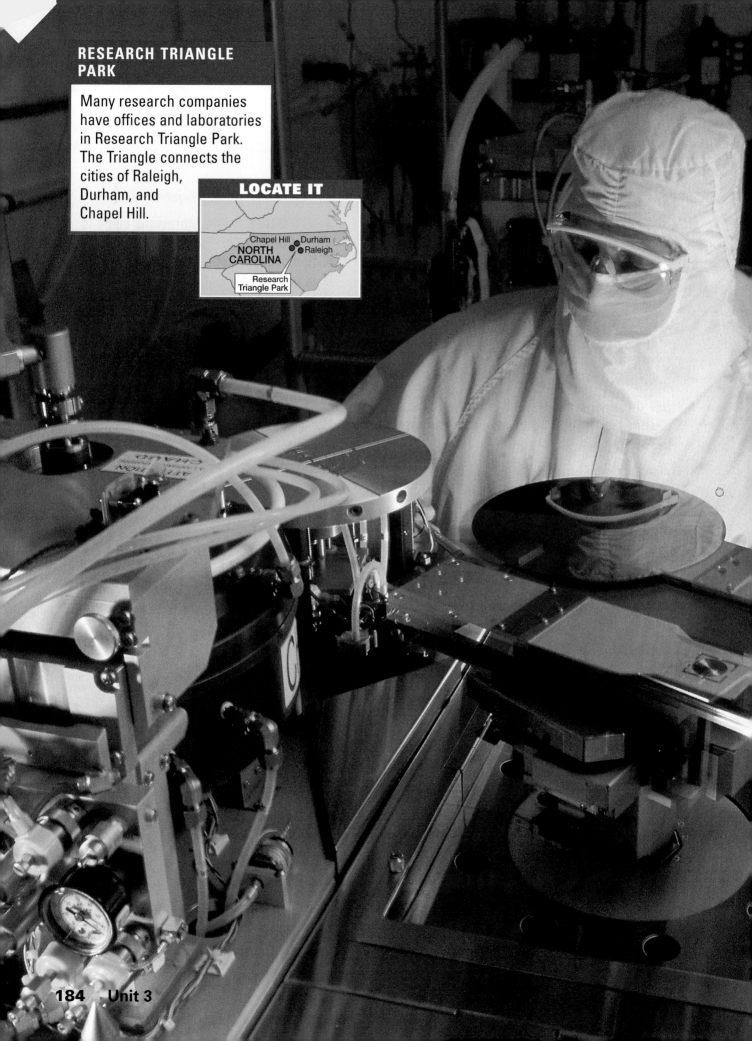

RESEARCH TRIANGLE PARK

Many research companies have offices and laboratories in Research Triangle Park. The Triangle connects the cities of Raleigh, Durham, and Chapel Hill.

LOCATE IT

Chapel Hill • • Durham
NORTH • Raleigh
CAROLINA
Research Triangle Park

6

The Piedmont Region Today

" Where there is research, there is industry. "

—Governor Luther Hodges, *Businessman in the Statehouse*, 1962

CHAPTER READING SKILL

Generalize

When you **generalize,** you make a broad statement about what you have read. The generalization is based on the facts and details you read. Words such as *many, some, most,* and *usually* signal a possible generalization.

As you read, use facts and details from each lesson to write generalizations.

FACTS GENERALIZATION

The Piedmont Urban Crescent

The Piedmont is the most heavily populated region of North Carolina. The region has almost all the state's large cities and much of its industry. Of the state's ten largest cities, seven are in the Piedmont—Charlotte, Raleigh, Greensboro, Durham, Winston-Salem, Cary, and High Point. Most of these cities, along with towns around them, form a 140-mile (225-km) curve-shaped region called the Piedmont Urban Crescent.

Greater Charlotte

With more than half a million people, Charlotte is the central city in the Piedmont's largest urban area. An **urban** area is the city and the surrounding area. The greater Charlotte metropolitan area, sometimes called Metrolina, covers counties in both North Carolina and South Carolina. A **metropolitan area** is a large city and its suburbs. A **suburb** is a town or small city near a large city.

FAST FACT Six cities in North Carolina have more than 100,000 people each. Five of them are in the Piedmont: Charlotte, Durham, Greensboro, Raleigh, and Winston-Salem. Only Fayetteville is outside the Piedmont.

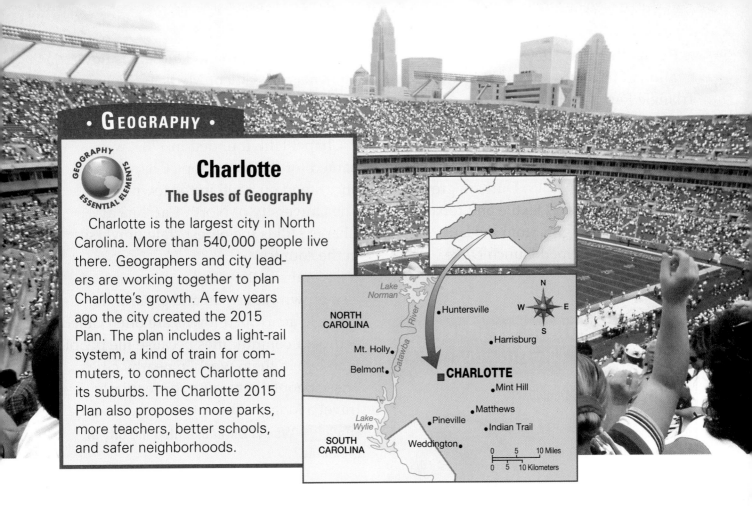

GEOGRAPHY ESSENTIAL ELEMENTS

Charlotte
The Uses of Geography

Charlotte is the largest city in North Carolina. More than 540,000 people live there. Geographers and city leaders are working together to plan Charlotte's growth. A few years ago the city created the 2015 Plan. The plan includes a light-rail system, a kind of train for commuters, to connect Charlotte and its suburbs. The Charlotte 2015 Plan also proposes more parks, more teachers, better schools, and safer neighborhoods.

Charlotte's first settlers were Scotch-Irish families who traveled south on the Great Wagon Road from Pennsylvania. In 1799 young Conrad Reed discovered a gold nugget in nearby Cabarrus County. For the next 50 years, Charlotte was a gold-mining center.

Charlotte's growth ended in 1849 when gold was discovered in California. The city grew again after the Civil War, when textile mills sprang up in the area. By 1920 more than 300 textile mills had been built. The mills attracted thousands of job seekers to the greater Charlotte area.

Charlotte grew even more rapidly after railroad lines were built. Charlotte merchants and mill owners brought cotton and other crops by rail from as far away as Mississippi and Alabama.

In the 1950s the city became a **hub**, or center, for the trucking industry when the federal government built two major interstate highways through Charlotte. Charlotte's airport is a major hub for air traffic as well. These highway and airline connections have helped make Charlotte a transportation hub for the southeastern United States.

REVIEW How did Charlotte become an urban center?

The Piedmont Triangle

The part of North Carolina called the Research Triangle is another large urban area in the Piedmont. The main cities that make up the Triangle are Raleigh, Durham, and Chapel Hill.

Raleigh was built in 1792 as the state capital and grew slowly until the late 1950s. Then business and government leaders created the Research Triangle Park, a center for research and technology.

Chapter 6 ■ 187

Research is the careful study or investigation of information. The Research Triangle Park attracted scientists and researchers from all over the world. This helped Raleigh become the state's second-largest city by the early 1990s.

Founded in the 1850s, Durham grew mainly because of its textile and tobacco industries. Large gifts from the Duke family fortune helped launch Duke

University in Durham. Durham is now known as the City of Medicine. People from all over the United States travel to Durham's hospitals for medical care.

Chapel Hill, founded in 1789, was named for the New Hope Chapel that once stood on a hill in the town center. The University of North Carolina at Chapel Hill is the oldest state university in the country.

Several smaller cities and towns have also grown rapidly in and around the Triangle area. Such towns are often called bedroom communities because the people who live in them work in nearby cities. These people **commute**, or regularly travel a long distance, to and from work.

REVIEW Why is Durham called the City of Medicine?

The Triad

The Triad (TRY•ad) is an area made up of three large cities and many smaller cities and towns in a 12-county area. *Triad* means "group of three." The Triad's three large cities are Greensboro, Winston-Salem,

POINTS OF VIEW
City Growth

KIKI DUNTON, lawyer

"As cities grow, houses, stores, and shopping malls eat up open spaces, increase traffic, and cause air and water pollution. We should set aside special open spaces."

MICHAEL SANDMAN, real estate developer

"Build up instead of out. An eight-story building with underground parking lots, restaurants and stores on the first floor, and offices and apartments on the floors above still leaves room for open space all around it."

Analyze the Viewpoints

1. How do Kiki Dunton and Michael Sandman think cities should provide open space?
2. What are some other views people might have about how cities should grow?

and High Point. Today Greensboro is the third-largest city in the state. Its economy first took off in the early 1890s. At that time the Cone brothers created the Cone Mills textile company. Greensboro has also thrived because of its many fine colleges and universities.

The Moravians founded the town of Salem in 1766. As it grew, Salem became the home of several textile mills. Much later, in 1849, the town of Winston grew up nearby. In 1874 Joshua Reynolds built a tobacco company that provided hundreds of jobs in the city. In 1913 Winston and Salem joined and earned the nickname Twin City.

Today Winston-Salem's excellent hospitals have made it a medical center. It also has several colleges, including Wake Forest University, Winston-Salem State University, and Salem College.

High Point grew because of its furniture industry. Today more than half of all furniture made in the United States is manufactured within 200 miles (322 km) of High Point. High Point has the nation's largest furniture market.

REVIEW Which industries helped Greensboro, Winston-Salem, and High Point grow?

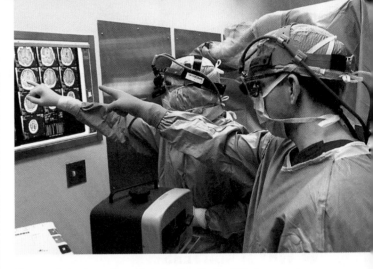

Some of the best hospitals in the United States are in the Research Triangle area.

LESSON 1 REVIEW

❶ **MAIN IDEA** What are the three major urban areas in the Piedmont?

❷ **WHY IT MATTERS** What are some important industries in the Piedmont Urban Crescent?

❸ **VOCABULARY** Use the words **suburb** and **commute** to describe life in the Piedmont.

❹ **READING SKILL—Generalize** What features do the three urban areas of the Piedmont have in common?

❺ **ECONOMICS** What makes Charlotte a transportation hub?

❻ **HISTORY** What event helped Greensboro's economy grow?

❼ **CRITICAL THINKING—Hypothesize** Why do you think some people choose to live in small towns and work in large cities?

PERFORMANCE—Design a Booklet Choose one Piedmont urban area. Read more about it. Design a booklet for people who want to move to that area. Include details about the area's industries, transportation, and important events.

189

·SKILLS·

MAP AND GLOBE

Read a Population Map

➡ **WHY IT MATTERS**

Think about where you live. Do many people live near you? If you live in a city, your neighboorhood may be full of people. If you live on a farm, there may be very few people nearby. A **population map** can show you how many people live in a certain area. Knowing how to read a population map can help you find out which places have few people and which places have many people.

A population map can help you find large cities. It can also show you country areas where few people live. North Carolina has country areas, cities, and everything in between.

➡ **WHAT YOU NEED TO KNOW**

Crowded and less-crowded areas have different population densities. **Population density** measures how many people live in an area of a certain size. The size is usually one square mile or one square kilometer. A square mile is a square piece of land. Each of its four sides is a mile long. A square kilometer is a square piece of land with sides that are each one kilometer long.

The map on page 191 shows the population density of North Carolina. Look at the map key. Each color stands for a different population density. Areas with the highest population density are red. Areas with the lowest population density are yellow.

Some parts of North Carolina are crowded. Other parts have very few people.

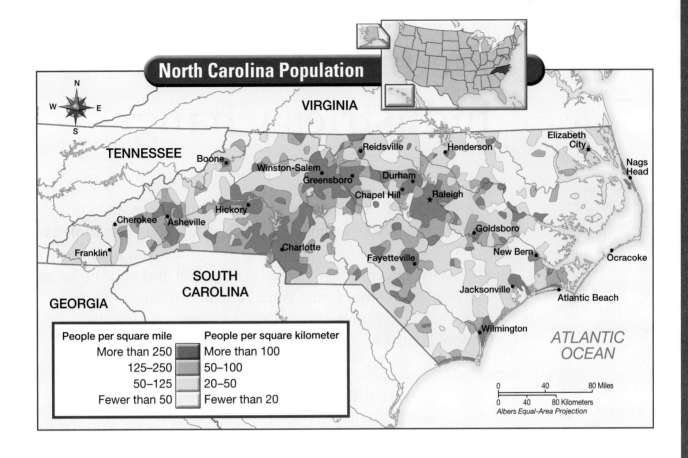

North Carolina Population

▶ PRACTICE THE SKILL

Use the North Carolina population map to answer these questions.

1. Find the map key. What population density is shown by red? What population density is shown by yellow?

2. What do you notice about the red areas? Are they near cities or far away from them?

3. Overall, is the population density higher around Fayetteville or around Boone? How can you tell?

4. Is the population density higher in the Piedmont area or near the coast? How can you tell?

▶ APPLY WHAT YOU LEARNED

Find a recent population map of the United States in an encyclopedia or an atlas. In which parts of the United States is the population density the highest? In which parts is it the lowest? Is North Carolina's population density higher or lower than that of Nevada? Is it higher or lower than that of Massachusetts?

Practice your map and globe skills with the **GeoSkills CD-ROM**.

MAIN IDEA
Read to learn about changes in manufacturing and technology in the Piedmont region.

WHY IT MATTERS
Changes in the Piedmont's industries have directly affected the way people live and work there.

VOCABULARY
technology
automate
synthetic fibers
diversify
service worker
innovation

Piedmont Industries Change

In the late 1950s Governor Luther Hodges wanted to bring high-paying jobs in technology to North Carolina. **Technology** is the way people use new ideas to make tools and machines. In 1962 the governor announced, "The heart and hope of North Carolina's industrial future is the Research Triangle." Today more than 50,000 people work in the research center that Hodges helped create.

Traditional Industries Change

Many Tar Heels in the Piedmont earn their living working in manufacturing jobs. Manufacturing provides more jobs for Tar Heels than any other field. Today, however, the products made

Textile manufacturing is one of the most important industries in the Piedmont. This worker is checking spools of thread before the thread is made into cloth.

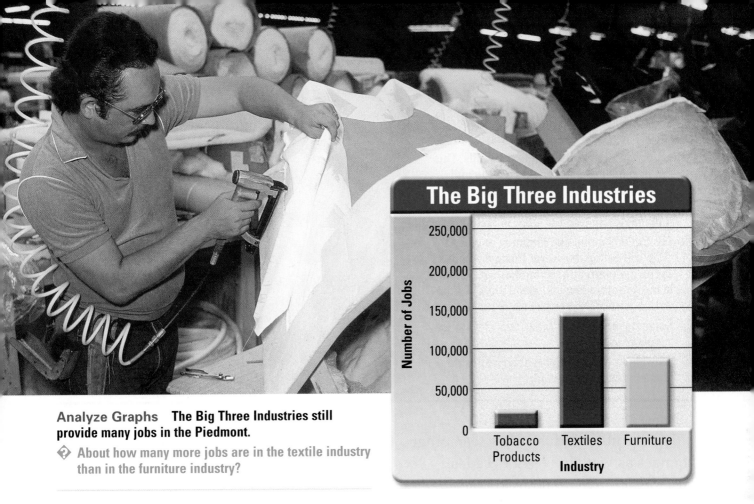

The Big Three Industries

Number of Jobs

- 250,000
- 200,000
- 150,000
- 100,000
- 50,000
- 0

Tobacco Products — Textiles — Furniture

Industry

Analyze Graphs The Big Three Industries still provide many jobs in the Piedmont.

❖ About how many more jobs are in the textile industry than in the furniture industry?

in the Piedmont are much more varied than they were in the past. One-third of factory workers have jobs in one of the Big Three industries—textiles, tobacco, and furniture. Other workers make a variety of other products, including chemicals, tires, machinery, trucks, and buses.

The number of jobs in the state's Big Three industries began to drop in the 1970s. At that time many companies, especially in the textile business, became more **automated**. This means that machines now did many of the jobs once handled by people.

Changes also took place in the materials used to make cloth. Many textiles are still made from cotton. However, some textiles are made from synthetic fibers. **Synthetic fibers** are made by people and not from plants or animal hairs.

Textile and clothing manufacturing are still leading industries in North Carolina. However, they provide fewer jobs than they did in the past.

The state's tobacco industry also has changed. Tobacco factories have become larger and more automated. Greater awareness of the dangers of smoking has reduced demand for tobacco products in the United States.

Some tobacco companies have recently diversified. To **diversify** is to increase the variety of people, places, and things. These companies are producing a greater variety of goods, such as food products.

The furniture industry has also become more automated. Workers now use computers to design furniture instead of creating it entirely by hand. Computer-controlled tools cut the wood to the exact sizes and shapes needed.

Analyze Primary Sources

Textile making has been an important industry in the Piedmont for many years. This photograph from 1908 shows the Loray Mill in Gastonia.

1 Young children worked in textile mills. This girl may have started working in the mill when she was only five or six years old. Later the government passed laws making it illegal for children to work in factories.

2 The threads going one direction in woven cloth are called the warp. These machines set up the warp threads for the loom. At the loom other threads, called the weft, will be woven across the warp to make cloth.

3 Spinning machines turned cotton into these spools of yarn.

❖ Why might a factory have been an unsafe place for children to work?

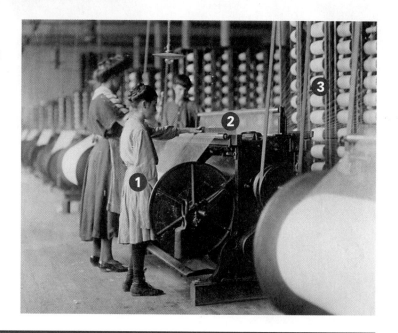

The furniture industry has seen other changes as well. In recent decades Americans have been buying more furniture imported from other countries. The cost of lumber has also gone up. As in the textile industry, the number of people working in the furniture industry has dropped.

REVIEW How have the textile, tobacco, and furniture industries changed?

Service Industries

The number of service jobs in North Carolina is growing, especially in the Piedmont.

Service workers do not make or sell products. **Service workers** do jobs or activities for others for pay. Service workers include teachers, bankers, government employees, and truck drivers.

One important kind of service in the Piedmont is research. Research jobs in laboratories and offices often result in new products and innovations. **Innovations** are new or better ways of doing things.

Other service jobs in North Carolina are in state government. Government workers provide many important services. They oversee the state's public schools, hospitals, highways, and parks. They take care of public health issues and work to protect the state's natural resources.

Train service and other forms of transportation provide many jobs for North Carolinians.

People who work in banking, tourism, teaching, and other fields have service jobs.

At every hour of the day and night, trucks cross the state to distant markets carrying products made in North Carolina. Most of the state's textile and clothing manufacturers ship their products by truck. Trucks deliver furniture and tobacco products as well.

Good airline connections are important to the success of many Piedmont businesses. The state's busiest airport is Charlotte-Douglas International Airport.

Trains connect the state with places all along the Atlantic Coast. Trains carry heavy cargo such as coal, paper, and lumber and also provide passenger service to points in the North and the South.

Innovations in communication are changing the way people in North Carolina live and work. North Carolina has a good "information highway" or set of communication links. Some Tar Heels are telecommuters, who work at home and communicate with their offices by e-mail, fax, and the Internet.

REVIEW How have service jobs contributed to North Carolina's economy?

LESSON 2
REVIEW

1 MAIN IDEA How has technology changed the way people work in the Piedmont?

2 WHY IT MATTERS How do service jobs in North Carolina help you in your daily life?

3 VOCABULARY Define **diversify** and **innovation**.

4 READING SKILL—Generalize Why is transportation important to the economy of the Piedmont?

5 CIVICS/GOVERNMENT What services do government workers provide?

6 ECONOMICS What are the Big Three industries?

7 CRITICAL THINKING—Evaluate Which industry would you most want to work in? Why?

PERFORMANCE—Write a Job Description Imagine that you work for a North Carolina business that is looking for new workers. Write a job description for one job. Include all the things the worker must know and do.

Dolley Madison

Dolley Payne was born on May 20, 1768, in what is now Greensboro. In 1790 she married a Philadelphia lawyer named John Todd, who died in 1793, when yellow fever struck Philadelphia. A widow at age 25, Dolley Payne Todd married James Madison, a representative in the United States Congress, in 1794. James Madison became President of the United States in 1809, and Dolley became First Lady. She is the only First Lady from North Carolina.

 FROM THE GREENSBORO HISTORICAL MUSEUM, GREENSBORO, NORTH CAROLINA

Engraved print (above) of Friends Meeting House in North Carolina kept by Dolley Madison. Daguerreotype portrait (left) of Dolley Madison in 1848 taken one year before her death. A daguerreotype is a photograph-like image on a piece of silver-plated copper.

Analyze the Primary Source

① What differences do you see between the portrait of Dolley Madison and the daguerreotype?

② Examine Dolley Madison's personal items. What do they tell you about her?

Silk velvet ball gown worn by Dolley Madison as First Lady.

Carved ivory calling-card case

ACTIVITY

Research a First Lady Select one First Lady to research for a presentation. Gather information about the time in which she was First Lady and her contributions to the country. Locate pictures of personal artifacts that can provide you with additional information about her life. Present your findings to the class.

RESEARCH

Visit The Learning Site at **www.harcourtschool.com/ primarysources** to research other primary sources.

Read a Line Graph

▶ WHY IT MATTERS

In the last 50 years, new industries have brought many people to North Carolina. The population of the state has grown. This growth is easier to understand when you see it on a line graph. A **line graph** is a kind of graph that shows changes over a period of time.

▶ WHAT YOU NEED TO KNOW

The line graph on page 199 shows how the population changed in North Carolina between 1950 and 2000. The numbers along the left side of the graph show the number of people. The numbers across the bottom of the graph show the years 1950 through 2000. The graph has one dot for every ten years. Each dot shows the population of North Carolina in one of those years. The line connects the dots to show the change in North Carolina's population.

1 Find 1950 on the bottom of the line graph. Move your finger up from 1950 until you reach the dot. Then move your finger to the left. Look at the closest number. Slightly more than 4,000,000 people lived in North Carolina in 1950. This number is an **estimate**, a close guess, of the population.

2 Now, find 1960 at the bottom of the graph. Repeat the process. About how many people lived in North Carolina in 1960?

As North Carolina's population grows, more people take part in community activities.

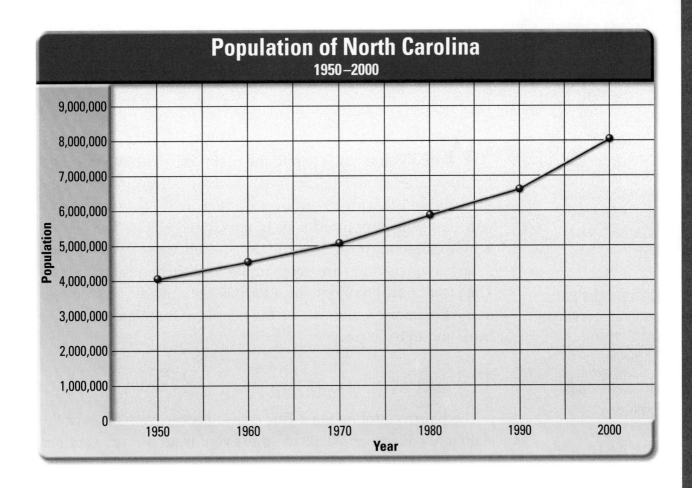

Population of North Carolina
1950–2000

(Line graph. Y-axis: Population, from 0 to 9,000,000 in increments of 1,000,000. X-axis: Year, 1950, 1960, 1970, 1980, 1990, 2000.)

▶ **PRACTICE THE SKILL**

Study the line graph titled *Population of North Carolina*. Then use the graph to answer these questions.

1 What was the population of North Carolina in 1970?

2 In which ten-year period did the population change the most?

3 About how much did the population grow between 1950 and 1960?

4 About how many more people lived in North Carolina in 2000 than in 1950?

▶ **APPLY WHAT YOU LEARNED**

Choose a North Carolina city that you would like to research. Gather population figures for that city since 1950 from your library or from other sources. Create a line graph showing how the population of that city has changed since 1950. Study the information shown on your graph. In what ten-year period did the population of the city you chose change the most? Explain how you know this.

3

MAIN IDEA
Read to learn about exciting and interesting things to do in North Carolina's Piedmont region.

WHY IT MATTERS
By participating in the Piedmont region's activities and attractions, people can learn about North Carolina's diversity and heritage.

VOCABULARY
professional team
living museum
pottery

Life in the Piedmont

Would you enjoy a trip to the plains of Africa, where gorillas, giraffes, and zebras live? The North Carolina Zoological Park, spread out over more than 500 acres, is one of only two state-supported zoos in the United States. The other is in Minnesota. At the North Carolina Zoo, most animals live in environments that are very similar to their natural habitats. The North Carolina Zoological Park is just one of many places in the Piedmont region where the people of our state go to learn and to have fun.

Piedmont Activities

The North Carolina State Fair draws people from all over the state to the Piedmont. This ten-day event is held every October in Raleigh. One of the largest state fairs in the United States, it attracts more than 700,000 visitors each year. Some want to

LOCATE IT

NORTH CAROLINA

University of North Carolina, Charlotte

Students at the University of North Carolina at Charlotte perform Asian dances at an international festival.

ride the roller coaster or sample the popcorn. Others like the cooking contests, flower and garden shows, and livestock exhibits and competitions. The fair began in 1853 as a way for farmers to get together to show off their best crops, livestock, and farm machinery.

Throughout the year people in the Piedmont find ways to celebrate their diversity. The Fiesta del Pueblo takes place in September in Chapel Hill. The fiesta brings together 40,000 people who celebrate Latin American art, music, and traditions.

Many cities in North Carolina have international festivals. Both Charlotte and Raleigh have yearly events where people share their customs and traditions. In Raleigh people crowd into the downtown convention center to watch folk dances and to sample foods from other nations. At the University of North Carolina at Charlotte, international students perform music and dance and display arts and crafts from more than 50 countries. These festivals honor the many different groups that call North Carolina home.

College basketball is serious business for North Carolina's sports fans. Tar Heels enjoy rooting for one of the sixteen teams of the state university system. Fans cheer for teams from the University of North Carolina, Duke University, Wake Forest University, and other schools.

North Carolinians also enjoy professional sports. The Carolina Panthers are the state's professional football team.

People enjoy the rides at the North Carolina State Fair.

A **professional team** is made up of players who are paid for playing a sport. North Carolina's professional hockey team is the Carolina Hurricanes. The Wilmington Hammerheads is the professional soccer team.

NASCAR, the National Association of Stock Car Racing, sponsors a popular sport. Each year several races are held in the North Carolina Speedway in Rockingham. Thousands of spectators crowd the stands to watch drivers speed cars around the 1.017-mile (1,637-km) oval track.

REVIEW How do the people of the Piedmont show pride in their diversity?

Basketball fans have many teams to enjoy in North Carolina.

Dinosaur fossils are a star attraction at the Museum of Natural Sciences.

Museums of All Kinds

Charlotte's Discovery Place can give you an insider's look at a space shuttle and a space station. In the museum's three-story-tall rain forest, you can see tropical birds, iguanas, and more than 50 kinds of plants and animals.

For lovers of rocks, minerals, snakes, or dinosaurs, the North Carolina State Museum of Natural Sciences is a must-see. It has the world's only known skeleton of the 40-foot (about 12-m), 110-million-year-old, meat-eating dinosaur called Acrocanthosaurus.

Raleigh's Exploris Museum offers visitors a chance to make connections with people and places around the world through hands-on activities. At Durham's Museum of Life and Science, visitors to the Magic Wings Butterfly House can see more than 50 unusual kinds of butterflies.

Visitors also enjoy the Morehead Planetarium at the University of North Carolina in Chapel Hill.

It was the first planetarium to be owned by a university. Russian and American astronauts trained there for a joint space mission.

Many attractions in North Carolina focus on the history of the state. Visitors to Old Salem seem to step back in time more than 200 years. This living museum in Winston-Salem is a town that has been carefully restored, or rebuilt. A **living museum** is a museum where people dress up and act like people of an earlier time. Now the town looks as Salem did in the early 1800s.

The Mattye Reed African Heritage Center is on the campus of North Carolina A & T State University in Greensboro. It houses one of the country's best collections devoted to African culture. The Heritage Center displays arts and crafts from more than 30 African nations.

REVIEW What are some types of museums in the Piedmont?

Meet a tropical bird at Discovery Place.

Arts and Crafts

Art is meant to be shared, and in the Piedmont it certainly is. The North Carolina Museum of Art in Raleigh is the oldest state-funded art museum in the country. Charlotte's Mint Museum of Art is the oldest art museum in the state. It was once the home of a United States mint built after North Carolina's gold rush in the early 1800s. In the 1930s the building was taken apart and rebuilt in a new location in Charlotte as a museum.

Music and dance are alive in North Carolina. The American Dance Festival in Durham attracts famous dance companies from all over the world.

About 20 potteries, or places where pottery is made, can be found in and around Seagrove, south of Asheboro. **Pottery** is the name given to pots, bowls, dishes, and other items made from clay that is baked to harden. In Seagrove companies have been making pottery since the mid-1700s.

REVIEW **What are some of the ways people in the Piedmont can enjoy the arts?**

• HERITAGE •

Seagrove Pottery

The early settlers of the Piedmont made pottery because they had to. Settlers around Seagrove, a small town about 30 miles from the Triad, made their own cups, bowls, plates, butter churns, jugs, and other pots. Some of the early settlers came from Staffordshire, a part of England that is famous for its pottery. They and other settlers started making pots for other people. They sold pots for a nickel or a dime or traded them for nails and horseshoes. Pottery was only sold locally until about 1922. Then a magazine article about Seagrove pottery made it famous across the country.

Today, many artists in Seagrove work full-time making pots to sell. Some families have made pottery for five generations!

LESSON 3 REVIEW

1 **MAIN IDEA** What are five activities people enjoy in the Piedmont?

2 **WHY IT MATTERS** How do people learn about North Carolina's heritage from museums?

3 **VOCABULARY** Use **professional team** and **pottery** in a paragraph about activities in the Piedmont.

4 **READING SKILL—Generalize** Why do people hold international festivals?

5 **CULTURE** What is celebrated at the Fiesta del Pueblo?

6 **HISTORY** What is the oldest state-funded art museum in the country?

7 **CRITICAL THINKING—Analyze** Why are arts and crafts important to North Carolina's culture?

 PERFORMANCE—Plan a Museum With a small group, plan a Discovery Museum for your school or community. Decide what objects and pictures to display. Write a description of your museum and share it with your classmates.

6 Review and Test Preparation

USE YOUR READING SKILLS

Complete this graphic organizer to help you make generalizations about the Piedmont region. A copy of this graphic organizer appears on page 66 of the Activity Book.

The Piedmont Urban Crescent

FACTS		GENERALIZATION
Railroads made trade easier. The government built two major highways through Charlotte.	→	Transportation helped the Piedmont's cities grow.

Piedmont Industries Change

FACTS		GENERALIZATION
	→	

Life in the Piedmont

FACTS		GENERALIZATION
	→	

THINK & WRITE

Write a Research Plan Imagine that your school has raised money to build a new playground and sports area. You have been asked to help by doing some research on playgrounds and equipment. Describe what information and research materials you will have to get to make an informed decision. Make a five-step research plan as a way to organize your search.

Write a Newspaper Report You are visiting the North Carolina State Fair. Write a story about your trip for your school or home-town newspaper. If you need to, read more about the fair before you write. Describe the events you would attend and things you would see. Use details and descriptions to make your article interesting to read. Also include important information such as the dates and times of events at the fair.

USE VOCABULARY

Match each vocabulary word to its definition.

metropolitan area (p. 186)

commute (p. 188)

technology (p. 192)

innovation (p. 194)

pottery (p. 203)

1 a better way to do something

2 pots and dishes made from clay

3 to travel a long distance to work

4 a large city and its suburbs

5 how people use new ideas to make tools and machines

RECALL FACTS

Answer these questions.

6 What are the three large cities in the Triad?

7 Name two reasons for Charlotte's growth.

8 Where in North Carolina did Russian and American astronauts train?

Write the letter of the best choice.

9 **TEST PREP**   Seagrove is famous for—
A textiles.
B furniture.
C medical schools.
D pottery.

10 **TEST PREP**   Charlotte grew rapidly after—
F textile mills closed.
G the Research Triangle Park opened.
H railroad lines were built.
J Joshua Reynolds built a tobacco company.

11 **TEST PREP**   Most of North Carolina's textile manufacturers ship their products by—
A truck.
B boat.
C railroad.
D airplane.

THINK CRITICALLY

12 In industry, is it a good idea to automate jobs? Why or why not?

13 How have changes in transportation affected life in the Piedmont?

APPLY SKILLS

Read a Population Map

14 Look at the map on page 191. Is the population density highest in the Mountain region, the Piedmont, or the Coastal Plain? How do you know?

15 Which cities have the highest population in the Mountain region?

Read a Line Graph

16 Use the graph on page 199. Did North Carolina's population change more between 1950 and 1960 or between 1990 and 2000?

17 About how many more people were in North Carolina in 1980 than in 1950?

OLD SALEM

GET READY

African Americans began living in the Moravian community of Salem, North Carolina, in the late 1700s. Although they were enslaved, they lived and worked alongside the Moravians. For a time, some African Americans worshiped at the Home Moravian Church. Some lived in the Single Sisters' and Single Brothers' houses. African Americans provided important services in the community. They were skilled brickmakers, potters, blacksmiths, and carpenters.

At the restored village of Old Salem, visitors can take a walking tour of sites related to the African Americans who lived in, worked in, and helped build the community.

WHAT TO SEE

At New Salem, actors take on the roles of villagers from long ago.

Villagers work together to sharpen an axe.

LOCATE IT

Old Salem

NORTH CAROLINA

African Americans worshiped at the Log Church, built in 1823.

The Single Brothers' House looks much as it did in the late 1700s.

Actors dressed in historic clothing stop to chat outside the Miksch House.

TAKE A FIELD TRIP

GO ONLINE

A VIRTUAL TOUR
Visit The Learning Site at **www.harcourtschool.com/tours** to take virtual tours of other historic places.

CNN
Turner Le@rning

A VIDEO TOUR
Check your media center or classroom library for a videotape tour of Old Salem.

3 Review and Test Preparation

VISUAL SUMMARY

Write a Study Guide Study the pictures and captions below to help you review Unit 3. Then choose two pictures. Write a guide to help another student study those events. Describe why the events were important.

USE VOCABULARY

Write a definition of the first word in each pair. Use the second word in the definition.

1 **pioneer** (p. 156), **relocate** (p. 156)

2 **manufacturing** (p. 163), **technology** (p. 192)

3 **commute** (p. 188), **suburb** (p. 186)

4 **Emancipation Proclamation** (p. 174), **abolitionist** (p. 167)

RECALL FACTS

Answer these questions.

5 What were the names of the first two Moravian settlements in North Carolina?

6 How was the economy of the South different from the economy of the North before the Civil War?

7 What makes Charlotte a transportation hub?

Write the letter of the best choice.

8 **TEST PREP** Settlers from Pennsylvania in the 1730s traveled on—
A new railroad lines.
B the Great Wagon Road.
C highways.
D the Underground Railroad.

9 **TEST PREP** Why were Southerners against higher taxes before the Civil War?
F They feared the taxes would end slavery.
G They wanted to buy goods from the North.
H They wanted to sell cotton to Britain.
J They wanted to protect their factories.

10 **TEST PREP** Which of these people work in service jobs?
A textile manufacturers
B government workers
C cotton farmers
D furniture makers

Visual Summary

1750

1800

1766 Moravians found Salem p. 189

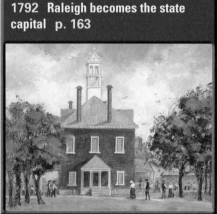

1792 Raleigh becomes the state capital p. 163

1816 First North Carolina textile mill is built p. 177

208

11 TEST PREP The North Carolina State Fair is held every October in—
F Charlotte.
G Durham.
H Greensboro.
J Raleigh.

12 TEST PREP The oldest art museum in North Carolina is—
A Discovery Place in Charlotte.
B Exploris Museum in Raleigh.
C North Carolina Museum of Art in Raleigh.
D Mint Museum of Art in Charlotte.

THINK CRITICALLY

13 Do you think North Carolina should try to attract new industries? If so, what industries would help North Carolina's economy?

14 Are museums important? Why or why not?

15 How has technology changed life in North Carolina? Have most of the consequences been good or bad? Explain your answer.

APPLY SKILLS

Read a Population Map
Use the population map on this page to answer the following questions.

16 If you wanted to find an area with fewer than 50 people per square mile, what color should you look for on the map?

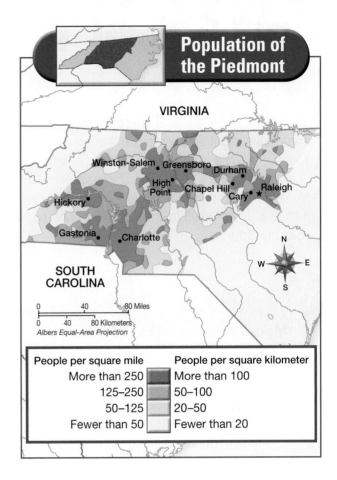

Population of the Piedmont

VIRGINIA

Winston-Salem • Greensboro • Durham
High Point • Chapel Hill • Cary ★ Raleigh
Hickory •
Gastonia • Charlotte

SOUTH CAROLINA

0   40   80 Miles
0   40   80 Kilometers
Albers Equal-Area Projection

People per square mile	People per square kilometer
More than 250	More than 100
125–250	50–100
50–125	20–50
Fewer than 50	Fewer than 20

17 What color shows an area with more than 250 people per square mile?

18 Where is the population density highest? Why do you think that is?

19 Where is the population density lowest?

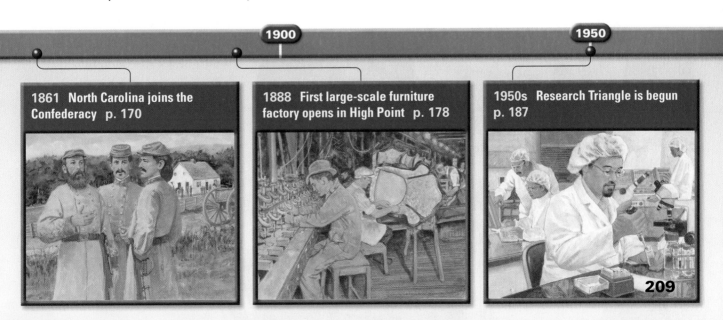

1900

1950

1861 North Carolina joins the Confederacy p. 170

1888 First large-scale furniture factory opens in High Point p. 178

1950s Research Triangle is begun p. 187

Unit Activities

 Visit The Learning Site at www.harcourtschool.com/socialstudies/activities for additional activities.

Write a Play

With a small group of students, write a short play about settlers in the Piedmont. You might write about Moravians in Salem or about pioneers on the Great Wagon Road. Make sure each person in your group has a part to play. If possible, present your play to your classmates.

Make a Collage

Make a collage of pictures about life in the Piedmont. Find pictures in old magazines or newspapers. You can also draw pictures to use. Cut out the pictures and make a collage. Put in things such as postcards or other objects if you want. Make sure your collage shows many different ways of life. Write a paragraph about your collage. Explain why you chose the pictures you did. Then display your collage and paragraph in your classroom.

VISIT YOUR LIBRARY

- *The Wagon* by Tony Johnston. Tambourine Books.

 - *Master of Mahogany* by Mary E. Lyons. Charles Scribner's Sons.

- *Who Comes with Cannons?* by Patricia Beatty. Morrow.

COMPLETE THE UNIT PROJECT

Create a Newcomers' Guide As a group, decide how you want to organize the information in your newcomers' guide. Include historical and cultural information about the Piedmont region, and describe what the Piedmont is like today. Combine your work with your classmates'. Publish your guide and display it during a classroom fair.

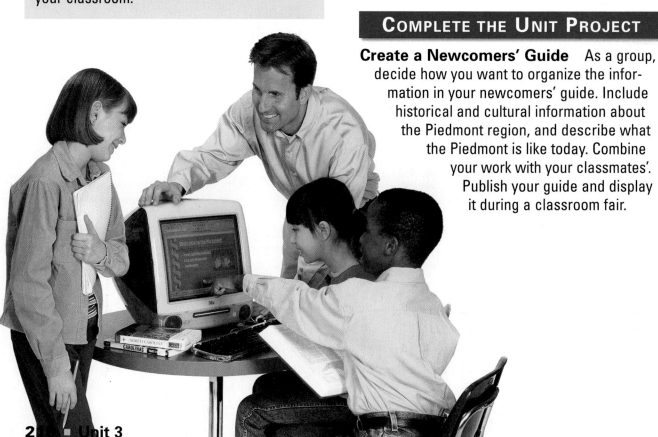

The Mountain Region

Fiddle

The Great Smoky Mountains National Park

4

The Mountain Region

" Shaconage, the place of blue smoke "

—Cherokee description of the Great Smoky Mountains

Preview the Content

Look at the pictures, tables, graphs, and maps in this unit. What do they show? Make a list of topics you think will be important in this unit. As you read, use your list to remind you of important ideas.

Preview the Vocabulary

Suffixes The suffixes *–tion* and *–ation* often change a verb, or action word, into a noun. If you know the meaning of the verb, you can easily understand the meaning of the noun. Look up each verb in a dictionary. Then tell what you think the meaning of each noun below might be.

VERB	MEANING	NOUN	MEANING
generate		generation	
reserve		reservation	
conserve		conservation	

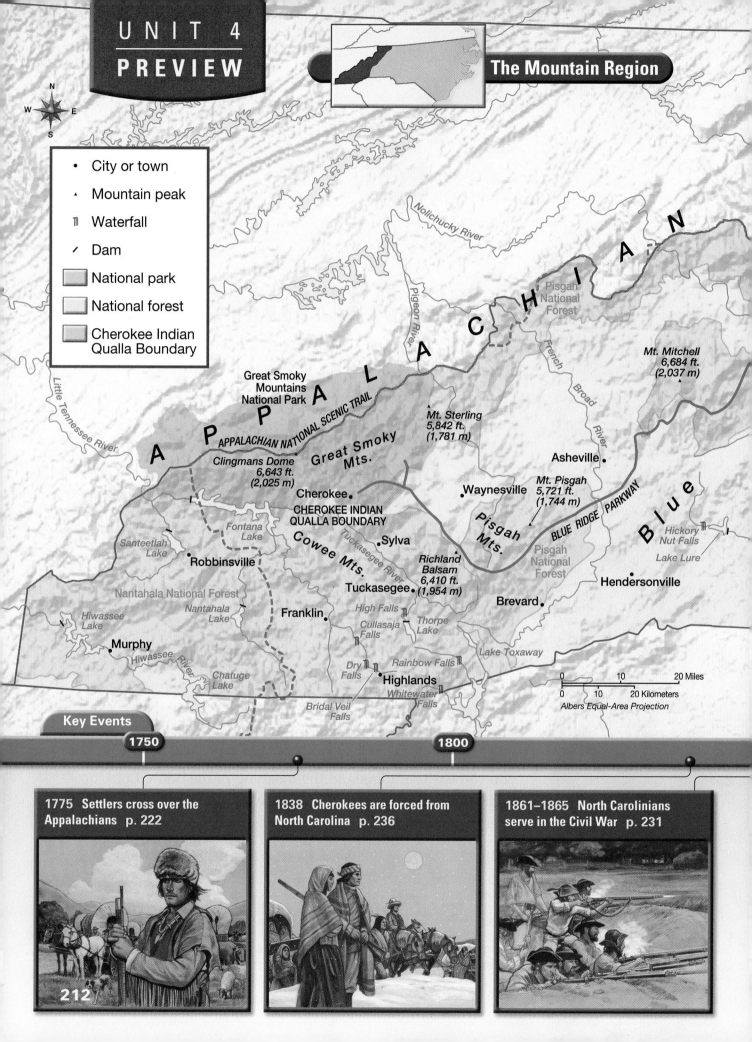

Map Legend

- City or town
- Mountain peak
- Waterfall
- Dam
- National park
- National forest
- Cherokee Indian Qualla Boundary

Nolichucky River

Pisgah National Forest

Mt. Mitchell
6,684 ft.
(2,037 m)

APPALACHIAN

Pigeon River

French Broad River

Great Smoky Mountains National Park

APPALACHIAN NATIONAL SCENIC TRAIL

Great Smoky Mts.

Mt. Sterling
5,842 ft.
(1,781 m)

Asheville

Clingmans Dome
6,643 ft.
(2,025 m)

Cherokee

Waynesville

Mt. Pisgah
5,721 ft.
(1,744 m)

BLUE RIDGE PARKWAY

Blue

CHEROKEE INDIAN QUALLA BOUNDARY

Little Tennessee River

Fontana Lake

Sylva

Tuckasegee River

Pisgah Mts.

Pisgah National Forest

Hickory Nut Falls

Santeetlah Lake

Cowee Mts.

Richland Balsam
6,410 ft.
(1,954 m)

Lake Lure

Robbinsville

Tuckasegee

Hendersonville

Nantahala National Forest

Nantahala Lake

Franklin

High Falls

Thorpe Lake

Brevard

Hiwassee Lake

Cullasaja Falls

Lake Toxaway

Murphy

Chatuge Lake

Dry Falls

Rainbow Falls

Highlands

Hiwassee River

Bridal Veil Falls

Whitewater Falls

0   10   20 Miles
0   10   20 Kilometers
Albers Equal-Area Projection

Key Events

1750

1800

1775 Settlers cross over the Appalachians p. 222

1838 Cherokees are forced from North Carolina p. 236

1861–1865 North Carolinians serve in the Civil War p. 231

212

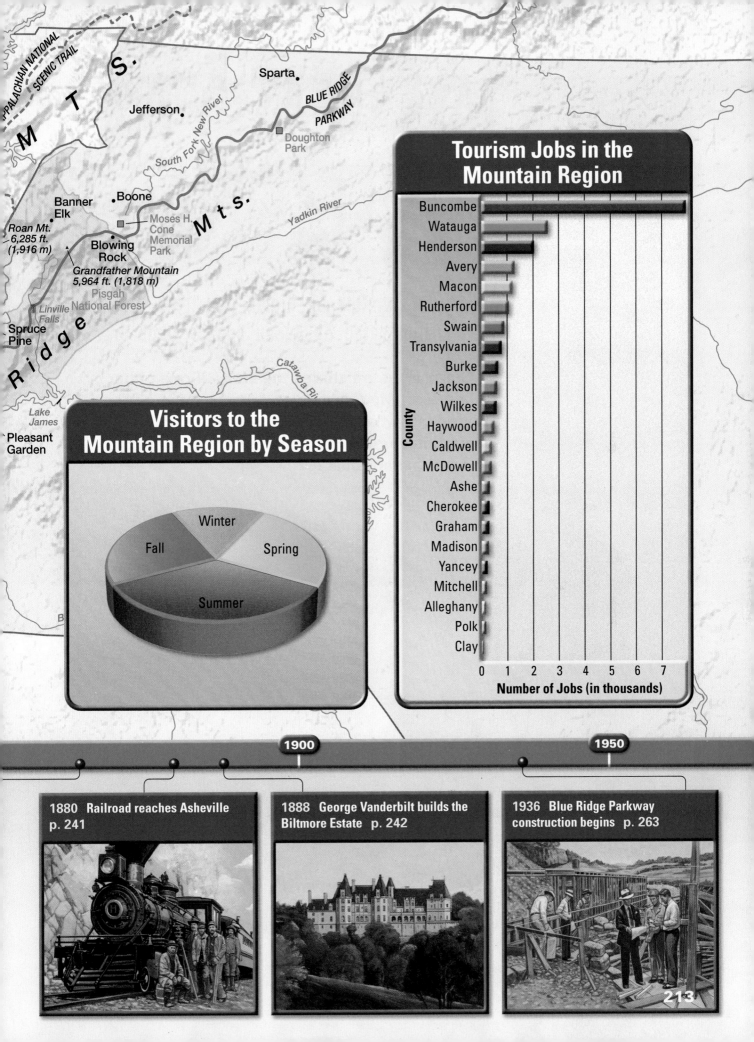

Tourism Jobs in the Mountain Region

County (top to bottom):
- Buncombe
- Watauga
- Henderson
- Avery
- Macon
- Rutherford
- Swain
- Transylvania
- Burke
- Jackson
- Wilkes
- Haywood
- Caldwell
- McDowell
- Ashe
- Cherokee
- Graham
- Madison
- Yancey
- Mitchell
- Alleghany
- Polk
- Clay

Number of Jobs (in thousands): 0 1 2 3 4 5 6 7

Visitors to the Mountain Region by Season

Winter, Spring, Summer, Fall

1880 Railroad reaches Asheville p. 241

1888 George Vanderbilt builds the Biltmore Estate p. 242

1936 Blue Ridge Parkway construction begins p. 263

1900   1950

MY GREAT-AUNT ~ARIZONA~

written by Gloria Houston
illustrated by Susan Condie Lamb

Gloria Houston shares the story of one of her relatives in *My Great-Aunt Arizona*. Read now to find out what life was like growing up in a mountain community and how Arizona worked to achieve her goals.

My great-aunt Arizona was born in a log cabin her papa built in the meadow on Henson Creek in the Blue Ridge Mountains. When she was born, the mailman rode across the bridge on his big bay horse with a letter.

The letter was from her brother, Galen, who was in the cavalry, far away in the West. The letter said, "If the baby is a girl, please name her Arizona, and she will be beautiful, like this land."

Arizona was a very tall little girl. She wore her long brown hair in braids. She wore long full dresses, and a pretty white apron. She wore high-button shoes, and many petticoats, too. Arizona liked to grow flowers.

She liked to read, And sing, And square dance to the music of the fiddler on Saturday night.

Arizona had a little brother, Jim. They played together on the farm. In summer they went barefoot and caught tadpoles in the creek. In the fall they climbed the mountains searching for galax and ginseng roots. In the winter they made snow cream with sugar, snow, and sweet cream from Mama's cows.

When spring came, they helped Papa tap the maple trees and catch the sap in buckets. Then they made maple syrup and maple sugar to eat, like candy.

Arizona and her brother Jim walked up the road that wound by the creek to the one-room school. All the students in all the grades were there, together in one room. All the students read their lessons aloud at the same time. They made a great deal of noise, so the room was called a blab school.

The students carried their lunches in lard buckets made of tin. They brought ham and biscuits. Sometimes they had a fried apple pie. They drank cool water from the spring at the bottom of the hill. At recess they played games like tag and William Matrimmatoe.

* * * *

When Arizona's mother died, Arizona had to leave school and stay home to care for Papa and her brother Jim. She still loved to read—and dream about the faraway places she would visit one day. So she read and she dreamed, but she took care of Papa and Jim.

Then one day Papa brought home a new wife. Arizona could go away to school, where she could learn to be a teacher. Aunt Suzie invited Arizona to live at her house and help with the chores. Aunt Suzie made her work very hard. But at night Arizona could study— and dream of all the faraway places she would visit one day.

Finally, Arizona returned to her home on Henson Creek. She was a teacher at last.

She taught in the one-room school where she and Jim had sat. She made new chalkboards out of lumber from Papa's sawmill, and covered them with black polish made for stoves.

She still wore long full dresses and a pretty white apron. She wore high-button shoes and many petticoats, too. She grew flowers in every window. She taught students about words and numbers and the faraway places they would visit someday. "Have you been there?" the students asked. "Only in my mind," she answered. "But someday you will go."

Analyze the Literature

1. What is the origin of the main character's name in the story?

2. How can you tell this story takes place in the Mountain region?

3. Write a paragraph describing one of the members of your family.

READ A BOOK

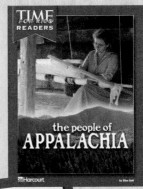

START THE UNIT PROJECT

Make a Mountain Atlas Make an atlas of the Mountain region. With a small group of classmates, choose some activities people enjoy in the mountains, such as hiking, skiing, craft festivals, or whitewater rafting. As you read the unit, make notes about where people might enjoy these activities. Mark these locations on a map.

USE TECHNOLOGY

Visit The Learning Site at **www.harcourtschool.com/ socialstudies** for additional activities, primary sources, and other resources to use in this unit.

THE BILTMORE ESTATE

The Biltmore Estate is the largest private home in the United States. It was built in 1889. At that time, many wealthy people constructed homes in the Mountain region to enjoy its climate and scenery. Today the Biltmore Estate is a popular tourist site.

LOCATE IT

NORTH CAROLINA

Biltmore Estate

7

The Mountain Region Long Ago

❝ The most beautiful place in the world ❞

—George Washington Vanderbilt, 1888

CHAPTER READING SKILL

Identify Cause and Effect

When you read about history, it is important to remember the difference between a cause and an effect. A **cause** is an event or action that makes something else happen. An **effect** is what happens as a result of that event or action.

CAUSE → EFFECT

MAIN IDEA
Read to learn how early pioneers explored and settled the Western frontier.

WHY IT MATTERS
Trailblazing explorers and early frontier families led many settlers to the mountains.

VOCABULARY
frontier
gap
log cabin
generation
barter

Settling the Western Mountains

1750   1800   1850   1900

1751–1775

The western mountains of North Carolina were first settled by the Cherokees more than 1,000 years ago. People of European heritage first settled in North Carolina in the 1600s, but few went to the Mountain region which they called "Cherokee land." This western area was the **frontier**, the area beyond the European settlement. In the late 1700s some European settlers began to move onto the frontier, looking for new opportunities and a better life.

Daniel Boone and the Wilderness Road

The descendants of Scotch-Irish and German immigrants who settled in the Piedmont were among the first European settlers of the Mountain region. Their families had come

FAST FACT
Early European settlers kept many Cherokee place names. Both the Cullasaja River and Cullasaja Falls are named for a Cherokee village that once stood along the riverbank.

south on the Great Wagon Road from Pennsylvania. They had joined other settlers in the Piedmont in the early 1700s.

By the time colonists began fighting the American Revolution, many settlers had moved to the Piedmont. Some settlers were pioneers who wanted to go farther west. However, high mountains and thick forests covered the lands to the west. Often the route was a narrow trail covered with leaves and branches. Pioneers needed experienced guides to find their way across the mountains.

Daniel Boone proved to be such a guide. He was one of the first pioneers to blaze trails in the Blue Ridge Mountains, guiding settlers from the Piedmont across the mountains through what is now the state of Tennessee and into Kentucky. At that time, Tennessee was called Tennessee Country and was part of the North Carolina colony.

Born in Pennsylvania, Boone moved with his family to the Yadkin River valley in what is now North Carolina in 1751, when he was in his teens. The family traveled south on the Great Wagon Road. The Boones made their home in what is today Rowan County in the Piedmont. Daniel Boone was an experienced guide and an expert hunter and trapper. He tracked game in the woods of western North Carolina and knew the trails of the area. Boone became interested in Kentucky when he heard stories about the good soil to be found west of the Appalachian Mountains.

In 1769 Boone followed an old

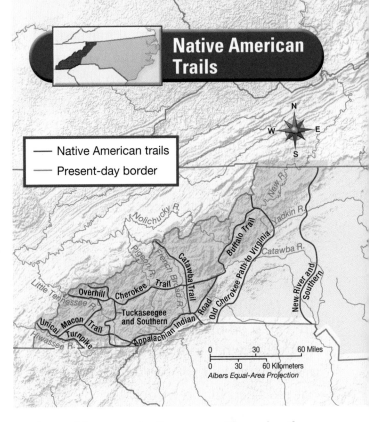

Native American Trails

— Native American trails
— Present-day border

Movement **European settlers migrating to North Carolina followed paths that had been used by Native Americans.**

❖ **Which trails followed the French Broad River?**

Native American trail called the Warriors Path across the mountains and into Virginia. He then went through the mountains from Virginia into Kentucky, which was then part of the Virginia colony at what is now called the Cumberland Gap. A **gap** is an opening or a low place between mountains. In 1775 Boone and some 30 men using axes chopped a trail through the wilderness. This trail later became the Wilderness Road. It grew wider as hundreds of wagons rattled and bumped across it on their way west.

Daniel Boone helped open the Mountain region to pioneers.

When the route was well marked, many pioneers followed the Wilderness Road and other trails west to what are today Kentucky and Tennessee. After the American Revolution ended, many pioneers heading west stopped and settled in the North Carolina mountains.

REVIEW What route led pioneers to the western lands of Tennessee and Kentucky?

Early Mountain Settlements

Moving to the frontier meant separation from family and friends. The painful first step on the pioneers' journey was to decide what to leave behind. Next, families packed up everything they would need in the wilderness. By the time the journey began, packs filled with clothes, dried food, rifles, and tools weighed down the horses. Usually adults walked beside the horses. The youngest child rode in a basket attached to a horse's pack saddle. Older children cared for cattle and hogs, keeping them safe along the dangerous trails.

Pioneer families in a new settlement usually built a lean-to shack as their first shelter. It was made of poles and covered with branches to keep out the wind and rain. A blanket spread over a pile of leaves on the ground served as a bed. After the family had cut and split enough logs, they built a **log cabin**. Settlers of the Mountain region had learned how to build log cabins from German settlers back in Pennsylvania.

Most log cabins had just one room with a dirt floor and no windows. Inside it was dirty and dark. The only light came through an opening in the wall and from the fire that burned day and night in the fireplace. There, wood and bear fat burned for warmth and for cooking. After dark, families also used candles or oil lamps and went to bed early.

At the end of the cabin farthest from the door, the family cooked and ate around the fireplace. They put their beds in another corner. This left only a small space for sitting and entertaining.

Mountain region settlers brought cooking pots, tools, oil lamps, spinning wheels and quilts with them.

Analyze Primary Sources

Early Mountain settlers built cabins from logs. If they could, they cut the logs into rough boards first. This cabin near Blowing Rock shows how the settlers used the resources they found in the mountains.

❶ The cabin is made of huge chestnut logs. Settlers used chestnut trees because the wood did not rot easily. Unfortunately, a disease killed most of the chestnut trees in the early 1900s.

❷ The roof extends out at the edges to keep rain from spilling onto the walls or into the cabin.

❸ Early Mountain settlers had no glass for windows. Often windows, if there were any, were left uncovered. Settlers sometimes used wooden shutters to close the windows at night and when it rained. Other times, windows were covered with oiled paper.

◈ The chimney is large. Why do you think the settlers needed a big fireplace?

Frontier cabins were often quite crowded. Many settlers had large families. In the mountains two or three generations of a family might live in the same log cabin their entire lives. A **generation** is a group of people of about the same age, such as brothers and sisters. Each family added what they could to make the cabin more comfortable. One generation might add windows. Another might cover the dirt floor with boards.

REVIEW Why was life on the frontier difficult for settlers?

People in the Mountain region helped each other. When it was time to harvest corn, they held husking parties to get the corn ready to use.

A Rugged Life

Mountain life could be hard and lonely. Men hunted for food in the forests. Women hauled water from creeks for cooking and washing. They fed the chickens and hogs, milked the cows, split wood, and made fires. They also tended the garden and prepared vegetables for the winter. They did the spinning, weaving, and sewing to make their families' clothes.

Mothers depended on their daughters to help them with the chores and to look after younger children. Boys went hunting with their fathers as soon as they were old enough.

Store-bought goods were rare. In the mountains, settlers had to travel many miles to the nearest store.

Many settlers in the Mountain region lived far from their neighbors. Before roads and railroads came to the Mountain region, settlers had to be self-sufficient. To be self-sufficient, settlers had to make or grow almost everything they needed. They raised their food and made most of their clothes and furniture.

Most people got what they needed by bartering with their neighbors. When people **barter**, they trade goods for other goods without using money. They might trade corn for a chicken, or a pig or animal skins for tools.

There were few doctors on the frontier. Settlers had to care for themselves. They treated aches, cuts, and fevers with medicines made from plants.

Although they were independent, the Mountain pioneers also helped each other.

Musical instruments such as this banjo provided entertainment for Mountain pioneers.

Neighbors came together for special events such as barn raisings and corn huskings. At a corn husking, everyone pitched in to strip the leaves from newly harvested ears of corn. Sometimes settlers divided into teams to see who could husk the most corn in the least amount of time. Working together like this, they finished jobs quickly. Often there was time left for eating, music, dancing, and storytelling.

Mountain neighbors also got together to help each other build cabins and barns. Usually the men did the heavy work of raising the frame of the barn, while the women prepared huge platters of food and cared for the children.

Settlers knew they could rely on their neighbors for help. After a fire, flood, or other disaster, families gave comfort and helped one another rebuild in the same ways people do today.

REVIEW Why did settlers in the Mountain region have to be self-sufficient?

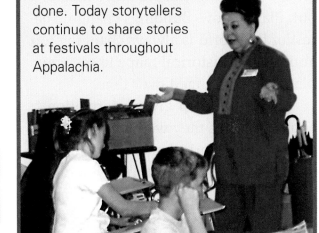

• HERITAGE •

Appalachian Storytelling

People have told stories in the Mountain region for hundreds of years. The early Scotch-Irish settlers brought stories with them from Britain. Some of these stories came from British books written in the 1700s. Others have been passed down from person to person for centuries. Mountain people told stories to pass the time while they worked and when the work was done. Today storytellers continue to share stories at festivals throughout Appalachia.

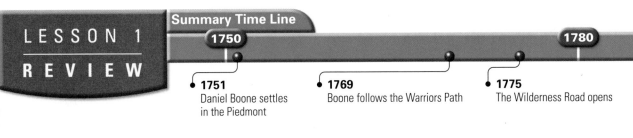

LESSON 1
REVIEW

Summary Time Line

1750 — 1780

1751 Daniel Boone settles in the Piedmont

1769 Boone follows the Warriors Path

1775 The Wilderness Road opens

1 **MAIN IDEA** How did early Mountain settlers live?

2 **WHY IT MATTERS** What brought the early settlers to the Mountain region?

3 **VOCABULARY** Use the terms **generation** and **log cabin** in a sentence that describes how early pioneers lived.

4 **TIME LINE** When did Daniel Boone first follow the Warriors Path?

5 **READING SKILL—Identify Cause and Effect** What happened when the Wilderness Road opened?

6 **CULTURE** What different jobs did men and women handle on the frontier?

7 **ECONOMICS** How did Mountain settlers exchange goods with neighbors?

8 **CRITICAL THINKING—Apply** Who do you think are modern pioneers? Why do you think so?

PERFORMANCE—Draw a Diagram Use information from the lesson to draw a diagram of the inside of a log cabin. Show where people slept, cooked, and ate. Label your diagram clearly.

·SKILLS·

MAP AND GLOBE

Compare Historical Maps

➤ WHY IT MATTERS

Think about your neighborhood. It is always changing. People move in and out. Plants grow. Buildings change. The rest of the world is always changing too. You can use historical maps to see how places have changed over time.

A **historical map** gives information about places as they were in the past. By comparing historical maps that show the same place at different times, you can see how the place has changed over time.

➤ WHAT YOU NEED TO KNOW

You have read about settlers in North Carolina. As farmland in the eastern part of the state became scarce, pioneers moved west. They made trails and roads which allowed others to follow them.

The map on this page and the map on the next page show the eastern part of what is now the United States. Each map shows a different year. Map A shows the British colonies at the beginning of the Revolutionary War. Map B shows

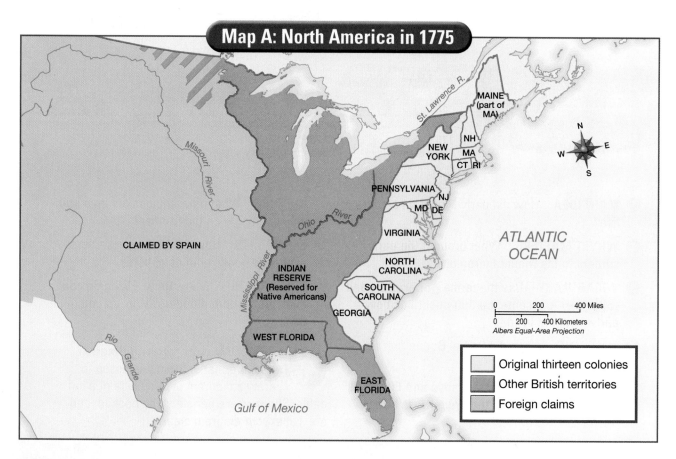

Map A: North America in 1775

MAINE (part of MA)

St. Lawrence R.

NH
NEW YORK MA
CT RI

PENNSYLVANIA
NJ
MD DE

VIRGINIA

Missouri River

CLAIMED BY SPAIN

Ohio River

NORTH CAROLINA

INDIAN RESERVE (Reserved for Native Americans)

SOUTH CAROLINA

Mississippi River

GEORGIA

WEST FLORIDA

Rio Grande

EAST FLORIDA

Gulf of Mexico

ATLANTIC OCEAN

0   200   400 Miles
0   200   400 Kilometers
Albers Equal-Area Projection

Original thirteen colonies
Other British territories
Foreign claims

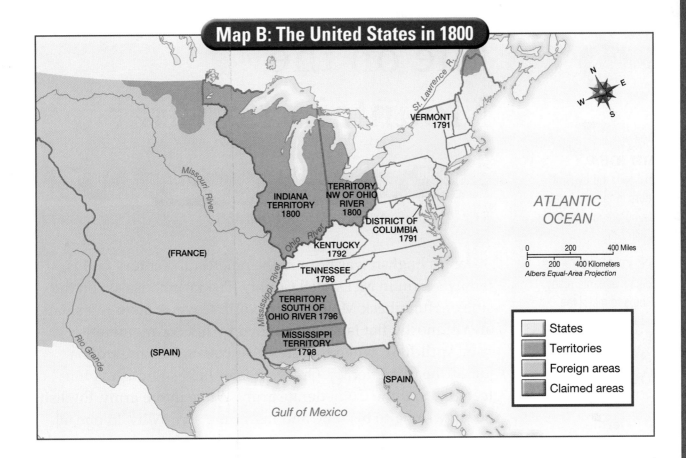

Map B: The United States in 1800

VERMONT 1791

INDIANA TERRITORY 1800

TERRITORY NW OF OHIO RIVER 1800

DISTRICT OF COLUMBIA 1791

KENTUCKY 1792

TENNESSEE 1796

TERRITORY SOUTH OF OHIO RIVER 1796

MISSISSIPPI TERRITORY 1798

(FRANCE)

(SPAIN)

(SPAIN)

Missouri River

Ohio River

Mississippi River

Rio Grande

St. Lawrence R.

ATLANTIC OCEAN

Gulf of Mexico

0 200 400 Miles
0 200 400 Kilometers
Albers Equal-Area Projection

States
Territories
Foreign areas
Claimed areas

the same area 25 years later. By looking at the two maps, you can see how the United States grew. The original 13 colonies became states. Other areas became states or territories. A **territory** is an area that belongs to a country but does not have the same rights as a state.

▶ PRACTICE THE SKILL

Look at the map keys to learn what each color and each symbol means. Then use the maps to answer these questions.

1 What happened to the British territories between 1775 and 1800?

2 What states are labeled on the 1800 map? When did they become states?

3 How did the land controlled by Spain change between 1775 and 1800?

4 How did the area directly west of North Carolina change?

▶ APPLY WHAT YOU LEARNED

Write three or four sentences about these two maps. Include the dates of the maps in your sentences but leave blanks where dates belong. Then trade papers with a partner. Have your partner fill in the correct map dates to complete the sentences.

Practice your map and globe skills with the **GeoSkills CD-ROM**.

Life on the Mountain Frontier

MAIN IDEA
Learn about the lives of pioneers in the Mountain region before and during the Civil War.

WHY IT MATTERS
Pioneers overcame many hardships to make the Mountain region their home.

VOCABULARY

cove

fertile

| 1750 | 1800 | 1850 | 1900 |

1780–1865

James English was born in the nineteenth century on his family's farm in McDowell County. The farmhouse sat on the side of Humpback Mountain in North Cove. A **cove** is a small area of mostly flat land surrounded by hills or mountains.

In April 1861, when the Civil War began, North Carolina joined the Confederacy. One year later James English volunteered to join the Confederate army. While in the army, English began writing to his wife and his young son, Willy. In one of his letters, he reminded his son, "You must be a good boy and mind what your mother and aunt say to you."

Setting Down Roots

In the years before the American Revolution, most people living in the mountains were Cherokees. The British had issued a declaration that did not allow Europeans to settle west of the Blue Ridge Mountains. The British wanted to avoid conflict between Cherokees and European settlers.

This painting shows the kind of landscapes early mountain settlers saw.

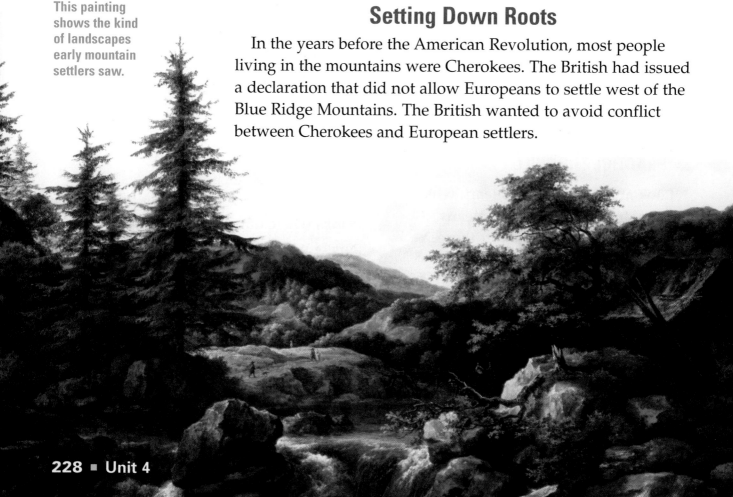

Governor Zebulon Vance (above right), a grandson of David Vance, grew up at the Vance farm. Today visitors to the farm, now part of the Vance Homestead State Historic Site, can see the Vances' kitchen and other rooms.

Because of this, the Cherokees fought for the British in the American Revolution. The British defeat was the Cherokees' loss as well. It opened the Mountain region to new settlers because the British had lost control of the land. North Carolina's leaders had promised western lands to Patriot soldiers. Many families followed the trails made by Daniel Boone and others to Tennessee and Kentucky. Many people moving into the mountains were European settlers who had first settled on the Coastal Plain and in the Piedmont.

David Vance was a Scotch-Irish immigrant who had moved to the Piedmont with his family in the mid-1700s. During the American Revolution, Vance served with General Washington. After the war he moved west and settled in Buncombe County. He worked there as a teacher, lawyer, and land surveyor. By 1795 he had earned enough money to buy a farm. His farm is now a historical site.

Although travel to the Mountain region was possible in the 1800s, it was still difficult. Most settlers traveled on paths and rough roads along streams and rivers. They usually settled in the river valleys where the soil was **fertile**, or good for growing crops. The mountains had rocky ground, so farms had to be small. As more settlers arrived, the population in the Mountain region grew. Some settlers moved on to Tennessee and Kentucky.

REVIEW Why did more settlers move to the Mountain region after the American Revolution ended?

North Carolinians who served in the Civil War lived in military camps between battles.

Slavery in the Mountain Region

In the rocky land of the Mountain region, there was not enough flat land for large plantations like those on the Coastal Plain. Few farmers in the mountains owned slaves.

Enslaved African Americans in the Mountain region often did work other than farming. Some were blacksmiths, tailors, or wagon builders. Mine owners used slave labor to mine mica, copper, and gold. Enslaved people were also forced to work on large road-building projects. As in other parts of the state, wealthy families used slave labor for child care, cooking, cleaning, planting crops, and caring for livestock.

Later in the 1800s tourists began visiting the Mountain region to enjoy the cooling mountain breezes. Some enslaved African Americans then served as cooks, butlers, laundry workers, or nurses for children. Others drove carriages or tended horses.

REVIEW What work did enslaved African Americans do in the Mountain region?

The Civil War in the Mountains

People in the Mountain region disagreed strongly about whether North Carolina should leave the Union. Some families were Unionists. Unionists supported the North and opposed secession. Others supported the South and favored joining the Confederacy and forming a new country.

Some slaves had to wear identification tags, such as this slave badge.

After Governor Zebulon Vance, David Vance's grandson, declared that North Carolina would leave the Union, support for the Confederacy grew in the Mountain region. Many settlers joined the Confederate army. They wanted to show their loyalty to their state. They were self-reliant, or independent, people who did not want the federal, or national, government to tell them what to do.

The Civil War brought many hardships to the region's soldiers and their loved ones. Throughout the Mountain region, wives and mothers of soldiers had to manage family farms. Mothers depended on their children to help them plant and harvest crops.

REVIEW How did people in the Mountain region react to the Civil War?

POINTS OF VIEW
Secession

W. W. HOLDEN, newspaper editor, 1860

66 No reason exists why North Carolina should contemplate [consider] at this time a dissolution [breaking up] of the Union. 99

MATTHIAS E. MANLY, judge, 1860

66 If [the Northern states] insist upon regarding slaves in the South as a moral taint [wrong] which it is their duty to eradicate [remove], we must quit [leave] them. 99

Analyze the Viewpoints

1. What views did W. W. Holden and Matthias Manly have about seceding from the Union?

2. **Make It Relevant** What are some community issues about which North Carolinians might disagree today?

LESSON 2 REVIEW

Summary Time Line

1780 — 1865

1795 — David Vance buys mountain farm

1861 — The Civil War begins

1. **MAIN IDEA** How were the lives of pioneers affected by the Civil War?

2. **WHY IT MATTERS** What hardships did Mountain people face during the Civil War?

3. **VOCABULARY** Use the words **cove** and **fertile** in a sentence about mountain farming.

4. **TIME LINE** When did the Civil War begin?

5. **READING SKILL—Identify Cause and Effect** What caused increased support for the Confederacy?

6. **CULTURE** Why did North Carolina choose to secede?

7. **CRITICAL THINKING—Analyze** How were the lives of enslaved African Americans in the Mountain region different from those of slaves on the Coastal Plain?

PERFORMANCE—Give a Speech Imagine that you are Governor Zebulon Vance. Write a speech to convince people in the Mountain region to join the Confederate army. Give your speech to the class.

North Carolina Arts and Crafts

Native Americans and European immigrants both loved the seclusion of North Carolina's western mountains. With this isolation, however, came the need to create everyday forms of arts and crafts. Natives and pioneers built their homes, crafted furniture, dolls, and toys, carved musical instruments, shaped pottery, and made baskets. Many descendants of early North Carolinians still practice their arts and crafts in the mountains of the state's western corridor.

FROM PENLAND SCHOOL OF CRAFTS, PENLAND, NORTH CAROLINA

Basketry

Wood, reeds, and other materials are woven together to make baskets. Complicated patterns in the weaving often have special meanings. Traditionally, baskets were used to carry or hold items. Today they are also collected for their beauty.

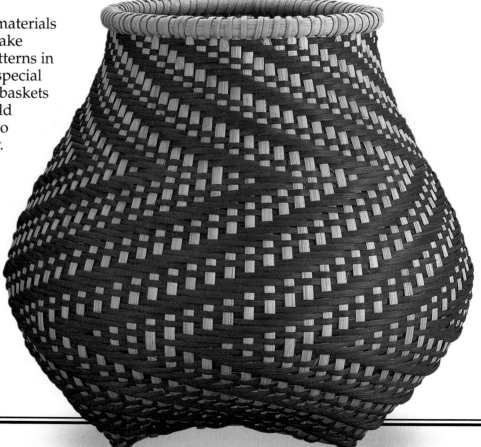

Analyze the Primary Source

❶ What resources can be used to make arts and crafts?

❷ How are basketry, glassware, and earthenware similar?

Glassware

Glass is one of the most useful and ornamental materials on Earth. It is made from silica sand, soda ash, and limestone. It can be stronger than steel or more fragile than an eggshell. It is heated to extremely high temperatures and can be spun, shaped, or blown like a bubble.

Earthenware

Earthenware is one of the oldest kinds of pottery. It is made from clay that is pressed into a mold or shaped by hand and then baked to harden. Earthenware can be painted or left undecorated.

ACTIVITY

Make a Collage Collect images of different kinds of North Carolina arts and crafts from newspapers, magazines, and the Internet. Compare the materials and techniques used in making this art. Arrange your findings in a collage to be displayed in the class.

RESEARCH

Visit The Learning Site at **www.harcourtschool.com/ primarysources** to research other primary sources.

MAIN IDEA
Read to find out about the history of the North Carolina Cherokees.

WHY IT MATTERS
Many Cherokees were forced to leave their land in the past. Today some Cherokees still live in the Mountain region.

VOCABULARY
epidemic
treaty
reservation

The Cherokees in North Carolina

1750   1800   1850   1900

1820–1870

In his book *The Path to Snowbird Mountain*, Cherokee writer Traveller Bird described his grandfather's home in Graham County near the Great Smoky Mountains. He wrote,

> **To me this region is the top of the whole world—the land of the Sky People.**

Over the years Traveller Bird's love of the Mountain region has been shared by many Cherokees.

Europeans and the Cherokees

By the time Spanish explorer Hernando de Soto and his men first came in 1540, the Cherokees had lived in what is now North Carolina for more than 1,000 years. Their homeland included parts of present-day South Carolina, northern Georgia, northeastern Alabama, and eastern Tennessee.

Spanish explorers came looking for gold, silver, and other treasures. However, they brought with them deadly diseases such as smallpox. These diseases spread rapidly, causing epidemics that wiped out entire Cherokee villages. During an **epidemic** many people have the same disease at the same time. The Native American population fell sharply because of these diseases.

Col-lee (left) was a Cherokee leader in the 1700s. Below is an axe used by Cherokee people.

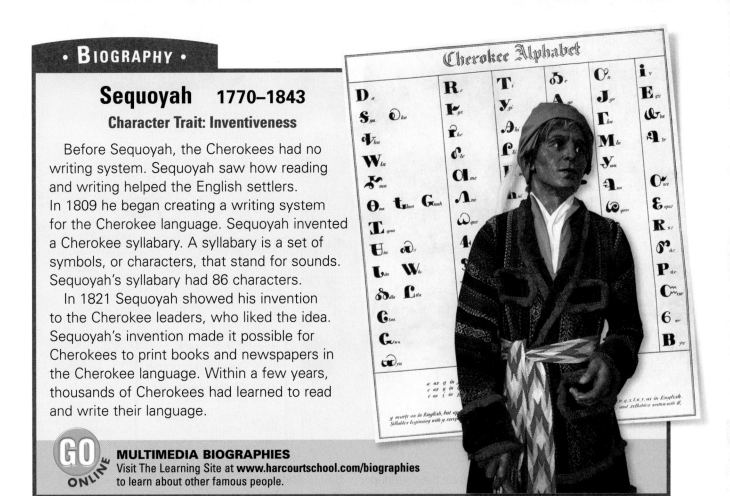

Sequoyah 1770–1843

Character Trait: Inventiveness

Before Sequoyah, the Cherokees had no writing system. Sequoyah saw how reading and writing helped the English settlers. In 1809 he began creating a writing system for the Cherokee language. Sequoyah invented a Cherokee syllabary. A syllabary is a set of symbols, or characters, that stand for sounds. Sequoyah's syllabary had 86 characters.

In 1821 Sequoyah showed his invention to the Cherokee leaders, who liked the idea. Sequoyah's invention made it possible for Cherokees to print books and newspapers in the Cherokee language. Within a few years, thousands of Cherokees had learned to read and write their language.

GO ONLINE

MULTIMEDIA BIOGRAPHIES
Visit The Learning Site at www.harcourtschool.com/biographies to learn about other famous people.

By the late 1600s English settlers in the Carolina Colony began to trade with the Cherokees. The Cherokees exchanged animal skins for metal tools such as hoes and knife blades. They also bought guns and ammunition. Over time, the Cherokees came to depend on these European goods.

During the American Revolution the Cherokees sided with the British because Britain had tried to stop colonists from moving onto Cherokee land. After the war, the Cherokees lost much of their land east of the Appalachians to the United States. The United States government made treaties with their leaders. A **treaty** is a written agreement. With each treaty, the Cherokees sold land for very little money and moved farther west.

In return, each treaty promised that the government would not take more land. However, these promises were soon broken. By 1785 pioneers were building log cabins in what are today Yancey, Mitchell, Avery, Madison, and Buncombe Counties. By 1800 the Cherokees in North Carolina held only a small area of land.

REVIEW Why did the Cherokees support the British in the American Revolution?

The Trail of Tears

The Cherokees had worked hard to become a part of the American way of life. They became farmers and built schools. Cherokee leaders created a constitution and organized a government. The Cherokee leader Sequoyah developed a written Cherokee language.

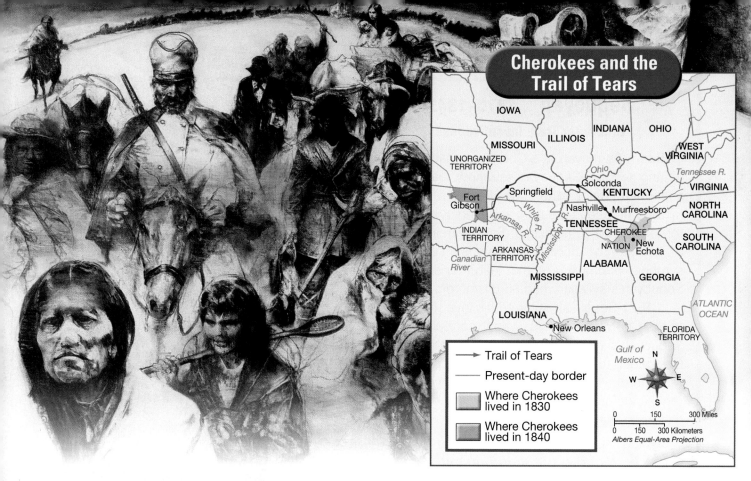

Cherokees and the Trail of Tears

Trail of Tears
Present-day border
Where Cherokees lived in 1830
Where Cherokees lived in 1840

0   150   300 Miles
0   150   300 Kilometers
Albers Equal-Area Projection

GEOGRAPHY THEME

Movement Cherokees from the southeastern United States were forced to move to what is now Oklahoma during the journey known as the Trail of Tears (background picture).

⬦ About how many miles did the Cherokees travel?

Then, in 1829, prospectors discovered gold on Cherokee land in northern Georgia. Ignoring earlier treaties, thousands of settlers took over Cherokee land. These settlers and Georgia officials asked the government to open up more land to settlers.

In 1830, lawmakers reacted by passing the Indian Removal Act. This law required Native Americans living east of the Mississippi River to leave their land. They were forced to move west to the Indian Territory in what is today Oklahoma. The Cherokees fought the Indian Removal Act in the United States courts. In 1832 the highest court ruled that the Cherokees and their lands should be protected. However, President Andrew Jackson ignored the court's decision. In May 1838 soldiers were sent to force more than 15,000 Cherokees to leave their homes.

The Native Americans were first taken to forts, or camps, where they stayed in cramped conditions. Then the Cherokees were forced to walk 1,000 miles (1,609 km) to the Indian Territory. No one had enough warm clothes, blankets, or food. Many people became ill. Before the journey ended, more than 4,000 Cherokees had died of cold, disease, or hunger. This terrible journey became known as the Trail of Tears.

REVIEW When did the Trail of Tears begin?

Those Who Stayed

During the Indian Removal a group of about 1,000 Cherokees in North Carolina escaped capture and hid in the Great Smoky Mountains. In 1868 the government officially recognized the Cherokees of western North Carolina as the Eastern Band of Cherokee.

Today more than 12,000 people belong to the Eastern Band of Cherokee. Some are descendants of the native people who escaped removal by hiding in the mountians. Most Cherokees in North Carolina live in or near the Qualla (KWAH•luh) Boundary Reservation. A **reservation** is land set aside by the government for use by Native Americans.

Visitors can stop at the Museum of the Cherokee Indian. There they can also attend the outdoor drama *Unto These Hills*, which describes the events of the 1830s.

REVIEW How did some Cherokees escape capture?

This craft shop was one of the first buildings constructed on the Qualla Boundary Reservation.

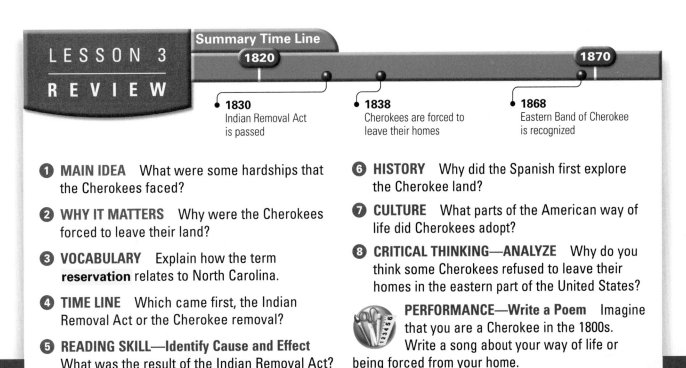

LESSON 3 REVIEW

Summary Time Line

1820 — 1870

1830 Indian Removal Act is passed

1838 Cherokees are forced to leave their homes

1868 Eastern Band of Cherokee is recognized

❶ **MAIN IDEA** What were some hardships that the Cherokees faced?

❷ **WHY IT MATTERS** Why were the Cherokees forced to leave their land?

❸ **VOCABULARY** Explain how the term **reservation** relates to North Carolina.

❹ **TIME LINE** Which came first, the Indian Removal Act or the Cherokee removal?

❺ **READING SKILL—Identify Cause and Effect** What was the result of the Indian Removal Act?

❻ **HISTORY** Why did the Spanish first explore the Cherokee land?

❼ **CULTURE** What parts of the American way of life did Cherokees adopt?

❽ **CRITICAL THINKING—ANALYZE** Why do you think some Cherokees refused to leave their homes in the eastern part of the United States?

PERFORMANCE—Write a Poem Imagine that you are a Cherokee in the 1800s. Write a song about your way of life or being forced from your home.

Determine Point of View

VOCABULARY

point of view

▶ WHY IT MATTERS

A writer's feelings and beliefs about a subject can help you understand what you read. They can also tell you why the writer wrote as he or she did. These feelings and beliefs are called the writer's **point of view**.

▶ WHAT YOU NEED TO KNOW

In 1838 the Cherokees were forced to leave their lands in North Carolina. A Cherokee named Aitooweyah (eye•too•WAY•uh) said: "We . . . the people think only of the love we have for our land . . . we do love the land where we were brought up." The United States government had a very different view.

President Andrew Jackson said: "The . . . speedy removal will be important to the U.S., to individual states, and to Indians themselves. . . it will enable them to pursue happiness in their own way. . . ."

▶ PRACTICE THE SKILL

Follow these steps to identify each writer's point of view.

❶ What was Andrew Jackson's point of view about the Cherokees' move? How do you know?

❷ What point of view did Aitooweyah have about the Cherokees' move? How do you know?

❸ How are the two points of view different?

▶ APPLY WHAT YOU LEARNED

Look for a newspaper article that presents a strong point of view. What is the writer's point of view? How do you know what the point of view is?

An artist's view of what the Trail of Tears might have been like.

Growth in the Mountain Region

1875–1890

MAIN IDEA
Read to learn about growth in the Mountain region after the Civil War.

WHY IT MATTERS
After the Civil War, the growth of railroads and tourism brought others in closer contact with the Mountain region.

VOCABULARY
spring
estate
conservation
forestry

After the Civil War many changes came to the Mountain region. Tourists began to visit the region to enjoy its cool waters, clean air, and beautiful views. Many visitors traveled on the Western North Carolina Railroad. Building this train line required blasting seven tunnels through the solid rock of the mountains. In 1878 many tourists took the long train ride from Salisbury to Mud Cut to see the tunnels in the mountains.

Mountain Resorts

Tourists began visiting the Mountain region as early as the 1780s. Health resorts in Hot Springs in Madison County attracted visitors who wanted to drink from the mineral springs or to bathe in them. A **spring** is a place where underground water comes out of the ground. Many people believed that some springs could cure illness. By the early 1800s wealthy families from the coastal Carolinas and Georgia were traveling to the mountains for their health.

Mountain resorts, such as this one in Hot Springs, attracted people of all ages to North Carolina.

Many "summer people," as the local people called these tourists, built large houses in the area. Families from Charleston and other parts of coastal South Carolina went to Flat Rock in Henderson County for the summer months. Wealthy plantation owners also chose this town as a summer retreat.

Blowing Rock in Watauga County first attracted summer residents in the 1880s. It is located high in the mountains, at an elevation of 4,000 feet (1,219 m). Because of this, its summer temperatures rarely climb above 80°F (27°C).

To attract more tourists, business leaders in the Mountain region built large hotels that had elevators and steam heat. Guests sat on wide porches, enjoying the views. They played golf or tennis or went horseback riding. Among these early hotels were the Mountain Park Hotel in Hot Springs and the Green Park Hotel in Blowing Rock.

REVIEW Why did many tourists want to spend the summer in Mountain towns?

The Railroad Brings More People

Extending the railroads into the mountains helped tourism grow. The Western North Carolina Railroad linked the far western counties with the rest of the state. In 1869 the railroad reached Old Fort in McDowell County. Construction

• GEOGRAPHY •

Mount Mitchell
Understanding Environment and Society

By the early 1900s, loggers had cleared out many of the trees on Mount Mitchell. Some people worried that soon there would not be any forests left. On March 3, 1915, the area surrounding Mount Mitchell became the first state forest in North Carolina— Mount Mitchell State Park. People began to visit the mountain to see its beautiful views. At first tourists drove their cars up old logging roads or followed old railroad tracks. The Blue Ridge Parkway, built in the 1940s, brought even more people to Mount Mitchell.

TN
Pisgah National Forest
North... R.
N
W E
S
Spruce Pine
Pisgah
Faust
French Broad R.
Mars Hill
Little Switzerland
National
Forest
MOUNT MITCHELL ■
L. James
Black Mountain
Marion
40
Asheville
40
0   10   20 Miles
0 10   20 Kilometers

slowed because workers had to lay tracks along steep mountain slopes and blast tunnels through the Blue Ridge Mountains. The work was hard and dangerous. The last tunnel built through the hard rock of the mountains was the 1,832-foot (558-m) Swannanoa Tunnel. It took the railroad into Asheville in 1880.

Workers built trestles, or bridges with railroad tracks on them, to carry the trains across deep valleys. When the Western North Carolina Railroad was completed, travel to the Mountain region became much easier.

Good transportation was important to business. At that time railroads were the fastest form of transportation for passengers and for goods. The railroads helped small towns attract new businesses. New businesses created more jobs and drew more people to the Mountain region.

REVIEW How did the extension of railroads into the region affect western North Carolina?

Asheville Grows

The first train steamed into Asheville on October 3, 1880. The railroad helped Asheville become the transportation hub of the Mountain region. Before 1880 Asheville was a small, hard-to-reach town surrounded by many mountains. With the railroad the town grew into a city. Hotels, banks, and other kinds of businesses opened. One of the city's first hotels was the Battery Park, built in 1886.

In the 20-year period from 1880 to 1900, Asheville's year-round population rose from 2,600 to almost 15,000. As many as 20,000 more people spent a part of each year there.

Today Asheville is the Mountain region's largest city. Its population still soars each summer when tourists arrive. It is the center for shopping, banking, education, and government services in the region.

REVIEW What helped Asheville grow?

The Biltmore Estate

In 1888 George Vanderbilt, a member of one of the richest families in the United States, visited the Mountain region. He liked the mountain views and the climate so much that he decided to build a home there. Vanderbilt bought more than 125,000 acres of land near Asheville. The home he built was no ordinary vacation house. It has more than 250 rooms and is the largest private home in the United States. The house and the land are called the Biltmore Estate. An **estate** is a large piece of land with a huge house on it. It took hundreds of workers more than five years to build the house.

Vanderbilt wanted to produce farm and forest products. He hired Gifford Pinchot (PIN•choh) to oversee the development of the forests. Pinchot had studied forest management in France. He became one of the first people to urge Americans to think about conservation. **Conservation** is the protection and wise use of natural resources such as trees.

Managing forests was a new idea for people in North Carolina in the late 1800s. Lumber had long been a leading product. Lumber companies cut down trees and sold the lumber. They did not replace the trees. Farmers burned trees to clear areas for their cattle to graze. These actions destroyed forests and left mountainsides bare. Without trees, the topsoil streamed down hillsides when it rained. However, the furniture industry boomed. The demand for wood grew.

Vanderbilt and Pinchot worked to save forests in the Mountain region. Pinchot began restoring the forests. He ordered diseased trees cut down and healthy ones planted. After Pinchot left the Biltmore Estate, Vanderbilt hired German forester

Today tourists visit the Biltmore Estate and the forests around it.

FAST FACT

The Biltmore Estate has more than 250 rooms, including 43 bathrooms, and 3 kitchens. When built, it featured North Carolina's first electric elevator.

The Pisgah National Forest was once part of George Vanderbilt's land.

Carl Schenck to manage the estate's forests. There Schenck started the first forestry school in the United States. **Forestry** is the science of managing and protecting forests and forest resources.

After Vanderbilt died, nearly 87,000 acres of Biltmore's forestland was turned over to the government. Today this land is the Pisgah National Forest, North Carolina's first national forest. It has become a Mountain region treasure everyone can share.

REVIEW How did Pinchot and Schenck change lumbering in North Carolina?

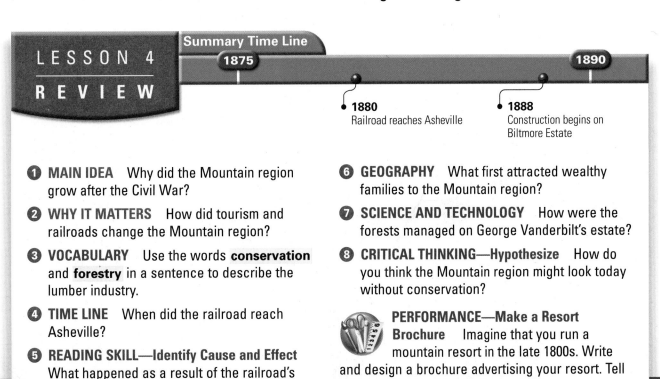

LESSON 4
REVIEW

Summary Time Line

1875 — 1890

1880
Railroad reaches Asheville

1888
Construction begins on Biltmore Estate

1 **MAIN IDEA** Why did the Mountain region grow after the Civil War?

2 **WHY IT MATTERS** How did tourism and railroads change the Mountain region?

3 **VOCABULARY** Use the words **conservation** and **forestry** in a sentence to describe the lumber industry.

4 **TIME LINE** When did the railroad reach Asheville?

5 **READING SKILL—Identify Cause and Effect** What happened as a result of the railroad's arrival in Asheville?

6 **GEOGRAPHY** What first attracted wealthy families to the Mountain region?

7 **SCIENCE AND TECHNOLOGY** How were the forests managed on George Vanderbilt's estate?

8 **CRITICAL THINKING—Hypothesize** How do you think the Mountain region might look today without conservation?

PERFORMANCE—Make a Resort Brochure Imagine that you run a mountain resort in the late 1800s. Write and design a brochure advertising your resort. Tell why people should visit the mountains.

7 Review and Test Preparation

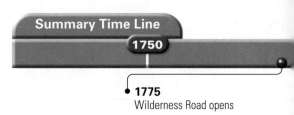

Summary Time Line

1750

1775
Wilderness Road opens

USE YOUR READING SKILLS

Use this graphic organizer to help you understand some of the causes and effects of the events you read about in Chapter 7. A copy of this graphic organizer appears on page 76 of the Activity Book.

The Mountain Region Long Ago

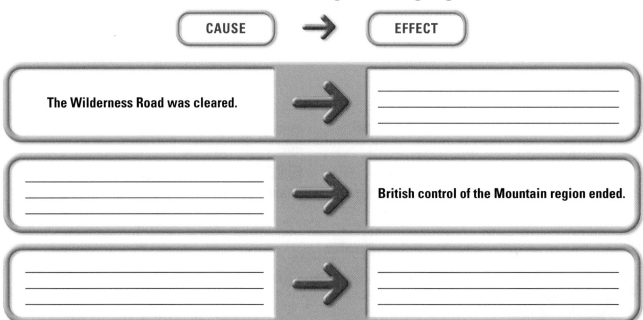

CAUSE → EFFECT

The Wilderness Road was cleared. →

→ British control of the Mountain region ended.

→

THINK & WRITE

Write a Journal Entry Imagine that you are an early pioneer in the Mountain region. Write a journal entry about your life compared with the life you had in your old home. Include the challenges you faced. Also write about your hopes for the future in the Mountain region.

Write a Booklet Imagine that you live in North Carolina in the 1830s. Write a booklet to hand out to people in a mountain town. Explain your point of view on the Indian Removal Act, the court decision to protect the Cherokees, and President Jackson's response. Explain your opinions.

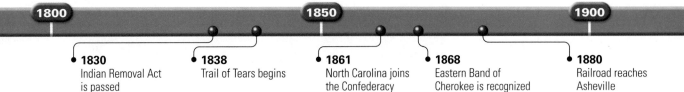

1800 | 1850 | 1900

1830
Indian Removal Act
is passed

1838
Trail of Tears begins

1861
North Carolina joins
the Confederacy

1868
Eastern Band of
Cherokee is recognized

1880
Railroad reaches
Asheville

USE THE TIME LINE

Use the chapter summary time line to answer these questions.

1 When did North Carolina join the Confederacy?

2 How many years after the Wilderness Road opened did the railroad reach Asheville?

USE VOCABULARY

In each of the following sentences, fill in the blank with the correct term.

log cabin (p. 222)

barter (p. 224)

fertile (p. 229)

reservation (p. 237)

estate (p. 242)

3 We visited a ____ to learn about Cherokee culture and crafts.

4 Early pioneer families often lived in a ____.

5 The wealthy family bought a huge ____ in the country.

6 Instead of using money to buy goods, mountain settlers would ____ for what they needed.

7 Crops grow well on ____ land.

RECALL FACTS

Answer these questions.

8 Why did Europeans settle the frontier?

9 How did parents in the Mountain region depend on their children?

10 How did George Vanderbilt protect forests?

Write the letter of the best choice.

11 **TEST PREP** Most settlers in the western mountains of North Carolina were—
  A descendants of Scotch-Irish and German immigrants.
  B Cherokees.
  C Spanish explorers.
  D British.

12 **TEST PREP** People of the Mountain region supported the Confederate army mainly because—
  F they were loyal to their state.
  G they wanted new land.
  H they wanted to keep their slaves.
  J the governor pushed them to join.

THINK CRITICALLY

13 Why might people in the mountains have disagreed with city people about slavery?

14 How might life in the Mountain region have been different if the Cherokees had not been forced to leave the state?

APPLY SKILLS

Compare Historical Maps

15 Use the historical maps on pages 226–227 to name three territories that were new in 1800.

Determine Point of View

16 Find a magazine or newspaper article that expresses a point of view on an important issue. Write a summary of the issue from your point of view.

1800 **Chapter 7 ■ 245**

MOSES CONE MEMORIAL PARK

Moses Cone Memorial Park is one of the many scenic areas along the Blue Ridge Parkway. The land belonged to Moses Cone, a denim cloth manufacturer. After he died, the land was given to the United States government. The government has kept it as a park.

LOCATE IT

NORTH CAROLINA

Moses Cone
Memorial Park

8

The Mountain Region Today

66 I've never seen nothing to beat these mountains. 99
—Davitus Gosnell, a 90-year-old farmer

CHAPTER READING SKILL

Draw Conclusions

A conclusion is a decision or an idea reached by using evidence from what you read and what you already know about a subject. To **draw a conclusion**, combine new facts with the facts you already know.

As you read this chapter, use evidence and what you already know to draw conclusions about North Carolina.

EVIDENCE
KNOWLEDGE

CONCLUSION

1

Living in the Mountain Region

MAIN IDEA

Read to find out about the Mountain region's communities and cultural heritage.

WHY IT MATTERS

The people of the Mountain region are proud of their rich cultural heritage and enjoy sharing it with others.

VOCABULARY

retirement
community
clogging
ballad
bluegrass music

In 1980 Ray Greene, Walt Davis, and other musicians who first played music with one another in the 1920s started getting together again. They went to the town of Black Mountain to play what they called "old-time mountain m ↑ y played folk songs, country music, fiddle tunes, and bl s. Many people who gathered to hear these musicians remembered this music from childhood.

Mountain Communities

With more than 63,000 people, Asheville is the Mountain region's largest city. It is a regional center for government and medical care. Some people who live there work for the federal, state, and local governments. Others are doctors or nurses at the three hospitals in the city.

People in Asheville work in many other jobs as well. Some are craftspeople, such as potters, glassmakers, and weavers. Some are businesspeople who own the shops and galleries that display the work of the artists and craftspeople. (↑ h or

FAST FACT Asheville is named for Samuel Ashe. He was governor of North Carolina from 1795 to 1798. Ashe County and Asheboro are also named for him.

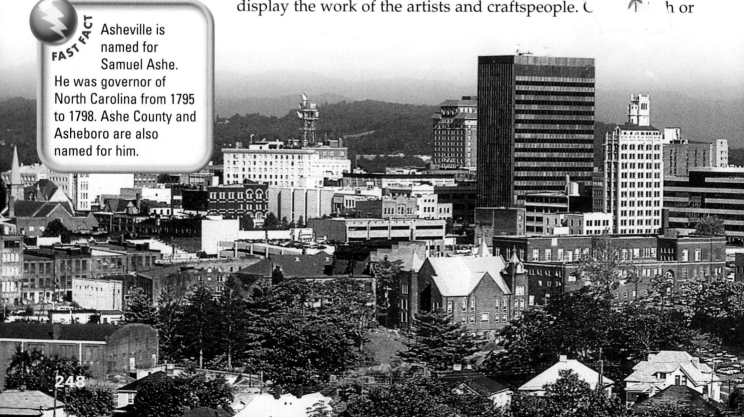

248

North Carolina artist Romare Bearden showed folk musicians in this untitled work.

go to school at the University of North Carolina at Asheville or work in banking or manufacturing.

Many people who live in Asheville work in the tourist industry. Some run motels or inns. Others work as tour guides. Tourists enjoy visiting such places as the Biltmore Estate and the house where Thomas Wolfe, a famous author, grew up. The city is a base for many vacationers exploring the Mountain region.

Asheville, Hendersonville, and other western North Carolina towns have become popular retirement communities. **Retirement communities** are places where older people live when they no longer work at full-time jobs.

LOCATE IT

NORTH CAROLINA

Asheville

Many people who are retired, called retirees, move to western North Carolina from all over the United States. They choose this area because of its mild climate and scenic mountain views.

When retirees move to a town, they help the ᴀ ᴛy. They buy houses, food, and clothing. They go to movies, attend community college classes, and shop at area malls. Many give help to the community through volunteer work.

About 30 years ago the leaders of Hendersonville wanted to attract more people to the downtown area. They turned some streets into walking streets for shoppers. They fixed up historic buildings and storefronts on Main Street. New shops and restaurants opened. Today the town is popular as a retirement community and as a tourist area.

Black Mountain also worked to make its downtown an inviting place. Today Black Mountain has many visitors. It is called "the front porch of western North Carolina." The town attracts people for its views of the Blue Ridge Mountains and for the historic area on Cherry Street.

Boone is a busy college town in the Blue Ridge Mountains. It was named for trailblazer Daniel Boone. During the winter months, students at Appalachian State University study hard all week. On weekends they go to ski at nearby Beech or Sugar Mountain. The area has some of the best ski trails in the eastern United States.

Businesses in Watauga County, in towns such as Boone, Banner Elk, and Blowing Rock, have been helped by their nearness to ski resorts. Vacationers not only rent cars and skis but also spend money on food, motels, and movies.

REVIEW **What has helped the cities and towns in the Mountain region grow?**

Ski resorts such as Sugar Mountain attract many tourists to the Mountain region.

Freeman Owle   1946–

Character Trait: Self-Discipline

Freeman Owle is a master Cherokee carver and storyteller. He grew up in Birdtown on the Qualla Boundary, a Cherokee reservation in Swain County. When Owle was in high school, he started making wooden bowls. Owle later used soapstone, which can be easily chipped and carved. Today Owle is both an artist and a teacher. He travels to museums, schools, and other places telling Cherokee stories and talking about his carvings.

GO ONLINE

MULTIMEDIA BIOGRAPHIES
Visit The Learning Site at www.harcourtschool.com/biographies to learn about other famous people.

Mountain Arts and Crafts

In 1920 Lucy Morgan, a North Carolina native, moved to the Mountain region's Mitchell County. She helped her brother Rufus run a school for children in the town of Penland for four years.

Morgan also started a program for the women of Mitchell County. She wanted people to be proud of their traditional crafts while making money ⋀ families.

Today the school founded ⋀ n has 40 buildings. People travel to the P⋀ l from many countries. T veaving, photography, pottery, glassmaking, and wood carving.

Many people collect quilts. They hang them on walls instead of using them as bedcovers. One of the best places to see and buy quilts and other Mountain crafts is the Folk Art Center on the B⋀ ge Parkway. The center also sells of the Southern Highland Craf This is a group of artists who r tery, baskets, quilts, candles, w cornhusk dolls, and wood carvings.

Near the town of Cherokee, tourists enjoy stopping at the Qualla Arts and Crafts Mutual. It is the largest Native American–owned crafts center in the country. It offers Cherokee beadwork, baskets, wood carvings, pottery, and other crafts.

One Cherokee craftworker is Freeman Owle. He is a famous Cherokee carver who is also a storyteller. He makes carvings of plants, animals, and objects he sees in his environment.

⋀ at are some traditional and crafts?

Craftspeople in the mountain region make pottery such as this "ugly jug."

Music, Dance, and Storytelling

In the 1920s John and Olive Campbell were working with the pe[ople] [of] Brasstown to preserve the[ir] crafts and music. Olive C[ampbell] worked with Lucy Morgan from Penland and others to organize the Southern Highland Craft Guild.

In 1925 Olive Campbell started the John C. Campbell Folk School to preserve Mountain arts and crafts. Today the school offers classes in dance, music, and storytelling as well as in [a]rts and crafts.

Clogging [is] one kind of traditional folk dancing taught at the Campbell Folk School. This fast, toe-tapping dance started in the southern Appalachian Mountains.

A dulcimer used in mountain music

Its roots are in dances brought to the area by Scottish, Irish, and English settlers.

Cloggers dance to lively country music. Country music developed from the folk songs and ballads of the English, Irish, and Scottish settlers of the Southeast. A **ballad** is a song that tells a story. A style of country music that dates back to the 1920s is **bluegrass music**. Bluegrass music has its roots in African American blues and gospel music.

Some mountain musicians play the dulcimer. The dulcimer is a traditional Appalachian instrument us[ed in] [playin]g folk music. Musicians hold [them in] their laps and play them b[y] [pluckin]g strumming the strings. In North Carolina, there are a number of dulcimer clubs.

Storytelling has been practiced in the mountains since the arrival of the first Native Americans. The Cherokees have [...] [...] hat date back many centuries. [...] brought with them stories from England, Scotland, and Ireland. In the past, storytelling was the main form of entertainment.

One of North Carolina's master storytellers is Ray Hicks, who lives in Beech Creek in Watauga County. He is best known for telling Jack tales, such as "Jack and the Beanstalk."

Every year people from all over the world attend many festivals that display the heritage of song, dance, arts, and crafts. The Mountain Dance and Folk Festival and the Southern Highland Craft Guild Fair are both held in Asheville. The ten-day Folkmoot USA attracts dance groups from all over the world.

REVIEW **How do the people of the Mountain region share their culture through their arts and crafts?**

Storytelling is an important part of Cherokee culture.

LESSON 1 REVIEW

❶ **MAIN IDEA** What communities are in the Mountain region, and how do they attract tourists?

❷ **WHY IT MATTERS** How do people in the Mountain region celebrate their heritage?

❸ **VOCABULARY** How do **clogging** and **bluegrass music** differ?

❹ **READING SKILL—Draw Conclusions** What can you conclude about Lucy Morgan, based on her work?

❺ **CULTURE** What do tourists find at the Qualla Arts and Crafts Mutual?

❻ **CRITICAL THINKING—Analyze** Why do you think many retired people choose to move to the mountains?

PERFORMANCE—Write a Letter Your grandparents have just moved to a retirement community in the Mountain region. Write a short letter they could send telling why you might want to visit.

MAIN IDEA
Read to find out about the various industries of the Mountain region.

WHY IT MATTERS
The Mountain region's natural resources and location have influenced the region's economic activities.

VOCABULARY
orchard
reforestation
smog
haze

Working in the Mountain Region

At the Sky Top Apple Orchard, in Flat Rock, Henderson County, the Butler family offers tourists Granny Smith apples and 29 other kinds of apples. An **orchard** is a large group of fruit trees. David Butler and his family have been raising and selling apples for 30 years. Many Sky Top customers return every fall to buy apples at his orchard.

Farming in the Mountains

Today North Carolina is one of the largest apple-growing states. The mild winters and cool summers in the valleys are just right for growing many kinds of apples. Most of the apples from North Carolina are grown in the Mountain region.

Apples need warm days, cool nights, and winter temperatures below 45°F (7°C). The Mountain region is cold enough in the winter and has the cooler summer temperatures that apples need in order to grow.

An apple tree bears fruit in about 8 to 10 years. A full-grown tree can produce up to 20 bushels, or baskets, of apples a year.

Apple orchards are found throughout the Mountain region.

Christmas Tree Production

YEAR	CHRISTMAS TREE SALES
1993	🌲🌲🌲🌲🌲🌲🌲
1994	🌲🌲🌲🌲🌲🌲🌲
1995	🌲🌲🌲🌲🌲🌲🌲
1996	🌲🌲🌲🌲🌲🌲
1997	🌲🌲🌲🌲🌲🌲🌲
1998	🌲🌲🌲🌲🌲🌲🌲
1999	🌲🌲🌲🌲🌲🌲🌲🌲
2000	🌲🌲🌲🌲🌲🌲🌲🌲

🌲 = $10 million

Analyze Graphs The farming of Christmas trees is an important business in North Carolina.

◆ How much more money was made from Christmas tree sales in 2000 than in 1996?

Applesauce and juice companies buy about three-fifths of North Carolina's apples. The rest are sold as whole fruit or are made into cider.

Christmas trees are another important Mountain crop. North Carolina farmers grow about one-fifth of all the Christmas trees in the United States. Many of these are Fraser firs, the most common evergreens in the Mountain region. Fraser firs from North Carolina have been used eight times to decorate the White House at Christmas. Trees used for the White House have to be 16 to 18 feet (5 to 6 m) tall.

In North Carolina many people drive to tree farms in the mountains to choose a tree for the Christmas holiday. When spring comes, tree farmers plant new trees to replace those sold in December. An average-size Christmas tree takes about 12 years to grow.

Apples, Christmas trees, and tobacco are the three main crops in the Mountain region. Mountain farmers grow many other crops too, such as potatoes, cabbage, corn, and soybeans. They also raise beef and dairy cattle on the good grazing land in the valleys.

REVIEW What are the most important crops raised in the Mountain region?

Mining and Forestry

If you're looking for gems in North Carolina, start in Alexander County. In 1998 James Hill dug up many emeralds near his hometown of Hiddenite. Nine years earlier the largest emerald ever found in North America was discovered at the Rist Mine in Hiddenite.

This emerald, from the Rist Mine, is the largest ever found in North America.

Of course, such finds are rare. Still, North Carolina lawmakers made the emerald the official state gem.

Ordinary rocks and stones are not as exciting as emeralds. Yet in the Mountain region, mines that produce gravel and stone are more important to the economy.

Throughout the Mountain region, trucks carry crushed stone away from local quarries. The construction industry uses more than two-thirds of this crushed stone to make concrete and to build highways.

Logging is also an important industry. Lumber companies provide jobs for many people. Loggers cut down trees to provide wood for houses and furniture and for paper products such as newspapers, books, and magazines.

Forests cover much of the Mountain region. Lumber companies and private citizens own some of this forestland. Other forests are protected in national or state parks or national forests. Most of the trees in these areas cannot be cut down.

The Mountain region has two national forests, the Nantahala (nan•tuh•HAY•luh) and the Pisgah. The Nantahala is the larger of the two. Its name comes from a Cherokee word meaning "land of the noonday sun." In the Nantahala Forest the deep valleys get sunlight only in the middle of the day, when the sun is directly overhead.

FAST FACT The biggest pine tree in North Carolina is an Eastern white pine in Henderson County. It is 178 feet (54 m) tall, almost twice as tall as the state capitol in Raleigh.

Paper mills, such as this one in Haywood County, use trees from North Carolina forests. The trees are carried on trucks to the paper mill.

Forests are important for many reasons. They provide homes for wildlife. They offer places for fishing, camping, and other forms of recreation. Forests also help the environment. The root systems of trees hold soil in place, preventing erosion. The leaves of trees also contribute to clean air.

North Carolina's forests have to be managed wisely. Caring for a forest means cutting down sick or older trees so that younger, healthy trees can grow. Workers also cut down some trees in crowded forests to give the other trees more room. Then the trees that are left have enough nutrients, sunlight, and water.

Sometimes forests need to be replanted, or reforested. **Reforestation** is a program for planting seedlings, or young trees, to replace trees that have been cut down for lumber. The North Carolina government protects forests so people can enjoy them for years to come. People do not always agree about how forests should be managed. The benefits that living trees give to the environment must be balanced with the need to use trees for lumber.

REVIEW What are some ways forests are managed in the Mountain region?

Manufacturing

Forest products make up one of North Carolina's largest manufacturing industries. Almost every county in the mountains has factories and mills that make wood products.

Some factory workers build furniture. Workers in paper and pulp mills in Waynesville and Canton in Haywood County make many kinds of products, including papers used for magazines and books. Most large paper mills are built near the forests that supply wood. They are also located near rivers and streams. Water from the rivers and streams is used to manufacture paper goods.

Linn Cove Viaduct

The Linn Cove Viaduct was built in 1987. A viaduct is an elevated road or bridge that rests on a series of narrow concrete piers or columns. Engineers made parts of the viaduct indoors in a building a few miles from the site. As a result, they did not damage the mountain while they worked. Also, they could work during the winter. When the viaduct was finished, it was 1,243 feet (379 m) long. There were 153 concrete sections. Each section weighed 50 tons, about as much as ten elephants!

In the 1980s people who lived in the Mountain region became worried about the environment. They thought that chemicals and other wastes from manufacturing might get into the waterways. Health officials warned people not to eat fish from rivers or lakes. Now government officials are working to cut down on pollution.

Food processing is also done in the mountains. Factories make baked goods, bottle soft drinks, and process food crops. Other factories make machinery, clothing and leather goods, and building equipment.

Along with positive changes, industrial growth brings air pollution. Much of this pollution is caused by power plants that burn coal in North Carolina and the neighboring states. Winds carry pollution throughout those states. Cars and factories add to air pollution. The smoke from power plants, factories, and cars often gets trapped in the valleys between the mountains, causing smog. **Smog** is a mixture of smoke and fog. It harms people as well as trees and other plants.

Haze also occurs in the mountains. **Haze** is produced by dust, smoke, or mist in the air. Haze makes it hard to see.

Today government leaders and scientists in North Carolina, Tennessee, and other southeastern states are working together to come up with solutions to pollution problems. The states in the South know they must cooperate to clean up the air in order to protect the environment and people.

REVIEW What are some manufacturing industries in the Mountain region?

Service Industries and Tourism

Workers hold many service jobs in the Mountain region. Some work in schools as teachers or in stores as salesclerks. Others are doctors and nurses in hospitals.

The most important service industry in the Mountain region is tourism. Tourism provides jobs for thousands of people and is very important to the economy of the region. Many people hold jobs in restaurants, hotels, and inns. Others care for parks and forests. Some pump gas at service stations. Others work as guides, helping tourists raft safely down fast-flowing rivers or climb up mountain trails. Tourism boosts the economy of the Mountain region.

REVIEW **Why is tourism important to the economy of the Mountain region?**

Rafting guides lead people on exciting trips down North Carolina's mountain rivers.

LESSON 2 REVIEW

1. **MAIN IDEA** What are some industries of the Mountain region?

2. **WHY IT MATTERS** How do industries in the Mountain region use the region's natural resources?

3. **VOCABULARY** What are **smog** and **haze**, and how can they cause problems?

4. **READING SKILL—Draw Conclusions** Do people in the Mountain region protect natural resources? Explain your answer.

5. **GEOGRAPHY** Why are there so many apple orchards in the Mountain region?

6. **ECONOMICS** Which is more important to the Mountain region's economy, emeralds or gravel? Why?

7. **CRITICAL THINKING—Apply** How can North Carolina help prevent pollution?

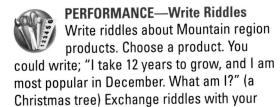

PERFORMANCE—Write Riddles
Write riddles about Mountain region products. Choose a product. You could write; "I take 12 years to grow, and I am most popular in December. What am I?" (a Christmas tree) Exchange riddles with your classmates.

Read a Double-Bar Graph

➡ WHY IT MATTERS

A good way to compare **statistics**, or facts shown with numbers, is by making a graph. A **double-bar graph** makes it easy to compare two sets of statistics. The graph uses two sets of bars to show different information. The bars make it easy to compare information quickly.

➡ WHAT YOU NEED TO KNOW

Look at the title of the double-bar graph on page 261. It tells what is being compared. The graph compares the number of acres of trees cut down with the number of acres of trees planted in the national forests of North Carolina over a four-year period. Use these steps as a guide to study the graph.

Step 1 The years are shown at the bottom of the graph. The number of acres appears along the left side of the graph.

Step 2 Look at the two bars for each year. The green bar shows the acres of trees cut. The blue bar shows the acres of trees planted.

Step 3 Read the graph by placing your finger at the top of each bar and then moving your finger left to the number. If the top of the bar is between two numbers, the exact number of acres is between those two numbers.

Thousands of acres of trees are cut down every year in North Carolina.

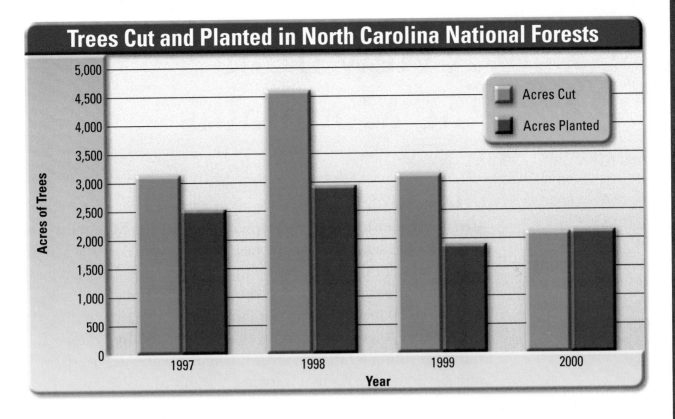

Trees Cut and Planted in North Carolina National Forests

Acres of Trees (y-axis): 0, 500, 1,000, 1,500, 2,000, 2,500, 3,000, 3,500, 4,000, 4,500, 5,000

Year (x-axis): 1997, 1998, 1999, 2000

Key:
- Acres Cut
- Acres Planted

PRACTICE THE SKILL

1. Compare the information in each set of bars. In what year was the number of acres cut closest to the number of acres planted?

2. In what year was there the biggest difference?

3. In general, were more acres cut or planted between 1997 and 2000?

New trees take the place of trees that were cut down.

APPLY WHAT YOU LEARNED

Make a double-bar graph that compares two of your daily activities. Compare the time you spend doing homework and the time you spend on a daily activity of your choice. Then draw the graph. Label the bottom with the days of the week. List the number of hours along the left side. Make two bars for each day. One is for homework time. The other is for your activity. Include a title and a key for your graph. Write several sentences telling what you discovered by using the graph.

3

A View from the Mountains

In May 2001 a Raleigh newspaper printed a debate between two of its reporters. The subject was whether the Mountain region or the seashore was the best place to vacation. Joe Miller was in favor of the mountains. "In the mountains," he said, "you can ride some of the best mountain bike trails in the East, gaining 3,000 feet of altitude or more on a single ride. In the mountains, you can go white-water rafting." **White-water** rafting is riding a raft on a river where the water moves so quickly around rocks that it foams.

Along the Blue Ridge Parkway

One of the treasures of the Mountain region is the Blue Ridge Parkway. This winding, scenic road connects the Great Smoky Mountains National Park in North Carolina with the Shenandoah National Park in Virginia. About half of its 470 miles (756 km) are in North Carolina.

TENNESSEE

NORTH CAROLINA

Trees and flowers are easy to see along this road because no billboards or trucks are allowed. Fall is leaf lovers' favorite season. Leaves on many trees turn red, yellow, gold, and orange. In spring, wildflowers dot the fields. Houck (HOWK) Medford grew up in Waynesville near the Blue Ridge Parkway. After working as a dentist in Winston-Salem for 20 years, he returned to the mountains. He started a group that built the Water Rock Knob Visitors Center at the southern end of the parkway. A knob is a rounded hill or mountain, usually standing alone.

Medford's group has collected stories of people who have lived or worked along the parkway. Medford explains why he and other Mountain people like the parkway. "Everybody has some sort of connection to the parkway, whether it's a Mother's Day drive or the fall tour, or camping or hiking or biking."

Workers began building the Blue Ridge Parkway in 1936. At that time the United States was in the middle of hard economic times. Millions of people were out of work. Building the parkway gave many people jobs. Most of the work was finished in 1967, but one last part was not finished until 1987.

A CLOSER LOOK
The Blue Ridge Parkway

You can see many different parts of the Mountain region from the Blue Ridge Parkway.

1. The parkway enters North Carolina near Cumberland Knob. This was the first part of the parkway built.
2. Linville Falls is just off the parkway. The Linville River drops 120 feet (37 m) from the side of Grandfather Mountain into Linville Gorge.
3. The parkway passes near Mount Mitchell, the tallest mountain east of the Mississippi River.
4. The headquarters for the whole parkway is in Asheville.
5. The southern end of the parkway is in Cherokee, near the Qualla Boundary Reservation.

❖ What part of the parkway would you most like to visit? Why?

VIRGINIA

Visitors traveling south along the Blue Ridge Parkway from Virginia cross into North Carolina near Cumberland Knob. About 60 miles (97 km) farther south, many cars park to get a view of Blowing Rock. This is a huge cliff that hangs over the John's River Gorge. A **gorge** is a deep passageway cut through rocks by water.

At Milepost 304 on the parkway, visitors can see the Linn Cove Viaduct. This road winds around Grandfather Mountain. People can walk across the Mile High Swinging Bridge on Grandfather Mountain. They can also camp and hike.

Many cars stop at overlooks near Linville Falls. An **overlook** is a place where cars can pull off the road and passengers can look down on the scenery below. The Cherokees called Linville Falls the River of Cliffs. Waterfalls come crashing through the Linville Gorge.

The Linville Gorge is the deepest gorge east of the Grand Canyon in Arizona.

The parkway continues south through Mount Mitchell State Park. There travelers can get close to the top of Mount Mitchell. This is the highest point east of the Mississippi River. Mount Mitchell was named for Dr. Elisha Mitchell, who measured the elevations of the Black Mountains in the 1800s.

After Asheville the parkway enters Pisgah National Forest. At the Cradle of Forestry, travelers can learn about the work of Gifford Pinchot and Carl Schenck. Both men helped establish the first forestry school in the United States.

The final stop on the southern end of the Blue Ridge Parkway is Great Smoky Mountains National Park. It is the most visited park in the national park system.

REVIEW What are some places to visit along the Blue Ridge Parkway?

Lakes and Rivers

There are many ways to enjoy the lakes and rivers of the Mountain region. At Lake Lure you can sit around a campfire cooking fresh fish caught from the lake. Dams on the Hiwassee, Little Tennessee, and Tuckasegee (tuh•kuh•SEE•jee) Rivers provide hydroelectricity and flood control. Fontana Dam stretches more than a half mile across a gorge on the Little Tennessee River. It is the highest dam in the eastern United States. Reservoirs formed by these dams offer places for recreation. A **reservoir** is a human-made lake that stores water.

For vacationers who like rafting, a trip down the roaring Nantahala River offers plenty of excitement. The French Broad and Nolichucky (nah•luh•CHUH•kee) Rivers are other popular places for white-water rafting.

Some people visit the mountains to go white-water kayaking or canoeing. The Nantahala River is the official training center for United States athletes preparing for the white-water canoeing and kayaking competition in the Olympic Games. Athletes from other countries also train near the Nantahala.

REVIEW What are some ways to enjoy the lakes and rivers of the Mountain region?

• GEOGRAPHY •

Nantahala River
Understanding Environment and Society

The Nantahala River is one of North Carolina's popular outdoor recreation areas. Visitors can rent a raft, a kayak, a canoe, or a boat. The nearly 9-mile (14-km) trip down the river includes many rapids, areas where the water gets rough. The river's flow is controlled by a series of dams run by the Nantahala hydroelectric plant. The plant uses the river's rushing water to make electricity. The Nantahala is one of the most popular white-water rivers in the country. Visitors can hike, bike, or ride a horse to Nantahala Lake to fish for trout. They can even spend a night or two under the stars in the Nantahala National Forest.

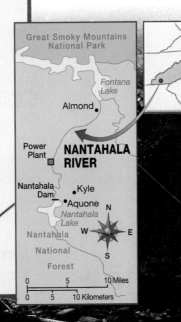

Bagpipers lead the parade of clans at the Grandfather Mountain Highland Games.

The Gathering of the Clans

Bagpipes and sheepdogs are part of one of the most exciting festivals in the Mountain region. The celebration is officially called the Grandfather Mountain Highland Games and Gathering of Scottish Clans. A clan is a group of families with the same ancestors. The games have been held yearly for almost 50 years.

Clan members gather at MacRae Meadows. The festival opens with a torch-lit ceremony known as the Calling of the Clans.

For the next three days, large crowds watch athletes compete in tests of speed and strength. Events include wrestling, archery, foot races, tugs of war, and Highland dancing. Musicians give harp, fiddle, and bagpipe concerts. There are also demonstrations of sheepherding using sheepdogs.

The festival ends on Sunday with clan members marching across the field in their **kilts**, or skirts. Each clan wears a kilt with a different plaid pattern, called a tartan.

REVIEW How do the Highland Games reflect the heritage of the Highland Scots?

LESSON 3
REVIEW

❶ **MAIN IDEA**   What are some physical features of the Mountain region?

❷ **WHY IT MATTERS**   Why do people enjoy visiting the Mountain region?

❸ **VOCABULARY**   Describe the Mountain region's rivers, using the terms **white-water** and **reservoir**.

❹ **READING SKILL—Draw Conclusions**   Based on this lesson, what can you conclude about tourism in the Mountain region?

❺ **HISTORY**   When did workers begin building the Blue Ridge Parkway?

❻ **CULTURE**   What are some of the competitions held at the Highland Games?

❼ **CRITICAL THINKING—Hypothesize**   What jobs in the Mountain region might be affected by a decrease in tourism?

 PERFORMANCE—Draw a Picture   Draw a picture showing some ways people enjoy the Mountain region. Show both physical features and outdoor activities.

·SKILLS· Identify Fact and Opinion

READING

▶ WHY IT MATTERS

A good reader or listener can tell facts from opinions. A **fact** is a statement that can be checked and proved to be true. An **opinion** is a statement that tells what someone thinks or believes. Knowing how to tell a fact from an opinion can help you better understand what you read or hear.

▶ WHAT YOU NEED TO KNOW

In this unit you have read about the history of the Mountain region and about life there today. Some things you read were facts. Others, especially people's quotes, were opinions.

Read the fact about Daniel Boone below. Then read the opinion about Mountain people. The fact gives you information you can check. The opinion tells you what one person thinks.

▶ PRACTICE THE SKILL

Facts often give numbers or specific information. Reference books and other sources can be used to check facts.

Opinions are what speakers or writers believe. Look for key words such as *I think* and *in my opinion*. Also look for words that **evaluate**, or judge, an event. Words such as *wonderful* are clues to a writer's opinion.

Historians study both facts and opinions. Facts help historians know what happened. Opinions tell historians what people thought about what happened.

▶ APPLY WHAT YOU LEARNED

Compare a newspaper story and an editorial. Identify facts and opinions in each. Which gives more opinions?

FACT

In 1769 Boone followed an old Native American trail across the mountains into Kentucky.

Facts can be checked in books, in encyclopedias, and on official papers.

OPINION

Alfred Adams described his neighbors. "The mountain people are very independent. If they tell you they'll do something, they'll do it."

Opinions are beliefs or feelings.
Opinions cannot be checked as facts can.

READING SKILLS

8 Review and Test Preparation

USE YOUR READING SKILLS

Complete this graphic organizer to draw conclusions about the Mountain region's industries, resources, and way of life. A copy of this graphic organizer appears on page 83 of the Activity Book.

The Mountain Region Today

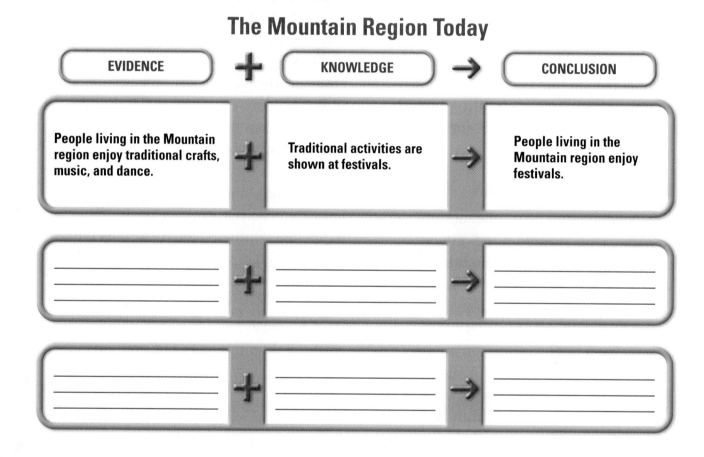

EVIDENCE	+	KNOWLEDGE	→	CONCLUSION
People living in the Mountain region enjoy traditional crafts, music, and dance.	+	Traditional activities are shown at festivals.	→	People living in the Mountain region enjoy festivals.

THINK & WRITE

Design a Bumper Sticker   Make up a saying about the natural beauty of the Mountain region. Then write your saying on a long strip of paper. Add a picture to make people notice your sticker. Post your bumper sticker in your classroom.

Write a Dialogue   Imagine that you are listening to a conversation between two people. One lives and works in the Mountain region. The other is a visitor. Write what they might say. Include the ideas and experiences of each person.

USE VOCABULARY

Write a paragraph to persuade a visitor to spend a summer in the Mountain region. Use these four vocabulary words from this chapter in your paragraph.

ballad (p. 252)

white-water (p. 262)

kilt (p. 266)

clogging (p. 252)

RECALL FACTS

Answer these questions.

1 What is the largest city in the Mountain region?

2 What is the state gem of North Carolina?

3 What is the most important service industry in the Mountain region?

Write the letter of the best choice.

4 **TEST PREP** The Penland School is a—
A university in the Blue Ridge Mountains.
B Native American–owned craft center.
C school for learning traditional crafts.
D dance school.

5 **TEST PREP** Which of the following North Carolina trees was used in the White House?
F apple
G oak
H Fraser fir
J pine

6 **TEST PREP** Which is the most visited park in the national park system?
A Great Smoky Mountains National Park
B Shenandoah National Park
C Hot Springs National Park
D Sequoia and Kings Canyon National Park

THINK CRITICALLY

7 Why do you think George Vanderbilt wanted to conserve the forests around the Biltmore Estate?

8 How would the economy of the Mountain region be different without the Blue Ridge Parkway?

APPLY SKILLS

Read a Double-Bar Graph
Use the graph on page 261.

9 About how many fewer acres of trees were planted in 1999 than in 1998?

Identify Fact and Opinion
Write *fact* if the sentence is a fact. Write *opinion* if it is an opinion.

10 In 1925 Olive Campbell founded the John C. Campbell Folk School.

11 Clogging is an exciting Mountain folk dance.

12 The Mountain region is full of beautiful scenery.

13 Many factories and mills make wood products in the Mountain region.

VISIT

A FOLK ART CENTER

GET READY

At the Blue Ridge Parkway's Folk Art Center, artists display and sell contemporary and traditional crafts of the Southern Appalachian region. Located near Asheville, the center welcomes more than 300,000 visitors a year. Visitors to the Folk Art Center have the opportunity to see artists at work and to learn more about the culture and traditions of the Mountain region. If you visit, you can watch crafts-people weave baskets, shape dolls from corn husks, or carve wooden figures. You can even try your own hand at decorating a clay pot.

WHAT TO SEE

A visitor enjoys looking at items on display in the Folk Art Center's main gallery.

LOCATE IT

NORTH CAROLINA

Asheville

The Blue Ridge Parkway's Folk Art Center

Visitors can learn how crafts are made. This artist demonstrates a craft called *marbling*.

This Native American doll is made from corn husks.

This woven bedspread is decorated with colorful animals.

An artist carved this bear from wood.

TAKE A FIELD TRIP

GO ONLINE

A VIRTUAL TOUR
Visit The Learning Site at **www.harcourtschool.com/tours** to find virtual tours of other art museums in the United States.

Turner Le@rning.

A VIDEO TOUR
Check your media center or classroom library for a videotape tour of the Blue Ridge Parkway's Folk Art Center.

4 Review and Test Preparation

VISUAL SUMMARY

Review the pictures and captions below to help you study Unit 4. Then choose three pictures. Write three sentences about the event shown in each picture. Identify what happened, why it happened, and what effects the event caused.

USE VOCABULARY

Match each word to its definition.

conservation (p. 242) **frontier** (p. 220)

overlook (p. 264) **orchard** (p. 254)

territory (p. 227)

1. a large group of fruit trees
2. a place to look at scenery from a high road
3. an area that belongs to a country
4. the western edge of European settlement
5. protection of natural resources

RECALL FACTS

Answer these questions.

6. Why did early pioneers in the Mountain region need to be self-sufficient?
7. When did the Western North Carolina Railroad reach Asheville?
8. Who are the Eastern Band of Cherokee?
9. How did early pioneers change the land of the Mountain region?

Write the letter of the best choice.

10. **TEST PREP** What happened to the 87,000 acres of the Biltmore Estate that were turned over to the government?
A The land is used for logging.
B The land was used to build the Blue Ridge Parkway.
C The government built offices on this land.
D The land is now Pisgah National Forest.

11. **TEST PREP** The Blue Ridge Parkway runs from the Great Smoky Mountains National Park to—
F the North Carolina coast.
G Cherokee, North Carolina.
H Raleigh, North Carolina.
J the Shenandoah National Park in Virginia.

Visual Summary

1750 — 1800

1775 Settlers cross over the Appalachians p. 222

1838 Cherokees are forced from North Carolina p. 236

1861–1865 North Carolinians serve in the Civil War p. 231

272

12 TEST PREP Where would you go to learn traditional Mountain folk dance, music, and storytelling?

A the Qualla Arts and Crafts Mutual
B the John C. Campbell Folk School
C Black Mountain
D Blowing Rock

THINK CRITICALLY

13 Why is tourism important to the economy of the Mountain region?

14 How is the life of a traditional craftsman like the life of a tree farm manager? How is it different?

15 Why do you think Cherokees choose to live in North Carolina today?

APPLY SKILLS

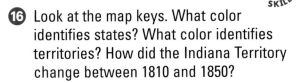

Compare Historical Maps
Use the maps on this page to answer these questions.

16 Look at the map keys. What color identifies states? What color identifies territories? How did the Indiana Territory change between 1810 and 1850?

17 How did the United States grow between 1810 and 1850?

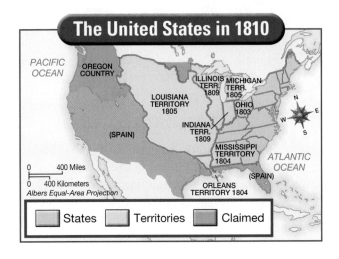

The United States in 1810

PACIFIC OCEAN

OREGON COUNTRY

ILLINOIS TERR. 1809
MICHIGAN TERR. 1805
LOUISIANA TERRITORY 1805
OHIO 1803
INDIANA TERR. 1809

(SPAIN)

MISSISSIPPI TERRITORY 1804

ATLANTIC OCEAN

(SPAIN)

ORLEANS TERRITORY 1804

0   400 Miles
0   400 Kilometers
Albers Equal-Area Projection

States   Territories   Claimed

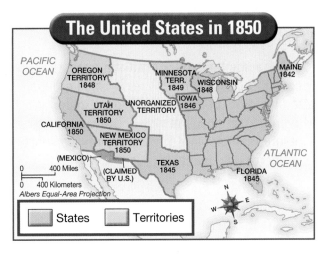

The United States in 1850

PACIFIC OCEAN

OREGON TERRITORY 1848
MINNESOTA TERR. 1849
WISCONSIN 1848
MAINE 1842

UTAH TERRITORY 1850
UNORGANIZED TERRITORY
IOWA 1846

CALIFORNIA 1850
NEW MEXICO TERRITORY 1850

(MEXICO)
(CLAIMED BY U.S.)
TEXAS 1845

ATLANTIC OCEAN

FLORIDA 1845

0   400 Miles
0   400 Kilometers
Albers Equal-Area Projection

States   Territories

18 What are five states that joined the United States between 1810 and 1850?

19 Compare United States territories in 1810 and 1850.

1900

1950

1880 Railroad reaches Asheville p. 241

1888 George Vanderbilt builds the Biltmore Estate p. 242

1936 Blue Ridge Parkway construction begins p. 263

273

Unit Activities

GO ONLINE

Visit The Learning Site at www.harcourtschool.com/socialstudies/activities for additional activities.

Have a Mountain Region Job Fair

As a class, create a plan for a job fair in the Mountain region. Think of different jobs in the region. Then design displays showing these jobs. Include as much job information as you can. Design a bulletin board showing your class plan.

Plan a Movie

Imagine that you are making a movie called *The Mountains*. Work in small groups to plan parts of the movie. Choose important events to show in the movie. Draw sketches of important scenes. If you can, write a short script for one scene.

VISIT YOUR LIBRARY

■ *Mountain Jack Tales* by Gail E. Haley. Parkway Publishers.

■ *The Journal of Jesse Smoke: A Cherokee Boy* by Joseph Bruchac. Scholastic.

■ *The Christmas Barn* by C.L. Davis. Pleasant Company Publications.

COMPLETE THE UNIT PROJECT

Make a Mountain Atlas
Continue making your mountain atlas. First, make a list of recreation activities in North Carolina's mountains. Name places in the mountains where people can enjoy the activities. Then write a description of each place and activity. Make maps showing where these activities occur.

North Carolina
in the
Modern World

The Wright brothers'
stopwatch

The Wright Brothers National Memorial on the Outer Banks of North Carolina

North Carolina in the Modern World

" Success. Four flights Thursday morning. "

—Wilbur Wright and Orville Wright, in a telegram to their father from Kitty Hawk, December 17, 1903

Preview the Content

Read the title of each lesson in this unit. Write two or three questions you have about each lesson.

Preview the Vocabulary

Multiple Meanings A word can often have several meanings. You may know one meaning but not another. Use the Glossary to look up each of the terms listed below. Then use each term in a sentence.

(interest) ⇉ _____   (cabinet) ⇉ _____

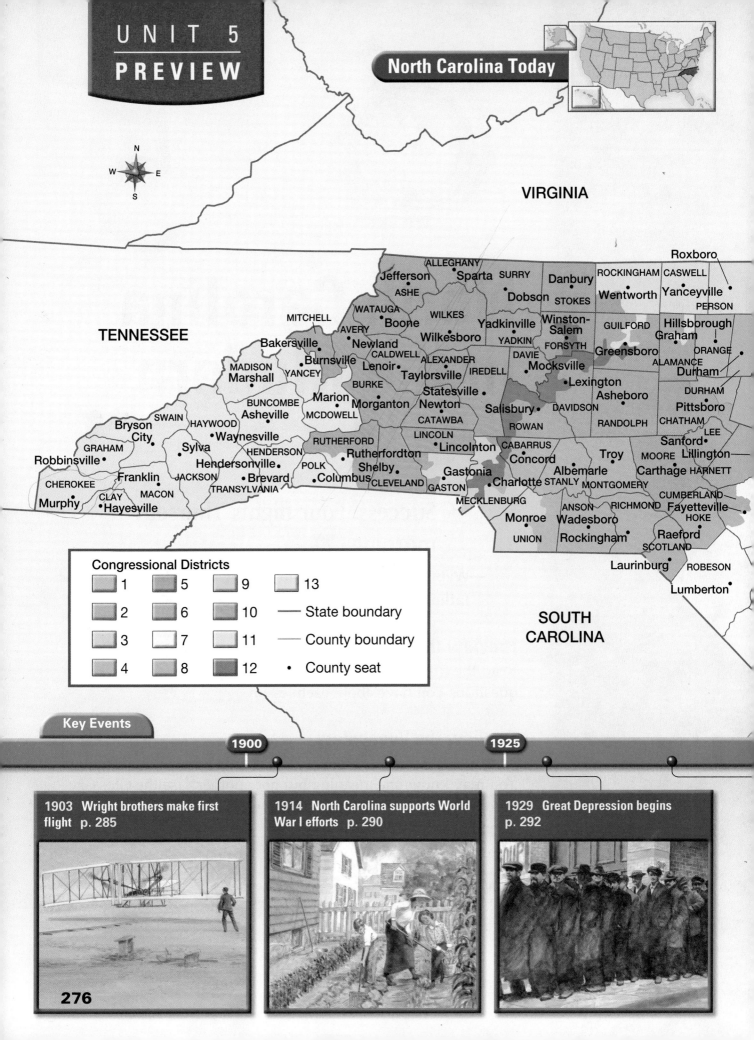

North Carolina Today

VIRGINIA

TENNESSEE

Roxboro

ALLEGHANY
Jefferson · Sparta   SURRY   Danbury   ROCKINGHAM   CASWELL
ASHE   Dobson   STOKES   Wentworth   Yanceyville
WATAUGA   PERSON
MITCHELL   · Boone   WILKES   Yadkinville   Winston-Salem   GUILFORD   Hillsborough
AVERY   Wilkesboro   YADKIN   Salem   FORSYTH   Greensboro   Graham
Bakersville   Newland   CALDWELL   ALEXANDER   DAVIE   ALAMANCE   ORANGE   Durham
MADISON   Burnsville   Lenoir   Taylorsville   IREDELL   · Mocksville   DURHAM
Marshall   YANCEY   BURKE   Lexington   Asheboro   Pittsboro
BUNCOMBE   Marion   Morganton   Statesville   Newton   Salisbury   DAVIDSON   RANDOLPH   CHATHAM
SWAIN   Asheville   MCDOWELL   CATAWBA   Salisbury   ROWAN   LEE
Bryson   HAYWOOD   Waynesville   LINCOLN   CABARRUS   Sanford
City   GRAHAM   RUTHERFORD   Lincolnton   Concord   Troy   MOORE   Lillington
Robbinsville ·   Sylva   HENDERSON   Rutherfordton   Shelby   Gastonia   Albemarle   Carthage   HARNETT
Franklin   JACKSON   · Brevard   POLK   CLEVELAND   GASTON   STANLY   MONTGOMERY   CUMBERLAND
CHEROKEE   MACON   TRANSYLVANIA   Columbus   Charlotte   ANSON   RICHMOND   Fayetteville
Murphy   CLAY   · Hayesville   MECKLENBURG   Monroe   Wadesboro   HOKE   Raeford
                                            UNION   Rockingham   SCOTLAND
                                                              Laurinburg   ROBESON
SOUTH
CAROLINA   Lumberton

Congressional Districts

1	5	9	13
2	6	10	— State boundary
3	7	11	— County boundary
4	8	12	• County seat

Key Events

1900 ———————————— 1925

1903 **Wright brothers make first flight** p. 285

1914 **North Carolina supports World War I efforts** p. 290

1929 **Great Depression begins** p. 292

North Carolina Population, 1900–2000

Year / Population (in millions)

Ethnic Groups in North Carolina

ETHNIC GROUP	POPULATION
European descent	
African American	
Hispanic American	
Asian American	
Native American	
Native Hawaiian/Pacific Islander	
More than one race	
Other	

🚶 = 250,000 persons

VANCE
WARREN
Oxford
NORTHAMPTON
GATES
CURRITUCK
CAMDEN
Warrenton
Gatesville
PASQUOTANK
Currituck
Jackson
Winton
Camden
Henderson
Halifax
HERTFORD
PERQUIMANS
Elizabeth City
GRANVILLE
HALIFAX
CHOWAN
Hertford
Louisburg
BERTIE
FRANKLIN
NASH
Windsor
Edenton
Nashville
Tarboro
MARTIN
Columbia
Manteo
Raleigh
EDGECOMBE
Plymouth
TYRRELL
Williamston
WASHINGTON
DARE
WAKE
Wilson
PITT
WILSON
Greenville
Smithfield
GREENE
Washington
HYDE
Snow Hill
Swan Quarter
JOHNSTON
BEAUFORT
Goldsboro
Kinston
WAYNE
LENOIR
CRAVEN
New Bern
Bayboro
SAMPSON
Trenton
Clinton
JONES
PAMLICO
Kenansville
DUPLIN
ONSLOW
CARTERET
Jacksonville
Beaufort
Elizabethtown
Burgaw
BLADEN
PENDER
Whiteville
NEW HANOVER
Wilmington
COLUMBUS
Bolivia
BRUNSWICK

ATLANTIC OCEAN

0   20   40 Miles
0   20   40 Kilometers
Albers Equal-Area Projection

1975

2000

1941 United States enters World War II p. 294

1960 Greensboro sit-in takes place p. 297

PRESENT North Carolina's population is more diverse than ever p. 306

START with a SONG

The Old North State

words by William Gaston

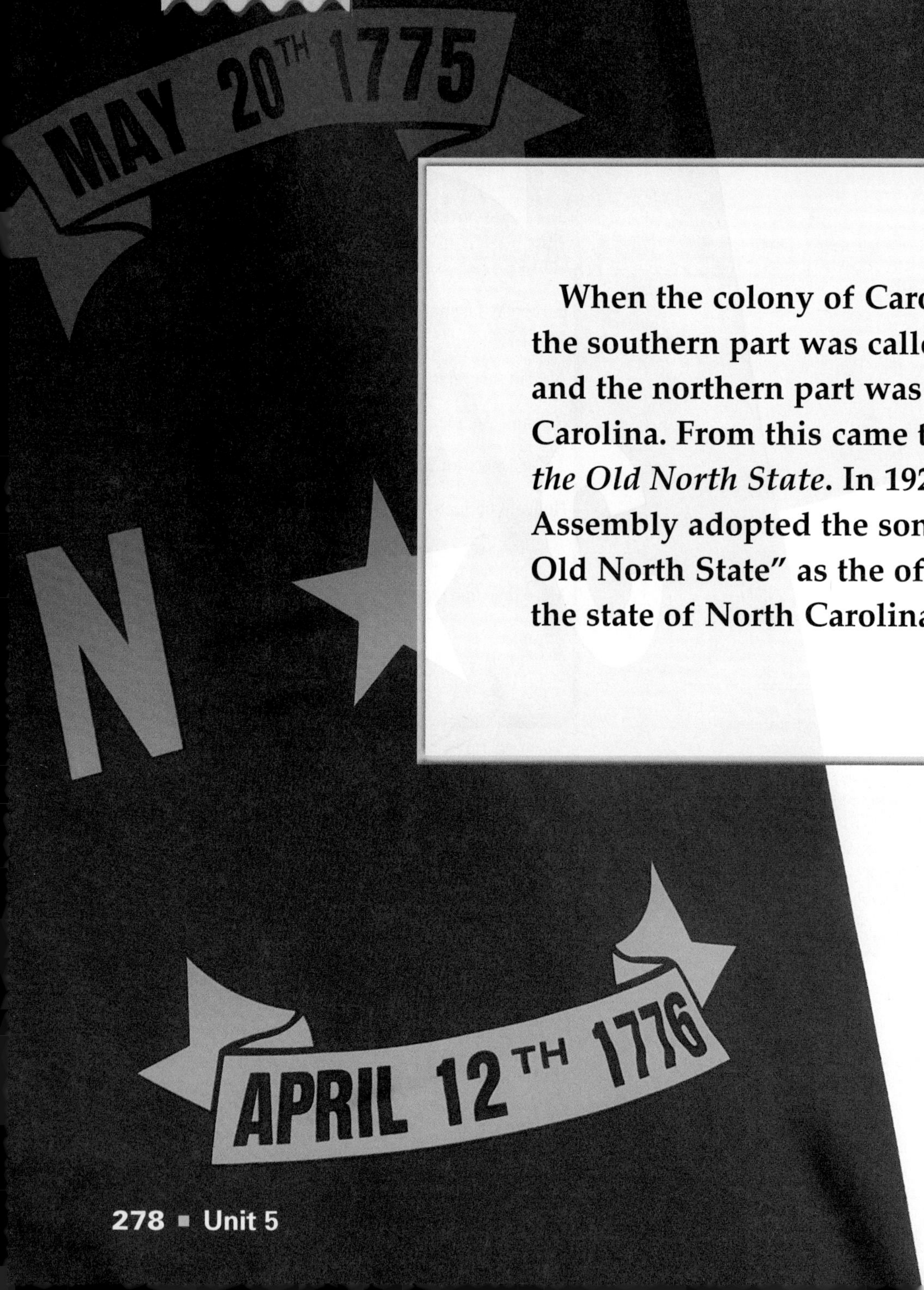
MAY 20TH 1775
N
APRIL 12TH 1776

When the colony of Carolina was divided, the southern part was called South Carolina and the northern part was called North Carolina. From this came the nickname *the Old North State*. In 1927, the General Assembly adopted the song titled "The Old North State" as the official song of the state of North Carolina.

Carolina! Carolina!
    heaven's blessings attend her,
While we live we will cherish,
    protect and defend her,
Tho' the scorner may sneer at
    and witlings defame her,
Still our hearts swell with gladness
    whenever we name her.

Refrain:
Hurrah! Hurrah!
    the Old North State forever,
Hurrah! Hurrah!
    the good Old North State.

Analyze the Literature

1 State and national anthems remind people about
  special times in history. They also can remind
  citizens of their responsibilities to their state or
  country. What responsibilities does the North
  Carolina state song remind you of?

2 Write your own anthem about either North Carolina
  or the United States. You can set your words to the
  tune of a song you know.

READ A BOOK

START THE
UNIT PROJECT

Future Invention Book With your
classmates, create a book of designs
for scientific inventions for the twenty-
first century. As you read this unit, take
notes on key inventions from the
twentieth century. Your notes can help
you decide what inventions could
assist North Carolinians in the future.

USE TECHNOLOGY

Visit The Learning Site at
**www.harcourtschool.com/
socialstudies** for additional
activities, primary sources,
and other resources to use in this unit.

WILMINGTON'S PORT

The USS *North Carolina* played a large role in World War II. Today the ship is a museum. It is anchored in Wilmington's port. You can visit it to learn more about the war and the people who fought in it.

LOCATE IT

NORTH CAROLINA

• Wilmington

North Carolina: the Twentieth Century and Beyond

" Uncommon valor was a common virtue. "

—Admiral Chester Nimitz, referring to American soldiers in World War II, 1945

CHAPTER READING SKILL

Make Inferences

When you read, sometimes you need to make inferences. An **inference** is an educated guess based on the facts you have read and your own knowledge and experience.

As you read each lesson in the chapter, use the details and your own knowledge and experience to make inferences.

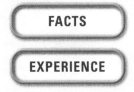

FACTS

EXPERIENCE

INFERENCE

1

A New Century Brings Change

MAIN IDEA
Read to find out about changes in North Carolina transportation from 1900 to the present.

WHY IT MATTERS
Improved ways of transportation have affected where and how people in North Carolina live, work, and play.

VOCABULARY
mass production
primary road
secondary road
interstate highway
aviation
glider
canal

1850   1900   1950   2000

1895–1955

Beginning in the 1890s about 300 different people tried to build cars powered by gasoline. One of the inventors was Gilbert Waters of New Bern, North Carolina. Waters built what he called the Buggymobile.

Gilbert Waters could not find anyone to invest money to manufacture his invention. His banker told him, "Buggies without horses will never be practical. They would be too expensive and dangerous." However, as the new century began, North Carolina and the country entered a new age in transportation—the Automobile Age.

FAST FACT In 1916 Henry Ford opened a car assembly factory in Charlotte. The plant made Model Ts and other Ford cars until it closed in 1932.

Analyze Primary Sources

Believe it or not, this is a car. It was called the Buggymobile. Gilbert Waters built it in New Bern in 1903. It could travel 35 miles per hour.

1 The body and wheels of the car came from a horse-drawn buggy. It was easier for Waters to use a buggy frame than to make a new one. He put a gasoline engine on the buggy frame to make a car.

2 There was no steering wheel. Instead the driver used a bar to turn the car. The bar is a lot like the handle-bars on a bicycle. The driver pulled the bar to turn the car.

3 Roads were mostly made of dirt. The car was open to dust, rain, and anything else that might fly by. Drivers wore goggles to protect their eyes and gloves to protect their hands. They also wore long coats called dusters to cover their clothes.

◆ How is the Buggymobile similar to cars you know about? How is it different?

North Carolina and the Automobile

The first automobiles were manufactured for sale in 1895. They were very expensive because they had to be made one at a time. In 1913 Henry Ford was the first person to use an assembly line to produce automobiles. He set up the assembly line at his Ford Motor Company factory in Detroit, Michigan. On the assembly line, the frame of each car traveled on a moving belt as workers added parts. The assembly-line method of making cars made the mass production of automobiles possible. **Mass production** is the making of products in large numbers.

At Henry Ford's factories, workers turned out automobiles faster than ever before. Ford was able to sell his cars at a lower price and still make money. In 1908, before Ford used the assembly line, his Model T sold for $850. By 1914 it cost

only $290. Soon other automakers were copying what Ford was doing.

In 1905 there were only 550 automobiles in the entire state of North Carolina. Five years later there were 3,220 cars on the roads of North Carolina.

By 1919 other American automakers were mass-producing engines that ran on gasoline. The discovery of oil in Texas helped lower the price of gasoline, which is made from oil. As both cars and gasoline became cheaper, the number of cars on North Carolina roads rose to more than 109,000.

As the number of people with cars grew, a new sport called auto racing became popular. Charlotte Motor Speedway opened in October 1924. Thousands of people came to see cars race around its wooden track. Today the Speedway still draws loyal fans.

REVIEW What helped make the automobile popular in North Carolina in the 1900s?

Roads and Highways

As more and more people bought cars, the state faced a new problem. It needed better roads and highways.

In the early 1900s most of North Carolina's roads were in poor condition. Dirt roads turned to mud when it rained. County governments were in charge of building and repairing roads. However, most counties did not have the money to do so. Mecklenburg, Buncombe, and Guilford Counties required citizens to pay taxes to help build and repair roads.

In 1902 some North Carolinians formed the North Carolina Good Roads Association. A state government worker, Harriet Morehead Berry, became one of its leaders. In 1918 Berry suggested that the state government provide money to build a highway system.

Because of Berry's hard work, state lawmakers passed the Highway Act of 1921. At that time North Carolina had only 135 miles (217 km) of hard-surfaced roads. These were made of concrete or

An early gasoline pump

asphalt. The Highway Act of 1921 provided the money that the state needed to build new primary roads.

Primary roads are roads that run between major towns and government centers in each county. By 1930 there were at least a few miles of hard-surfaced roads in each of the state's 100 counties.

In the 1930s work on the state's highways slowed because the United States faced hard times. The government had little money for roads.

After World War II ended, road building started again. In the late 1940s Governor William Kerr Scott urged the state to build new secondary roads. **Secondary roads** run between rural areas and the state's towns and cities. Scott wanted farmers to be able to get their crops to market. During Scott's years as governor, the state built many new roads and bridges.

At the same time, the federal government began building an

North Carolina's roads were almost impossible to use in the early twentieth century.

Harriet Morehead Berry   1877–1940

Character Trait: Civic Virtue

Harriet Morehead Berry is a big part of the reason why people call North Carolina the Good Roads State. She worked for a geologist, a scientist who studies rocks and minerals, who worked for state government. In 1902 she helped create the North Carolina Good Roads Association. She worked hard to get county leaders, road builders, and citizens to come to meetings. At the meetings Berry and other people spoke about how good roads could help North Carolina's economy. In 1921 the legislature finally passed a law putting the state in charge of all the highways. Thanks to her work, Berry is called the Mother of Good Roads in North Carolina.

GO ONLINE

MULTIMEDIA BIOGRAPHIES
Visit The Learning Site at www.harcourtschool.com/biographies to learn about other famous people.

interstate highway. This highway connected North Carolina with other states. It also made travel within the state easier. During Scott's term the state paved more than 12,000 miles (19,300 km) of secondary roads. By 1955 North Carolina had almost 68,000 miles (109,500 km) of roads and highways. It earned the nickname the Good Roads State.

REVIEW What was the Highway Act of 1921?

First in Flight

In 1903 two bicycle makers from Dayton, Ohio, made aviation (ay•vee•AY•shuhn) history at Kitty Hawk, North Carolina. **Aviation** is the making and flying of airplanes. In the fall of 1900, Orville and Wilbur Wright went to the Outer Banks. They had chosen the Outer Banks as the best place to experiment with kites, gliders, and a motor-driven airplane.

A **glider** is an aircraft without an engine. The Wright brothers chose Kitty Hawk because the wind there was ideal for glider practice. The brothers returned to Kitty Hawk during the next three years. Their efforts led to many scrapes, bruises, and crash landings.

The Wright Flyer soars over the Outer Banks.

On December 17, 1903, the Wright brothers' hard work finally paid off. Several young men from the nearby Life Saving Station were there to help with the Wright brothers' plane. With Orville at the controls, the world's first power-driven airplane flew 120 feet (37 m). That same day, Wilbur's flight lasted 59 seconds and covered a distance of 852 feet (260 m).

Today North Carolina honors this aviation event in several ways. Tar-Heel cars have the slogan *First in Flight* on their license plates. Also, the state chose an image of the first flight for the North Carolina quarter made by the United States Mint.

In 1925 the national government gave a boost to the airline industry by using planes to carry mail. By 1930 there were 43 airlines carrying more than 385,000 passengers throughout the United States.

Today airports in Charlotte, Greensboro, and Raleigh-Durham serve as regional centers for air travelers. More than 11 million passengers a year take flights into and out of Charlotte/Douglas International Airport. At this airport, named for Charlotte's mayor Ben Elbert Douglas, passengers can fly to places across the United States and throughout the world.

REVIEW How did the Wright brothers' flights in 1903 make aviation history?

The Atlantic Intracoastal Waterway

In the 1900s North Carolina built good roads and played an important part in aviation history. However, the state still had problems shipping goods by water.

Today boats of all kinds and sizes use the Intracoastal Waterway.

The national government and the state government helped improve shipping in North Carolina.

In 1936 the national government completed building the Atlantic Intracoastal Waterway. The waterway runs from Boston, Massachusetts, to Key West, Florida. On this waterway, ships can travel along the Atlantic coast without facing the dangers of the open seas. The rivers, bays, sounds, and inlets of the waterway are connected by canals.

A **canal** is a human-made waterway that is dug across land, to be used by boats and ships. Today both commercial ships and pleasure boats use the waterway in North Carolina. In 1952 the state government helped Wilmington and Morehead City build ports to handle oceangoing ships. In 2001, engineers began planning to make the Cape Fear channel deeper for larger ships.

REVIEW How is the Atlantic Intracoastal Waterway important to North Carolina?

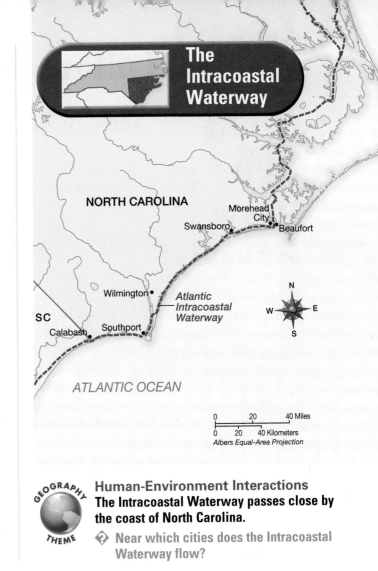

The Intracoastal Waterway

NORTH CAROLINA

Morehead City
Swansboro
Beaufort
Wilmington
Atlantic Intracoastal Waterway
SC
Calabash
Southport

ATLANTIC OCEAN

0   20   40 Miles
0   20   40 Kilometers
Albers Equal-Area Projection

GEOGRAPHY THEME

Human-Environment Interactions
The Intracoastal Waterway passes close by the coast of North Carolina.

❖ Near which cities does the Intracoastal Waterway flow?

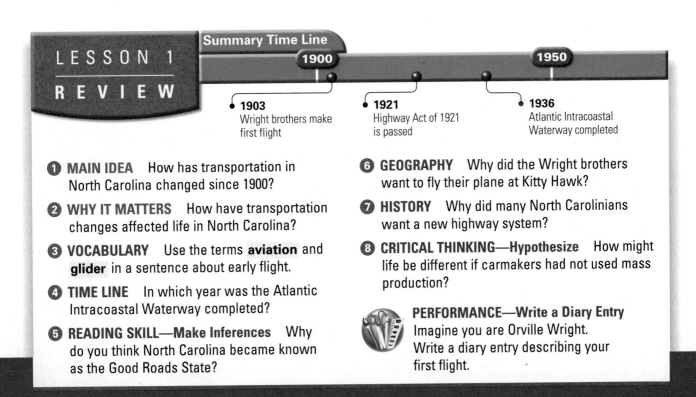

LESSON 1 REVIEW

Summary Time Line

1900   1950

1903
Wright brothers make first flight

1921
Highway Act of 1921 is passed

1936
Atlantic Intracoastal Waterway completed

① **MAIN IDEA** How has transportation in North Carolina changed since 1900?

② **WHY IT MATTERS** How have transportation changes affected life in North Carolina?

③ **VOCABULARY** Use the terms **aviation** and **glider** in a sentence about early flight.

④ **TIME LINE** In which year was the Atlantic Intracoastal Waterway completed?

⑤ **READING SKILL—Make Inferences** Why do you think North Carolina became known as the Good Roads State?

⑥ **GEOGRAPHY** Why did the Wright brothers want to fly their plane at Kitty Hawk?

⑦ **HISTORY** Why did many North Carolinians want a new highway system?

⑧ **CRITICAL THINKING—Hypothesize** How might life be different if carmakers had not used mass production?

PERFORMANCE—Write a Diary Entry
Imagine you are Orville Wright. Write a diary entry describing your first flight.

·SKILLS· Follow Routes on a Map

MAP AND GLOBE

VOCABULARY

route

▶ **WHY IT MATTERS**

Two kinds of trains operate in North Carolina—passenger trains and freight trains. The state's passenger trains carry more than 200,000 people yearly. Unlike passenger trains, freight trains carry goods only.

Look back at page 157 in Chapter 5. The map there shows the route of the Great Wagon Road. A **route** is a path you follow to get from one place to another. The map on page 289 shows another kind of route. The routes on this map are for passenger trains in North Carolina. The map shows in which direction the trains travel, where the trains stop along the way, and where the routes of the trains end.

▶ **WHAT YOU NEED TO KNOW**

There are six passenger-train routes in North Carolina. The name of each train route is listed in the map key. Each route is marked in a different color. The dots along the routes are the cities where the trains stop. If more than one line passes through a dot, more than one train stops in that city.

You can see on the map that some trains go outside of North Carolina. The arrows at the end of each route are labeled. The labels list other cities where the train stops. The labels do not list all the cities outside of North Carolina where the train stops. Only the largest cities are listed.

Some North Carolina road maps also show train routes.

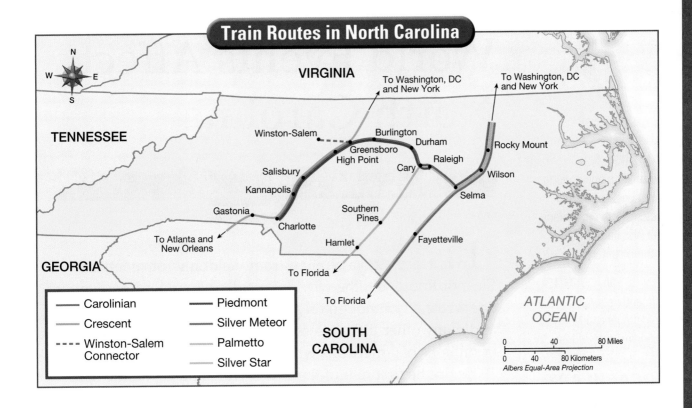

Train Routes in North Carolina

VIRGINIA

To Washington, DC and New York

To Washington, DC and New York

TENNESSEE

Winston-Salem
Burlington
Durham
Greensboro
High Point
Raleigh
Rocky Mount
Cary
Salisbury
Wilson
Kannapolis
Selma
Gastonia
Southern Pines
Charlotte
To Atlanta and New Orleans
Hamlet
Fayetteville

To Florida

GEORGIA

To Florida

ATLANTIC OCEAN

SOUTH CAROLINA

Key

— Carolinian
— Crescent
- - - Winston-Salem Connector
— Piedmont
— Silver Meteor
— Palmetto
— Silver Star

0   40   80 Miles
0   40   80 Kilometers
Albers Equal-Area Projection

► PRACTICE THE SKILL

Use the map and map key to answer these questions about passenger trains in North Carolina.

1 What color stands for the Silver Palm route? What color stands for the Silver Star?

2 What cities are along the Silver Palm route?

3 Which colors stand for the trains that go from Charlotte to Durham? What are the names of the trains?

4 How many train stations are on the Silver Meteor route?

5 What is the name of the train that goes from New York to New Orleans?

6 Which two routes go through Burlington?

► APPLY WHAT YOU LEARNED

Use the map to plan a train trip in North Carolina. Start in Charlotte. Decide which cities you would like to visit. Remember that you can only change trains in a city where more than one route meets. Write a plan for your trip. Give the names of the trains and cities. Trade plans with a classmate. See if you can follow your classmate's plan on the map.

Practice your map and globe skills with the **GeoSkills CD-ROM**.

MAIN IDEA
Read to learn about world and national events that affected North Carolinians in the first half of the twentieth century.

WHY IT MATTERS
World and national events influenced North Carolinians' way of life.

VOCABULARY
war bond
interest
shortage
suffrage
consumer good
depression
unemployment
rationing

World Events Affect North Carolina

1914–1945

In January 1935 a woman from Weldon wrote a letter to Eleanor Roosevelt, the wife of President Franklin Roosevelt. She wrote, "I cannot go on getting in debt for food, milk, coal, and many other little necessary things." This woman was one of millions of Americans who faced economic problems in the 1930s. In the first half of the 1900s, wars and economic hard times changed the way Americans, including North Carolinians, lived.

World War I

In 1914 a war started in Europe. Britain, France, and Russia fought against Germany, Austria-Hungary, and Turkey. This conflict is known today as World War I. It was fought on battle-fields in Europe. During the first three years of the war, the United States remained neutral. It did not take sides in the fighting. On May 7, 1915, however, torpedoes launched from a German submarine caused the British passenger ship *Lusitania* to sink. Many passengers, including 128 Americans died. After German submarines also sank several American ships, President Woodrow Wilson asked Congress to declare war on Germany.

The national government set up three training camps for troops in North Carolina. They were Camp Greene in Charlotte, Camp Polk in Raleigh, and Fort Bragg near Fayetteville.

World War I medals and helmet

World War I was the first war in which soldiers used tanks and other advanced war technology.

After the war, the first two camps were closed. Only Fort Bragg continued to grow. Today Fort Bragg is one of the largest military bases in the world.

More than 86,000 North Carolina men served in the armed forces during World War I. Also, 195 North Carolina women served overseas as nurses. During the war many North Carolina women took over office and factory jobs when soldiers went to war. Other women worked for the Red Cross and other groups helping the troops.

North Carolinians also helped the war effort by buying war bonds. Buying **war bonds** was a way of lending money to the government to help pay for the war. When people bought war bonds, they lent their money for a certain amount of time. When that time had

passed, the government returned the money with interest. **Interest** is the money that a bank or a government pays for using people's money.

The war caused shortages of food and other goods. A **shortage** means that there is not enough of something for everyone. To make up for the shortages, citizens took action. Families turned empty lots, yards, and school grounds into gardens for growing vegetables. They called them victory gardens.

American forces helped bring an end to World War I. In 1918 Germany surrendered. The war was over. More than 2,340 North Carolinians had died in the war in battle or from disease.

(REVIEW) How did North Carolinians at home help fight the war?

Ring it again

BUY A
United States Government Bond of the
SECOND
LIBERTY LOAN
of 1917
Help Your Country and Yourself

This poster advertised war bonds.

Gertrude Weil (far left) and other suffrage workers fought to make sure women gained the right to vote.

Women and the Right to Vote

In the late 1880s a group of North Carolina women began to fight for the right to vote, or **suffrage**. Many lawmakers in North Carolina opposed these efforts. Still, the women did not give up. By 1913 a few men and more women had joined local suffrage groups in Morganton, Charlotte, and a dozen other cities. Yet little progress was made until World War I ended.

As the war came to an end, President Wilson and other government leaders recognized how much women had helped in the war effort. When the war ended in 1918, Congress began work on a new amendment to the United States Constitution. This amendment would give women the right to vote.

In North Carolina Gertrude Weil (WYL) of Goldsboro, president of the state's Equal Suffrage League, helped lead the cause. Weil began a letter-writing campaign to get representatives in the United States Congress to support the women's voting rights amendment.

Support for woman suffrage was strong in many states. By August 1920 the Nineteenth Amendment became a law. This meant that women across the United States had the right to vote.

REVIEW How did women in North Carolina fight for the right to vote?

The Great Depression

The years after World War I brought many changes to American life. In the 1920s the United States economy boomed. Factories began turning out new products. These included washing machines, radios, and other electrical appliances. Many of these new items were consumer goods. A **consumer good** is a product made for personal use. As people bought more new products, factories hired more workers and produced more goods.

In 1929 the good times ended. North Carolina and the rest of the United States suffered an economic depression. A **depression** is a time when there are few jobs and very little money. The depression of the 1930s became known as the Great Depression.

In the early 1930s demand for goods dropped sharply. Factories began laying off workers. People who lost their jobs had less money to spend. This caused more businesses to fail. For much of the 1930s, **unemployment**, or the number of people without jobs, was high.

Many people who had borrowed money from banks could not repay it. As a result, banks began to fail, or close down. By February 1932 more than 200 banks had failed in North Carolina. The life savings, farms, and homes of many North Carolinians were lost. People in North Carolina and the rest of the country looked to the United States government for help.

Elected in 1932, President Franklin D. Roosevelt developed a plan to make things better. He called his plan the New Deal. Under the plan, the national government began paying people to build post offices, schools, and other public buildings. In North Carolina, work on the Blue Ridge Parkway started, providing hundreds of jobs. Other New Deal programs created jobs paving roads or building water and sewer systems.

One of the most popular New Deal programs was the Civilian Conservation Corps. This program provided young men with jobs in conservation and forestry, such as planting trees and cleaning up parks. These jobs gave people money and a feeling of usefulness and hope.

REVIEW How did Roosevelt's New Deal help Americans during the Great Depression?

The Civilian Conservation Corps worked on many projects in North Carolina.

World War II

By the end of the 1930s, the United States faced another world war. The war began in 1939 with Germany fighting Britain and other European nations. At first, the United States stayed out of the fighting. Then Japan dropped bombs on American ships at Pearl Harbor, Hawaii, on December 7, 1941.

The United States declared war on Japan. Soon the war was clearly a world war. On one side of the fighting in World War II were the Axis Powers of Germany, Italy, and Japan. On the other side were the Allies, which included Britain, France, the United States, and the Soviet Union.

North Carolina played an important part in World War II. By the end of the war more servicemen and servicewomen had been trained in North Carolina than in any other state. Troops came from all over the United States to Fort Bragg, Camp Lejeune (luh•JOON), Cherry Point, Seymour Johnson Air Base at Goldsboro, and the Coast Guard station at Elizabeth City. These bases in North Carolina still train large numbers of troops.

In World War II most of the 361,000 North Carolinians in the armed forces were men. Women served as doctors and nurses, drivers, telephone operators, airplane mechanics, and parachute workers.

During World War II, families also had victory gardens and took part in rationing to help the troops. **Rationing** means that people can buy only a limited amount of goods such as sugar, butter, meat, coffee, and gasoline.

Women worked at many different jobs during World War II.

VICTORY WAITS ON YOUR FINGERS—

KEEP 'EM FLYING

UNCLE SAM NEEDS STENOGRAPHERS! • GET CIVIL SERVICE
U.S. CIVIL SERVICE COMMISSION

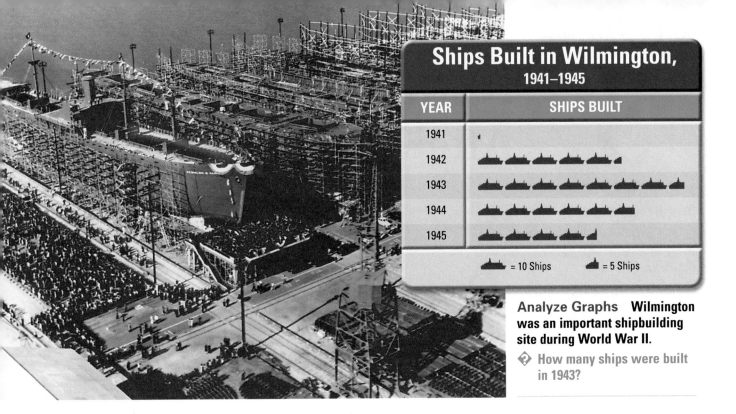

Ships Built in Wilmington, 1941–1945

YEAR	SHIPS BUILT
1941	
1942	
1943	
1944	
1945	

= 10 Ships   = 5 Ships

Analyze Graphs Wilmington was an important shipbuilding site during World War II.

◆ How many ships were built in 1943?

Women once again filled men's jobs. They worked at shipyards in New Bern, Wilmington, and Elizabeth City. They built military planes in Burlington. They made parachutes, sheets, towels, blankets, and socks for the armed services at factories in the Piedmont.

World War II ended in 1945 with the defeat of the Axis Powers and the reorganization of many nations. About 400,000 Americans died in the war, including 4,100 North Carolinians.

REVIEW How did North Carolina contribute to the war effort?

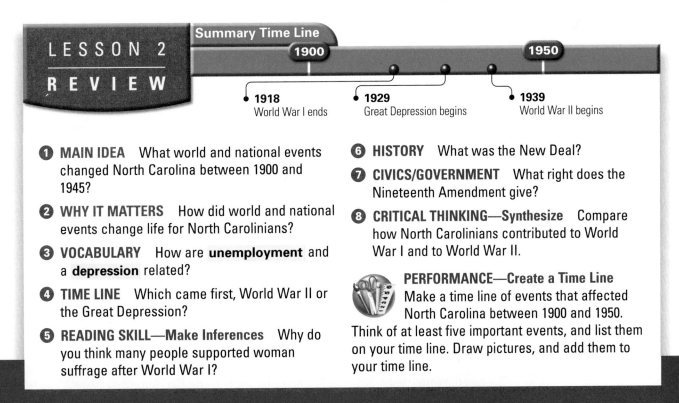

LESSON 2 REVIEW

Summary Time Line

1900 — 1950

1918 World War I ends

1929 Great Depression begins

1939 World War II begins

1. **MAIN IDEA** What world and national events changed North Carolina between 1900 and 1945?

2. **WHY IT MATTERS** How did world and national events change life for North Carolinians?

3. **VOCABULARY** How are **unemployment** and a **depression** related?

4. **TIME LINE** Which came first, World War II or the Great Depression?

5. **READING SKILL—Make Inferences** Why do you think many people supported woman suffrage after World War I?

6. **HISTORY** What was the New Deal?

7. **CIVICS/GOVERNMENT** What right does the Nineteenth Amendment give?

8. **CRITICAL THINKING—Synthesize** Compare how North Carolinians contributed to World War I and to World War II.

PERFORMANCE—Create a Time Line Make a time line of events that affected North Carolina between 1900 and 1950. Think of at least five important events, and list them on your time line. Draw pictures, and add them to your time line.

3

MAIN IDEA
Read to discover how citizens of North Carolina responded to changes after World War II.

WHY IT MATTERS
North Carolinians' ability to adapt to changing times shaped the way they live and think today.

VOCABULARY
veteran
leisure
civil rights
Cold War
satellite
astronaut

North Carolina After World War II

1945–Present

O n February 1, 1960, four African American college students sat down at a lunch counter in a store in Greensboro to protest unfair treatment. Their actions helped start a movement for freedom and equal treatment for African Americans. One of the young men, David Richmond, remembered how the students felt before they took action. "All of us were afraid," said David Richmond, "but we went and did it." Their actions and those of others brought many changes to North Carolina.

North Carolina Faces Changes

When World War II ended, thousands of North Carolina soldiers came home. Many of them returned to college or took new jobs. A **veteran** is a person who has served in the armed forces. The GI Bill of Rights, passed by Congress in 1944, provided money for education, job training, homes, and medical care. Americans again had money to buy products to meet their needs and wants.

Many North Carolina families had money to buy cars. Families moved farther from downtown areas. They had to commute, or travel to and from their city jobs. As a result, the number of highways and shopping centers grew.

Americans made more money and were able to work fewer hours. They had more **leisure** time, or time away from work. Many families spent some leisure time enjoying television. The television set was the most popular new household product of the 1950s.

REVIEW How did the lives of North Carolinians change after World War II?

The end of World War II led to better times for many North Carolinians.

The Fight for Civil Rights

After World War II, segregation was still allowed by law. Segregation is the separation of people because of their race, religion, or where they come from. Segregation laws took away many of the civil rights of African Americans. **Civil rights** are rights given to all citizens by the Constitution.

Most Southern states and some other states passed segregation laws. African Americans were not allowed to go to the same schools, movie theaters, and other public places as white people.

In 1954 the United States courts ruled that separate schools were against the law. Three years later, North Carolina integrated its public schools, opening them equally to all students.

By the 1960s many people throughout the United States had joined the fight for civil rights. Dr. Martin Luther King, Jr., an African American minister from Georgia, had been leading the fight against segregation. He and other civil rights leaders led marches and protests to get equal rights for all.

In 1964 the Civil Rights Act became law, making segregation illegal. Since the 1960s many groups have worked to gain civil rights. These groups include Native

Dr. Martin Luther King, Jr.

Americans, women, people with disabilities, and a number of other groups. North Carolina strongly supports equal rights for all its people.

REVIEW How did people work for civil rights after World War II?

CITIZENSHIP

DEMOCRATIC VALUES
Justice

The Greensboro Sit-In

February 1, 1960, started like any other day at the South Elm Street Woolworth store in Greensboro. Then Franklin McCain, Joseph McNeil, Ezell Blair, Jr., and David Richmond sat down at the lunch counter. They politely asked to buy lunch. They were refused because they were African Americans. The four men told the people at the counter that they would not leave until they were served. This kind of protest is called a sit-in.

Before long hundreds of African Americans and other people were protesting at other lunch counters. People in other cities started their own sit-ins. Six months later, the Woolworth stores and other stores ended segregation at their lunch counters. The Greensboro sit-in was one of the most important events in the Civil Rights movement.

Analyze the Value

❶ Why do you think the four men started a sit-in at the lunch counter?

❷ How did the sit-ins help African Americans get equal rights?

❸ **Make It Relevant** Think of something in your community you want to change. Write a list of ways you could protest peacefully. How would your protest encourage people to change what they do?

Into the Space Age

The United States and the Soviet Union had fought side by side to win World War II. After the war their political differences led to serious conflict. This conflict became known as the **Cold War** because most of the time the war was fought with words rather than with soldiers and weapons.

In 1957 the Soviet Union surprised the world by putting the first satellite into space. A **satellite** is an object that circles a larger object. Within ten years, the United States also had many successes in space. In May 1961 astronaut Alan B. Shepard, Jr., became the first American to go into space. An **astronaut** is anyone training for or serving as a crew member on a space-craft. Nine months later, American astronaut John H. Glenn, Jr., became the first American to orbit, or circle, Earth.

In July 1969 Neil Armstrong became the first person to walk on the moon. North Carolina's first astronaut was Charles M. Duke, Jr., of Charlotte. Duke flew on the *Apollo 16* mission and spent more than 70 hours walking on the moon.

Today astronauts orbit Earth in space shuttles. The space shuttles are reuseable spacecraft that launch and repair satellites and carry out science experiments in space.

The United States launched its first space shuttle in 1981. Five years later, the space shuttle *Challenger* exploded after liftoff, killing the seven crew members. Among them was pilot Michael J. Smith, born in Beaufort, North Carolina.

Charles M. Duke, Jr.

The lunar lander (left) and lunar rover (right) were some of the tools Charles Duke and other astronauts used on the moon.

After this disaster, scientists worked to make the shuttle program safer. Today astronauts continue to do important work in space. North Carolina astronauts include Charles E. Brady, Jr., of Robbins, Curtis L. Brown of Elizabethtown, and William S. McArthur of Wakulla.

Although the United States and Russia once competed in space programs, they have been partners since 1994. One example of this cooperation was Russia's *Mir* (MEER) Space Station. Several United States astronauts spent many months as part of the *Mir* crew. In 1995 Ellen Baker, who was born in Fayetteville, was part of the crew of the first space shuttle to dock, or connect, with *Mir*. Today the United States is part of an international space project. Twenty-two nations are working together to build the International Space Station. At the space station astronauts from a variety of countries carry out scientific research.

The Saturn V rocket carried *Apollo 16*'s astronauts into space.

REVIEW Who are some astronauts from North Carolina?

· GEOGRAPHY ·

GEOGRAPHY ESSENTIAL ELEMENTS

North Carolina Vietnam Veterans Memorial

Understanding Places and Regions

On May 27, 1991, North Carolinians dedicated a memorial to the brave veterans of the Vietnam War. The North Carolina Vietnam Veterans Memorial is about 5 miles (8 km) north of Lexington, along Interstate 85. It was built to honor every one of the 216,000 North Carolinians who fought in the Vietnam War.

The center of the memorial is a curving wall made of North Carolina brick. On the wall are plaques with the names of more than 1,600 Tar Heels who died in the war or who are still missing. Another part of the memorial stretches from the wall all the way to Greensboro. The North Carolina Forest Service planted 58,000 North Carolina pine trees on that land. Each tree stands for one of the 58,000 people from across the United States who died fighting the Vietnam War.

War and Peace

During the 1960s the United States took part in a war in Vietnam in Asia. Vietnam was divided into two countries—North Vietnam and South Vietnam. The United States sided with South Vietnam while the Soviet Union sided with North Vietnam. Many of the troops who fought in Vietnam trained at Fort Bragg. One group was the Special Forces unit, or the Green Berets. In 1973 the United States withdrew from the fight. About 1,570 North Carolinians died in that war.

After the Vietnam War ended in 1975, the Cold War continued for another 16 years. Today Russia and the United States are working together on space projects and in many other ways.

Employees at this North Carolina research center work with scientists from countries around the world.

On September 11, 2001, airplanes flown by terrorists crashed into buildings near Washington, D.C., and in New York City. Thousands of people were killed. Since then, the United States government has sought to bring those responsible to justice. Many members of the United States military involved in this effort have been trained at military bases in North Carolina.

REVIEW In what ways did the Vietnam War affect North Carolina?

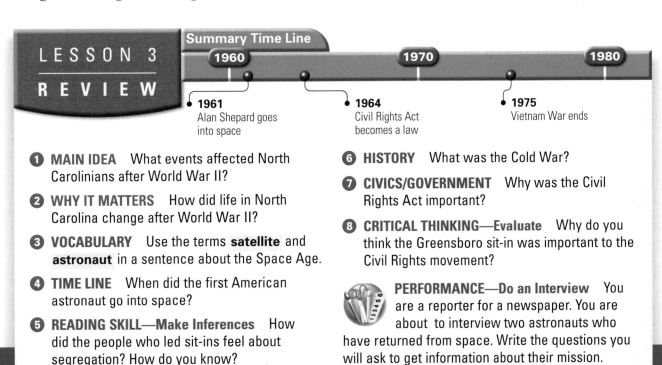

LESSON 3 REVIEW

Summary Time Line

1960 — 1970 — 1980

1961 Alan Shepard goes into space

1964 Civil Rights Act becomes a law

1975 Vietnam War ends

1 MAIN IDEA What events affected North Carolinians after World War II?

2 WHY IT MATTERS How did life in North Carolina change after World War II?

3 VOCABULARY Use the terms **satellite** and **astronaut** in a sentence about the Space Age.

4 TIME LINE When did the first American astronaut go into space?

5 READING SKILL—Make Inferences How did the people who led sit-ins feel about segregation? How do you know?

6 HISTORY What was the Cold War?

7 CIVICS/GOVERNMENT Why was the Civil Rights Act important?

8 CRITICAL THINKING—Evaluate Why do you think the Greensboro sit-in was important to the Civil Rights movement?

PERFORMANCE—Do an Interview You are a reporter for a newspaper. You are about to interview two astronauts who have returned from space. Write the questions you will ask to get information about their mission.

9 Review and Test Preparation

1903
The Wright brothers
make their first flight

USE YOUR READING SKILLS

Complete this graphic organizer to help you make inferences about North Carolina in the twentieth century. A copy of this graphic organizer appears on page 90 of the Activity Book.

North Carolina in the Twentieth Century

Fact The first automobiles were very expensive.	**Inference** _____ _____
Experience Most people cannot afford expensive goods.	_____ _____

Fact The United States tried to remain neutral in World War I.	**Inference** _____ _____
Experience _____ _____	_____ _____

Fact The economy of the United States was strong in the years following World War II.	**Inference** _____ _____
Experience _____ _____	_____ _____

THINK & WRITE

Write a Persuasive Letter   Imagine that you are living at a time before the Nineteenth Amendment has been passed. Write a letter to a member of the United States Congress. Explain how you feel about suffrage. Try to persuade the member of Congress to support the same view that you hold. Share your letter with a classmate.

Write Newspaper Headlines   Imagine that you edit a newspaper during the twentieth century. Choose five events that took place in the century. Write a headline for each event. Your events should be from different times in the twentieth century. Make your headlines interesting so that people will want to buy your newspaper.

1918
World War I
ends

1939
World War II
begins

1961
Alan Shepard goes
into space

1975
The Vietnam War ends

**September 11,
2001**
Terrorist attacks
in United States

USE THE TIME LINE

Use the chapter summary time line to
answer these questions.

1 When did the Vietnam War end?

2 How many years after the end of World
War I did World War II begin?

USE VOCABULARY

Write a sentence using each term below.

3 **mass production** (p. 283)

4 **shortage** (p. 291)

5 **consumer good** (p. 293)

6 **veteran** (p. 296)

7 **civil rights** (p. 297)

RECALL FACTS

Answer these questions.

8 What did the Highway Act of 1921 do?

9 Why was the Civilian Conservation Corps
popular?

10 Which astronauts from North Carolina
participated in the space program?

Write the letter of the best choice.

11 **TEST PREP** Why did Governor W. Kerr
Scott want more secondary roads?
   A He wanted people to commute to work.
   B He wanted to give people jobs during the
   Great Depression.
   C He wanted to help farmers get their crops
   to market.
   D He wanted better roads between
   major towns.

12 **TEST PREP** Who proposed the
New Deal?
   F Henry Ford
   G Harriet Morehead Berry
   H Woodrow Wilson
   J Franklin D. Roosevelt

13 **TEST PREP** Who was the first person
to walk on the moon?
   A Alan Shepard
   B John Glenn
   C Neil Armstrong
   D Ellen Baker

THINK CRITICALLY

14 What do you think was the most important
event in North Carolina in the twentieth
century? Why?

15 Do you think the New Deal was successful?
Why or why not?

16 Why is good transportation important to
North Carolina's economy?

17 Why do you think citizens of North Carolina
are proud that their state was "first in flight"?

18 What are some ways North Carolinians
honor the people who were killed on
September 11, 2001?

APPLY SKILLS

Follow Routes on a Map
Use the map on page 289 to
answer the questions.

19 Which trains could take you from
Florida to New York?

20 Which trains go through both Salisbury
and Burlington?

North Carolina's state capitol is at Union Square in Raleigh. It was built in 1840. The building is made of gneiss (NYS) stones that were from the area nearby. The building is more than 97 feet (30 m) tall.

LOCATE IT

NORTH
CAROLINA

Raleigh

North Carolina Today

" As a state, our greatest strength lies in our willingness and our ability to reach out to all people. . . . **"**

> —Governor Michael Easley,
> Office of the Governor,
> state of North Carolina
> Web Site

CHAPTER READING SKILL

Identify Fact and Opinion

A **fact** is a statement that can be checked and proved. An **opinion** tells what a person thinks or believes. It cannot be proved.

As you read this chapter, identify facts about topics and then write your opinions about things related to the topics.

FACT OPINION

Into the Twenty-First Century

MAIN IDEA
Read to find out how people of many races and beliefs cooperate in North Carolina today.

WHY IT MATTERS
In a peaceful society, people of many cultural backgrounds live and work together.

VOCABULARY
migrant worker
ethnic group
interdependent
international trade

Each morning Steve Norwood, the principal of Hillandale Elementary School in East Flat Rock, greets students in English and Spanish. One-fourth of the students in this Mountain region school are Hispanic. In Asheville, Jerry Tudela, who came from Bolivia in South America, recalls how he felt when he first arrived. "When I came here almost 12 years ago, I thought I was the only Hispanic here," said Tudela. "Now we have a lot of folks coming here."

A Changing Population

For a long time young people moved away from North Carolina to find good jobs. Beginning in the 1970s, many new industries moved into the state, including high-tech and research companies. The state welcomed the new businesses, and many Tar Heels who had left returned home.

Today North Carolina is one of the nation's fastest-growing states. Its population rose by one-fifth between 1990 and 2000. Many new

FAST FACT
People in Hickory call a local school the little United Nations because the students come from so many places.

Many retired people enjoy participating in sports and outdoor activities in North Carolina.

arrivals came from states in the Northeast and from other states, especially New York, New Jersey, Florida, Virginia, and Georgia. Today more than 8 million people call North Carolina home. More than half of them live in cities. The rest live in towns and rural areas.

North Carolina's climate makes it a popular place for people of all ages to live. Many older Americans choose North Carolina as a place to retire. About half of them move to the Mountain region. Others choose the Piedmont or places along the coast.

Older residents contribute to their communities. They buy homes, shop, and join in art and leisure activities. Many retirees enjoy doing work in the community, often without pay. Their experience in businesses and other activities is helpful to others.

REVIEW Why do people of all ages choose to live in North Carolina?

A Mix of People

In the new century North Carolina's population is more diverse than it was in the past. The first settlers in North Carolina were the Cherokees and other Native American groups. Today the state has more than 99,500 Native Americans. More than half of them are Lumbees. Most Lumbees live in Robeson, Hoke, Cumberland, and Scotland Counties. The second-largest group of Native Americans is the Eastern Band of Cherokees. Only five other states have larger Native American populations.

The first European settlers of North Carolina were the English and the Highland Scots. Today almost three out of four of all North Carolinians are of European background.

About one out of every five people in North Carolina is African American. Most of them are descendants of people who were brought to the colonies as slaves.

Native Americans in North Carolina Today

GROUP	LOCATION
Lumbee	Robeson, Hoke, Scotland, and Cumberland Counties
Eastern Band of Cherokees	Swain, Graham, and Jackson Counties and the Qualla Boundary
Coharie	Sampson and Harnett Counties
Waccamaw-Siouan	Bladen and Columbus Counties
Haliwa-Saponi	Halifax and Warren Counties
Indians of Person County	Person County
Meherrin	Hertford County

Analyze Tables Native Americans live in many parts of North Carolina today.

◈ In which counties do many Waccamaw-Siouan people live?

At one time African American professionals left North Carolina to find better-paying, high-level jobs. Today many have returned to work in North Carolina's high-tech industries.

There are now four times as many Hispanics living in North Carolina as there were in 1990. At one time most Hispanics in North Carolina were migrant workers. A **migrant worker** is a person who moves from farm to farm to harvest crops. In the last ten years, many farmworkers have settled in one place. Many have found year-round jobs at food-processing plants and hog farms in eastern North Carolina. Others have settled in the state's larger cities to work in building and service jobs. Today almost 380,000 Hispanics live in the state. They make up almost 5 percent of the state's population.

Bailian Li of Raleigh is Chinese American. He is one of more than 114,000 Asians who moved to North Carolina during the 1990s. The number of Asians in North Carolina has more than doubled during the last ten years. Many live and work in the Research Triangle area. Most Asian Americans are from India, China, or Taiwan, but others have come from Korea, Japan, Vietnam, or the Philippines.

REVIEW In what ways is the population of North Carolina more diverse today than in the past?

Sharing Traditions

North Carolinians have many things in common. The people in the state all live under the same laws and have equal rights. State government leaders are the same for all citizens. Everyone shares the state's many natural resources.

At the same time, Tar Heels today come from many ethnic groups. An **ethnic group** is a group made up of people who come from the same country or speak the same language and share certain customs and beliefs. Ethnic differences can be seen in the languages that people speak, the kinds of music they enjoy, the foods they eat, and the holidays they celebrate.

When Marco Badillo moved to Sanford eight years ago, he saw little that reminded him of Mexico. "People . . . didn't speak our language," he said. Now new immigrants can find lawyers and doctors who speak Spanish and churches with many Spanish-speaking members. There are stores that sell tortillas and restaurants that serve Mexican food. There are outdoor markets that specialize in selling Hispanic goods. There are also television and radio programs in Spanish as well as in English.

Throughout the state Tar Heels have found many ways to celebrate their cultures. The Lumbees hold powwows twice a year in Lumberton. At the spring and fall gatherings, the Lumbees celebrate their traditions in songs and dances. In Fayetteville, families of Greek descent have a festival that raises money for the Greek churches. Every year Greek food, music, and dances attract thousands to this celebration.

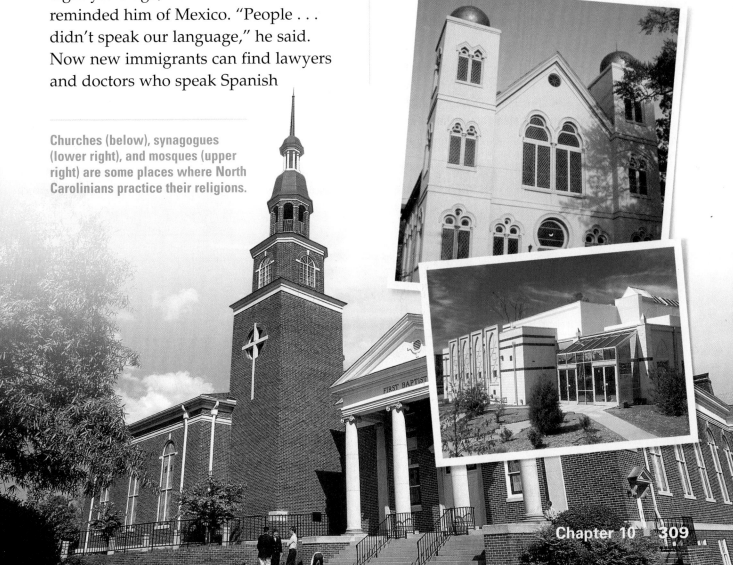

Churches (below), synagogues (lower right), and mosques (upper right) are some places where North Carolinians practice their religions.

Religious diversity, too, is increasing in the state. Many North Carolinians are Christians. Some are Roman Catholics, and others are Protestants. Among the largest Protestant groups are the Baptists, Methodists, Presbyterians, and Lutherans. Many cities in the Piedmont also have Quaker meetinghouses.

Most of the state's large cities have synagogues, where Jewish people attend services. Boone, Chapel Hill, and Greensboro are some of the cities with Buddhist temples or retreat centers. Both Charlotte and the Triangle area have temples where Hindus worship. Mosques, which are used by Muslims—people who practice the religion of Islam—can be found in the Triad, in the Triangle area, and in smaller cities in the state.

REVIEW **What are some ways people from different ethnic groups celebrate their traditions?**

Growing Interdependence

As in other states, North Carolina's farmers and workers do not grow or make everything that people need. For example, fruits such as oranges and grapefruits grow well only in warmer climates. Store owners in North Carolina buy those fruits from farmers in Florida and California. Farmers in North Carolina grow crops such as peanuts, soybeans, and apples. Many states depend on North Carolina for these crops.

Although North Carolina farmers grow cotton, they cannot supply all the cotton needed by the state's textile mills. Tar Heel mills buy cotton grown in Texas and other states. In turn, Texans buy cotton products, such as towels and clothing that are made in North Carolina. The 50 states in the United States are interdependent. **Interdependent** places,

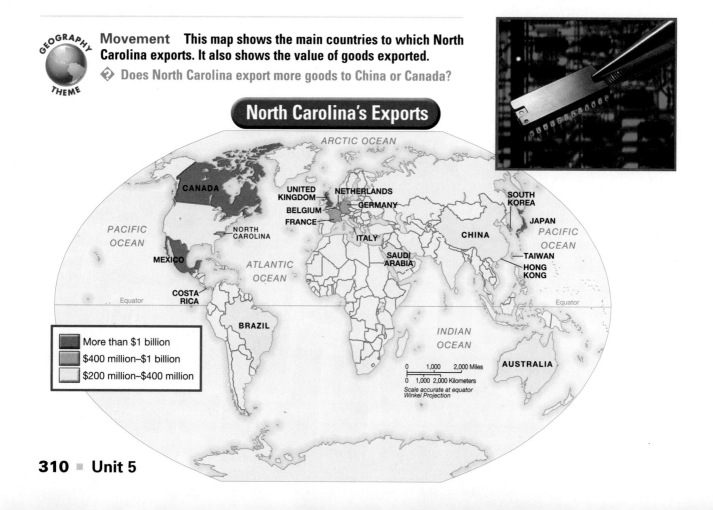

Movement This map shows the main countries to which North Carolina exports. It also shows the value of goods exported.

◈ Does North Carolina export more goods to China or Canada?

North Carolina's Exports

Legend:
- More than $1 billion
- $400 million–$1 billion
- $200 million–$400 million

Bald eagle

Cape Fear shiners

Box turtle

North Carolinians are working to protect rivers, streams, and other animal habitats.

regions, or states depend on one another for goods and services.

Countries are also interdependent. The United States trades with countries around the world. It is a part of the world economy. North Carolina's crops, such as soybeans, peanuts, and tobacco are bought by countries as far away as China. Countries around the world buy North Carolina's goods. **International trade**, or trade among nations, helps North Carolina's economy.

Today some of North Carolina's most important trade partners are Canada, Mexico, Japan, and the United Kingdom. Canada buys computers, trucks, telephones, and other products made in North Carolina. Japan buys goods such as soybeans and tobacco.

Companies in North Carolina buy lumber and paper from Canada and televisions and other electronic equipment

from Japan. North Carolina buys food, clothing, and furniture from Mexico. More than 750 international companies have branches of their businesses in North Carolina. These businesses not only support the network of international trade, but they also provide jobs for thousands of North Carolina workers.

REVIEW How is North Carolina part of the world economy?

Changes Bring Challenges

As North Carolina grows, the state faces new challenges. Every year hundreds of acres of forests and wetlands in North Carolina are cleared. Roads, houses, shopping centers, and parking lots are built where trees or marshes once stood. Some North Carolinians want to protect and preserve wetland and wilderness areas.

In 1974 the state government passed the Coastal Area Management Act, or CAMA. This law limits the number of buildings in certain coastal areas. Many people believe that more rules are needed to make sure wildlife habitats, water, and air are protected. In the Mountain region some communities have rules that stop building on mountaintops.

Heavy traffic is a problem caused by population growth in urban areas. Leaders in some cities are planning to provide more public transportation to lessen the traffic jams.

In the future, North Carolinians may have to make hard choices about land use. Some want public parks to be places for baseball, tennis, or golf. Others want to limit forest use to hiking trails. To decide on land use, North Carolinians will have to work together.

REVIEW What problems have been caused by North Carolina's rapid population growth?

Parks and hiking trails are two uses of land.

1. **MAIN IDEA** How has the population of North Carolina changed since 1990?

2. **WHY IT MATTERS** What are some ways that people from many backgrounds work together in North Carolina?

3. **VOCABULARY** How are the words **interdependent** and **international trade** related?

4. **READING SKILL—Identify Fact and Opinion** Does the following sentence state a fact or an opinion? "The best way to deal with heavy traffic is to create more roads."

5. **CULTURE** What are some ways in which people in North Carolina celebrate their cultures?

6. **CIVICS/GOVERNMENT** Why was the Coastal Area Management Act passed?

7. **CRITICAL THINKING—Apply** What are some ways North Carolinians can solve the problems caused by a growing population?

PERFORMANCE—Make a Collage In a small group, make a collage showing the many ethnic groups of North Carolina. Use pictures from magazines or newspapers or pictures you draw. Post your collage in your classroom.

Make Economic Choices

VOCABULARY

trade-off
opportunity cost

▶ WHY IT MATTERS

People make economic decisions daily. When you buy or do one thing, you give up the chance to buy or do something else. Giving up one thing to get another is called a **trade-off**. What you give up is called the **opportunity cost** of what you get.

▶ WHAT YOU NEED TO KNOW

The following steps can help you make better economic choices:

Step 1 **Identify what you want to buy.**

Step 2 **Figure out how much you can spend.**

Step 3 **Think about trade-offs and opportunity costs.**

▶ PRACTICE THE SKILL

Imagine that you are the treasurer of a small town. The town council wants to build a new park and a new office building. Your town does not have enough money to pay for both. How can you decide which to do? List the benefits, trade-offs, and opportunity costs of each choice.

▶ APPLY WHAT YOU LEARNED

You and a friend made $15 selling fresh-squeezed lemonade. Your friend wants to spend the money to go to a movie. You want to use it to buy more lemons. Think about the consequences and opportunity costs. Write a paragraph explaining your decision.

Local leaders must make economic choices as they plan their town's growth.

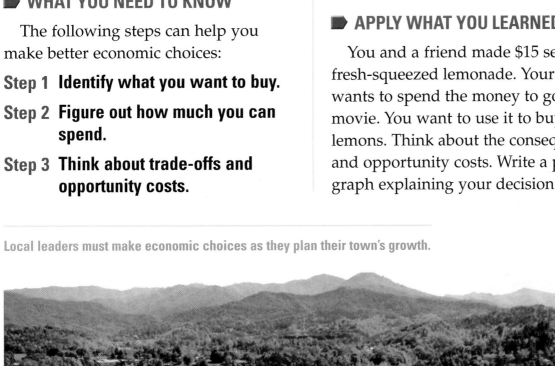

2

MAIN IDEA
Read to learn how North Carolina's state government works.

WHY IT MATTERS
The state government influences the lives of all North Carolinians.

VOCABULARY
legislative branch
executive branch
judicial branch
budget
veto
treasurer
attorney general
jury trial

Government in North Carolina Today

For many years Ashley's mother had a rule—no bike riding without a helmet. Sometimes Ashley was the only child in her neighborhood who wore a helmet. "Now all of my friends have one," said Ashley, a fifth grader. In 2001, North Carolina lawmakers passed a helmet law. This law requires everyone in North Carolina under the age of 16 to wear a helmet when biking. Al Deitch, who works for the state government, supported passing this law. Doctors who have treated children with head injuries also supported it. A group that studied bike accidents also worked to get the law passed.

The North Carolina Constitution

A state constitution is a written plan for state government. It tells how the state government should be set up. It also describes the powers and duties of each branch of the government. The state constitution says that the purpose of government is to help people.

Since becoming a state North Carolina has had three constitutions. The first was approved in 1776 and amended, or changed, in 1835. North Carolinians wrote the next Constitution in 1868, after the state rejoined the United States following the Civil War. By 1970, Tar Heels had made so many changes to the 1868 Constitution that citizens voted to have a new one. The Constitution in use today was written in 1971.

The Constitution includes a part called the Declaration of Rights, which lists the rights of North Carolina's citizens. The state Constitution contains the same rights that are listed in the United States Constitution. These rights protect the freedoms of the people.

State governments make decisions about issues that affect citizens. Wearing a helmet while riding a bike is one such decision.

North Carolina's State Government

LEGISLATIVE BRANCH

North Carolina House of Representatives and North Carolina Senate

EXECUTIVE BRANCH

Governor and State Agencies

JUDICIAL BRANCH

Courts

Analyze Diagram The three branches of North Carolina's government work together. Each branch has its own responsibilities.

◆ What parts of the government are included in the executive branch?

The North Carolina Constitution protects freedom of speech. It states that the government cannot stop people from expressing opinions in nonviolent ways. People also have the right to meet in protest or support of issues. Citizens' rights include freedom of religion, too. This means that the government cannot favor one religion over another.

The North Carolina Constitution sets up a state government with three branches, or parts. The **legislative** (LEH•juhs•lay•tiv) **branch** makes the laws. The **executive** (ig•ZEH•kyuh•tiv) **branch** sees that the laws are carried out. The **judicial** (ju•DIH•shuhl) **branch** judges people accused of breaking the law and decides whether laws are fair.

REVIEW What are some freedoms included in the North Carolina Declaration of Rights?

The Legislative Branch

The legislative branch makes the state's laws. The General Assembly is the group elected to do this. It is divided into two parts—the Senate and the House of Representatives. The Senate has 50 members, and the House of Representatives has 120 members. All the members are elected by the voters and serve two-year terms. The state is divided into voting districts made up of one or more counties. On Election Day, people in each district vote to decide who will go to the House and the Senate to represent their district.

Lawmakers in the General Assembly write bills, or plans for new laws. When they approve a bill, it can become a law. Lawmakers also vote on the budget prepared by the executive branch.

A gavel like this is used to call the General Assembly together.

A **budget** is a plan for spending money. The money raised from state taxes pays the costs of the state government. It also pays for many of the services that help the state run smoothly. These services include building and repairing state roads and state parks, running some hospitals, and caring for people who are poor or disabled. A large part of the budget is used for public schools and for state colleges and universities.

Before a bill is voted on, lawmakers in the House and the Senate talk about it. At first, some lawmakers were against having the bicycle helmet law. They said it was not needed. Other lawmakers and groups fought to have the law. A group that had studied bike accidents reported on the deaths and injuries that have happened when children rode bikes without wearing helmets. Doctors told lawmakers about head injuries caused by bike accidents. Both the House and the Senate studied the bill. State senator Allen Wellons of Smithfield supported it. He said that having the law would be a good way of "getting out the word on how important bicycle helmets are." To show how he felt, Wellons gave out hundreds of helmets in his district.

REVIEW What are the most important jobs of the legislature?

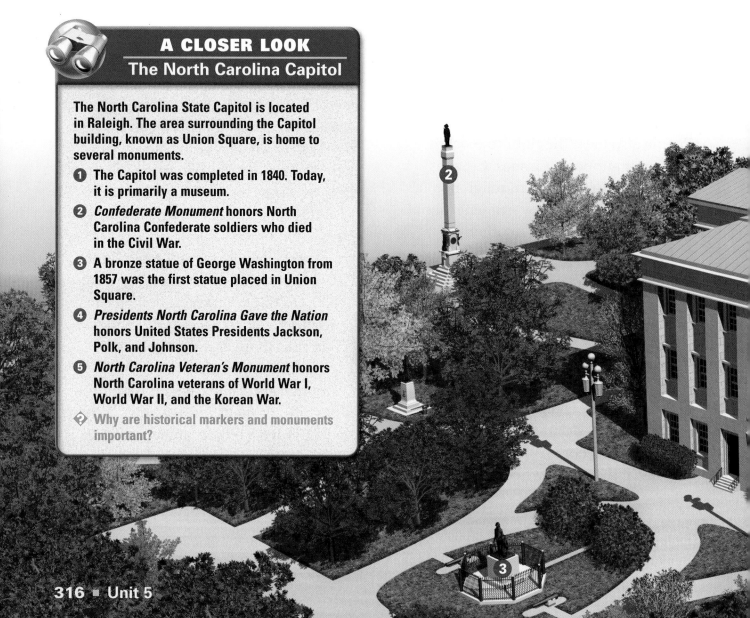

A CLOSER LOOK
The North Carolina Capitol

The North Carolina State Capitol is located in Raleigh. The area surrounding the Capitol building, known as Union Square, is home to several monuments.

❶ The Capitol was completed in 1840. Today, it is primarily a museum.

❷ *Confederate Monument* honors North Carolina Confederate soldiers who died in the Civil War.

❸ A bronze statue of George Washington from 1857 was the first statue placed in Union Square.

❹ *Presidents North Carolina Gave the Nation* honors United States Presidents Jackson, Polk, and Johnson.

❺ *North Carolina Veteran's Monument* honors North Carolina veterans of World War I, World War II, and the Korean War.

❖ Why are historical markers and monuments important?

The Executive Branch

The governor, or chief executive, leads the executive branch of government. North Carolina voters elect a governor for four years. No governor can serve more than two terms in a row. This branch carries out the laws passed by the General Assembly. It also has many other important duties. The governor can suggest new laws to the legislature. One big job of the executive branch is to prepare the state budget. The lawmakers may make some changes before the budget bill becomes a law.

A bill passed by the General Assembly is sent to the governor. He or she then has several choices. If the governor signs the bill, it becomes a law. If the governor does not sign a bill within ten days, it can still become a law. If the governor does not want the bill to become law, he or she can veto it. To **veto** a bill is to refuse to approve it. A veto stops the bill from becoming a law at that time. However, a bill vetoed by the governor still can become a law if three-fifths of the House and three-fifths of the Senate vote for it again.

When the bicycle helmet bill came to Governor Mike Easley, he signed it. He also visited an elementary school in Fuquay-Varina (FOO•kway•vuh•REE•nuh). There he said that the state planned to spend more than $280 million to buy bicycle helmets for the state's children.

Analyze Primary Sources

North Carolinians are proud of their history—and they show it on the flag.

1 The first date on the flag, May 20, 1775, refers to the Mecklenburg Declaration of Independence.

2 The second date on the flag, April 12, 1776, is when North Carolina adopted the Halifax Resolves. The resolves made North Carolina the very first colony to demand independence from Britain.

3 The same flag has flown over North Carolina since March 1885.

❖ How is the North Carolina state flag similiar to the flag of the United States?

Many state employees work with the governor to carry out the duties of the executive branch. Voters also elect the council of state, including the lieutenant (loo•TEH•nuhnt) governor, state treasurer (TRE•zhuh•ruhr), and attorney general. The **treasurer** is in charge of the state's money. The **attorney general** helps carry out state laws. The governor can also choose others to help him or her make decisions. Still other workers in the executive branch manage prisons, care for the state's highways, and make sure laws on food safety and pollution are obeyed.

REVIEW Who is the leader of the executive branch of North Carolina state government?

The Judicial Branch

The judicial branch makes sure that state laws agree with the state constitution. The branch has judges and courts that hear and decide cases. The judges decide how a person who breaks the law will be punished. The judicial branch works to make sure all citizens are treated fairly.

North Carolina has several levels of courts. In the low courts cases are tried by a jury. In a **jury trial** a group of citizens decides whether a person accused of a crime or other wrongdoing is guilty or not guilty. Jury trials are often held in superior or district courts. These courts handle almost three million cases each year.

The next level is the court of appeals, which has twelve judges. In an appeal, a person who has lost his or her case asks a higher court for changes in decisions made in a lower court. Sometimes the court changes the decisions. Other times it orders the lower court to hold a new trial. It may also agree with the lower court's decision.

The state's highest court is the state supreme court. It reviews decisions made in all the lower courts. Voters in North Carolina elect the seven judges on the supreme court. The judges serve

The North Carolina Supreme Court has seven judges, called justices.

eight-year terms. One of the judges serves as chief justice.

The North Carolina Supreme Court makes decisions on many issues. The Court must decide if state laws conflict with the state Constitution. The Court also reviews appeals from people who have already had their cases examined by the court of appeals. Four out of seven justices must agree on each decision. The Court listens to about 100 cases a year and makes decisions on them.

REVIEW **What is the highest court in North Carolina?**

LESSON 2
REVIEW

1 MAIN IDEA What are the three branches of North Carolina's state government? What are their duties?

2 WHY IT MATTERS How does the North Carolina state government affect your life?

3 VOCABULARY Use the terms **budget** and **veto** in a sentence about passing a bill.

4 READING SKILL—Identify Fact and Opinion Does the following sentence state a fact or an opinion? "The most important right in the constitution is freedom of speech."

5 CIVICS/GOVERNMENT What is the purpose of a state constitution?

6 ECONOMICS How does the state government use tax money?

7 CRITICAL THINKING—Evaluate Do you think the three-branch system of state government is effective? Why or why not?

 PERFORMANCE—Make a Diagram Make a diagram showing the three branches of government of the state of North Carolina. List the duties of each branch. Include the names and titles of important officials in each branch. Use the library or the Internet to find this information.

Follow a Flow Chart

VOCABULARY
flow chart
amendment

▶ WHY IT MATTERS

Some information is easier to understand when it is explained in a picture. The drawing on page 321 is a flow chart. A **flow chart** is a drawing that shows the order in which things happen. The arrows on a flow chart help you read the steps in the correct order.

▶ WHAT YOU NEED TO KNOW

The flow chart on page 321 shows how the North Carolina Constitution can be changed. A change to a constitution is called an **amendment**. The first two boxes show the two ways an amendment can start. Follow the arrows to see the steps in the process.

▶ PRACTICE THE SKILL

Answer these questions.

1 What are the two ways an amendment can start?

2 What happens after a convention writes an amendment?

3 How much of each house has to vote yes for the amendment process to continue?

4 Who finally decides if an amendment is added to the constitution?

▶ APPLY WHAT YOU LEARNED

Work with a partner to make a flow chart that shows how to make something. It can be as simple as making a paper airplane. Write each step on a strip of paper. Then paste the strips in order onto a sheet of posterboard. Connect the steps with arrows. Give your flow chart a title. Use it to teach your classmates how to make your item.

(7)

The Constitution, or Form of Government, agreed to and resolved upon by the Representatives of the Freemen of the State of North Carolina, elected and chosen for that particular Purpose, in Congress assembled, at Halifax, the Eighteenth Day of December, in the Year of our Lord One Thousand Seven Hundred and Seventy six.

WHEREAS Allegiance and Protection are in their Nature reciprocal, and the one should and whereas *George* the Third, King of *Great Britain*, and late Sovereign of the *British American* Colonies, hath not only withdrawn from them his Protection, but by an act of the *British* Legislature declared

North Carolina's Constitution is the basis for all the state's laws. Shown at left is a page from North Carolina's first Constitution, adopted in 1776.

Amending the Constitution

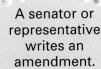 A senator or representative writes an amendment.

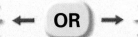 OR

A convention of the people writes an amendment.

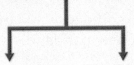 The House of Representatives and the Senate vote on the amendment.

If less than three-fifths of each house votes yes, the amendment is not added.

If three-fifths or more of each house votes yes, the amendment process continues.

The citizens of North Carolina vote on the amendment.

If most people vote **NO**, the amendment is not added to the state constitution.

If most people vote **YES**, the amendment becomes part of the state constitution.

CHART AND GRAPH SKILLS

MAIN IDEA
Read to find out about the different kinds of local governments and their roles.

WHY IT MATTERS
Communities depend on local governments to provide services and leadership.

VOCABULARY

county seat

county commissioner

sheriff

registrar of deeds

school board

municipal government

city council

mayor

zoning

Local Governments

In addition to having a state government, North Carolina has county and city governments. People who live in the counties and cities elect leaders of the local governments. Each year these leaders make hundreds of decisions that affect everyone in the community.

For example, in September 2000, Carteret County leaders decided to buy 20 acres of land to add to a park in the town of Smyrna. The park has two ball fields used for softball, football, and soccer. Many young people play games on these fields. However, there is still a need for additional fields for practice or other events. County leaders could decide to pay for building more fields on the 20 acres of new parkland.

North Carolina Counties

When North Carolina was still a colony, the Lords Proprietors divided it into four counties. Those counties were located in the northeastern corner of what is today North Carolina. These first counties were Currituck (KUHR•uh•tuhk), Pasquotank (PAS•kwoh•tangk), and Perquimans Counties,

Local governments provide important services such as police protection.

322

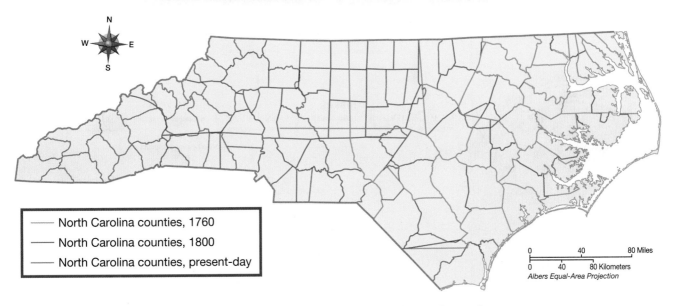

North Carolina Counties, 1760, 1800, and Today

N
W · E
S

— North Carolina counties, 1760
— North Carolina counties, 1800
— North Carolina counties, present-day

0   40   80 Miles
0   40   80 Kilometers
Albers Equal-Area Projection

GEOGRAPHY THEME

Region The number of counties in North Carolina has changed over time. Borders have also shifted.

❖ In what part of North Carolina were the most counties added after 1800?

which were all formed in 1668, and Chowan (chuh•WAHN) County, formed in 1670. The first counties were larger than today's counties. Over time, these larger counties were divided into several smaller ones to make it easier to govern growing populations. Hoke County, founded in 1911, is one example. It was the last county to be created, formed by taking land from Cumberland and Robeson Counties. With almost 948 square miles (2,455 sq km), Robeson County is the state's largest in size. Tyrrell County, with almost 392 square miles (1,015 sq km), is the state's smallest. Today the state has 100 counties. Mecklenburg County, with 695,000 people, has the most people. Tyrrell County, with 4,100 residents, has the fewest.

REVIEW How were the early counties different from today's counties?

County Governments

Each county has its own government. One town or city serves as the county seat. The **county seat** is the center of government for a county. Often, the county seat is the largest city in the county. Jacksonville is the county seat of Onslow County, and Burnsville is the county seat of Yancey County.

Each county in North Carolina has county commissioners. The **county commissioners** direct county activities. The commissioners decide how much citizens will have to pay to the county in taxes and how tax money will be spent on government services.

County services include elections, road care, and public schools.

WELCOME TO
WATAUGA CO.
LEAVING
AVERY CO.

Sign marking the borders of two North Carolina counties

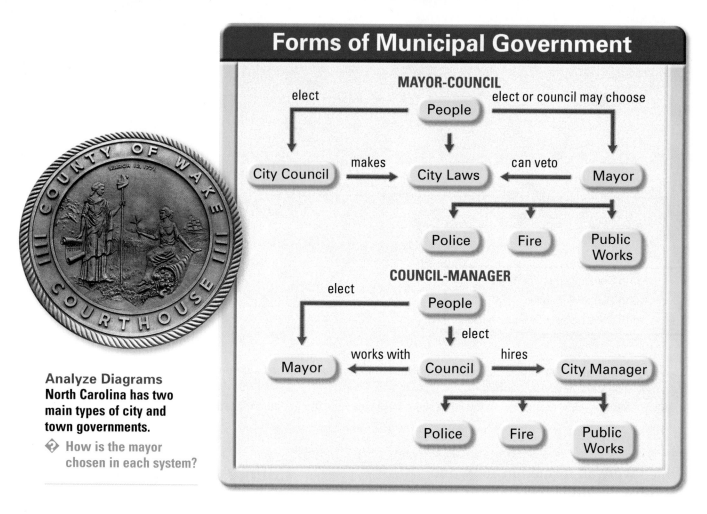

Forms of Municipal Government

MAYOR-COUNCIL

People

elect → City Council

elect or council may choose → Mayor

City Council — makes → City Laws

Mayor — can veto → City Laws

Police   Fire   Public Works

COUNCIL-MANAGER

People

elect → Mayor

elect → Council

Council — works with → Mayor

Council — hires → City Manager

Police   Fire   Public Works

Analyze Diagrams
North Carolina has two main types of city and town governments.

❖ How is the mayor chosen in each system?

The voters in each county elect the commissioners. For example, Wake County voters elect seven commissioners.

Voters also choose other county officials. In many counties the best-known official is the sheriff. The **sheriff** makes sure people obey the laws. Other elected officials include the county treasurer, who pays the county's bills, and the registrar of deeds. The **registrar of deeds** keeps the county records, such as land sales.

Voters also elect members of the local school board. The **school board** works with public schools in a school district. The school board helps manage local schools and decides how schools are paid for.

REVIEW What are some ways in which county governments help the people of North Carolina?

Municipal Governments

Each North Carolina city or town has a municipal (myoo•NI•suh•puhl) government. A **municipal government** is a city or town government. Municipal governments keep communities safe by providing services such as firefighting and police protection. Many cities provide clean water, build and maintain streets and sidewalks, and pick up garbage. They also plan and care for city parks, put up traffic lights, and plant trees in public areas.

There are two forms of municipal government in North Carolina. Most cities and towns have either a mayor-council or council-manager form of government.

In a mayor-council government, the voters elect both the mayor and the city council members. The **city council** makes laws for the city and collects city taxes. The **mayor** is the leader of this kind of government. The mayor leads council meetings and may hire city officials.

Some mayors have moved from city government to state government or to the United States Congress. Howard Lee, who was mayor of Chapel Hill for six years, now serves in the North Carolina Senate. Sue Myrick, who was mayor of Charlotte, is a member of the United States House of Representatives.

Other cities and towns have a council-manager form of local government. The elected city council members make the laws. Often a mayor is elected as well. The council then chooses and hires a city manager to run the city. The city manager takes charge of all city services and chooses department heads.

Municipal governments decide how to keep towns and cities running well. They pay for city projects, such as road beautification.

325

Some of the most difficult decisions a city council makes are about zoning. **Zoning** is the way a city plans how it will grow, and how its land will be used. For example, the council may decide whether a shopping center can be built in a neighborhood. Cities have industrial zones, or areas where factories, stores, and offices may be located.

In Salisbury, a property owner in a historic district wanted to rent her house to a business. In a historic district, old buildings must be kept as they were in the past. The house in the Salisbury historic district was built in 1912. The zoning for the district of 160 houses was zoned only for homes.

The property owner explained that she would not change the outside of the house in any way. However, some groups did not want a business in the area.

The city council and other government groups debated the problem. Finally, the five city council members voted not to allow a business in the historic district.

REVIEW What services do municipal governments provide?

One of the responsibilities of Salisbury's city council is to decide how the city's historic buildings can be used.

LESSON 3
REVIEW

1 MAIN IDEA What are the roles of a county government and a municipal government?

2 WHY IT MATTERS How do local governments help their communities?

3 VOCABULARY How are the jobs of a **mayor** and a **sheriff** different?

4 READING SKILL—Identify Fact and Opinion Does the following sentence state a fact or an opinion? "More taxes should be spent on public school education."

5 GEOGRAPHY How many counties does North Carolina have?

6 CIVICS/GOVERNMENT What is the role of the county commissioners?

7 CRITICAL THINKING—Hypothesize How might life be different if local governments were not elected by voters?

PERFORMANCE—Write a Story Write a story about a local issue that interests you. Your story should include characters who are active in local government. You might include a mayor, county commissioners, or members of a school board.

SALISBURY

The National Government

MAIN IDEA
Read to learn how the national government works and about leaders who have represented North Carolina in Washington, D.C.

WHY IT MATTERS
Good national leaders make the government strong for all the people.

VOCABULARY
federal government
Pledge of Allegiance
republic
Senate
House of Representatives
Cabinet
Supreme Court
impeach

After North Carolina was hit hard by flooding from Hurricane Floyd in 1999, the federal government helped people recover. The **federal government** is another term for the national government. In 1999, federal offices provided money for North Carolinians to rebuild their homes or to buy new ones. Helping Americans in emergencies is just one of the ways the federal government works for its citizens.

Branches of the Federal Government

The flag and the Pledge of Allegiance are symbols of the United States. The **Pledge of Allegiance** is a promise to be loyal to the United States. The pledge calls the United States a republic. A **republic** is a form of government in which people elect representatives to run the country for them. The government of the United States is also a democracy. A democracy is a form of government in which the people take part.

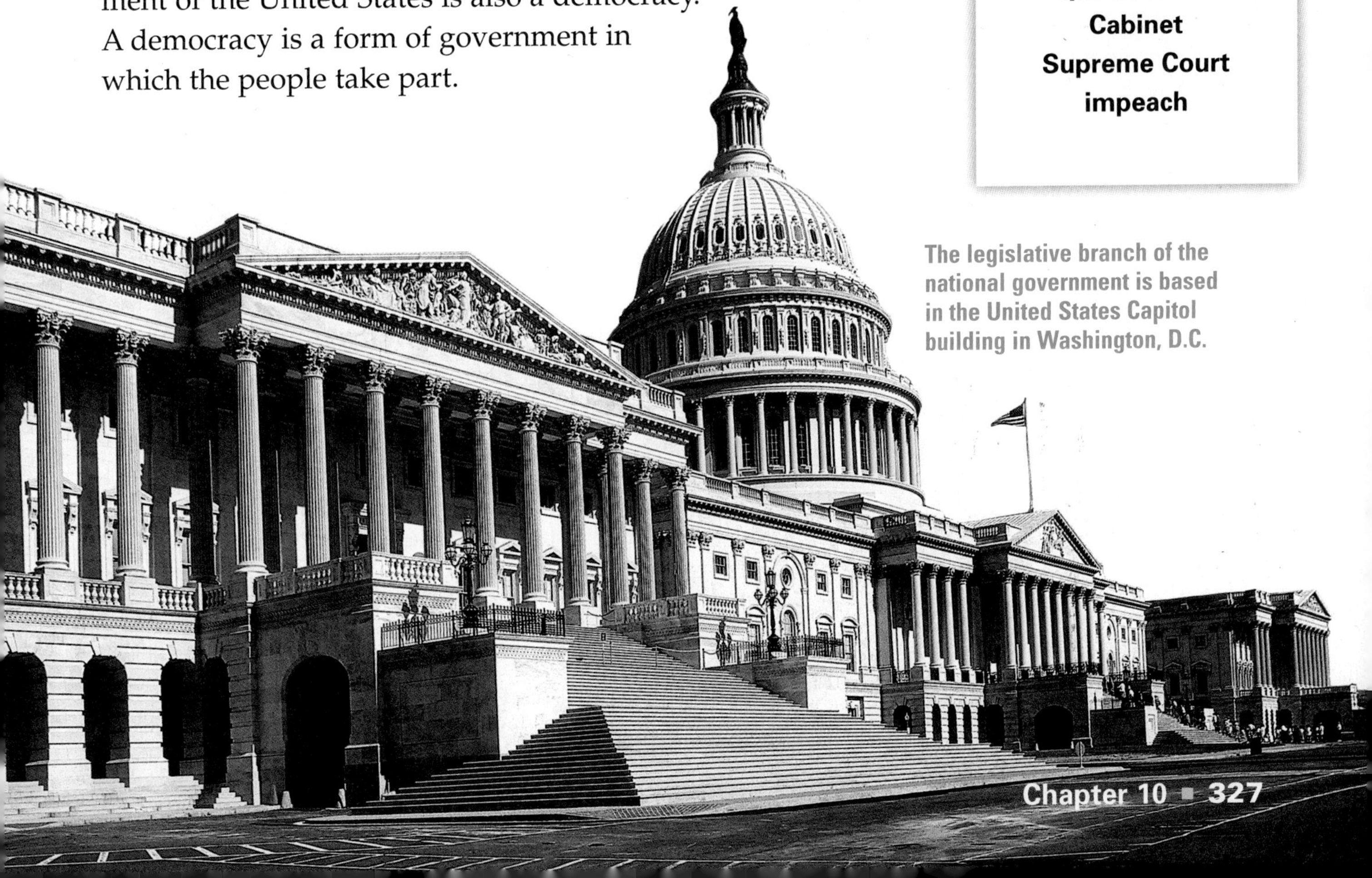

The legislative branch of the national government is based in the United States Capitol building in Washington, D.C.

DEMOCRATIC VALUES
Separation of Powers

In both the North Carolina Constitution and the United States Constitution, the work of the government is divided among three branches. Each branch has certain powers. Each branch also keeps watch over the other two. That way, no branch can become too powerful. For example, in the federal government, the legislative branch can pass laws, but they must be approved by the executive branch. Then the judicial branch makes sure the laws follow the Constitution. The President, the head of the executive branch, appoints justices to the Supreme Court. The appointments, however, have to be approved by the legislative branch.

Analyze the Value

1. Why is it important for one branch of the government to approve the action of another branch?

2. **Make it Relevant** Look in magazines or newpapers for examples of one branch of the federal government limiting the power of another branch.

The Senate meets in the United States Capitol. (top) The President lives and works in the White House. (bottom)

The federal government, like North Carolina's state government, is divided into three branches—legislative, executive, and judicial. These three branches have many of the same duties that state governments have.

The United States Congress is the legislative, or lawmaking, branch of the federal government. It is made up of two parts, the **Senate** and the **House of Representatives**. In every state, voters elect two senators to represent their state in the United States Senate. Senators look out for the interests of their state and of the whole country. Every state also elects a certain number of lawmakers to represent it in the House of Representatives. The number of each state's lawmakers in the House of Representatives depends on the state's population.

The 2000 Census showed that North Carolina had grown rapidly. As a result, the state gained one more representative. It now has 13 representatives.

The President of the United States is the chief executive, or leader of the executive branch. The Vice President works with the President. The executive branch is responsible for carrying out the laws passed by the Congress. The President and those who work with the President decide on the best ways to solve national problems. The President is also the commander in chief of the armed forces.

The President selects a Cabinet. A **Cabinet** is a group of officials who advise the President. Each person in the Cabinet heads one government department, such as transportation.

The third branch of the federal government is the judicial branch. The judicial branch explains the law and makes sure it is carried out fairly. The highest court in the United States is the **Supreme Court**. Its nine judges decide whether laws and decisions of lower courts agree with the United States Constitution.

REVIEW What are the duties of the three branches of the federal government?

Presidents from North Carolina

Three people from North Carolina served as Presidents of the United States. They were Andrew Jackson, James Knox Polk, and Andrew Johnson.

Jackson was born in 1767, near Waxhaw. Because his home was close to the border between North Carolina and South Carolina, both states claim him. He was a lawyer, but he was better known for his bravery in the War of 1812. Jackson's troops called him Old Hickory. Wood from hickory trees is very hard.

Jackson became the seventh President in 1829. He served two terms. His supporters saw him as a man who helped poor farmers. Many people, however, did not agree with his policies toward Native Americans.

The second North Carolinian to become President was James K. Polk. He was born near Pineville in 1795. He served seven terms in the United States House of Representatives. Then Polk became the eleventh President in 1845. Polk was successful in getting more land in the West for the United States.

President Andrew Jackson

President James K. Polk

President Andrew Johnson

Andrew Johnson, the third President from North Carolina, was born in 1808 in Raleigh. He served as Vice President under President Abraham Lincoln. When Lincoln was shot in 1865, Johnson became the nation's seventeenth President. He often fought with Northern lawmakers about how the South should be treated after the Civil War. He was the first President to be impeached by Congress. To **impeach** is to accuse an official of wrongdoing. At his trial by the Senate, lawmakers found him not guilty by one vote.

REVIEW Who were the three Presidents born in North Carolina?

Other Well-Known Leaders

North Carolinians have been leaders in all branches of the federal government. One of the state's best-loved and most-respected senators was Sam J. Ervin, Jr., better known as "Senator Sam." Ervin was born in Morganton in 1896 and went to the University of North Carolina.

He served on the state supreme court, in the state legislature, and in the United States House of Representatives. In 1954 he was elected as a United States senator. He represented North Carolina in the Senate for the next 20 years.

Ervin was known for being wise, honest, and funny. He described himself as an "old country lawyer," but he was an expert on the United States Constitution. He believed that Americans should value "their most precious heritage, the right to vote in a free election."

Another of North Carolina's best-known lawmakers is Jesse Helms, who served in the United States Senate for 30 years. Senator Helms was born in Monroe in 1921. He was head of the Senate committee on world affairs.

North Carolina voters elected John Edwards to the United States Senate

• BIOGRAPHY •

Elizabeth Dole   1936–

Character Trait: Patriotism

Elizabeth Dole was born in Salisbury and has had a long career in public service. She has held three different jobs in the United States government. In 1971 President Richard Nixon chose her to be a member of the Federal Trade Commission. Then, in 1983, President Ronald Reagan named Dole Secretary of Transportation. In 1989 President George Bush named her Secretary of Labor. In 1991 she left the government to become president of the American Red Cross. In 2000 Elizabeth Dole left her job with the American Red Cross to take part in the presidential election. In 2001 and 2002 she campaigned to become a senator from North Carolina.

MULTIMEDIA BIOGRAPHIES
Visit The Learning Site at www.harcourtschool.com/biographies to learn about other famous people.
GO ONLINE

Senator Sam Ervin and Representative Eva Clayton both represented North Carolina in the United States Congress.

in 1998. As a senator, he has shown his ability to work for North Carolina and the country.

Women from North Carolina have also held key jobs in the federal government. Eva Clayton was the first woman from North Carolina to serve in Congress. Voters in eastern North Carolina elected her to the House of Representatives in 1992. She served there for five terms and retired in 2002. In Congress she worked hard to improve the lives of rural farmers and African Americans.

REVIEW Who are some of the North Carolinians who have served in the federal government?

LESSON 4
REVIEW

1 MAIN IDEA What are the main parts of each branch of the federal government?

2 WHY IT MATTERS How does the federal government affect the lives of Americans?

3 VOCABULARY Write a sentence about the United States Congress. Use the words **Senate** and **republic**.

4 READING SKILL—Identify Fact and Opinion Does the following sentence state a fact or an opinion? "Andrew Jackson's nickname was Old Hickory."

5 HISTORY How did Andrew Johnson become President?

6 CIVICS/GOVERNMENT Who are some of the leaders of our country who came from North Carolina?

7 CRITICAL THINKING—Evaluate Why is it important for each state to have representatives in Congress?

 PERFORMANCE—Write a Letter Pretend that you are writing a letter to someone in another country. Explain how the United States federal government works.

A North Carolina Monument

Located on the grounds of the North Carolina Capitol Building is the *Monument to Presidents born in North Carolina: James K. Polk, Andrew Jackson, and Andrew Johnson.* Artist Charles Keck completed the monument in 1948. Even though North Carolina is the birthplace of these three Presidents, all three were living in the neighboring state of Tennessee when they were elected.

 FROM THE NORTH CAROLINA CAPITOL BUILDING, RALEIGH, NORTH CAROLINA

Artists sometimes work with clay models before creating a final sculpture.

Keck used clay and sculpting tools (left) to create his models.

This monument shows what each President was best known for.

James K. Polk was President when the United States expanded.

Andrew Jackson was a military leader in the Revolutionary War and the War of 1812.

Andrew Johnson was the first President to be impeached, or accused of wrongdoing, by the House of Representatives.

Analyze the Primary Source

1 Why do you think President Jackson is riding a horse?

2 Why do you think President Polk is holding a map?

3 Why do you think President Johnson is holding the United States Constitution?

1795   1849
JAMES KNOX POLK
OF
MECKLENBURG COUNTY
PRESIDENT
1845—1849
HE ENLARGED OUR
NATIONAL BOUNDARIES

1767   1845
ANDREW JACKSON
OF
UNION COUNTY
PRESIDENT
1829—1837
HE REVITALIZED
AMERICAN DEMOCRACY

1808   1875
ANDREW JOHNSON
OF
WAKE COUNTY
PRESIDENT
1865—1869
HE DEFENDED
THE CONSTITUTION

ACTIVITY

Design a Monument Choose a person who is important to North Carolina history. Select a symbol to represent his or her achievements. Design a monument that includes the symbol, and sketch or describe it.

RESEARCH

GO ONLINE

Visit The Learning Site at **www.harcourtschool.com/ primarysources** to research other primary sources.

5

MAIN IDEA
Read to learn about the rights and responsibilities of citizens of the United States and of North Carolina.

WHY IT MATTERS
Good citizens know about their government, and they know their rights.

VOCABULARY
naturalized citizen
public office
register
volunteer

North Carolina Citizenship

On October 5, 2001, a dozen people from different parts of North Carolina gathered at the Federal Building in Raleigh. The 12 people were there for a special ceremony. Many of them had brought their families and friends. They were in Raleigh to become United States citizens. After the ceremony a college group sang "America the Beautiful." Parts of the United States Constitution were read aloud. It was a day to celebrate being an American.

Mandy Khanpour was born in Iran. She now lives in Holly Springs. She was one of the people who became citizens that day. "I love to be an American," she said. Billy Wei agrees. He now lives in Raleigh, but he was born in China. He became a citizen, too, along with Anastasia Sigounas from Greece. Sigounas, who now lives in Greenville, proudly showed the red, white, and blue ribbon pinned to her shirt. "I'm honored to wear it," she said.

Becoming a Citizen

To be a citizen of a country is an important privilege. People who were born in this country are citizens of the United States. A person who was born in another country and decides to live in this country can become a naturalized citizen. A **naturalized citizen** is a person who has gone through the steps of becoming a citizen.

Mandy Khanpour, Billy Wei, and Anastasia Sigounas all became naturalized citizens. When adults such as these three become United States citizens, their children under 18 years of age become citizens as well.

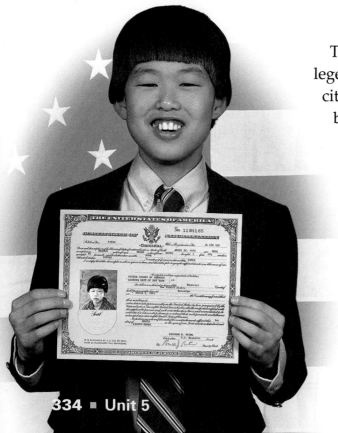

People from all over the world want to become citizens of the United States.

Becoming a Citizen

STEP 1: IMMIGRATION

Immigrants move to the United States.

STEP 2: APPLICATION

They write a judge asking to become a citizen.

STEP 3: TEST

They must take and pass a test about the United States.

STEP 4: CEREMONY

They promise to be loyal to the United States.

Analyze Diagrams   New immigrants follow these steps to become naturalized citizens.

◈ What must an immigrant who wants to be a citizen do after writing to a judge?

By law most immigrants cannot apply to become citizens until they have lived in the United States for five years. If an immigrant is married to a United States citizen, the waiting time is three years.

After the waiting period, immigrants must complete some final steps to become a citizen. First, the person must write to a judge to ask to become a citizen of the United States. Next, the person must take a test. The person answers questions about the history and government of the United States.

By passing the test, the person shows that he or she can read, write, and speak English.

Finally, there is a ceremony like the one held at the Federal Building in Raleigh. A judge asks the person if he or she promises to be loyal to the United States. After the ceremony, the naturalized citizen gets his or her citizenship papers. From then on, he or she has the same rights as other citizens.

REVIEW How do immigrants become citizens of the United States?

The Rights of Citizens

United States citizens have important rights. Citizens have the right to vote if they are 18 years old or older. Citizens also have the right to hold public office. **Public office** is an elected job in the local, state, or national government.

Citizens have all the rights promised by the Bill of Rights in the United States Constitution. These rights include freedom of speech, freedom of the press, freedom of religion, and freedom to gather in groups. Citizens also have the right to a fair trial if they are accused of a crime. Some American citizens travel or work in other countries. When abroad, these citizens have the right to seek help from the United States government.

• HERITAGE •

Naturalization Ceremony in Southport

The coastal town of Southport welcomes new citizens every Fourth of July. The tradition started more than ten years ago. Lois Gable of Oak Island saw a naturalization ceremony on the Fourth of July in another state. She said, "I found myself thinking . . . this is what the Fourth of July is all about." She liked the ceremony so much that she decided to start the same sort of ceremony in Southport.

Southport starts its Fourth of July celebration with a naturalization ceremony every year. Boats spurting red, white, and blue water come down the river. Bands play, choirs sing, and homes have flags waving. In 2000, Southport's ceremony was at Fort Johnston. There were 160 new citizens that day! They came from 50 different countries.

Fort Johnston is the site of Southport's annual Fourth of July citizenship ceremony.

The federal government cannot take away a citizen's rights unless that person has been found guilty of certain crimes. A person who is guilty of serious crimes can lose the right to vote.

The government can place certain limits on a citizen's rights. For example, federal law says that a citizen must be 18 years old to vote. Every state has laws and rules that say when and how a citizen **registers**, or signs up to vote.

People in this country who are not citizens have many of the same rights as citizens. However, they cannot vote, hold public office, or be on a trial jury.

REVIEW What are the rights of citizens?

The Responsibilities of Citizens

Along with their rights, citizens also have responsibilities, or duties. One of the most important responsibilities of citizens is to vote. In a democracy it is important for every citizen to vote on every Election Day. A related duty of citizens is to learn about the people who are running for political office and what they stand for.

Citizens have other duties too. They have to pay taxes, obey laws, and serve on a jury if they are asked.

Many of the responsibilities of citizenship are for adults. Some duties are for young and old alike. One way of being a good citizen is to help make the community a better place to live. Many Tar Heels **volunteer** (vah•luhn•TIR), or work without pay, to help others in the community.

There are many ways to volunteer. Some school volunteers read books to younger children or help them with schoolwork. Others help collect toys, clothes, or school supplies for needy families. Some volunteers collect cans of food and take them to local food banks. Others spend several hours each week helping at the local library or animal shelter.

Volunteers at work at an animal shelter

These volunteers are building a new house for a needy family.

Many volunteers take part in local cleanup projects. Shawn Garner of Roanoke Rapids persuaded the other Boy Scouts of his troop to help fix up Medoc Mountain State Park in northeastern North Carolina. The park had been damaged by Hurricane Floyd. Garner led the volunteers in planting trees and fixing up the trails. "I felt," he said, "that for all the times the Scouts used the park, we should help give something back."

Volunteering can be done in your own neighborhood. Young people can volunteer to help recycle paper and other materials. They can also volunteer in many ways at home and at school.

REVIEW **What are some responsibilities that citizens have?**

LESSON 5
REVIEW

1 MAIN IDEA What are some rights and responsibilities of United States citizens?

2 WHY IT MATTERS Why do good citizens need to know about their government?

3 VOCABULARY Write sentences about voting. Use the terms **public office** and **register**.

4 READING SKILL—Identify Fact and Opinion Is the following sentence a fact or an opinion? "Many citizenship ceremonies take place on September 17, Citizenship Day."

5 CIVICS/GOVERNMENT What are the four steps to becoming a naturalized citizen of the United States?

6 CIVICS/GOVERNMENT What is the Bill of Rights?

7 CRITICAL THINKING—Synthesize Why do citizens have responsibilities as well as rights?

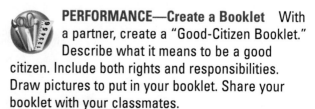
PERFORMANCE—Create a Booklet With a partner, create a "Good-Citizen Booklet." Describe what it means to be a good citizen. Include both rights and responsibilities. Draw pictures to put in your booklet. Share your booklet with your classmates.

· SKILLS ·
CITIZENSHIP

Act as a Responsible Citizen

▶ WHY IT MATTERS

When a responsible person sees a problem, he or she takes action to help solve it. Responsible citizens are informed about their country, their state, and their city. Being informed helps them choose their leaders wisely. It also helps them be active in their communities.

▶ WHAT YOU NEED TO KNOW

There are many ways to act responsibly. Think of a time when you acted responsibly. Maybe you cleaned up a mess or helped another student. What did you do? How did you feel doing it? When you act responsibly, you set a good example for others.

▶ PRACTICE THE SKILL

Here are steps to help you act responsibly.

1. Identify the problems around you. Learn more about them.

2. Think about ways to solve these problems. Try to think of solutions that would be good for other people as well as for you.

3. Decide what you can do to help. You might do something alone or with other people.

4. Remember to be careful. Never do something unsafe to solve a problem. Get help from others to do what you cannot do alone.

▶ APPLY WHAT YOU LEARNED

List some things you can do to show that you want to be a good citizen of your community. Include things you can do by yourself and things you would need help to do. Explain why they are responsible things to do.

You can be a responsible citizen by paying attention to your community's needs.

339

10 Review and Test Preparation

USE YOUR READING SKILLS

Complete this graphic organizer. Read each sentence. If the sentence is a fact, put an X in the FACT column. If it is an opinion, put an X in the OPINION column. A copy of this graphic organizer appears on page 101 of the Activity Book.

STATEMENT	FACT	OPINION
North Carolina is a great place to live and work.		X
The population of North Carolina is growing and becoming more diverse.		
North Carolina's industries are becoming more interdependent.		
Voting is a way for citizens to become involved in the democratic process.		
The best government officials are from North Carolina.		
Voters can influence issues that are important to them and their communities.		

THINK & WRITE

Write an Election Speech   Imagine that you are running for office in your city or town. Think about some of the issues that are important to you and your community. Write a speech to persuade voters to elect you. Explain some of the changes you would like to make in your community. Describe what laws you would support, and tell why.

Write a Poem   Think about the different ethnic groups who live in North Carolina. Write a poem to celebrate the many cultures of your state. Use descriptions and precise language to make your poem more interesting. Write your poem in a creative way on a sheet of paper and illustrate it, if you wish. Display your poem in the classroom.

Use Vocabulary

For each sentence below, fill in the blank with one of the vocabulary terms from the word bank.

ethnic group (p. 309)

jury trial (p. 318)

zoning (p. 326)

Supreme Court (p. 329)

volunteer (p. 337)

1 The reporter wrote about a _____ in which a woman was found guilty of robbing a bank.

2 Sarah likes to _____ at a food bank every Thanksgiving.

3 The town planners made sure that they obeyed all _____ laws.

4 The international food festival included dishes from every _____ in the community.

5 The confusing results of the election were argued all the way to the _____.

Recall Facts

Answer these questions.

6 What are the two kinds of local government found most often in North Carolina?

7 Who is the head of the executive branch of the United States government?

Write the letter of the best choice.

8 **TEST PREP** Which government official is responsible for the state's money?
  A the attorney general
  B the treasurer
  C the governor
  D the lieutenant governor

9 **TEST PREP** Members of North Carolina's council of state include all of the following except the—
  F treasurer.
  G lieutenant governor.
  H governor.
  J attorney general.

10 **TEST PREP** What is the largest county in size in North Carolina today?
  A Robeson County
  B Tyrrell County
  C Hoke County
  D Yancey County

Think Critically

11 Why is it important that local, state, and federal governments work together? Explain your opinion.

12 Do you think the responsibilities of United States citizens are fair? Why or why not?

Apply Skills

Follow a Flow Chart
Use the chart on page 321.

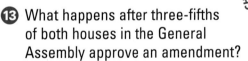

13 What happens after three-fifths of both houses in the General Assembly approve an amendment?

Make Economic Choices

14 You have ten dollars. List some things you can do with the money, such as spend it, save it, or donate it to charity. What are the opportunity costs of each choice?

Act as a Responsible Citizen

15 Choose a person you know who you think is a responsible citizen. Make a list of reasons you have this opinion.

VISIT

KITTY HAWK

GET READY

When Orville and Wilbur Wright made the first airplane flights at Kitty Hawk in 1903, they changed the world forever. A monument atop 90-foot (27-m) Kill Devil Hill, where the historic flight took place, commemorates their achievement. Visitors to the Wright Brothers National Memorial can tour a museum of aviation history. They can also attend a presentation conducted by a park ranger and learn many interesting facts about the Wright brothers. Inside the huge granite monument, stairs lead to an observation deck. Nearby, you can trace with your footsteps the trail of the very first flight. People who visit the Wright Brothers National Memorial leave with an awakened appreciation of Orville and Wilbur Wright's gift of flight.

LOCATE IT

Kitty Hawk

NORTH CAROLINA

On this side of the monument are engraved the words "In commemoration of the conquest of the air."

Visitors can tour a reconstructed workroom like the one used by the Wright brothers.

This photograph of Orville Wright was taken on December 17, 1903.

This boulder marks the take-off spot of the first successful airplane flight.

A model of the Wright brothers' original plane is on display at the visitor center.

TAKE A FIELD TRIP

GO ONLINE

A VIRTUAL TOUR
Visit The Learning Site at **www.harcourtschool.com/tours** to find virtual tours of other historic sites in the United States.

CNN
Turner Le@rning

A VIDEO TOUR
Check your media center or classroom library for a videotape tour of Kitty Hawk.

· U N I T ·

5 Review and Test Preparation

VISUAL SUMMARY

Make Outlines   Study the pictures and captions below to help you review Unit 5. Then make a short outline for each picture. Include key information about the event shown in the picture.

USE VOCABULARY

For each pair of terms, write a sentence or two showing how they are related.

1 **primary roads** (p. 284), **interstate highways** (p. 285)

2 **civil rights** (p. 297), **ethnic group** (p. 314)

3 **Senate** (p. 328), **House of Representatives** (p. 328)

RECALL FACTS

Answer these questions.

4 Why did work on North Carolina's roads slow down during the 1930s?

5 How did war bonds help the government during World War I?

6 Who was Dr. Martin Luther King, Jr.?

7 How are members of a school board selected and what are their duties?

Write the letter of the best choice.

8 **TEST PREP**   People created victory gardens during World War I—
   A to celebrate the end of the war.
   B because there were shortages of food.
   C to make their communities beautiful.
   D because they had more land than they needed and more free time.

9 **TEST PREP**   How did Gertrude Weil help lead the fight for woman suffrage?
   F She organized a letter-writing campaign.
   G She held a sit-in.
   H She wrote an amendment to the U.S. Constitution.
   J She ran for Congress.

10 **TEST PREP**   Which branch of government is responsible for making laws?
   A the judicial branch
   B the municipal branch
   C the executive branch
   D the legislative branch

Visual Summary

1900   1925

1903 Wright brothers make first flight p. 285

1914 North Carolina supports World War I efforts p. 290

1929 Great Depression begins p. 292

344

11 TEST PREP Which of the following is NOT a responsibility of being a citizen?
  F gather in groups
  G pay taxes
  H volunteer
  J serve on a jury

THINK CRITICALLY

12 Why do you think it is important that women were given the right to vote?

13 If you were running for public office, what position would you choose to run for? Explain your answer.

14 Why do you think the North Carolina state government has three branches?

15 How can students be good citizens? How can adults be good citizens?

APPLY SKILLS

Follow Routes on a Map
Use the bus map on this page to answer the following questions.

16 Which bus route would you use to go to Double Oaks Recreation Center?

17 What is the main street that bus #11 follows?

18 Which bus could you use to reach the Amtrak station?

Charlotte Bus Routes

Norris Avenue
Rachel Street
Lucena Street
Double Oaks Road
21
77
Double Oaks Recreation Center
13
22
21
CE
11
277
Dalton Avenue
Amtrak Station
12
North Tryon Street
North College Street
277

0   1/4   1/2 Mile
0   1/4   1/2 Kilometer

19 Which bus route uses Norris Avenue and Rachel Street?

20 Name two ways you could get to Dalton Avenue from Lucena Street.

21 Which street shown on the map do you think is the busiest? Explain.

1975

2000

1941 United States enters World War II p. 294

1960 Greensboro sit-in takes place p. 297

PRESENT North Carolina's population is more diverse than ever p. 307

Unit Activities

 Visit The Learning Site at www.harcourtschool.com/ socialstudies/activities for additional activities.

Hold a Debate

As a class, choose an issue in your community. Divide your class into three groups. One group will act as a county commission. Each of the other groups should choose a different point of view about the issue. Assign each person a role. Hold a debate about the issue in class. Each side should try to persuade the county commissioners to do something about the issue. At the end of the debate, have the county commissioners vote on the issue.

Make a Scrapbook

Make a scrapbook showing what it means to you to live in North Carolina. Collect pictures of important places, things, and events. Write a description of each picture. Explain what the picture shows about North Carolina and why it is important to you. Include pictures of many kinds of things in your scrapbook.

VISIT YOUR LIBRARY

- **Sidewalk Chalk: Poems of the City** by Carole Boston Weatherford. Wordsong/ Boyd's Mill Press.

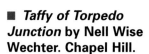

- **Taking Flight** by Stephen Krensky. Simon and Schuster.

- **Taffy of Torpedo Junction** by Nell Wise Wechter. Chapel Hill.

COMPLETE THE UNIT PROJECT

Future Inventions Book Decide what invention you will design. Draw a picture of your invention. Write a description that tells what the invention will do to help North Carolina in the future. Publish your invention with your classmates' inventions in a book.

For Your Reference

Almanac
Facts About North Carolina

North Carolina				
LAND	**SIZE**	**CLIMATE**	**POPULATION***	**LEADING PRODUCTS**
Highest Point: Mount Mitchell in the Black Mountain range 6,684 feet (2,037 m) **Lowest Point:** Atlantic Coast sea level	**Area:** 52,672 square miles (136,410 sq km) **Greatest Distance North/South:** 188 miles (303 km) **Greatest Distance East/West:** 499 miles (803 km)	**Highest Recorded Temperature:** 110°F (43°C) at Fayetteville on August 21, 1983 **Lowest Recorded Temperature:** -34°F (-37°C) on Mount Mitchell on January 21, 1985 **Average Temperature:** 77°F (25°C) in July 41°F (5°C) in January **Average Yearly Rainfall:** 49 inches (124 cm)	8,049,313 * 2000 Census population figures	**Crops:** Tobacco, cotton, soybeans, corn, wheat, peanuts, sweet potatoes, apples, potatoes, cucumbers **Livestock:** Hogs, chickens, turkeys, cattle and calves, sheep and lambs **Fishing:** Blue crabs, clams, flounder, shrimp, trout **Manufacturing:** Chemicals, textiles, machinery, electrical equipment, food products, furniture, tobacco products **Mining:** Limestone, lithium, phosphate rock, sand and gravel, feldspar, mica, olivine, clay, granite, marble, talc

Charlotte is the largest city in North Carolina, with a population of more than 540,000. Known as the Queen City of the South, Charlotte is a leading banking, distribution, and transportation center. It ranks as the second-largest financial center in the country, behind New York City.

The United States

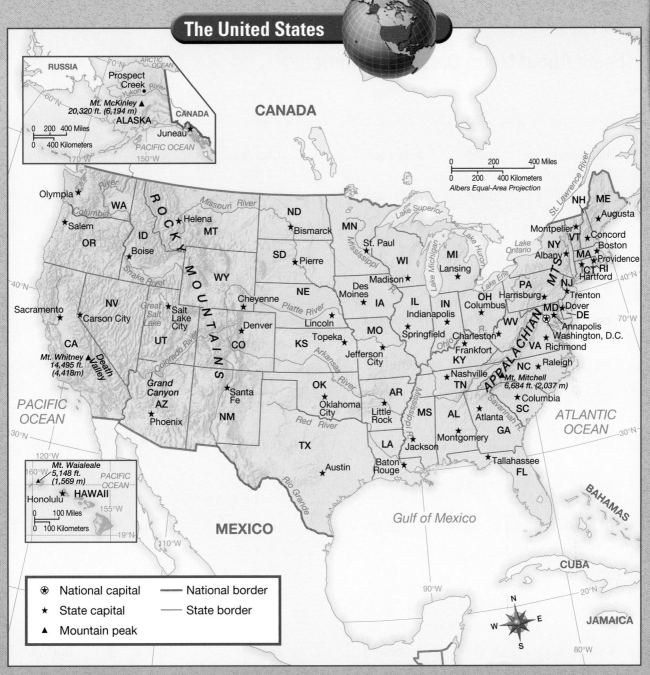

RUSSIA
ARCTIC OCEAN
70°N
Prospect Creek
Yukon River
60°N
Mt. McKinley ▲
20,320 ft. (6,194 m)
CANADA
ALASKA
Juneau
0 200 400 Miles
0 400 Kilometers
PACIFIC OCEAN
170°W
150°W

CANADA

0 200 400 Miles
0 200 400 Kilometers
Albers Equal-Area Projection

Olympia ★
WA
ROCKY MOUNTAINS
Columbia River
Salem ★
OR
Helena ★
MT
ID
Boise ●
ND
Bismarck ★
Missouri River
MN
St. Paul ★
Lake Superior
St. Lawrence River
NH
ME
Augusta ★
Montpelier ★
VT
Concord ★
Boston ★
NY
Albany ★
MA
Providence ★
CT RI
Hartford ★
40°N

40°N
Sacramento ★
NV
Carson City ★
Great Salt Lake
UT
Salt Lake City ★
WY
Cheyenne ★
Denver ★
CO
SD
Pierre ★
NE
Lincoln ★
Platte River
Des Moines ★
IA
Madison ★
WI
MI
Lansing ★
Lake Michigan
Lake Huron
Lake Ontario
Lake Erie
OH
Columbus ★
PA
Harrisburg ★
Trenton ★
NJ
APPALACHIAN MTS.
MD
Dover ★
DE
Annapolis ★
Washington, D.C. ⊛
70°W

CA
Mt. Whitney ▲
14,495 ft. (4,418m)
Death Valley
Colorado River
Grand Canyon
AZ
Phoenix ●
NM
Santa Fe ★
KS
Topeka ★
MO
Jefferson City ★
IL
Springfield ★
IN
Indianapolis ★
Charleston ★
WV
Frankfort ★
KY
Ohio R.
VA
Richmond ★
NC
Raleigh ★
Nashville ★
TN
Mt. Mitchell ▲
6,684 ft. (2,037 m)
Columbia ★
SC

Snake River

PACIFIC OCEAN
30°N
OK
Oklahoma City ★
AR
Little Rock ★
Red River
Arkansas River
MS
Jackson ★
AL
Montgomery ★
Atlanta ★
GA
Savannah R.
Tallahassee ★
FL
ATLANTIC OCEAN
30°N

120°W
Mt. Waialeale ▲
5,148 ft. (1,569 m)
160°W
PACIFIC OCEAN
HAWAII
Honolulu ★
155°W
0 100 Miles
0 100 Kilometers
19°N
110°W

TX
Austin ★
LA
Baton Rouge ★
Mississippi R.
Rio Grande

MEXICO

Gulf of Mexico

BAHAMAS

90°W

CUBA
20°N

JAMAICA
80°W

Legend
⊛ National capital — National border
★ State capital — State border
▲ Mountain peak

N
W E
S

Raleigh has served as the state capital since 1792. The present capitol building was built between 1833 and 1840.

North Carolina has more than 1,700 elementary schools.

Almanac

Facts About North Carolina Counties

County	Population*	County Seat	County	Population*	County Seat
Alamance	130,800	Graham	Cherokee	24,298	Murphy
Alexander	33,603	Taylorsville	Chowan	14,526	Edenton
Alleghany	10,677	Sparta	Clay	8,775	Hayesville
Anson	25,275	Wadesboro	Cleveland	96,287	Shelby
Ashe	24,384	Jefferson	Columbus	54,749	Whiteville
Avery	17,167	Newland	Craven	91,436	New Bern
Beaufort	44,958	Washington	Cumberland	302,963	Fayetteville
Bertie	19,773	Windsor	Currituck	18,190	Currituck
Bladen	32,278	Elizabethtown	Dare	29,967	Manteo
Brunswick	73,143	Bolivia	Davidson	147,246	Lexington
Buncombe	206,330	Asheville	Davie	34,835	Mocksville
Burke	89,148	Morganton	Duplin	49,063	Kenansville
Cabarrus	131,063	Concord	Durham	223,314	Durham
Caldwell	77,415	Lenoir	Edgecombe	55,606	Tarboro
Camden	6,885	Camden	Forsyth	306,067	Winston-Salem
Carteret	59,383	Beaufort	Franklin	47,260	Louisburg
Caswell	23,501	Yanceyville	Gaston	190,365	Gastonia
Catawba	141,685	Newton	Gates	10,516	Gatesville
Chatham	49,329	Pittsboro	Graham	7,993	Robbinsville

County	Population*	County Seat	County	Population*	County Seat
Granville	48,498	Oxford	Mecklenburg	695,454	Charlotte
Greene	18,974	Snow Hill	Mitchell	15,687	Bakersville
Guilford	421,048	Greensboro	Montgomery	26,822	Troy
Halifax	57,370	Halifax	Moore	74,769	Carthage
Harnett	91,025	Lillington	Nash	87,420	Nashville
Haywood	54,033	Waynesville	New Hanover	160,307	Wilmington
Henderson	89,173	Hendersonville	Northampton	22,086	Jackson
Hertford	22,601	Winton	Onslow	150,355	Jacksonville
Hoke	33,646	Raeford	Orange	118,227	Hillsborough
Hyde	5,826	Swan Quarter	Pamlico	12,934	Bayboro
Iredell	122,660	Statesville	Pasquotank	34,897	Elizabeth City
Jackson	33,121	Sylva	Pender	41,082	Burgaw
Johnston	121,965	Smithfield	Perquimans	11,368	Hertford
Jones	10,381	Trenton	Person	35,623	Roxboro
Lee	49,040	Sanford	Pitt	133,798	Greenville
Lenoir	59,648	Kinston	Polk	18,324	Columbus
Lincoln	63,780	Lincolnton	Randolph	130,454	Asheboro
Macon	29,811	Franklin	Richmond	46,564	Rockingham
Madison	19,635	Marshall	Robeson	123,339	Lumberton
Martin	25,593	Williamston	Rockingham	91,928	Wentworth
McDowell	42,151	Marion	Rowan	130,340	Salisbury

*The population figures give the most recent estimates.

County	Population*	County Seat	County	Population*	County Seat
Rutherford	62,899	Rutherfordton	Vance	42,954	Henderson
Sampson	60,161	Clinton	Wake	627,846	Raleigh
Scotland	35,998	Laurinburg	Warren	19,972	Warrenton
Stanly	58,100	Albemarle	Washington	13,723	Plymouth
Stokes	44,711	Danbury	Watauga	42,695	Boone
Surry	71,219	Dobson	Wayne	113,329	Goldsboro
Swain	12,968	Bryson City	Wilkes	65,632	Wilkesboro
Transylvania	29,334	Brevard	Wilson	73,814	Wilson
Tyrrell	4,149	Columbia	Yadkin	36,348	Yadkinville
Union	123,677	Monroe	Yancey	17,774	Burnsville

Almanac

Facts About North Carolina Governors

Governor	Term	Governor	Term
Richard Caswell	1776–1780	Jesse Franklin	1820–1821
Abner Nash	1780–1781	Gabriel Holmes	1821–1824
Thomas Burke	1781–1782	Hutchins G. Burton	1824–1827
Alexander Martin	1782–1784	James Iredell, Jr.	1827–1828
Richard Caswell	1784–1787	John Owen	1828–1830
Samuel Johnston	1787–1789	Montford Stokes	1830–1832
Alexander Martin	1789–1792	David L. Swain	1832–1835
Richard D. Spaight, Sr.	1792–1795	Richard D. Spaight, Jr.	1835–1836
Samuel Ashe	1795–1798	Edward B. Dudley	1836–1841
William R. Davie	1798–1799	John M. Morehead	1841–1845
Benjamin Williams	1799–1802	William A. Graham	1845–1849
James Turner	1802–1805	Charles Manly	1849–1850
Nathaniel Alexander	1805–1807	David S. Reid	1851–1854
Benjamin Williams	1807–1808	Warren Winslow	1854–1855
David Stone	1808–1810	Thomas Bragg	1855–1859
Benjamin Smith	1810–1811	John W. Ellis	1859–1861
William Hawkins	1811–1814	Henry T. Clark	1861–1862
William Miller	1814–1817	Zebulon B. Vance	1862–1865
John Branch	1817–1820	William W. Holden	1865

Governor	Term	Governor	Term
Jonathan Worth	1865–1868	Angus W. McLean	1925–1929
William W. Holden	1868–1870	Oliver M. Gardner	1929–1933
Tod R. Caldwell	1870–1874	John C. B. Ehringhaus	1933–1937
Curtis H. Brogden	1874–1877	Clyde R. Hoey	1937–1941
Zebulon B. Vance	1877–1879	Joseph M. Broughton	1941–1945
Thomas J. Jarvis	1879–1885	Robert G. Cherry	1945–1949
James L. Robinson*	1883	William K. Scott	1949–1953
Alfred M. Scales	1885–1889	William B. Umstead	1953–1954
David G. Fowle	1889–1891	Luther H. Hodges	1954–1961
Thomas M. Holt	1891–1893	Terry Sanford	1961–1965
Elias Carr	1893–1897	Daniel K. Moore	1965–1969
Daniel L. Russell	1897–1901	Robert W. Scott	1969–1973
Charles B. Aycock	1901–1905	James E. Holshouser, Jr.	1973–1977
Robert B. Glenn	1905–1909	James B. Hunt, Jr.	1977–1985
William W. Kitchin	1909–1913	James G. Martin	1985–1993
Locke Craig	1913–1917	James B. Hunt, Jr.	1993–2001
Thomas W. Bickett	1917–1921	Michael F. Easley	2001–
Cameron Morrison	1921–1925		

* Served while Thomas J. Jarvis was traveling outside of the state

Biographical Dictionary

This list gives facts about the famous people in North Carolina history whom you read about in this book. The page number tells where you can read about each person. Also listed are some other famous Tar Heels you might like to know about.

A

Amadas, Philip *1550-1618* English navigator who commanded ships in Sir Walter Raleigh's expeditions to North America in the 1500s. p. 92, 94

Armstrong, Neil A. *1930–* Astronaut who was the first person to set foot on the moon, July 20, 1969. p. 298

Ayllón, Lucas Vasquez de (eye•YOHN, LOO•kuhs VAHS•kayz day) *1475–1526* Spanish explorer who started a settlement near the mouth of the Cape Fear River in 1526. p. 93

B

Baker, Ellen S. *1953–* Astronaut who flew on the first space shuttle to dock with the Russian space station *Mir*, in 1995; born in Fayetteville. p. 299

Barker, Penelope *1728–1796* North Carolina colonist who organized the Edenton Tea Party in 1774 to protest the British tax on tea. p. 113

Barlowe, Arthur English navigator who commanded ships in Sir Walter Raleigh's expeditions to North America in the late 1500s. p. 92, 94

Batts, Nathaniel *1620–1679* First permanent English settler to settle in North Carolina, about 1655. p. 99

Bennett, James Owner of the farmhouse where Confederate General Joseph E. Johnston surrendered to the Union General William Tecumseh Sherman after the Battle of Bentonville during the Civil War. p. 174

Berry, Harriet Morehead *1877–1940* State official who led the movement to establish a state highway system in North Carolina in 1918. p. 284

Betts, Doris *1932–* Author and journalist; born in Statesville.

Blount, William *1749–1800* North Carolina signer of the United States Constitution.

Bonny, Anne *1697?–?* Pirate who robbed ships off the coast of the Carolinas in the 1700s. p. 105

Boone, Daniel *1734–1820* One of the first pioneers to cross the Appalachian Mountains. p. 221

Brady, Charles E., Jr. *1951–* Astronaut from Robbins. p. 299

Brinkley, David *1920–* Broadcast journalist; born in Wilmington.

Brown, Curtis L. *1956–* Astronaut from Elizabethtown. p. 299

C

Cannon, James W. *1852–1921* Founder of the textile mill that produced the first manufactured towels in the South. p. 177

Carver, George Washington *1864–1943* African American scientist who became well known for his research on the uses of peanuts and on ways to improve farming.

Caswell, Richard *1729–1789* Hero at the Battle of Moores Creek Bridge during the American Revolution and the first governor of the state of North Carolina.

Charles I *1600–1649* King of England, Scotland, and Ireland from 1625 to 1649; gave Sir Robert Heath the Carolina territory in 1629. p. 99

Charles II *1630–1685* King of England, Scotland, and Ireland from 1660 to 1685; gave the Carolina territory to the Lords Proprietors. p. 99

Chavis, John *1763–1838* African American minister who set up schools for both African Americans and whites in Raleigh in the early 1800s.

Chesnutt, Charles W. *1858–1932* Author from Fayetteville who wrote about African Americans and their life under segregation.

Clayton, Eva *1933–* In 1992 became the first woman from North Carolina elected to the U.S. House of Representatives. p. 331

Clement, Lillian Exum *1894–1924* In 1920 became the first woman elected to the North Carolina state legislature.

Coffin, Katherine *1803–1881* Quaker leader who, with her husband, Levi, helped slaves escape on the Underground Railroad. p. 167

Coffin, Levi *1798–1877* Quaker leader who, with his wife, Katherine, helped slaves escape on the Underground Railroad. p. 167

Coleman, Warren C. *1849–1903* First African American to own a textile mill in North Carolina.

Coltrane, John *1926–1967* Jazz musician; born in Hamlet.

Cornwallis, Charles *1738–1805* British general during the American Revolution. p. 115

Cosell, Howard *1920–1995* Television sports announcer; born in Winston-Salem.

Culpeper, John *1633–1692* North Carolina colonist who was one of the leaders of Culpeper's Rebellion, in 1677. p. 101

D

Dare, Virginia *1587–?* First English child born in North America; born on Roanoke Island. p. 95

Davie, William R. *1756–1820* North Carolina delegate to the United States Constitutional Convention.

Davis, Archie *1911–1998* Business leader who helped develop Research Triangle Park.

Davis, Jefferson *1808–1889* President of the Confederate States of America. p. 169

Day, Thomas *1801?–1861* African American furniture maker; lived in Milton. p. 178

de Soto, Hernando (day SOH•toh) *1496?–1542* Spanish explorer who led an expedition into what is today the southeastern United States. p. 93

Dole, Elizabeth H. *1936–* Former head of the American Red Cross; former secretary of transportation and secretary of labor; born in Salisbury. p. 330

Drake, Francis *1543–1596* English explorer; rescued England's first North American colonists from Roanoke Island. p. 94

Drummond, William *1620–1677* First governor of the Carolina colony, from 1664 to 1667.

Duke, Charles M., Jr. *1935–* Astronaut who was the tenth person to walk on the moon, in 1972; born in Charlotte. p. 298

Duke, James Buchanan "Buck" *1856–1925* Head of the American Tobacco Company in the 1890s. p. 36

Durant, George *1632–1693* North Carolina colonist who was one of the leaders of Culpeper's Rebellion, in 1677. p. 101

E

Edwards, John *1953–* United States senator from North Carolina; elected in 1998. p. 330

Elizabeth I *1533–1603* Queen of England from 1558 to 1603. p. 92

Ervin, Samuel J., Jr. *1896–1985* United States senator from North Carolina from 1954 to 1975. p. 330

F

Faircloth, Lauch *1928–* United States senator from North Carolina; first elected in 1992.

G

Gardner, Ava *1922–1990* Movie actor; born in Smithfield.

Gaston, William *1778–1844* Member of the U.S. House of Representatives, North Carolina Supreme Court justice, and author of the state song "The Old North State."

Glenn, John H., Jr. *1921–* Astronaut who was the first American to orbit Earth, in 1962. p. 298

Graham, Billy *1918–* Well-known Baptist minister; born near Charlotte.

Griffith, Andy *1926–* Television actor; born in Mount Airy.

H

Heath, Robert *1575–1649* English lawyer who once owned the land between Virginia and Spanish Florida. p. 99

Helms, Jesse *1921–* United States senator from North Carolina; first elected in 1972. p. 330

Henry, O. *1862–1910* Pen name of William Sydney Porter, a popular short story writer; born in Greensboro.

Hewes, Joseph *1730–1779* North Carolina signer of the Declaration of Independence. p. 115

Hicks, Ray *1922–* Appalachian storyteller; famous for telling "Jack tales." p. 253

Hodges, Luther *1898–1974* Governor of North Carolina 1954–1961; led the creation of Research Triangle Park. p. 192

Holt, Edwin *1807–1884* Textile mill owner from Alamance County.

Hooper, William *1742–1790* North Carolina signer of the Declaration of Independence. p. 115

Howe, Robert *1732–1786* Representative to the North Carolina congress at which the Halifax Resolves were written.

Humphreys, Henry Founder of the first steam-powered textile mill in North Carolina, in 1828.

J

Jackson, Andrew *1767–1845* 7th U.S. President; born near Waxhaw. p. 329

Johnson, Andrew *1808–1875* 17th U.S. President; born in Raleigh. p. 329

Johnston, Joseph E. *1807–1891* Confederate general. p. 174

Jordan, Michael *1963–* Professional basketball player who earlier had played for the University of North Carolina Tar Heels.

K

Kilmer, (Alfred) Joyce *1886–1918* Poet who wrote the poem "Trees."

King, Dr. Martin Luther, Jr. *1929–1968* African American civil rights leader who worked in nonviolent ways to end segregation. p. 297

Kuralt, Charles *1934–1997* Broadcast journalist; born in Wilmington.

L

Lane, Ralph *1530?–1603* Governor of the first Roanoke colony. p. 94

Lawson, John *1674-1711* Designer of the street plan for the town of Bath. p. 102

Lee, Howard *1934–* African American politician and businessman; served as mayor of Chapel Hill and in the state senate. p. 325

Lee, Robert E. *1807–1870* Commander of the Confederate army. p. 174

Leonard, "Sugar" Ray *1956–* World boxing champion; born in Wilmington.

Lincoln, Abraham *1809–1865* 16th U.S. President, leader of the Union during the Civil War, and signer of the Emancipation Proclamation. p. 168

Lowrie, Henry Berry *1846?–1872* Lumbee leader.

M

MacDonald, Donald F. *1926–* Cofounder of Highland Games at Grandfather Mountain, journalist, essayist, college professor.

Madison, Dorothea "Dolley" *1768–1849* Wife of President James Madison; born in Guilford County. p. 196

Martin, Alexander *1740–1807* North Carolina delegate to the United States Constitutional Convention; governor of North Carolina from 1782 to 1784 and from 1789 to 1792.

Martin, Josiah *1737–1786* Royal governor of North Carolina during the American Revolution.

McArthur, William S. *1951–* Astronaut from Wakulla. p. 299

Milsap, Ronnie *1943–* Country music singer; born in Robbinsville.

Mitchell, Elisha *1793–1857* Geologist who surveyed the Black Mountains in western North Carolina in the mid-1800s; Mount Mitchell named after him.

Monk, Thelonious *1920–1982* Jazz musician; born in Rocky Mount.

Moore, James *1737–1777* American commander at the Battle of Moores Creek Bridge during the American Revolution.

Morgan, Lucy *1889–1981* Founder of the Penland School of Crafts. p. 251

Morton, Agnes McRae *1897–1982* Cofounder of the Highland Games at Grandfather Mountain.

Murphey, Archibald D. *1777–1832* State legislator in the early 1800s who favored setting up public schools. p. 164

Murrow, Edward R. *1908–1965* Broadcast journalist; born in Greensboro.

Myrick, Sue *1941–* Member of the U.S. House of Representatives from North Carolina; former mayor of Charlotte. p. 325

O

Owle, Freeman *1946–* Cherokee carver and teacher. p. 251

P

Pearson, James Larkin *1879–1981* Poet laureate of North Carolina from 1953 until his death.

Penn, John *1741?–1788* North Carolina signer of the Declaration of Independence. p. 115

Petty, Richard *1938–* Stock-car racer; born in Level Cross.

Pinchot, Gifford (PIN•shoh) *1865–1946* Manager of the forest at Biltmore Estate. p. 242

Polk, James K. *1795–1849* 11th U.S. President; born near Pineville. p. 329

Pratt, Eliza Jane *1902–1981* First woman from North Carolina to serve in the U.S. House of Representatives.

R

Raleigh, Walter (RAH•lee) *1554–1618* English explorer who set up England's first colony in North America on Roanoke Island in 1585. p. 94

Reed, Conrad Young farm boy who discovered gold near Charlotte in 1799. p. 38

Reed, Mattye African American patron of the arts.

Reynolds, (Richard) Joshua *1906–1964* Founder of the R.J. Reynolds Company. p. 189

Roosevelt, Franklin Delano *1882–1945* 32nd U.S. President; created work programs that helped lead the nation out of the Great Depression. p. 293

S

Sandburg, Carl *1878–1967* Poet and historian; lived in Flat Rock.

Schenck, Carl *1868–1955* Founder of the first forestry school in the United States, at Biltmore Estate. p. 243

Schenck, Michael *1771–1847* Founder of the first water-powered textile mill in North Carolina. p. 177

Scruggs, Earl *1924–* Bluegrass musician; born in Flint Hill.

Sequoyah (sih•KWOY•uh) *1770?–1843* Cherokee leader who developed a system for writing the Cherokee language. p. 235

Sharp, Susie *1907–1996* First woman elected to serve on the North Carolina Supreme Court and the first woman to serve as Chief Justice.

Shepard, Alan B., Jr. *1923–1998* Astronaut who was the first American launched into space, in 1961. p. 298

Sherman, William Tecumseh *1820–1891* Union general. p. 174

Smith, Michael J. *1945–1986* Astronaut from Beaufort; died in the explosion of the space shuttle *Challenger*. p. 298

Spaight, Richard Dobbs *1758–1802* North Carolina signer of the United States Constitution.

Spencer, Cornelia Phillips *1825–1908* Author who wrote about North Carolina.

T

Teach, Edward *1680–1718* English pirate, also known as Blackbeard, who robbed ships off the coast of the Carolinas in the 1700s. p. 105

Travis, Randy *1959–* Country music singer; born in Marshville.

Tsali (SAH•lee) *1800s* Cherokee hero.

Vance, Zebulon *1830–1894* Governor of North Carolina from 1862 to 1865 and from 1877 to 1879; led North Carolina during the Civil War. p. 231

Vanderbilt, George Washington *1862–1914* Millionaire who built Biltmore Estate near Asheville in the 1890s. p. 242

Verrazano, Giovanni da (vair•uh•ZAH•noh, joh•VAH•nee dah) *1485?–1528?* Italian explorer for France who explored the area around the Cape Fear River and Pamlico Sound in 1524. p. 92

W

Washington, George *1732–1799* First U.S. President and commander of the Continental army during the American Revolution. p. 115

Watson, Arthel "Doc" *1923–* Bluegrass musician; born in Deep Gap.

Weil, Gertrude *1879–1971* Women's suffrage activist; born in Goldsboro. p. 292

White, David Founder, with his brother, William, of one of the first furniture factories in North Carolina, in 1881. p. 178

White, John *?–1593?* English painter and mapmaker who led the second group of colonists who settled on Roanoke Island. p. 63

Williamson, Hugh *1735–1819* North Carolina signer of the United States Constitution.

Wilson, Woodrow *1856–1924* 28th U.S. President; led the nation during World War I. p. 290

Wolfe, Thomas *1900–1938* Novelist; born in Asheville.

Wright, Orville *1871–1948* Pioneer in American aviation who, with his brother Wilbur, made and flew the first successful airplane, at Kitty Hawk in 1903. p. 285

Wright, Wilbur *1867–1912* Pioneer in American aviation who, with his brother Orville, made and flew the first successful airplane, at Kitty Hawk in 1903. p. 285

BIOGRAPHICAL DICTIONARY

Gazetteer

The Gazetteer is a geographical dictionary that will help you locate places discussed in this book. The page number tells where each place appears on a map.

A

Albemarle Sound A sound on the northern coast of North Carolina that separates the mainland from the Outer Banks. p. 26

Appalachian Mountain Range (a•puh•LAY•chee•uhn) A mountain range in the eastern United States; stretches through the western part of North Carolina. p. 212

Appalachian National Scenic Trail One of the nation's longest marked walking paths; extends for about 2,000 miles (3,219 km) from Springer Mountain, Georgia, to Mount Katahdin, Maine; passes through southwestern North Carolina. p. 212

Asheboro A town in the central Piedmont region; the county seat of Randolph County. (36°N, 80°W) p. 148

Asheville The largest city in the Mountain region; the county seat of Buncombe County. (36°N, 83°W) p. 26

Atlantic Beach A town on the central coast of North Carolina. (35°N, 77°W) p. 191

Atlantic Ocean One of the world's four oceans. p. 36

Averasboro (A•vuh•ruhs•buh•roh) The site of a Civil War battle. (35°N, 79°W) p. 174

B

B. Everett Jordan Lake A lake in the east-central Piedmont region; located on the Haw River. p. 35

Bath A town on the central coast of North Carolina; the first town in the state settled by Europeans, about 1690. (35°N, 77°W) p. 84

Beaufort (BOH•fert) A town on the central coast of North Carolina; the county seat of Carteret County; an early settlement in the state. (35°N, 77°W) p. 174

Bentonville The site of a Civil War battle. (36°N, 78°W) p. 174

Biltmore Estate The estate near Asheville built by George Washington Vanderbilt in the early 1900s. (36°N, 83°W) p. 218

Blewett Falls Lake (BLOO•uht) A lake in the southern Piedmont region; located on the Pee Dee River. (35°N, 80°W) p. 35

Blowing Rock A resort town in the northern Mountain region. (36°N, 82°W) p. 212

Blue Ridge Mountains The easternmost mountain range in the Appalachian Mountains of North Carolina. p. 212

Blue Ridge Parkway A scenic road that winds for 470 miles (756 km) along the top of the Blue Ridge Mountains. p. 262

Boone A city in the northern Mountain region; the county seat of Watauga County. (36°N, 82°W) p. 26

Brevard (bruh•VAHRD) A town in the southern Mountain region; the county seat of Transylvania County. (35°N, 83°W) p. 212

Broad River A river that starts in western North Carolina and flows south into South Carolina. p. 35

Brunswick (BRUHNZ•wick) A town on the southern coast of North Carolina; an early settlement in the state. (34°N, 79°W) p. 114

Burlington (BUHR•ling•tuhn) A city in the central Piedmont region. (36°N, 79°W) p. 148

C

Camp Lejeune (luh•JOON) A major United States Marine Corps base near Jacksonville, North Carolina. (35°N, 77°W) p. 124

Cape Fear The southernmost of the three prominent capes along the coast of North Carolina. (34°N, 77°W) p. 26

Cape Fear River A river that begins in central North Carolina and flows south into the Atlantic Ocean. p. 26

Cape Hatteras (HA•tuh•ruhs) The northernmost of the three prominent capes along the coast of North Carolina. (35°N, 75°W) p. 26

Cape Hatteras National Seashore A national park on the outer banks of North Carolina; includes parts of Bodie Island, Pea Island, Hatteras Island, and Ocracoke Island. p. 84

Cape Lookout The central cape of three prominent capes along the coast of North Carolina. (35°N, 77°W) p. 26

Cary A city in the east-central Piedmont region. (36°N, 79°W) p. 148

Catawba River (kuh•TAW•buh) A river that begins in western North Carolina and flows east and then south into South Carolina, where it is known as the Wateree River. p. 35

Chapel Hill A city in the east-central Piedmont region. (36°N, 79°W) p. 26

Charlotte (SHAHR•luht) The largest city in North Carolina; located in the south-central Piedmont region; the county seat of Mecklenburg County. p. 26

Cherokee (CHAIR•uh•kee) A city in the southern Mountain region. (35°N, 83°W) p. 191

Chowan River (chuh•WAHN) A river that begins in northeastern North Carolina and flows southeast into Albemarle Sound. p. 35

Clingmans Dome The highest mountain in the Great Smoky Mountains, with an elevation of 6,643 feet (2,025 m). (36°N, 83°W) p. 31

Clinton A town in the west-central Coastal Plain region; the county seat of Sampson County. (35°N, 78°W) p. 84

Coastal Plain region One of the three landform regions in North Carolina. p. 26

Concord A city in the central Piedmont; the county seat of Cabarrus County. (35°N, 81°W) p. 148

GAZETTEER

GAZETTEER

Cowee Mountains (KOW•ee) A mountain range in western North Carolina. p. 212

Currituck Sound (KUHR•ih•tuhk) A sound on the northern coast of North Carolina that separates the Currituck Banks from the mainland. p. 84

Durham (DUHR•uhm) A city located in the east-central Piedmont region; the county seat of Durham County. (36°N, 79°W) p. 26

East Dismal Swamp A swamp on the northern coast of North Carolina. (36°N, 77°W) p. 145

Edenton (EE•duhn•tuhn) A town on the northern coast of North Carolina; the county seat of Chowan County; the site of the Edenton Tea Party in 1774. (36°N, 77°W) p. 145

Elizabeth City A city on the northern coast of North Carolina; the county seat of Pasquotank County. (36°N, 76°W) p. 125

F

Fayetteville (FAY•uht•vihl) The largest city in the Coastal Plain region; the county seat of Cumberland County. (35°N, 79°W) p. 26

Fontana Lake A lake on the Little Tennessee River. (35°N, 84°W) p. 35

Fort Bragg A United States Army base near Fayetteville. (35°N, 79°W) p. 124

Fort Clark The site of a Civil War battle. (35°N, 76°W) p. 174

Fort Fisher The site of a Civil War battle. (34°N, 78°W) p. 174

Fort Hatteras The site of a Civil War battle. (35°N, 75°W) p. 174

Fort Macon The site of a Civil War battle. (35°N, 77°W) p. 174

Franklin A city in the southern Mountain region; the county seat of Macon County. (35°N, 83°W) p. 26

French Broad River A tributary of the Holston River in Tennessee. p. 35

G

Gastonia (ga•STOH•nee•uh) A city in the southwestern Piedmont region; the county seat of Gaston County. (35°N, 81°W) p. 148

Goldsboro A city in the central Coastal Plain region; the county seat of Wayne County. (35°N, 78°W) p. 125

Grandfather Mountain The highest mountain in the Blue Ridge Mountains, with an elevation of 5,964 feet (1,818 m). (36°N, 82°W) p. 31

Great Dismal Swamp A swamp in southeastern Virginia and northeastern North Carolina. (36°N, 76°W) p. 26

Great Smoky Mountains A mountain range in the Appalachian Mountains that forms part of the North Carolina–Tennessee border. p. 212

Great Smoky Mountains National Park A national park in western North Carolina and eastern Tennessee. p. 212

Greensboro A city in the north-central Piedmont region; the county seat of Guilford County. (36°N, 80°W) p. 26

Green Swamp A swamp in southeastern North Carolina. (34°N, 78°W) p. 145

Greenville A city in the central Coastal Plain region; the county seat of Pitt County. (36°N, 77°W) p. 114

Guilford Courthouse (GIL•fuhrd) The site of a Revolutionary War battle. (36°N, 80°W) p. 114

Hanging Rock State Park A state park in the northern Piedmont region. (36°N, 80°W) p. 16

Havelock (HAV•lahk) A town on the central coast of North Carolina. (35°N, 77°W) p. 125

Hendersonville A city in the southern Mountain region; the county seat of Henderson County. (35°N, 82°W) p. 212

Hickory A city in the west-central Piedmont region. (36°N, 81°W) p. 148

Highlands A town in the southern Mountain region. (35°N, 83°W) p. 212

High Point A city in the central Piedmont region. (36°N, 80°W) p. 148

High Rock Lake A lake on the Yadkin River in the central Piedmont region. (36°N, 80°W) p. 35

Hiwassee River A tributary of the Tennessee River. p. 221

Hyco Lake A lake on the Hyco River in the northern Piedmont region. (36°N, 79°W) p. 35

Intracoastal Waterway A series of canals and waterways that extends along the Atlantic coast of the United States; passes along the coast of North Carolina. p. 287

Jacksonville A city on the central coast of North Carolina; the county seat of Onslow County. (35°N, 77°W) p. 125

Jefferson A town in the northern Mountain region; the county seat of Ashe County. (36°N, 81°W) p. 212

K

Kannapolis (kuh•NAP•uh•luhs) A city in the central Piedmont region. (35°N, 81°W) p. 148

Kings Mountain The site of a battle of the American Revolution. (35°N, 81°W) p. 114

Kinston A town in the central Coastal Plain region; the county seat of Lenoir County; an early settlement in the state. (35°N, 78°W) p. 114

Kitty Hawk A town on the northern Outer Banks; the site of the Wright brothers' first airplane flight, in 1903. (36°N, 76°W) p. 26

L

Lake Gaston A lake in the northeastern Piedmont region; located on the Roanoke River. (36°N, 78°W) p. 35

Lake Hickory A lake in the west-central Piedmont region; located on the Catawba River. (36°N, 81°W) p. 35

Lake Mattamuskeet (mat•uh•muh•SKEET) The largest natural lake in North Carolina; located in the central Coastal Plain region. (35°N, 76°W) p. 35

Lake Norman The largest reservoir in North Carolina; located on the Catawba River in the south-central Piedmont region. (35°N, 81°W) p. 35

Lake Waccamaw A large natural lake in the southern Coastal Plain region. (34°N, 79°W) p. 35

Laurinburg (LAWR•uhn•buhrg) A town in the southwestern Coastal Plain region; the county seat of Scotland County. (35°N, 79°W) p. 125

Lincolnton A town in the southwestern Piedmont region; the county seat of Lincoln County. (35°N, 81°W) p. 31

Little Tennessee River A tributary of the Tennessee River. p. 35

Long Bay A bay on the North Carolina coast that stretches from Cape Fear southwest to Cape Romain, South Carolina. p. 84

Lumber River A tributary of the Pee Dee River. p. 35

Lumberton A city in the southern Coastal Plain region; the county seat of Robeson County. (35°N, 79°W) p. 125

M

Manteo A town on Roanoke Island in the Outer Banks of North Carolina; the county seat of Dare County. (36°N, 76°W) p. 90

Moores Creek Bridge The site of a battle of the American Revolution. (34°N, 78°W) p. 114

Morrow Mountain State Park A state park in the southern Piedmont region; in the Uwharrie Mountains. (35°N, 80°W) p. 27

Moses Cone Memorial Park A state park in the northern Mountain region. p. 246

Mount Mitchell The highest point in the eastern United States, with an elevation of 6,684 feet (2,037 m). (35°N, 82°W) p. 240

Mountain region One of the three landform regions in North Carolina. p. 26

Murphy A town in the southern Mountain region; the county seat of Cherokee County. (35°N, 84°W) p. 212

N

Nags Head A town on the Outer Banks. (36°N, 76°W) p. 26

Nantahala River (nan•tuh•HAY•luh) A river that begins in the southwestern Mountain region and flows into the Little Tennessee River at Fontana Lake. p. 265

Neuse River (NOOS) A river that begins in north-central North Carolina and flows southeast into Pamlico Sound. p. 35

New Bern A town on the central coast of North Carolina; the county seat of Craven County; the second-oldest town in the state settled by Europeans. (35°N, 77°W) p. 26

New River A river that begins in northwestern North Carolina and flows north into Virginia. p. 212

Nolichucky River (nahl•uh•CHUHK•ee) A tributary of the French Broad River. p. 221

North America One of the seven continents; contains Canada, the United States, and Mexico. p. 20

Northeast Cape Fear River A tributary of the Cape Fear River. p. 84

O

Occaneechi (oh•kuh•NEE•chee) A Native American village in the Piedmont region, discovered by archaeologists. p. 54

Ocracoke (OH•kruh•kohk) A town on the Outer Banks; an early settlement in North Carolina. (35°N, 76°W) p. 191

Onslow Bay (AHNZ•low) A bay on the North Carolina coast that stretches from Cape Fear north to Cape Lookout. p. 35

Outer Banks A long string of barrier islands off the coast of North Carolina. p. 85

P

Pamlico River (PAM•lih•koh) The name of the lower part of the Tar River; flows into Pamlico Sound. p. 35

Pamlico Sound The largest sound on the east coast of the United States; located off the central coast of North Carolina. p. 35

Pee Dee River A river that begins in central North Carolina and flows southeast into South Carolina. p. 35

Phelps Lake A large natural lake in the east-central Coastal Plain region. (36°N, 76°W) p. 35

Piedmont region (PEED•mahnt) One of the three landform regions in North Carolina. p. 26

Pigeon River A tributary of the French Broad River. p. 221

Pilot Mountain A mountain peak north of Winston-Salem, with an elevation of 2,421 feet (738 m). (36°N, 80°W) p. 31

Pisgah National Forest (PIZ•guh) A national forest in the central Mountain region. p 18

Plymouth (PLIM•uhth) A town in the north-central Coastal Plain region; the county seat of Washington County; an early settlement in the state; the site of a Civil War battle. (36°N, 77°W) p. 174·

Q

Qualla Boundary (KWAH•luh) a 56,572-acre (229 sq km) area of land in the southern Mountain region that belongs to the Cherokee and Oconaluftee Indians. (35°N, 83°W) p. 212

R

Raleigh (RAH•lee) The capital of North Carolina; the county seat of Wake County; located in the east-central Piedmont region. (35°N, 79°W) p. 26

Ramsour's Mill The site of a battle of the American Revolution. p. 114

Research Triangle Park The largest planned research park in the United States; located near Raleigh, Durham, and Chapel Hill. (36°N, 79°W) p. 184

Roan Mountain (ROHN) A mountain peak in western North Carolina, with an elevation of 6,285 feet (1,916 m). (36°N, 82°W) p. 31

Roanoke Island (ROH•uh•nohk) The site of the first English settlement in North Carolina in 1585; located on the northern coast of the state. (36°N, 76°W) p. 84

Roanoke Rapids A town in the northern Coastal Plain region. (36°N, 78°W) p. 125

Roanoke Rapids Lake A lake on the Roanoke River in the northwestern Coastal Plain region. (36°N, 78°W) p. 35

Roanoke River A river that begins in southern Virginia and flows southeast into North Carolina, where it empties into Albemarle Sound. p. 35

Rocky Mount A city in the central Coastal Plain region. (36°N, 78°W) p. 125

S

Salisbury (SAWLZ•behr•ee) A town in the central Piedmont region; the county seat of Rowan County. (36°N, 80°W) p. 148

Sanford A town in the central Piedmont region; the county seat of Lee County. (35°N, 79°W) p. 148

Seymour Johnson Air Force Base An Air Force base near Goldsboro in the central Coastal Plain region. (35°N, 78°W) p. 124

Smithfield A city in the Coastal Plain region; the county seat of Johnston County. (36°N, 78°W) p. 125

Southern Pines A town in the southwestern Coastal Plain region. (35°N, 79°W) p. 125

Statesville A city in the west-central Piedmont region; the county seat of Iredell County. (36°N, 81°W) p. 148

T

Tar River A river that begins in north-central North Carolina and flows southeast into the Pamlico River. p. 84

Town Creek Indian Mound A state historic site in the south-central Piedmont region; a ceremonial mound built by the Pee Dee Indians. (35°N, 80°W) p. 59

W

Waccamaw River A tributary of the Pee Dee River. p. 84

Waynesville A town in the Mountain region of North Carolina. p. 212

Wilmington (WIHL•ming•tuhn) A city on the southern coast of North Carolina; the county seat of New Hanover County; the largest deepwater port in the state. (34°N, 78°W) p. 26

Wilson A city in the west-central Coastal Plain region; the county seat of Wilson County. (36°N, 78°W) p. 125

Winston-Salem (wihn•stuhn•SAY•luhm) A city in the north-central Piedmont region; the county seat of Forsyth County. (36°N, 80°W), p. 26

Wrightsville Beach A city on the southern coast of North Carolina; located in New Hanover County; part of the Wilmington metro area. (34°N, 78°W) p. 136

Y

Yadkin River A tributary of the Pee Dee River. p. 26

Glossary

The Glossary contains important social studies words and their definitions. Each word is respelled as it would be in a dictionary. When you see this mark ´ after a syllable, pronounce that syllable with more force than the other syllables. The page number at the end of the definition tells where to find the word in your book.

add, āce, câre, pälm; end, ēqual; it, īce; odd, ōpen, ôrder; tŏŏk, pōōl; up, bûrn; yōō as *u* in *fuse*; oil; pout; ə as *a* in *above*, *e* in *sicken*, *i* in *possible*, *o* in *melon*, *u* in *circus*; check; ring; thin; this; zh as in *vision*

A

abolitionist (a•bə•li´shən•ist) A person who opposed slavery. p. 167

absolute location (ab´sə•lŏŏt lō•kā´shən) The exact position on Earth determined by using latitude and longitude. p. 22

agriculture (a´grə•kul•chər) Farming. p. 58

amendment (ə•mend´mənt) A change to a constitution. p. 174

analyze (a´nə•līz) To examine each part of something. p. 3

archaeologist (är•kē•ä´lə•jist) A scientist who studies artifacts left behind by people. p. 56

artifact (är´tə•fakt) Something people used in the past. p. 56

assembly (ə•sem´blē) A group of people elected to make laws and decide how money should be spent. p. 100

astronaut (as´trə•nät) Anyone training for or serving as a crew member on a spacecraft. p. 298

atlatl (ät´lä•təl) A carved stick with a hook on one end and a stone weight on the other; hunters used it to help them throw their spears farther. p. 57

attorney general (ə•tər´nē jen´ə•rəl) The person who carries out state laws. p. 318

automate (ô´tə•māt) To change an industry or job so that machines do much of the work once done by people. p. 193

aviation (ā•vē•ā´shən) The making and flying of airplanes. p. 285

B

backcountry (bak´kun•trē) The name given by early settlers to lands west of the Coastal Plain. p. 156

ballad (ba´ləd) A song that tells a story. p. 252

barrier island (bar´ē•ər ī´lənd) A low, narrow island between the ocean and the coastline of a mainland. p. 25

barter (bär´tər) To trade goods for other goods without using money. p. 224

Bill of Rights (bil uv rīts) A list of rights all citizens should have, such as freedom of speech and religion. p. 116

blockade (blä•kād´) An area blocked off to keep people and supplies from going in or out. p. 172

bluegrass music (blōō´gras myōō´zik) A style of country music that dates back to the 1920s and has its roots in African American blues and gospel music. p. 252

broadleaf (brôd´lēf) A tree that has wide, flat leaves that change color and fall off each autumn. p. 41

budget (bu´jət) A plan for spending money. p. 316

C

Cabinet (kab´nit) A group of officials who advise the President. p. 329

canal (kə•nal´) A waterway dug across the land and used by boats and ships. p. 287

cape (kāp) A point of land that sticks out into the sea. p. 26

capital (ka´pə•təl) The city in which a state's or country's government meets. p. 162

capital resources (ka´pə•təl rē´sôrs•əz) The money, buildings, machines, and tools needed to run a business. p. 179

cargo (kär´gō) The goods carried on a ship. p. 104

cash crop (kash kräp) A crop that people raise to sell to others instead of to use for themselves. p. 99

cause (kôz) The reason something happens. p. 75

channel (cha´nəl) The path that a river flows through. p. 35

charter (chär´tər) A written document that guarantees certain rights from a government or state to a person or group of people. p. 98

chronology (krə•nä´lə•jē) The order in which events take place. p. 2

city council (si´tē koun´səl) The group that makes laws for a city and collects city taxes. p. 325

civics (si´viks) The study of citizenship. p. 9

civil rights (si´vəl rīts) The rights given to all citizens by the Constitution. p. 297

clan (klan) A group tracing its roots from a common ancestor. p. 71

classify (kla´sə•fī) To sort into categories. p. 134

climate (klī´mət) The weather patterns a place has over a long time. p. 47

clogging (kläg′ing) A kind of traditional mountain folk dance. p. 252
coastal plain (kōs′təl plān) A lowland that lies along an ocean. p. 24
Cold War (kōld wôr) A conflict between the United States and the Soviet Union; it was fought with words and with economic and political actions instead of weapons. p. 298
colony (kä′lə•nē) A group of people living in one place and ruled by people in another place. p. 93
commute (kə•myo͞ot′) To regularly travel to and from work. p. 188
compare (kəm•pâr′) To say how two things are alike. p. 134
compromise (käm′prə•mīz) A settlement that calls for each side to give up something it wants in order to reach an agreement. p. 117
Confederacy (kən•fe′də•rə•sē) Another name for the Confederate States of America; the states that seceded from the Union. p. 169
confederation (kən•fe•də•rā′shən) A large group made up of several smaller groups. p. 72
congress (käng′grəs) A meeting where laws and decisions are made. p. 114
consequence (kän′sə•kwens) The result of a decision or an action. p. 171
conservation (kän•sər•vā′shən) The protection and wise use of natural resources. p. 242
constitution (kän•stə•to͞o′shən) The plan of government for a nation. p. 116
consumer good (kən•so͞om′ər go͝od) A product made for personal use. p. 293
continent (kän′tən•ənt) One of Earth's seven largest land areas. p. 21
contrast (kən•trast′) To say how two things are different. p. 134
council (koun′səl) A group of advisers or lawmakers. p. 69
county commissioners (koun′tē kə•mi′shə•nərz) The group of people that directs county activities. p. 323
county seat (kount′ē sēt) The city in which a county's government meets. p. 323
cove (kōv) A small area of mostly flat land surrounded by mountains. p. 228
cross-section (krôs′sek•shən) A slice or piece cut straight across something. p. 180
culture (kul′chər) The beliefs, traditions, and ways of life of people. p. 10
cutaway diagram (ku′tə•wā dī′ə•gram) A diagram that shows a cross-section of an object or building. p. 180

D

dam (dam) A structure that helps control the power of rushing water. p. 37
Declaration of Independence (de•klə•rā′shən uv in•də•pen′dəns) A statement telling why the colonies wanted to be free from Britain. p. 115
democracy (di•mä′krə•sē) A government in which the people take part. p. 69
depression (di•pre′shən) A time when jobs are scarce and there is very little money. p. 293
diversify (də•vûr′sə•fī) To increase the variety of people, places, or things. p. 193
diversity (də•vûr′sə•tē) A variety of different languages, religious beliefs, and customs among a group of people. p. 157
division of labor (də•vi′zhən uv lā′bər) The division of jobs among workers. p. 58
double-bar graph (du′bəl•bär graf) A type of graph that uses two sets of bars to compare two sets of statistics. p. 260
drought (drout) A time of extreme dryness that causes damage to crops. p. 49

E

economics (e•kə•nä′miks) The study of how money, goods, and services are used in a society. p. 8
economy (i•kä′nə•mē) The way people use resources to meet their needs. p. 8
effect (i•fekt′) Something that happens as a result of something else. p. 75
elevation (e•lə•vā′shən) The height of the land. p. 26
Emancipation Proclamation (i•man•sə•pā′shən prä•klə•mā′shən) A document that freed all enslaved people in the South. p. 174
entrepreneur (än•trə•prə•nûr′) A person who starts and runs a business. p. 176
epidemic (e•pə•de′mik) A situation in which many people have the same disease at the same time. p. 234
equator (i•kwā′tər) The imaginary line that separates the Northern and Southern Hemispheres. p. 21
erosion (i•rō′zhən) The wearing away of sand, soil, and gravel. p. 25
estate (is•tāt′) A large piece of land with a large house on it. p. 242
estimate (es′tə•mət) A close guess. p. 198
ethnic group (eth′nik gro͞op) A group of people from the same country, or people who speak the same language and share certain customs and beliefs. p. 309
evaluate (i•val′yə•wāt) To judge something. p. 267
evidence (e′və•dəns) Proof. p. 2
executive branch (ig•ze′kyə•tiv branch) The branch of federal or state government responsible for making sure laws are carried out. p. 315
expedition (ek•spə•di′shən) A journey into a new land to learn more about it. p. 92

export (ek′spôrt) A product sent from one country to another to be sold. p. 99

extinct (ik•stingt′) No longer living, like a kind of animal that has died out. p. 43

F

fact (fakt) A statement that can be checked and proved to be true. p. 267

fall line (fôl līn) A place along which rivers drop from higher to lower ground. p. 27

federal government (fe′dər•əl gu′vərn•mənt) Another name for the national government. p. 327

fertile (fûr′təl) Good for growing crops. p. 229

fertilizer (fûr′təl•ī•zər) A material that is added to the soil to help plants grow. p. 40

festival (fes′tə•vəl) A celebration. p. 139

floodplain (flud′plān) Flat land along a river that has been built up from soil deposited by the river. p. 35

flow chart (flō chärt) A drawing that shows the order in which things happen. p. 320

food processing (food prä′ses•ing) The turning of raw foods into food products. p. 131

forestry (fôr′ə•strē) The science of managing and protecting forests and forest resources. p. 243

free enterprise (frē en′tər•prīz) An economic system in which entrepreneurs are free to start and run their own businesses. p. 176

free state (frē stāt) A state where slavery was not allowed. p. 167

Freedmen's Bureau (frēd′menz byoor′ō) A group created by the federal government to help freed African Americans by providing food, clothing, and schools. p. 174

frontier (frun•tir′) The western edge of European settlement. p. 220

G

gap (gap) An opening or a low place between mountains. p. 221

generation (jen•ə•rā′shən) A group of people of about the same age. p. 223

geographer (jē•ä′grə•fər) A person who studies geography. p. 6

geography (jē•ä′grə•fē) The study of Earth and the people who live on it. p. 6

glider (glī′dər) An aircraft without an engine. p. 285

gorge (gôrj) A deep passageway cut through rocks by water. p. 264

government (gu′vərn•mənt) A system of leaders and laws that help people live together safely in a community, a state, or a country. p. 9

governor (gu′vər•nər) The leader of a colony or a state. p. 94

Green Corn Ceremony (grēn kôrn ser′ə•mō•nē) A Native American festival held to celebrate the harvest and the beginning of a new year. p. 73

growing season (grō′ing sē′zən) The time of year when the weather is warm enough for plants to grow. p. 49

H

habitat (ha′bə•tat) A place where animals find food and shelter. p. 41

haze (hāz) A condition of dust, smoke, or mist in the air that makes it hard to see. p. 258

hemisphere (he′mə•sfir) Each half of a sphere or a round object, such as Earth. p. 21

heritage (her′ə•tij) The ways of life that have been passed down through history. p. 10

historian (hi•stôr′ē•ən) A person who studies the past. p. 2

historical map (hi•stôr′i•kəl map) A map that gives information about places as they were in the past. p. 226

history (hi′stə•rē) The study of people, places, and events in the past. p. 2

House of Representatives (hous uv re•pri•zen′tə•tivz) One of the two branches, or parts, of the United States Congress. p. 328

hub (hub) The center for a business or industry. p. 187

human feature (hyoo′mən fē′chər) Something created by humans. p. 6

human resources (hyoo′mən rē′sôr•səz) Workers. p. 178

hurricane (hûr′ə•kān) A large storm with heavy rains and high winds that forms over warm ocean water. p. 51

hydroelectricity (hī•drō•i•lek•tri′sə•tē) Electricity made by using the power of rushing water. p. 37

I

immigrant (i′mi•grənt) A person who moves to one country from another. p. 107

impeach (im•pēch′) To accuse an official of wrongdoing. p. 330

import (im′pôrt) A good brought in from another country to be used or sold. p. 123

indentured servant (in•den′chərd sûr′vənt) A person who agreed to work for a colonist without pay for a number of years in exchange for travel to America. p. 107

inlet (in′let) An opening between islands. p. 25

innovation (i•nə•vā′shən) A new or better way of doing something. p. 194

interact (in•tər•akt′) To affect one another. p. 6

interdependent (in•tər•di•pen′dənt) Depending on each other for goods and services. p. 310

interest (in′trəst) The money that a bank or government pays for using people's money. p. 291

international trade (in•tər•na′shə•nəl trād) The trade among nations. p. 311

interstate highway (in′tər•stāt hī′wā) A highway that connects state to state. p. 285

J

judicial branch (jōō•di′shəl branch) The branch of the federal or state government responsible for seeing that the laws are fair and for judging the people accused of breaking the law. p. 315

jury trial (jŏŏr′ē trī′əl) A trial in which a group of citizens must decide whether a person accused of a crime is guilty or not guilty. p. 318

K

kilt (kilt) A plaid skirt worn by a Scottish clan member. p. 266

L

land use (land yōōs) The way most of the land in an area is used. p. 44

legislative branch (le′jəs•lā•tiv branch) The branch of federal or state government responsible for making the laws. p. 315

leisure (lē′zhər) Describes time away from work. p. 296

line graph (līn graf) A type of graph that shows changes over a period of time. p. 198

lines of latitude (līnz uv la′tə•tōōd) A set of imaginary lines running east and west around Earth. p. 22

lines of longitude (līnz uv län′jə•tōōd) A set of imaginary lines running from the North Pole to the South Pole. p. 22

livestock (līv′stäk) Farm animals that are raised to be sold. p. 130

living museum (li′ving myōō•zē′əm) A restored village or fort where people dress and act like the people of an earlier time. p. 202

location (lō•kā′shən) The place where something can be found. p. 6

log cabin (lôg ka′bən) A small house built from logs. p. 222

longhouse (lông′hous) A rectangular Native American house that has a wood frame covered with bark. p. 64

Loyalist (loi′ə•list) A colonist who was loyal to Britain during the Revolutionary War period. p. 113

M

manufacturing (man•yə•fak′chə•ring) The making of goods. p. 163

map scale (map skāl) The part of a map that compares a distance on the map to a distance in the real world. p. 126

mass production (mas prə•duk′shən) The making of goods in large quantities. p. 283

mayor (mā′ər) The leader of a city government. p. 325

meridian (mə•ri′dē•ən) A line of longitude. p. 22

metropolitan area (me•trə•pä′lə•tən âr′ē•ə) A large city and its suburbs. p. 186

migrant worker (mī′grənt wûr′kər) A person who moves from farm to farm harvesting crops. p. 308

migrate (mī′grāt) To move from one region to another and settle in that place. p. 56

military base (mil′ə•ter•ē bās) A place where people train or work for one of the armed services. p. 124

mixed farming (mikst färm′ing) A type of farming in which farmers grow more than one kind of crop. p. 129

municipal government (myōō•ni′sə•pəl gu′vərn•mənt) A city or town government. p. 324

N

national seashore (na′shən•əl sē′shôr) Coastal land and water areas protected by the United States govenment.

natural resource (na′chə•rəl rē′sôrs) Something found in nature that people can use. p. 38

naturalized citizen (na′chə•rə•līzd si′tə•zən) A person who has gone through the steps of becoming a citizen. p. 334

naval stores (nā′vəl stôrz) Tar, turpentine, and other products used to waterproof ships' wooden hulls. p. 107

needleleaf (nē′dəl•lēf) A tree whose thin, sharp, needlelike leaves stay green all year. p. 41

nomad (nō′mad) A person who keeps moving from place to place. p. 57

nonrenewable resource (nän•ri•nōō′ə•bəl rē′sôrs) A resource that, once used, cannot be replaced. p. 131

Northwest Passage (nôrth′west pa′sij) The water route that Europeans once thought crossed North America from the Atlantic Ocean to the Pacific Ocean. p. 92

O

opinion (ə•pin′yən) A statement that tells what someone thinks or believes. p. 267

opportunity cost (ä•pər•tōō′nə•tē kôst) What you give up when you buy or do one thing instead of another. p. 313

oral history (ôr'əl his'tə•rē) A story of an event, told aloud. p. 2

orchard (ôr'chərd) A group of fruit trees. p. 254

outcome (out'kum) The result of something. p. 95

overlook (ō'vər•lŏŏk) A place where cars can pull off the road and passengers can look down on the scenery below. p. 264

parallels (par'ə•lelz) Lines that are always the same distance from each other; another name for lines of latitude. p. 22

Patriot (pā'trē•ət) A colonist who favored independence from Britain. p. 113

physical feature (fi'zi•kəl fē'chər) A land feature that has been made by nature. p. 6

pioneer (pī•ə•nir') A person who is one of the first to settle in a place. p. 156

pirate (pī'rət) Someone who robs ships at sea. p. 104

plank road (plank rōd) A road made by placing split logs across a trail. p. 164

plantation (plan•tā'shən) A large farm that specializes in growing a single cash crop. p. 108

planter (plan'tər) A person who owns a plantation. p. 108

plateau (pla•tō') Flat land that rises above the surrounding land. p. 27

Pledge of Allegiance (plej uv ə•lē'jəns) A promise to be loyal to the United States. p. 327

pocosin (pə•kō'sən) A swampy area on high ground covered by bushes and shrubs. p. 26

point of view (point uv vyŏŏ) A person's feelings and beliefs about a subject. p. 3

pollution (pə•lŏŏ'shən) Anything that makes a natural resource dirty or unsafe to use. p. 41

population density (pä•pyə•lā'shən den'sə•tē) A measurement of how many people live in an area of a certain size. p. 190

population map (pä•pyə•lā'shən map) A map that shows how many people live in a certain area. p. 190

pottery (pä'tə•rē) Pots, bowls, dishes, and other items made from clay. p. 203

precipitation (pri•si•pə•tā'shən) Water that falls on Earth's surface as rain, sleet, or snow. p. 46

prediction (pri•dik'shən) A reasonable guess about what will happen next. p. 97

primary road (prī'mer•ē rōd) A road that connects main towns and government centers. p. 284

primary source (prī'mer•ē sôrs) A record made by someone who saw or took part in an event. p. 4

prime meridian (prīm mə•ri'dē•ən) A line of longitude that runs through Greenwich, a town near London, England, and is at a location of 0°. p. 23

product (prä'dəkt) Something people make or grow, usually to sell later. p. 38

professional team (prə•fe'shə•nəl tēm) A sports team made up of players who are paid for playing. p. 201

profit (prä'fət) The money left over after all costs have been paid. p. 177

proprietor (prə•prī'ə•tər) An owner of land or of a business. p. 99

public office (pub'lik ô'fəs) An elected job in local, state, or national government. p. 336

quarry (kwôr'ē) A place where stone is cut or blasted out of the ground. p. 40

ratify (ra'tə•fī) To accept officially. p. 117

rationing (ra'shə•ning) A system that limits how much people can buy of an item that many people want, such as sugar, butter, meat, or gasoline. p. 294

raw material (rô mə•tir'ē•əl) A natural resource, such as trees or minerals, that has not been changed in any way. p. 94

rebel (ri•bel') To turn against. p. 101

reconstruct (rē•kən•strukt') To rebuild. p. 174

reforestation (rē•fôr•ə•stā'shən) The planting of seedlings or young trees to replace trees that have been cut down for lumber. p. 257

region (rē'jən) An area with features that make it different from other areas. p. 6

register (re'jə•stər) To sign up to vote. p. 337

registrar of deeds (re'jə•strär uv dēdz) The official who keeps county records. p. 324

relative location (re'lə•tiv lō•kā'shən) Position in relation to other places. p. 19

relief (ri•lēf') Differences in elevation. p. 30

relocate (rē•lō'•kāt) To move to another place. p. 156

renewable resource (ri•nŏŏ'ə•bəl rē'sōrs) A resource that can be replaced after it is used. p. 131

republic (ri•pub'lik) A form of government in which people elect representatives to run the country for them. p. 327

research (ri•sûrch') The careful study or investigation of information. p. 188

reservation (re•zər•vā'shən) Land set aside by the government for use by Native Americans. p. 237

reservoir (re'sər•vwär) A human-made lake that stores water. p. 265

resources (rē'sōrs•əz) Products of the land. p. 44

retirement community (ri•tīr'mənt kə•myŏŏ'nə•tē) A place where older people live when they no longer work at full-time jobs. p. 249

revolution (re•və•lōō′shən) The sudden change or overthrow of a government. p. 113

river system (ri′vər sis′təm) A river and its tributaries. p. 37

route (rōōt) A path to follow to get from one place to another. p. 288

royal colony (roi′əl kä′lə•nē) A colony ruled by a king or queen. p. 107

S

satellite (sa′təl•īt) An object that circles a larger object. p. 298

scarce (skârs) Hard to find. p. 57

school board (skōōl bôrd) A group of people elected to help manage the public schools in a district. p. 324

secede (si•sēd′) To withdraw from the Union. p. 169

secondary road (se′kən•der•ē rōd) A road that connects a rural area to a town or city. p. 284

secondary source (se′kən•der•ē sôrs) A record of an event made by someone who was not there. p. 4

segregation (se•gri•gā′shən) The separation of people because of their race or culture. p. 175

self-sufficient (self•sə•fi′shənt) Producing everything one needs. p. 159

Senate (se′nət) One of the two houses, or parts, of the United States Congress. p. 328

service job (sûr′vəs jäb) An activity that people do for others for pay. p. 132

service worker (sûr′vəs wûr′kər) A worker who does jobs or activities for others for pay. p. 194

sharecropper (shâr′kräp•ər) A person who rents land, farms it, and pays the landowner a share of the crops. p. 174

sheriff (sher′əf) A county official who makes sure people obey the laws. p. 324

shortage (shôr′tij) A situation in which there is not enough of something for everyone. p. 291

slave (slāv) A person who is treated as property owned by another person and made to work without pay. p. 108

slave state (slāv stāt) A state where slavery was allowed by law. p. 167

smog (smäg) A mixture of smoke and fog. p. 258

society (sə•sī′ə•tē) A human group. p. 10

sound (sound) A body of water that lies between a mainland and an island. p. 35

specialize (spe′shə•līz) To work at just one job. p. 58

spring (spring) A place where underground water comes out of the Earth. p. 239

states' rights (stāts rīts) The idea that a state should be able to decide for itself about slavery, taxes, and other issues. p. 168

statistics (stə•tis′tiks) Facts shown with numbers. p. 260

suburb (su′bərb) A town or small city near a larger city. p. 186

suffrage (su′frij) The right to vote. p. 292

Supreme Court (sə•prēm′ kôrt) The highest court in the United States. p. 329

synthetic fibers (sin•the′tik fī′bərz) Fibers that are made by people, not from plants or animal hairs. p. 193

T

tax (taks) Money that a government collects from its citizens and that is most often used to pay for services. p. 100

technology (tek•nä′lə•jē) The way people use new ideas to make tools and machines. p. 192

temperature (tem′pər•ə•chŏŏr) The measurement of how hot or cold something is. p. 46

territory (târ′ə•tôr•ē) An area that belongs to a country but does not have the same rights as a state. p. 227

tide (tīd) The rising and falling of the oceans and the waters connected to them. p. 25

time line (tīm līn) A diagram that shows events or periods of time. p. 60

toll road (tōl rōd) A road that people must pay to use. p. 164

tornado (tôr•nā′dō) A funnel-shaped column of spinning air that forms under the clouds of intense thunderstorms. p. 50

tourism (tŏŏr′i•zəm) The selling of goods and services to people who travel to a place. p. 132

trade center (trād sen′tər) A community in which buying and selling goods is the main economic activity. p. 122

trade-off (trād′ ôf) The giving up of one thing to get another. p. 313

tradition (trə•di′shən) An idea or way of doing things that has been handed down through generations. p. 62

treasurer (tre′zhə•rər) The person in charge of a group's money. p. 318

treaty (trē′tē) A written agreement. p. 235

tribe (trīb) A group of people who share land, speak the same language, and have the same customs. p. 58

tributary (tri′byə•ter•ē) A river or stream that flows into a larger river. p. 36

Underground Railroad (un′dər•ground rā l′rōd) A series of routes and safe houses set up to help enslaved people on their journey north to freedom. p. 167

unemployment (un•im•ploi′mənt) The number of people without jobs. p. 293

Union (yōōn′yən) Another name for the United States. p. 169

urban (ûr′bən) Describing a city and the surrounding area. p. 186

veteran (ve′tər•ən) A person who has served in the armed forces. p. 296

veto (vē′tō) To refuse to approve a bill. p. 317

volunteer (vä•lən•tir′) To work without pay in order to help others in the community. p. 337

wampum (wäm′pəm) Beads made from cut and polished seashells and used to keep records, send messages to other tribes, barter for goods, or give as gifts. p. 65

war bond (wôr bänd) A paper stating that a person has loaned money to the government to help pay for a war. p. 291

weather (we′thər) The condition of the air outside on a particular day. p. 47

wetlands (wet′landz) Low-lying areas where the water level is always near or above the surface of the land. p. 26

white-water (hwīt′ wô•tər) Describes water that moves fast over rocks, rapids, and waterfalls. p. 262

wildlife refuge (wīld′līf ref′yōōj) A shelter or place where birds and animals are protected. p. 137

Z

zoning (zō′ning) The way a city plans how it will grow and how its land will be used. p. 326

Index

Page references for illustrations are set in italic type. An italic *m* indicates a map. Page references set in boldfaced type indicate the pages on which vocabulary terms are defined.

INDEX

INDEX

INDEX

For permission to reprint copyrighted material, grateful acknowledgment is made to the following sources:

Boyds Mills Press, Inc.: Cover illustration by Dimitrea Tokunbo from *Sidewalk Chalk: Poems of the City* by Carole Boston Weatherford. Illustration copyright © 2001 by Dimitrea Tokunbo.

Coastal Carolina Press, www.coastalcarolinapress.org, 910-362-9298: Cover illustration by Debi Davis from *Pale as the Moon* by Donna Campbell.

Dial Books for Young Readers, an imprint of Penguin Putnam Books for Young Readers, a division of Penguin Putnam Inc.: Cover illustration by Jerry Pinkney from *Back Home* by Gloria Jean Pinkney. Illustration copyright © 1992 by Jerry Pinkney.

Gallopade International: Cover from *The Big North Carolina Activity Book* by Carole Marsh. © 2000 by Carole Marsh/Gallopade International.

The Globe Pequot Press: From *North Carolina Is My Home* (Retitled: "Backroads and Byways") by Charles Kuralt and Loonis McGlohon, edited by Patty Davis. Text copyright © 1998, 1986 by The Globe Pequot Press.

HarperCollins Publishers: Cover illustration by Stephen Marchesi from *Who Comes With Cannons?* by Patricia Beatty. Illustration copyright © 1992 by Stephen Marchesi. From *My Great-Aunt Arizona* by Gloria Houston, illustrated by Susan Condie Lamb. Text copyright © 1992 by Gloria Houston; illustrations copyright © 1992 by Susan Condie Lamb. Cover illustration by James E. Ransome from *The Wagon* by Tony Johnston. Illustration copyright © 1996 by James E. Ransome.

Alfred A. Knopf Children's Books, a division of Random House, Inc.: Cover illustration by Don Demers from *Storm Warriors* by Elisa Carbone. Illustration copyright © 2001 by Don Demers.

Lee & Low Books, Inc., New York, NY 10016: "Children of Long Ago" (Part I), "Children of Long Ago" (Part II), from "All Dressed Up," and "Cornfield Leaves" from *Children of Long Ago* by Lessie Jones Little, illustrated by Jan Spivey Gilchrist. Text copyright © 2000 by Weston W. Little, Sr. Estate; text copyright © 1988 by Weston Little; illustrations copyright © 1988 by Jan Spivey Gilchrist.

Parkway Publishers, Inc.: Cover illustration from *Mountain Jack Tales* by Gail E. Haley. Copyright © 2002 by Gail E. Haley.

Pleasant Company Publications: Cover illustration by Raúl Colón from *The Christmas Barn* by C. L. Davis. Illustration © 2001 by Raúl Colón.

Simon & Schuster Books for Young Readers, an imprint of Simon & Schuster Children's Publishing Division: Cover illustration by Larry Day from *Taking Flight: The Story of the Wright Brothers* by Stephen Krensky. Illustration copyright © 2000 by Larry Day. From *An Island Scrapbook* by Virginia Wright-Frierson. Copyright © 1998 by Virginia Wright-Frierson.

The University of North Carolina Press, www.uncpress.unc.edu: Cover illustration from *Living Stories of the Cherokee,* collected and edited by Barbara R. Duncan. Copyright © 1998 by the University of North Carolina Press. Cover illustration by Ed Lindlof from *Taffy of Torpedo Junction* by Nell Wise Wechter. Cover illustration © by Ed Lindlof.

ILLUSTRATION CREDITS

Page 12, 13,56, 58, 80, 81, 156, Scott Cameron; 36, 48, Chuck Carter; 57, 60, Jeff Mangiat; 64, 68, 72, Luigi Galante; 84, 85, 144, 145, Bill Maughan; 108, Mike Lamble; 131, 179, 316, Patrick Gnan; 137, 262, Stephen Durke; 148, 149, 208, 209, 276, 277, 344, 345, Clifford Spohn; 172, Dale Gustavson; 181, Don Foley; 212, 213, 272, 273, George Gaadt. For permission to reprint copyrighted material, grateful acknowledgment is made to the following sources: Harper Collins Publishers: Cover illustration by Susan Condie Lamb from My Great-Aunt Arizona by Gloria Houston. Text copyright © 1992 by Gloria Houston. Illustration copyright © 1992 by Susan Condie Lamb. Lee & Low Books, Inc.: Cover illustration by Jan Spivey Gilchrist from Children of Long Ago by Lessie Jones Little. Text copyright © 2000 by Weston W. Little, Sr. Estate; copyright © 1988 by Weston Little. Illustration copyright © 1988 by Jan Spivey Gilchrist. Simon & Schuster Children's Publishing Division: Cover illustration by Virginia Wright-Frierson from An Island Scrapbook by Virginia Wright-Frierson. Copyright © 1998 by Virginia Wright-Frierson.

All maps by MAPQUEST.COM

PHOTO CREDITS

(By Page # Pos Credit except: Unit Openers (hard stock inserts with no page number) Almanac Title Page (bg) Audrey Gibson/Mark E. Gibson Photography; Title Page (object) Image Finders; 1 Image Finders; 2 (t) Mark E. Gibson Photography; 2 (c) Courtesy National Park Service Museum Management Program and Guilford Courthouse National Military Park, Lantern, BUDO 1623, http://www.cr.nps.gov/museum/exhibits/revwar/guco/gucoleisure.html; 2 (b) Courtesy National Park Service Museum Management Program and Guilford Courthouse National Military Park, Powder Bellows, GUCO 1496, http://www.cr.nps.gov/museum/exhibits/revwar/guco/gucoappear.html; 3 (t) Chuck Eaton/Transparencies, Inc; 3 (tc) Jerry Staats/Transparencies, Inc; 3 (c) Jim McGuire/Transparencies, Inc; 3 (bl) Dieter Melhorn/Transparencies, Inc; 3 (bc) Ginger Wagoner/Transparencies, Inc; 3 (br) Robert Cavin/Transparencies, Inc; 4 (t) (bl) Bettmann/CORBIS; 4 (r) Newsmakers/Getty Images; 5 (l) (c) Harcourt; 5 (r) Mike Booher/Transparencies, Inc; 7 (tl) Matthew Borkoski/Stock, Boston/PictureQuest; 7 (tr) Steve McBride/Picturesque Stock Photo; 7 (cl) Mark E. Gibson Photography; 7 (cr) Jeffery Muir Hamilton/Stock, Boston/PictureQuest; 7 (bl) Kevin Adams/Picturesque Stock Photo; 7 (br) David Young-Wolff/PhotoEdit/PictureQuest; 8 (t) Harcourt; 8 (bl) Robert Bailey/Transparencies, Inc.; 8 (br) Ron Chapple/FPG/Getty Images; 9 Ken Taylor/Wildlife Images; 10 (t) Murray & Associates/Picturesque; 10 (b) Otis Hairston, Jr.

UNIT 1

Unit 1 Opener (bg) Jane Faircloth/Transparencies, Inc.; Unit 1 Opener (object) Kelly Culpepper/Transparencies, Inc.; Unit 1 Opener (spread) Jane Faircloth/Transparencies, Inc.; 11 Kelly Culpepper/Transparencies, Inc.; 14-15 (c) Jim Hargan; 14 (l) Kelly Culpepper/Transparencies, Inc.; 15 (l) Mark E. Gibson; 16-17 (spread)

Laurence Parent Photography; 18 (b) Kevin Adams; 19 (l) Spencer Swager/Tom Stack & Associates; 19 (cl) Rod Patterson/Dembinsky Photo Associates; 19 (cr) Mark E. Gibson; 19 (r) Dusty Perin/Dembinsky Photo Associates; 20-21 (spread) Tim Barnwell/Stock, Boston; 24-25 (spread) Ken Taylor/Wildlife Images; 25 (br) (inset) Kevin Adams; 25 (cr) (inset) Ken Taylor/Wildlife Images; 27 (b) Jane Faircloth/Transparencies, Inc.; 27 (tr) David Muench/CORBIS/MAGMA; 28-29 (spread) Ken Taylor/Wildlife Images; 28 (br) (inset) Kevin Adams; 29(tr) WorldSat International Inc. – 2002; 30 (b) David Muench/CORBIS/MAGMA; 32 (t) Bob Daemmrich/Stock, Boston/PictureQuest; 32 (br) George Howard/Feldman & Associates; 32 (bl) (inset) Instituto e Museo di Storia della Scienza, Firenze; 32 (tr) (inset) Chris Hayes/Artbase Inc.; 33 (tl) (cr) (bl) Instituto e Museo di Storia della Scienza, Firenze; 34 (b) Billy E. Barnes/Transparencies, Inc.; 35 (cr) Ken Taylor/Wildlife Images; 36 (cl) Copyright National Portrait Gallery, Smithsonian Institution/Art Resource NY; 38 (bl) Ken Taylor/Wildlife Images; 39 (b) Billy E. Barnes; 40 (b) Billy E. Barnes/Transparencies, Inc.; 41 (tl) Laurence Parent; 41 (tr) J. Faircloth/Transparencies, Inc.; 41 (tl) (inset) Artbase Inc.; 41 (tr) (inset) Artbase Inc.; 42-43 (spread) Peter Armenia; 43 (tl) Ken Taylor/Wildlife Images; 43 (tc) Richard A. Cooke/CORBIS/MAGMA; 43 (tr) Ken Taylor/Wildlife Images; 44 (b) Steven McBride/Picturesque Inc.; 46 (b) Todd Bush; 47 (bc) Artbase Inc.; 49 (tr) Artbase Inc.; 50 (bc) Matt Alberts; 50 (c) (inset) Steve Exum Photography; 51 (t) NASA/SPL/ Photo Researchers; 51 (tr) Corey Lowenstein/The News & Observer; 51 (cr) Mel Nathanson/The News & Observer; 54-55 (spread) Peter Armenia; 58 (c) Marilyn "Angel" Wynn/Native Stock; 59 (t) Kelly Culpepper/Transparencies, Inc.; 60 (bl) Marie Freeman/Artbase Inc.; 61 (bl) The Appalachian Cultural Museum/Artbase Inc.; 61 (br) Brian Seed/© Copyright The British Museum; 62 (bl) Marilyn "Angel" Wynn/Native Stock; 63 (br) © Copyright The British Museum; 65 (tr) Marilyn "Angel" Wynn/Native Stock; 66 (cl) (inset) James Berringer/Salisbury Post; 66 (b) Donnie Roberts/The Dispatch, Lexington NC Newspaper; 67 (br) Martin Bennett/Journal Communications Inc.; 69 (cr) Marilyn "Angel" Wynn/Native Stock; 70 (bl) Ken Taylor/Wildlife Images; 71 (bc) Peggy Sanders Brennan; 73 (bc) Marilyn "Angel" Wynn/Native Stock; 74 (tr) Marilyn "Angel" Wynn/Native Stock; 74 (tl) Marilyn "Angel" Wynn/Native Stock; 78-79 (t) R. Norman Barrett/Bruce Coleman, Inc.; 78-79 (b) Steven McBride/Picturesque; 78 (c) (inset) Audrey Gibson/Mark E. Gibson Photography; 78 (bl) David Muench Photography; 79 (tl) (inset) (tcl) (inset) Ken Taylor/Wildlife Images; 79 (tr) (inset) Paul Epley/Transparencies, Inc.; 79 (tcr) (inset) Chris Ippolito/Transparencies, Inc.; 79 (bl) Mike Booher/Transparencies, Inc.; 82 (bl) Harcourt.

UNIT 2

Unit 2 Opener (bg) David Muench Photography; Unit 2 Opener (object) Diane Hardy, Courtesy NC Maritime Museum; Unit 2 Opener (spread) David Muench Photography; 83 Diane Hardy, Courtesy NC Maritime Museum; 86-87 (spread) Virginia Wright-Frierson; 86 (tr) Dave Starrett/Artbase Inc.; 87 (cl) Virginia Wright-

Frierson; 87 (br) Dave Starrett/Artbase Inc.; 86-87 (b) Dave Starrett/Artbase Inc.; 88-89 (b) Dave Starrett/Artbase Inc.; 88-89 (t) Virginia Wright-Frierson; 90-91 (spread) Wendell Metzen/Bruce Coleman, Inc.; 92 (bl) Bettmann/CORBIS/MAGMA; 92 (bc) Culver Pictures, Inc.; 93 (b) The Granger Collection, New York; 94 (tc) Archivo Iconografico, SA/CORBIS/MAGMA; 94 (bl) North Carolina Office of Archives and History; 94 (br) The Granger Collection, New York; 95 (tl) The Thomas Fisher Rare Book Library/© Copyright The British Museum; 95 (cl) The Granger Collection, New York; 96 (tr) The Granger Collection, New York; 97 (b) David Alan Harvey/National Geographic Image Collection; 98 (b) Ken Taylor/Wildlife Images; 98 (bl) (inset) Courtesy of Library of Congress/Documents of the Manuscript division/Thomas Jefferson Papers; 99 (t) Ken Taylor/Wildlife Images; 99 (tr) (inset) Gilbert Grant/Photo Researchers; 100 (b) North Carolina Office of Archives and History; 101 (tr) The Granger Collection, New York; 102 (b) Ken Taylor/Wildlife Images; 103 (tl) The Granger Collection, New York; 103 (bc) The Granger Collection, New York; 103 (tr) Marilyn "Angel" Wynn/Native Stock; 104 (t) Cindy Burnham/Nautilus Productions LLC; 104 (cr) Jim Bounds/The News & Observer; 105 (tc) Bettmann/CORBIS/MAGMA; 105 (cr) Bettmann/CORBIS/MAGMA; 106 (b) Ken Taylor/Wildlife Images; 107 (t) The Newark Museum/Art Resource NY; 107 (tr) (inset) The Provost and Fellows of Worcester College, Oxford/Worcester College Library; 107 (tl) (inset) Courtesy of The Historical Society of Pennsylvania, Atwater Kent Museum of Philadelphia; 110 (tl) The Granger Collection, New York; 110 (cl) North Carolina Office of Archives and History; 110(bc) North Carolina Department of Cultural Resources/Feldman & Associates; 110-111 (c) Diane Hardy/Courtesy of North Carolina Maritime Museum; 111 (r) North Carolina Office of Archives and History; 112 (bc) Courtesy of the Massachusetts Historical Society; 112 (br) Courtesy of the Massachusetts Historical Society; 112 (brr) Courtesy of the Massachusetts Historical Society; 112 (bl) Kelly Culpepper/Transparencies, Inc.; 113 (tr) The Granger Collection, New York; 114 (b) Jeff Babb; 114 (cr) Courtesy National Park Service, Museum Management Program and Guilford Court House National Military Park Powder horn, GUCO 1701 Photo by Khaled Bassim www.cr.nps/gov/museum exibit/rewar; 115 (tl) North Carolina Office of Archives and History; 115 (tc) North Carolina Office of Archives and History; 115 (tr) North Carolina Office of Archives and History; 116 (tr) Tony Freeman/PhotoEdit; 120-121 (spread) Billy E. Barnes; 122-123 (spread) William Fridrich; 124 (bc) Drew Griffin/Transparencies, Inc.; 124 (t) Reuters New Media Inc./CORBIS/MAGMA; 128 (bl) Kelly Culpepper/Transparencies, Inc.; 129 (tr) Artbase Inc.; 130 (t) Ann Purcell/Photo Researchers; 130 (bc) Artbase Inc.; 130 (tl) (inset) Pete A. Harris/AP Wide World Photos; 132 (cl) (inset) Courtesy of University of North Carolina at Wilmington; 132-133 (spread) Outer Banks Visitors Bureau; 134-135 (spread) Ken Taylor/Wildlife Images; 136 (b) Billy E. Barnes/Stock, Boston; 138 (b) Steve Exum; 138 (cr) (inset) Karen Kasmauski/National Geographic Image Collection; 139 (tr) Jane Faircloth/Transparencies, Inc.; 142-143 (bg) Ian

Adams/Danita Delimont; 142 (c) (inset) Ian Adams/Danita Delimont; 143 (tr) (inset) (cr) (inset) Jane Faircloth/Transparencies, Inc.; 143 (br) (inset) Ken Taylor/Wildlife Images; 143 (l) (inset)Ian Adams/Danita Delimont; 146 (br) Harcourt.

UNIT 3

Unit 3 Opener (bg) John Elk III; Unit 3 Opener (object) John Elk III; Unit 3 Opener (spread) John Elk III; 147 John Elk III; 150-151 (spread) Jan Spivey Gilchrist; 151 (cr) Jan Spivey Gilchrist; 152 (spread) Jan Spivey Gilchrist; 154-155 (spread) Raymond Gehman/CORBIS; 157 (br) Courtesy of the John Carter Brown Library at Brown University; 158 (tl) Audrey Gibson/Mark E. Gibson Photography; 158 (bc) Billy E. Barnes; 158 (tr) Marilyn "Angel" Wynn/Native Stock; 159 (b) The Granger Collection, New York; 160 (tr) Courtesy of High Point Museum and Historical Park, High Point, NC; 161 (b) North Carolina Office of Archives and History; 162 (bc) Guilford Courthouse National Military Park, NC.; 162 (tr) North Carolina Museum of History; 163 (b) Andre DeCoppet Collection/Princeton University Library; 164 (b) CORBIS/MAGMA; 165 (tr) North Carolina Office of Archives and History; 165 (tl) United States Department of Transportation; 166 (b) American School/Library of Congress, Washington DC, USA/Bridgeman Art Library; 167 (tr) The Granger Collection, New York; 168 (tr) North Carolina Office of Archives and History; 168 (tc) Culver Pictures, Inc.; 169 (tr) Harcourt; 169 (tr)(inset) Bettmann/CORBIS/MAGMA; 169 (tl) Harcourt; 169 (tl) (inset)Bettmann/CORBIS/MAGMA; 170 (tr) Bettmann/CORBIS/MAGMA; 173 (br) CSS Neuse SHS; 175 (tr) The Granger Collection, New York; 176 (bl) North Carolina Collection, University of North Carolina Library at Chapel Hill; 176 (br) (inset) Gaston County Museum of Art & History; 177 (t) Courtesy of North Carolina Office of Archives and History; 177 (tr) (inset) Jane Faircloth/Transparencies, Inc.; 177 (bc) Ken Taylor/Courtesy of the Estate of Bill Hatcher/Duke Homestead State Historic Site; 178 fgd North Carolina Office of Archives and History; 178 (tr) North Carolina Office of Archives and History; 179 (tl) William Early/photo courtesy of Bernhardt Furniture; 184-185 (spread) Richard Nowitz; 186 (b) Jane Faircloth/Transparencies, Inc.; 187 (t) Annie Griffiths Belt /CORBIS/MAGMA; 188-189 (spread) Tim Barnwell/Stock, Boston; 188 (cl) (inset) Kiki Dunton/Publicom; 188 (bl) (inset) Michael Sandman/Publicom; 189 (tr) Kraft Books/CORBIS SYGMA/MAGMA; 190 (b) Jane Faircloth/Transparencies, Inc.; 192 (b) Tim Wright/CORBIS/MAGMA; 193 (t) Robert Cavin/Transparencies, Inc.; 194 (br) Ernest H. Robl; 194 (tr) Lewis W. Hine/National Archives Reproduction; 195 (tl) Charles Gupton/Stock, Boston; 195 (tc) Ken Taylor/Wildlife Images; 195 (tr) Charles Gupton/Stock, Boston; 196 (tr) Bettmann/CORBIS/Feldman & Associates; 196 (cr) (bl) (inset) Greensboro Historical Museum/Feldman & Associates; 197 (tr) (l) Greenboro Historical Museum/Feldman & Associates; 198 (b) Bobbie Jamison/The Dispatch, Lexington NC Newspaper; 200 (b) Wade Bruton/UNC Charlotte; 201 (tr) Jim McDonald/CORBIS/MAGMA; 201 (bc) DUOMO/CORBIS/MAGMA; 202 (tr) Jane Faircloth/Transparencies, Inc.; 202 (tl) Francois Gohier/Photo Researchers; 202 (bc) Darrell

Gulin/CORBIS/MAGMA; 203 (cr) Paul Epley/Transparencies, Inc.; 206 (t) (inset) (b) (inset) Photo Courtesy of Old Salem; 206-207 (bg) Courtesy of Old Salem, N.C.; 207 (bl) (inset) Jane Faircloth/Transparencies, Inc.; 207 (br) (inset) John Elk, III/Bruce Coleman, Inc.; 207 (l) (inset) (t) (inset) Photo Courtesy of Old Salem; 210 (cl) Harcourt.

UNIT 4

Unit 4 Opener (bg) Jay Dickman/CORBIS; Unit 4 Opener (object) Jane Faircloth/Transparencies, Inc.; Unit 4 Opener (spread) Jay Dickman/COR-BIS; 211 Jane Faircloth/Transparencies, Inc.; 214-215 (bg) Susan Condie Lamb; 216 (t) Susan Condie Lamb; 217 (l) Susan Condie Lamb; 218-219 (bg) Steven McBride/Picturesque Stock Photo; 220 (b) Ken Taylor/Wildlife Images; 221 (bc) Bettmann/CORBIS/MAGMA; 222 (bc) The Appalachian Cultural Museum/Artbase Inc.; 222 (br) Hickory Ridge Homestead Museum/Artbase Inc.; 222 (bl) The Hickory Ridge Homestead Museum/Artbase Inc.; 223 (tr) North Carolina Office of Archives and History; 223 (bl) The Appalachian Cultural Museum/Artbase Inc.; 223 (br) Center Star with Corners Star Quilt, Unidentified member of Glick Family, Lancaster County, Pennsylvania, 1890-1900. Wool, with cotton backing, 76 3/4 inches x 82 1/2 inches (cropped), Photo Courtesy of Collection of American Folk Art Museum, New York; gift of Phyllis Haders 1985.3.1; 224 (t) North Carolina Office of Archives and History; 224 (bc) The Appalachian Cultural Museum/Artbase Inc.; 225 (cr) Richard Kolseth; 228 (b) North Carolina Museum of Art/CORBIS/MAGMA; 229 (t) Mike Booher/Transparencies, Inc.; 229 (tr) (inset) Bettmann/CORBIS/MAGMA; 230 (t) North Carolina Office of Archives and History; 230 (bc) The Charleston Museum, Charleston, South Carolina; 231 (tc) (inset) North Carolina Office of Archives and History; 231 (bc) (inset) North Carolina Office of Archives and History; 232 (tl) (bc) Robin Dreyer/Penland School of Crafts; 233 (cr) "Earth Series" by Clara Rountree Couch, Photo Tom Mills/Penland School of Crafts; 233 (tl) "Spiral Bowl" by Tommie Rush, Photo, Tom Mills/Penland School of Crafts; 233 (cl) "Fibanacci3" by Billie Ruth Sudduth, Photo, Tom Mills/Penland School of Crafts; 234 (bl) Gilcrease Museum, Tulsa; 234 (bc) Marilyn "Angel" Wynn/Native Stock; 235 (br) CORBIS/MAGMA; 235 (bc) Raymond Gehman/CORBIS/MAGMA; 236 (tl) Herbert Tauss/National Geographic Image Collection; 237 (tr) Marilyn "Angel" Wynn/Native Stock; 238 (b) The Granger Collection, New York; 239 (b) North Carolina Office of Archives and History; 240-241 (b) Ken Taylor/Wildlife Images; 242 (b) John Elk III/Stock, Boston; 243 (t) Kevin Adams; 246-247 (spread) Jonathan Wallen Photography; 248-249 (b) Tim Barnwell/Stock, Boston; 249 (t) Untitled by Romare Bearden ©Romare Bearden Foundation/Licensed by VAGA, New York, NY/Christie's Images/Corbis/Magma; 250 (b) Karl Weatherly/CORBIS/MAGMA; 251 (tr) Freeman Owle; 251 (bc) The Appalachian Cultural Museum/Artbase Inc.; 251 (cr) (inset) Freeman Owle; 252-253 (spread) Carol Shanks/Transparencies Inc.; 252 (tc) The Appalachian Cultural Museum/Artbase Inc.; 253 (tr) Marilyn "Angel" Wynn/Native Stock; 254 (b) Courtesy of Creasman Farms LLC; 254 (cl) Artbase Inc.; 255 (bc) Robert Miller/The News & Observer; 255 (t) Kelly